D1760607

THE CAMBRIDGE COMPANION TO
THE HEBREW BIBLE AND ETHICS

The Cambridge Companion to the Hebrew Bible and Ethics offers an engaging and informative response to a wide range of ethical issues. Drawing connections between ancient and contemporary ethical problems, the essays address a variety of topics, including student loan debt, criminal justice reform, ethnicity and inclusion, family systems, and military violence. The volume emphasizes the contextual nature of ethical reflection, stressing the importance of historical knowledge and understanding in illuminating the concerns, the logic, and the intentions of the biblical texts. Twenty essays, all specially commissioned for this volume, address the texts' historical and literary contexts and identify key social, political, and cultural factors affecting their ethical ideas. They also explore how these texts can contribute to contemporary ethical discussions. *The Cambridge Companion to the Hebrew Bible and Ethics* is suitable for use in undergraduate and graduate courses in liberal arts colleges and universities, as well as seminaries.

C. L. Crouch is the David Allan Hubbard Professor of Old Testament at Fuller Theological Seminary, California. She is the author of *War and Ethics in the Ancient Near East (2009)*, *The Making of Israel (2014)*, *Israel and the Assyrians (2014)*, *An Introduction to the Study of Jeremiah (2017)*, and, with J. M. Hutton, *Translating Empire (2019)*.

CAMBRIDGE COMPANIONS TO RELIGION
This is a series of companions to major topics and key figures in theology and religious studies. Each volume contains specially commissioned chapters by international scholars, which provide an accessible and stimulating introduction to the subject for new readers and nonspecialists.

Other Titles in the Series

AMERICAN ISLAM Edited by Juliane Hammer and Omid Safi

AMERICAN JUDAISM Edited by Dana Evan Kaplan

AMERICAN METHODISM Edited by Jason E. Vickers

ANCIENT MEDITERRANEAN RELIGIONS Edited by Barbette Stanley Spaeth

APOCALYPTIC LITERATURE Edited by Colin McAllister

AUGUSTINE'S "CONFESSIONS" Edited by Tarmo Toom

KARL BARTH Edited by John Webster

THE BIBLE, 2nd edition Edited by Bruce Chilton

THE BIBLE AND LITERATURE Edited by Calum Carmichael

BIBLICAL INTERPRETATION Edited by John Barton

BLACK THEOLOGY Edited by Dwight N. Hopkins and Edward P. Antonio

DIETRICH BONHOEFFER Edited by John de Gruchy

JOHN CALVIN Edited by Donald K. McKim

CHRISTIAN DOCTRINE Edited by Colin Gunton

CHRISTIAN ETHICS Edited by Robin Gill

CHRISTIAN MYSTICISM Edited by Amy Hollywood and Patricia Z. Beckman

CHRISTIAN PHILOSOPHICAL THEOLOGY Edited by Charles Taliaferro and Chad V. Meister

CHRISTIAN POLITICAL THEOLOGY Edited by Craig Hovey and Elizabeth Phillips

THE CISTERIAN ORDER Edited by Mette Birkedal Bruun

CLASSICAL ISLAMIC THEOLOGY Edited by Tim Winter

JONATHAN EDWARDS Edited by Stephen J. Stein

EVANGELICAL THEOLOGY Edited by Timothy Larsen and Daniel J. Treier

FEMINIST THEOLOGY Edited by Susan Frank Parsons

FRANCIS OF ASSISI Edited by Michael J. P. Robson

THE GOSPELS Edited by Stephen C. Barton

THE HEBREW BIBLE/OLD TESTAMENT Edited by Stephen B. Chapman and Marvin A. Sweeney

THE JESUITS Edited by Thomas Worcester

JESUS Edited by Markus Bockmuehl

JUDAISM AND LAW Edited by Christine Hayes

(continued after index)

THE CAMBRIDGE COMPANION TO

THE HEBREW BIBLE AND ETHICS

Edited by

C. L. Crouch
Fuller Theological Seminary / University of Pretoria

CAMBRIDGE
UNIVERSITY PRESS

CAMBRIDGE
UNIVERSITY PRESS

University Printing House, Cambridge CB2 8BS, United Kingdom

One Liberty Plaza, 20th Floor, New York, NY 10006, USA

477 Williamstown Road, Port Melbourne, VIC 3207, Australia

314–321, 3rd Floor, Plot 3, Splendor Forum, Jasola District Centre,
New Delhi – 110025, India

79 Anson Road, #06–04/06, Singapore 079906

Cambridge University Press is part of the University of Cambridge.

It furthers the University's mission by disseminating knowledge in the pursuit of
education, learning, and research at the highest international levels of excellence.

www.cambridge.org
Information on this title: www.cambridge.org/9781108473439
DOI: 10.1017/9781108562072

© Cambridge University Press 2021

This publication is in copyright. Subject to statutory exception
and to the provisions of relevant collective licensing agreements,
no reproduction of any part may take place without the written
permission of Cambridge University Press.

First published 2021

A catalogue record for this publication is available from the British Library.

ISBN 978-1-108-47343-9 Hardback
ISBN 978-1-108-46151-1 Paperback

Cambridge University Press has no responsibility for the persistence or accuracy of
URLs for external or third-party internet websites referred to in this publication
and does not guarantee that any content on such websites is, or will remain,
accurate or appropriate.

for John Barton
who made this possible

Contents

Notes on Contributors

Deborah Barer (PhD, University of Virginia) is Assistant Professor of Religious Studies at Towson University. Her current manuscript project explores rabbinic decision-making and is an expansion of her dissertation, "A Judge With No Courtroom: Law, Ethics, and the Rabbinic Idea of Lifnim Mi-Shurat Ha-Din."

Albino Barrera (PhD, Yale University) is Professor of Theology and Economics at Providence College. He is author of *God and the Evil of Scarcity: Moral Foundations of Economic Agency* (2005), *Economic Compulsion and Christian Ethics* (Cambridge University Press, 2005), *Globalization and Economic Ethics* (2007), *Market Complicity and Christian Ethics* (Cambridge University Press, 2011), and *Biblical Economic Ethics: Sacred Scripture's Teachings on Economic Life* (2013).

Mark G. Brett (PhD, University of Sheffield) is Professor of Hebrew Bible at Whitley College / University of Divinity and General Editor of *Journal of Biblical Literature*. He is editor of *Ethnicity and the Bible* (E.J. Brill, 1996) and author of *Genesis: Procreation and the Politics of Identity* (2000), *Decolonizing God: The Bible in the Tides of Empire* (2008), *Political Trauma and Healing: Biblical Ethics for a Postcolonial World* (2016), and *Locations of God: Political Theology in the Hebrew Bible* (2019).

Matthew J. M. Coomber (PhD, University of Sheffield) is Associate Professor of Biblical Studies at St Ambrose University. He is author of *Re-Reading the Prophets through Corporate Globalization: and an Episcopal priest. A Cultural-Evolutionary Approach to Understanding Economic Injustice in the Hebrew Bible* (2010) and editor of *Bible and Justice: Ancient Texts, Modern Challenges* (2011) and co-editor of the Fortress Commentary on the Bible: The Old Testament and Apocrypha (Fortress, 2014).

C. L. Crouch (DPhil, University of Oxford) is David Allan Hubbard Professor of Old Testament at Fuller Theological Seminary and Research Associate at the University of Pretoria. She is author of *War and Ethics in the Ancient Near East: Military Violence in Light of Cosmology and History* (2009), *Israel and the Assyrians: Deuteronomy, the Succession Treaty of Esarhaddon, and the Nature of Subversion* (2014), *The Making of Israel: Cultural Diversity in the Southern Levant and the Formation of Ethnic Identity in Deuteronomy* (2014) and, with J. M. Hutton, *Translating Empire: Tell Fekheriyeh, Deuteronomy, and the Assyrian Treaty Tradition* (2019).

Stacy Davis (PhD, University of Notre Dame) is Professor of Religious Studies and Department Chair at Saint Mary's College. She is author of *This Strange Story: Jewish and Christian Interpretation of the Curse of Canaan from Antiquity to 1865* (2008) and *Haggai and Malachi* (2015).

Julián Andrés González Holguín (PhD, Southern Methodist University) is Associate Professor of Old Testament at Church Divinity School of the Pacific / Pacific Lutheran Theological Seminary. He is author of *Cain, Abel, and the Politics of God: An Agambenian Reading of Gen. 4:1–16* (2017).

Else K. Holt (PhD, University of Aarhus) was Associate Professor of Old Testament at the University of Aarhus. She is author of *Prophesying the Past: The Use of Israel's History in the Book of Hosea* (1995), *Jeremias Bog fortolket* (1999) and *Kommentar til Salmernes Bog* (2004).

Bohdan Hrobon (DPhil, University of Oxford) is Professor of Old Testament at Trnava University. He is author of *Ethical Dimension of Cult in the Book of Isaiah* (2010).

Sandra Jacobs (PhD, University of Manchester) is Teaching Fellow at Leo Baeck College and Research Fellow at King's College London. She is author of *The Body as Property: Physical Disfigurement in Biblical Law* (2015).

Dominik Markl (PhD, University of Innsbruck) is Associate Professor of Old Testament Exegesis at the Pontifical Biblical Institute in Rome. He is author of *Der Dekalog als Verfassung des Gottesvolkes: Die Brennpunkte einer Rechtshermeneutik des Pentateuch in Exodus 19–24 und Deuteronomium 5* (2007), *Gottes Volk im Deuteronomium* (2012) and, with G. Fischer, *Das Buch Exodus* (2020) and editor of *The Decalogue and Its Cultural Influence* (2017).

Carolyn J. Pressler (PhD, Princeton Theological Seminary) is Emeritus Harry C. Piper Jr. Professor of Biblical Interpretation at United Theological Seminary of the Twin Cities. She is author of *The View of Women Found in Deuteronomic Family Laws* (1993), *Joshua, Judges and Ruth* (2002) and *Numbers* (2017) and, with L. Day, editor of *Engaging the Bible in a Gendered World: An Introduction to Feminist Biblical Interpretation in Honor of Katharine Doob Sakenfeld* (2006).

Brian Rainey (PhD, Brown University) is Assistant Professor at Princeton Theological Seminary. He is author of *Religion, Ethnicity and Xenophobia in the Bible: A Theoretical, Exegetical and Theological Survey* (2018).

Caryn A. Reeder (PhD, University of Cambridge) is Professor of New Testament at Westmont College. She is author of *Enemy in the Household: Family Violence in Deuteronomy and Beyond* (2012) and *Gendering War and Peace in the Gospel of Luke* (Cambridge University Press, 2018).

Matthew Richard Schlimm (PhD, Duke University) is Professor of Old Testament at University of Dubuque Theological Seminary. He is author of *From Fratricide to Forgiveness: The Language and Ethics of Anger in Genesis* (2011), *This Strange and Sacred Scripture: Wrestling with the Old Testament and Its Oddities* (2015) and *70 Hebrew Words Every Christian Should Know* (2018).

C.-L. Seow (PhD, Harvard University) is Vanderbilt, Buffington, Cupples Chair in Divinity and Distinguished Professor of Hebrew Bible at Vanderbilt University. He is author of *Myth, Drama, and the Politics of David's Dance* (1989), *A Grammar for Biblical Hebrew* (1987), *Ecclesiastes: A New Translation with Introduction and Commentary* (1997), *Daniel* (2003), *Job 1–21* (2013) and, with F. W. Dobbs-Allsopp, J. J. M. Roberts, and R. E. Whitaker, *Hebrew Inscriptions: Texts from the Biblical Period of the Monarchy* (2004).

Richard G. Smith (PhD, University of Cambridge) is Associate Professor of Biblical Studies at Taylor University. He is author of *The Fate of Justice and Righteousness during David's Reign: Narrative Ethics and Rereading the Court History According to 2 Samuel 8:15–20:26* (2009).

Anne W. Stewart (PhD, Emory University) is Vice President for External Relations at Princeton Theological Seminary. She is author of *Poetic Ethics in Proverbs: Wisdom Literature and the Shaping of the Moral Self* (Cambridge University Press, 2016).

C. A. Strine (DPhil, University of Oxford) is Senior Lecturer in Ancient Near Eastern History and Literature at University of Sheffield. He is author of *Sworn Enemies: The Divine Oath, the Book of Ezekiel, and the Polemics of Exile* (2013) and *Get Thee Out of Thy Country: Involuntary Migration and the Development of the Ancestral Narrative* (forthcoming) and, with C. M. Hays, B. Gallaher, J. Konstantinovsky, and R. Ounsworth, *When the Son of Man Didn't Come: A Constructive Proposal on the Delay of the Parousia* (2016).

Tarah Van De Wiele (PhD, University of Nottingham) is Honorary Assistant Professor of Religious Studies at University of Nottingham. Her current manuscript project is a revision of her dissertation, "Cast them out for their many crimes: Reading the violent psalmist as part of ancient Near Eastern legal culture."

Introduction

C. L. CROUCH

The study of ethics and the Hebrew Bible either side of the new millennium has generally fallen into two categories: a more traditional genre of 'Old Testament ethics', in which remarks on the biblical text are undertaken from a confessional and normative perspective, and more recent forays into the 'ethics of ancient Israel', which investigate the text from a historical perspective and reflect varying degrees of interest or attention to contemporary concerns. The aim of the essays in this volume is to bring these two scholarly enterprises into conversation.

*

Major works of Old Testament ethics include Christopher Wright's *Old Testament Ethics for the People of God*,[1] Bruce Birch's *Let Justice Roll Down*,[2] Andrew Sloane's *At Home in a Strange Land*,[3] and Hetty Lalleman's *Celebrating the Law? Rethinking Old Testament Ethics*.[4] All are compatriots and descendants of Walter Kaiser, Jr.'s classic *Toward an Old Testament Ethics*.[5] Such works are usually implicit or explicit attempts to grapple with the Hebrew Bible's moral content from a Christian perspective, reading the Old Testament in conjunction with and in light of the New Testament. The authoritative status of the Bible amongst evangelical Christians in particular has meant that many such

---

[1] C. J. H. Wright, *Old Testament Ethics for the People of God* (Downers Grove: InterVarsity, 2004), bringing together C. J. H. Wright, *Living as the People of God* (Downers Grove: InterVarsity, 1983) and C. J. H. Wright, *Walking in the Ways of the Lord* (Downers Grove: InterVarsity, 1995).

[2] B. C. Birch, *Let Justice Roll Down: The Old Testament, Ethics, and Christian Life* (Louisville: Westminster John Knox Press, 1991).

[3] A. Sloane, *At Home in a Strange Land: Using the Old Testament in Christian Ethics* (Peabody: Hendrickson, 2008).

[4] H. Lalleman, *Celebrating the Law? Rethinking Old Testament Ethics* (Milton Keynes: Paternoster, 2004).

[5] W. C. Kaiser, *Toward Old Testament Ethics* (Grand Rapids: Zondervan, 1991).

attempts have been undertaken from an evangelical perspective, as the status of the Bible dictates its normative authority and demands that it be reckoned with, at the same time that its frequently awkward, embarrassing, or confusing contents require exegesis and explanation. Thus far, efforts to engage the biblical texts from a normative but non-evangelical perspective have been concentrated primarily in edited volumes, such as M. Daniel Carroll R. and Jacqueline E. Lapsley's *Character Ethics and the Old Testament*,[6] John W. Rogerson, Margaret Davies, and M. Daniel Carroll R.'s *The Bible in Ethics*,[7] and Juliana Claassens and Bruce Birch's *Restorative Readings*.[8] John Rogerson's *Theory and Practice in Old Testament Ethics*[9] and Cyril Rodd's *Glimpses of a Strange Land*[10] are partial exceptions, although both are essentially single-author essay collections. Cheryl Anderson's *Ancient Laws*[11] *and Contemporary Controversies* and Mark Brett's *Political Trauma and Healing*[12] have been welcome exceptions in this regard.

Anderson and Brett also stand out as methological exceptions. Driven by normative aims, most works of Old Testament ethics tend to read the texts synchronically and systematically, smoothing out differences and seeking out one or a few unifying principles perceived to characterise the collection as a whole. Waldemar Janzen's *Old Testament Ethics: A Paradigmatic Approach*, for example, identifies five paradigms governing Old Testament ethical thinking and argues for an underlying interrelationship amongst them.[13] While differences of opinion within and amongst the biblical texts are sometimes acknowledged, normative works' ultimate interest in practical application has tended to favour an emphasis on unity and coherence. Such efforts are obliged, to greater or lesser degrees, to work against the heterogeneity of the Bible

---

[6] M. D. Carroll R. and J. E. Lapsley (eds), *Character Ethics and the Old Testament: Moral Dimensions of Scripture* (Louisville: Westminster John Knox, 2007).

[7] J. W. Rogerson, M. Davies, and M. D. Carroll R. (eds), *The Bible in Ethics: The Second Sheffield Colloquium*, JSOTSup 207 (Sheffield: JSOT, 1995).

[8] L. J. M. Claassens and B. C. Birch (eds), *Restorative Readings: The Old Testament, Ethics, and Human Dignity* (Eugene: Pickwick, 2015).

[9] J. W. Rogerson, *Theory and Practice in Old Testament Ethics*, JSOTSup 405 (London: T&T Clark, 2004).

[10] C. S. Rodd, *Glimpses of a Strange Land: Studies in Old Testament Ethics*, OTS (Edinburgh: T&T Clark, 2001).

[11] C. Anderson, *Ancient Laws and Contemporary Controversies: The Need for Inclusive Biblical Interpretation* (Oxford: Oxford University Press, 2009).

[12] M. Brett, *Political Trauma and Healing: Biblical Ethics for a Postcolonial World* (Grand Rapids: Eerdmans, 2018).

[13] W. Janzen, *Old Testament Ethics: A Paradigmatic Approach* (Louisville: Westminster John Knox, 1994).

itself: although the biblical texts contain a great deal of theological and ethical continuity, it is difficult ever simply to say, 'the Bible says', without further qualification. Yet, at the same time that this scriptural polyphony may be one of the most challenging aspects of the Hebrew Bible for those with normative concerns, it also has the potential to be one of its most exciting aspects; this vivacity is well reflected in the recent work by Anderson and Brett, which acknowledge and explore the text's responsiveness to changing circumstances and interpretations. Human moral experience is a diverse, complex phenomenon, and faithful readers are invited by the contributors of this volume to recognise the complexity of their own moral lives in the complexity of the biblical tradition's many voices.

Undoubtedly the most significant recent development in the study of the Hebrew Bible and ethics has been a rapidly proliferating attention to historical ethical concerns. In these works, the biblical texts are taken as a window into the moral world of ancient Israel, through which we may view the ethical thought processes of ancient Israelites. Insofar as they seek to unveil aspects ancient thinking, without making any judgements about it, such work may also be referred to as form of 'descriptive ethics'. Because it is interested in specific historical contexts, works in this category also tend to focus on individual texts or groups of texts.

Early, methodologically-groundbreaking works in this area include John Barton's *Ethics and the Old Testament*[14] and *Understanding Old Testament Ethics*,[15] capped off by his magnum opus, *Ethics in Ancient Israel*;[16] Gordon Wenham's *Story as Torah*[17] and *Psalms as Torah*;[18] and Eckart Otto's *Theologische Ethik des Alten Testaments*.[19] Although not an exclusively historical study, Eryl Davies's *The Immoral Bible* is similarly methodological in orientation.[20] These trailblazers have been followed by a veritable *floruit* of research undertaken from specific

---

[14]   J. Barton, *Ethics and the Old Testament* (Harrisburg: Trinity Press International, 1998).

[15]   J. Barton, *Understanding Old Testament Ethics: Approaches and Explorations* (Louisville: Westminster John Knox, 2003).

[16]   J. Barton, *Ethics in Ancient Israel* (Oxford: Oxford University Press, 2014).

[17]   G. J. Wenham, *Story as Torah: Reading Old Testament Narrative Ethically* (Grand Rapids: Baker, 2004).

[18]   G. J. Wenham, *Psalms as Torah: Reading Biblical Song Ethically*, Studies in Theological Interpretation (Grand Rapids: Baker, 2012).

[19]   E. Otto, *Theologische Ethik Des Alten Testaments*, Theologische Wissenschaft 3, 2 (Stuttgart: Kohlhammer, 1994).

[20]   E. W. Davies, *The Immoral Bible: Approaches to Old Testament Ethics* (London: T&T Clark, 2010).

genre- and text-based perspectives. Without claim to exhaustion, in this category are works such as Peter Lau's *Identity and Ethics in the Book of Ruth*,[21] Carol Newsom's *The Book of Job*,[22] Andrew Mein's *Ezekiel and the Ethics of Exile*,[23] Jonathan Rowe's *Michal's Moral Dilemma*,[24] and Harold Bennett's *Injustice Made Legal*.[25] Edited volumes taking a similarly historical tack include Dirk Human's *Psalmody and Poetry in Old Testament Ethics*[26] and Katharine Dell's *Ethical and Unethical in the Old Testament*.[27] Many of the contributors to the present volume have written ethical analyses of this kind, examining a particular book or a particular genre of the Hebrew Bible in search of its moral aims and assumptions.

Many of these works have been at pains to emphasise that historical investigations are not divorced from contemporary concerns, inherently anti-theological, or interested only in antiquity. Rather, they proceed from the basis that historical knowledge is essential for an accurate understanding of the ethical thinking of the Hebrew Bible and the ethical thinking of ancient Israel, as well of the intentions of the biblical texts vis-à-vis the moral formation of their audiences. Ethics, like theology, always happens in context. Investigating the ancient contexts of the biblical texts is thus a crucial part of the equation, if a student or a scholar wishes to consider how – or, indeed, whether – the texts are meaningful in the modern world. Historical work is thus a valuable undertaking in its own right, but also an essential prerequisite for normative work.

*

With this conversation between descriptive and normative ethics in mind, this volume seeks to balance historical and contemporary

[21] P. H. W. Lau, *Identity and Ethics in the Book of Ruth: A Social Identity Approach*, BZAW 416 (Berlin: de Gruyter, 2011).
[22] C. A. Newsom, *The Book of Job: A Contest of Moral Imaginations* (Oxford: Oxford University Press, 2009).
[23] A. Mein, *Ezekiel and the Ethics of Exile*, OTM (Oxford: Oxford University Press, 2006).
[24] J. Y. Rowe, *Michal's Moral Dilemma: A Literary, Anthropological, and Ethical Interpretation*, LHBOTS 533 (New York: T&T Clark, 2011).
[25] H. V. Bennett, *Injustice Made Legal: Deuteronomic Law and the Plight of Widows, Strangers, and Orphans in Ancient Israel*, The Bible in Its World (Grand Rapids: Eerdmans, 2002).
[26] D. J. Human (ed.), *Psalmody and Poetry in Old Testament Ethics* (New York: T&T Clark, 2012).
[27] K. J. Dell (ed.), *Ethical and Unethical in the Old Testament: God and Humans in Dialogue*, LHBOTS 528 (New York: T&T Clark, 2010).

concerns in an engaging and informative way, drawing connections between ancient and contemporary ethical problems and reflecting on both the advantages and the disadvantages of attempting to study these texts from an ethical perspective. Each contributor has been asked to address the historical and literary contexts of a book or a group of books, unpacking these texts' assumptions and concerns within their ancient contexts and identifying some of the key social, political, and cultural factors that have affected their ethical interests and aims. Each essay builds on these historical and literary foundations when they turn to contemporary concerns, examining the implications of their descriptive ethical analyses for normative ethical discussions. At times this is relatively straightforward and relatively uncontroversial, but often it is problematic – demanding careful, nuanced discussion of the relationship between ancient texts and contemporary contexts.

One of the specific aims of the volume is to recognise the contextual nature of ethical reflection. Moral imperatives exist in and relate to particular historical, political, social, and economic situations: ethics is always in context. Each of the essays in the volume conveys the importance of historical knowledge and understanding in illuminating the concerns, the logic, and the intentions of the biblical texts, especially if the author (or reader) wishes to consider the texts' normative ethical applications. The significance of context is reflected in the structure of the volume, with essays grouped into four, broadly genre-based sections: legal ethics, narrative ethics, prophetic ethics, and wisdom or poetic ethics. A fifth section addresses the role of the Hebrew Bible in Jewish and Christian ethical thought, both historically and in the contemporary context.

Finally: that the volume is not simply a series of topical essays is a way of recognising the polyphonic chorus that makes up the Hebrew Scriptures. Both the bane and the blessing of the Hebrew Bible when it comes to ethics is that it does not readily lend itself to simple 'dos and don'ts'. Instructions given in one place are complicated or contradicted elsewhere, and different ethical principles dominate different texts. The structure of this volume highlights the diversity of the Hebrew Bible's ethical thought processes and seeks, in turn, to encourage its readers to engage with a diverse array of approaches to contemporary ethical issues.

FURTHER READING

Anderson, C. *Ancient Laws and Contemporary Controversies: The Need for Inclusive Biblical Interpretation*. Oxford: Oxford University Press, 2009.

Barton, J. *Ethics in Ancient Israel*. Oxford: Oxford University Press, 2014.

Barton, J. *Understanding Old Testament Ethics: Approaches and Explorations*. Louisville: Westminster John Knox, 2003.

Birch, B. C. *Let Justice Roll Down: The Old Testament, Ethics, and Christian Life*. Louisville: Westminster John Knox Press, 1991.

Brett, M. G. *Political Trauma and Healing: Biblical Ethics for A Postcolonial World*. Grand Rapids: Eerdmans, 2016.

Byron, G. L., and V. Lovelace, eds. *Womanist Interpretations of the Bible: Expanding the Discourse*. Atlanta: Society of Biblical Literature, 2016.

Claassens, L. J. M., and B. C. Birch. *Restorative Readings: The Old Testament, Ethics, and Human Dignity*. Eugene: Pickwick, 2015.

Davies, E. W. *The Immoral Bible: Approaches to Old Testament Ethics*. London: T&T Clark, 2010.

Green, J. B., and J. E. Lapsley, eds. *The Old Testament and Ethics: A Book-by-Book Survey*. Grand Rapids: Baker, 2013.

Janzen, W. *Old Testament Ethics: A Paradigmatic Approach*. Louisville: Westminster John Knox, 1994.

Lalleman, H. *Celebrating the Law? Rethinking Old Testament Ethics*. Milton Keynes: Paternoster, 2004.

Rogerson, J. W. *Theory and Practice in Old Testament Ethics*. JSOTSup 405. London: T&T Clark, 2004.

Wenham, G. J. *Psalms as Torah: Reading Biblical Song Ethically*. Studies in Theological Interpretation. Grand Rapids: Baker, 2012.

Wenham, G. J. *Story as Torah: Reading Old Testament Narrative Ethically*. Grand Rapids: Baker, 2004.

Wright, C. J. H. *Old Testament Ethics for the People of God*. Downers Grove: InterVarsity, 2004.

Part I

Legal Ethics

1   The Decalogue: An Icon of Ethical Discourse
DOMINIK MARKL

But accursed be the man who stands up and says: "They are no longer binding." Accursed be he who teaches you, "Rise up and free yourselves of them! Lie, murder, and steal, whore, defile, and deliver your father and mother over to the knife, for that is human, and you should praise my name, because I proclaimed freedom to you."[1]

Thus speaks Moses at the culmination of Thomas Mann's *The Tables of the Law*, written in 1943. Mann's use of the Ten Commandments in his "antifascist manifesto" is a token of the Decalogue's symbolic role in discourses on ethical foundations in cultures that have been influenced by Judaism and Christianity.[2] While the quest for the origin and redactional development of the Decalogue's two versions in Exodus 20 and Deuteronomy 5 has been the focus of much exegetical work, these genetic questions are of limited relevance for understanding the Ten Commandments' ethical significance. I shall, therefore, concentrate here on some fundamental literary features of this text in its canonical contexts and its vast history of reception. Against this background, I shall consider the Decalogue as an icon of ethical discourse, which poses significant questions for contemporary ethical reflection.

---

[1] T. Mann, *The Tables of the Law*, trans. M. Faber and S. Lehman (Philadelphia: Paul Dry, 2010), 111. *Das Gesetz*, in *Sämtliche Erzählungen* (Frankfurt am Main: S. Fischer, 1963), 641–94, 694: "Aber Fluch dem Menschen, der da aufsteht und spricht: 'Sie gelten nicht mehr.' Fluch ihm, der euch lehrt: 'Auf, und seid ihrer ledig! Lügt, mordet und raubt, hurt, schändet und liefert Vater und Mutter ans Messer, denn so steht's dem Menschen an, und sollt meinen Namen preisen, weil ich euch Freiheit verkündete.'"

[2] J. Assmann, "Mose gegen Hitler: Die Zehn Gebote als antifaschistisches Manifest," *Thomas Mann Jahrbuch* 28 (2015): 47–61.

I.I THE DIVINE VOICE

"Has any people ever heard a divine voice speaking out of the fire, as you have heard, and lived?" asks Moses, reflecting on the unique experience of the theophany at Horeb (Deut 4:33; "Sinai" in Exodus). God "declared to you his covenant, which he charged you to observe: the Ten Words; and he wrote them on two tablets of stone" (Deut 4:13).

This theophany is a formative experience for Israel. Their "assembly" (qhl) becomes unique among the nations in its direct encounter with divine revelation.[3] According to the account in the book of Exodus, God appeared in awe-inspiring fire, clouds, and thunder, "so that his fear be upon your faces so that you do not sin" (Exod 20:20). The theophanic proclamation of the Decalogue thus serves a pedagogical purpose, preparing Israel's affective disposition not to transgress what is proclaimed in the theophany.

The relationship between the divine speaker and his addressees is established in the first words of this revelation: "I am YHWH, your God" ('nky yhwh elhyk, Exod 20:2; Deut 5:6; alt. "I, YHWH, am your God"). The expression establishes a relationship that defines the quality of the following discourse. In the literary context of the making of the Sinai covenant, it can be read as a speech act through which God declares the covenantal relationship.[4] The description of YHWH as the one "who brought you out of the land of Egypt, out of the house of slaves ['bdym]" refers to Israel's previous experience with God, summarizing the Exodus narrative. The liberation from Egypt sets the stage for the norms that follow, which are meant to protect Israel's freedom. The immediately subsequent prohibition of "serving" ('bd) other gods – that is, enslaving oneself to them – is, therefore, programmatic.

The encounter with the speaker – the divine voice – is presented as an overwhelming experience, which even leads to fear for one's life (Exod 20:19; Deut 5:25). At the same time, God is trustworthy, since he fought with his might to rescue Israel from oppression. The normative requirements that follow are thus grounded in a relationship of fear

---

[3] Both the "synagogue" and the "church" will later be able to identify with the assembly of Israel, since the "assembly" (qhl) of the revelation at Horeb will be rendered in the LXX both as "synagogue" (sunagōgē, Deut 5:22) and "church" (ekklēsia, Deut 9:10; 18:16; the expression is added in LXX Deut 4:10).

[4] D. Markl, Der Dekalog als Verfassung des Gottesvolkes: Die Brennpunkte einer Rechtshermeneutik des Pentateuch in Exodus 19–24 und Deuteronomium 5, HBS 49 (Freiburg im Breisgau: Herder, 2007), 98–103.

and gratitude. Psychologically, this resembles the relationship between parents and children in traditional societies. God is portrayed as an exalted father, very much in Sigmund Freud's sense. The addressees of the divine voice are supposed to obey God out of love and fear, just as children obey their parents.

But who, precisely, is addressed by the Decalogue? The prologue leaves no doubt that its "you" refers to the people of Israel as a whole, since it is the entire people whom God brought out of Egypt. That this "you" – grammatically singular throughout the Decalogue – should be understood both collectively and distributively certainly holds true for the following prohibition of "other gods" and idols: The making of the golden calf, the paradigmatic transgression of this principal prohibition, is portrayed as a collective sin. "They said, 'These are your gods, O Israel, who brought you up out of the land of Egypt!'" (Exod 32:4). This allusion to the Decalogue's prologue sarcastically portrays the people's sin in its unsurpassable gravity.

The you-addressee of the Decalogue, however, shifts and oscillates among different shades of reference. The Sabbath commandment is addressed to people in charge of a household that includes servants and livestock (Exod 20:10; Deut 5:14). "Coveting your neighbor's wife" is prohibited for men, though the general formulation of "you" in the second person masculine is hardly restricted to male addressees in the rest of the Decalogue, since it is difficult to assume that the divine voice should consider murder, theft, and other crimes permissible for women. In fact, Deuteronomy explicitly states that the assemblies in which the covenant is made, and in which the Torah is supposed to be taught in the future, involve women and men alike, and even children (Deut 29:9–10; 31:12).

The normativity of the Ten Words thus concerns both Israel as a collective and Israelites as individuals. Still, the you-address in the singular is rhetorically effective as it emphasizes the responsibility of the individual. Philo of Alexandria, who wrote the first commentary on the Ten Commandments that has come down to us, reasoned that the "most excellent lesson" given through the singular is "that each single person, when he is law-abiding and obedient to God, is equal in worth to a whole nation, even the most populous, or rather to all nations, and if we may go still farther, even to the whole world" (*Decal.* 37).[5]

---

[5]   For introduction and translation see S. J. Pearce, "On the Decalogue," in *Outside the Bible: Ancient Jewish Writings Related to Scripture 1*, ed. L. H. Feldman, J. L. Kugel, and L. H. Schiffman (Philadelphia: Jewish Publication Society, 2013), 989–1032.

Nineteen centuries later, Martin Buber wrote: "The soul of the Decalogue is the word 'Thou' .... Thanks to its 'thou,' the Decalogue means
the preservation of the Divine Voice."[6]

The immediacy established between the trans-human divine voice
and the human singular "you" is the basic form of normative instruction
in the Decalogue. The prohibitions' "you shall not," in their specific verbal
form (*yiqtol*) could also be translated "you will not." It is a strong prohibition, in the sense of "you must not," but it may even include a pedagogic
expression of trust: "I believe that you will not." The Ten Commandments
symbolically represent the epitome of what would later become the divine
command theory of ethics.[7] Modern criticism has unmasked the divine
voice as an exaltation of the internalized "father," and proposed that
humans should overcome such paternal authority in becoming mature
adults. Resistance against paternalizing moral claims – especially those of
ecclesial institutions – is probably at the root of the discomfort that the
Decalogue sometimes evokes in contemporary culture. It may be more
helpful today to view the Ten Commandments as an expression of the
moral character of God,[8] who cares for the well-being of humans and is an
example worth considering for imitation. Israelites are supposed to obey
the commandments not as slaves of God, but because noblesse oblige.[9]

Nevertheless, the question of the source of a normative authority that
transcends the interests of individuals or particular groups within society
remains relevant. If the divine voice is seen as a construct of ethical
authority that transcends human claims to power and self-interest, this
is a supreme achievement of the Decalogue's narrative staging.

1.2 ETHICAL VALUES OF CONSTITUTIONAL SIGNIFICANCE

The Decalogue's literary context is concerned not only with the
morality of individuals but with the making of a nation. While it is

---

[6] M. Buber, *Moses: The Revelation and the Covenant* (New York: Harper & Row, 1958),
     130.
[7] J. Barton, *Ethics in Ancient Israel* (Oxford: Oxford University Press, 2014), esp. 129.
     Significantly, Barton's book shows that divine command is not the only approach to
     ethics found in the Hebrew Bible.
[8] R. Brague, *The Law of God: The Philosophical History of an Idea*, trans. L. G.
     Cochrane (Chicago: University of Chicago Press, 2007), 57, views the Ten
     Commandments from the perspective of what they say about their speaker. For
     discussions on the moral character of God see Barton, *Ethics in Ancient Israel*,
     245–72.
[9] Brague, *The Law of God*, 58.

one of several "ethical digests" in the Hebrew Bible, it is also more than that.[10] Israel is about to become a "kingdom of priests and a holy nation" in the covenant with their God (Exod 19:3–6). "YHVH unites himself," as Martin Buber put it, "with Israel into a political, theo-political unity."[11] From the perspective of constitutional theory, the Decalogue's prohibitions against the veneration of other gods, divine images, and abuse of the divine name protect the authority of the lawgiver.[12] A modern theorist of political order, Eric Voegelin, likewise observed that "the Decalogue is not a catechism of religious and moral precepts, but a proclamation of the God-King laying down the fundamental rules for the order of the new domain."[13]

Philo thus considered the Ten Commandments "both laws and heads summarizing the particular laws" (*kai nomous ... kai tōn en merei kaphalaia, Decal.* 19) that would constitute Israel as a polity (*politeia, Decal.* 14). The Decalogue precedes law collections both in Exodus and Deuteronomy: the Book of the Covenant (Exod 20:22–23:33) and the laws of Deuteronomy (chs 12–26). This arrangement is the result of systematic reflection on the hierarchy of norms. In a series of concise formulations, the Decalogue protects essential relationships – with God, the family, and the wider social sphere – and fundamental values. The only two positive commandments – keeping the Sabbath and honoring one's parents – both concern the social realm of the family; they appear at the center of the Decalogue and have theological implications. The Sabbath creates a space of common rest among the members of the household, which means a temporary suspension of class distinctions.[14] Honoring one's parents is related to long life in the divinely given land. The subsequent prohibitions – of murder, adultery, theft, false witness, and covetousness – protect, positively speaking, Israel's values concerning the wider social realm: the integrity of life, the marital relationship, and property. The prohibition of covetousness reinforces the protection of marriage and property by addressing even the motivational origins and preparatory machinations that endanger them.

---

[10] On "ethical digests" in the Hebrew Bible see Barton, *Ethics in Ancient Israel*, 227–44.
[11] Buber, *Moses*, 115.
[12] Markl, *Der Dekalog als Verfassung des Gottesvolkes*, 167.
[13] E. Voegelin, *Israel and Revelation* (Baton Rouge: Louisiana State University Press, 1956), 425.
[14] J. L. Ska, "Biblical Law and the Origins of Democracy," in *The Ten Commandments: The Reciprocity of Faithfulness*, ed. W. P. Brown (Louisville: John Knox, 2004), 146–58, here 152.

Several proposals have been made relating the structures of the Book of the Covenant and the laws of Deuteronomy to the sequence of the Ten Commandments. Such proposals may not be entirely convincing. The most obvious similarity is that, like the Decalogue, the law collections commence with religious concerns and then move on to social legislation. Most likely, the formulation of the Decalogue was inspired by preexisting law collections. It is thus able to serve as a prelude or exposition that formulates the basic melody of the laws, but the law collections are not necessarily ordered or redacted according to the Ten Commandments.

The Decalogue addresses legal matters that are treated in greater detail in other laws of the Pentateuch, such as murder, theft, and adultery, as well as matters that cannot be subject to human legal procedure. Both are integral parts of the divine, normative proclamations that constitute Israel in the covenant as the people of God.[15] According to the Pentateuch, society is not based on laws that are binding because of human power, nor can all laws be enforced by a human judiciary. The integrity of a society governed by divine constitution rests on ethical attitudes and on respect for the law in its more specific sense. Notably, Israel is portrayed as a theo-polity: No king or any other official is mentioned in the Decalogue. In the midst of the Pentateuchal narrative, this appears natural. The Sinai revelation addresses the kingless people of Israel in the desert. Historically, the lack of interest in political institutions may presuppose their collapse during the Babylonian exile.

The function of the Decalogue may thus be compared to the role of constitutional documents in modern states. They identify the authoritative voice of the legislator ("we, the people of..."; note that in some constitutional documents this is preceded by "in the name of God") and invoke the ethical values that are fundamental for the legal constitution of the nation, such as human dignity. While the authors and redactors of the Pentateuch were hardly concerned with modern constitutional theory, the symbolic force of the Decalogue may have indirectly influenced the conception of modern constitutional documents. The Decalogue remains an ancient witness to the idea that ethical values should form the foundation of the legal constitution of society. Moreover, Israel's free acceptance of the covenant's instructions

---

[15]   On the overlapping realms of law and ethics in the Hebrew Bible see E. Otto, "The Study of Law and Ethics in the Hebrew Bible / Old Testament," in *Hebrew Bible / Old Testament. III: From Modernism to Post-Modernism*, ed. M. Sæbø (Göttingen: Vandenhoeck & Ruprecht, 2015), 594–621.

(Exod 19:8; 24:3, 7) may be seen as the origin of the idea of constitutional consensus: The law's validity rests on the people's (ideally assumed) acceptance of it.[16]

1.3 BETWEEN IMMUTABILITY AND INTERPRETIVE FLUIDITY

No other text of the Bible is as profoundly underwritten by divine authority as the Decalogue. It is proclaimed out of the theophanic fire and written into tablets of stone by the "finger of God" (Exod 31:18; Deut 9:10). Indeed,

> The divine writer is not represented in a pose like that of an Egyptian scribe with reed pen and ink, nor like a Babylonian with his stylus: he writes with his finger, as one writes in the sand, without any mediating instrument. This use of the body expresses a personal engagement: in giving the Law, God gives of his own and of himself.[17]

The stone symbolizes eternal durability. The tablets are even made of rock from Sinai, the mountain of the theophany. As a material token of the "utopian" origin of divine revelation in "the desert, a nonterritory, literally a no man's land," they are transferred to Jerusalem and lie in the center of the Temple's Holy of Holies (1 Kgs 8:9).[18]

The Decalogue is portrayed as a monument of normativity, an ultimate iconic text of the immutable will of God. It is consequently surprising that Moses' quotation of the Decalogue in Deuteronomy diverges from the version found in Exodus. Forty years after the revelation, the tablets now being carried in the ark, Moses solemnly quotes the commandments, twice underlining that he is referring to what "YHWH your God commanded you" at Horeb (Deut 5:12, 16). The words that he quotes, however, are not identical to those previously reported.

To see the significance of this, it will suffice to look at two of the most important differences. First, while the Sabbath commandment in Exodus is motivated by God's own rest on the seventh day of creation (Exod 20:11), in Deuteronomy Moses claims that God's mighty liberation of his people from Egypt is the reason for the Sabbath

---

[16]   Ska, "Biblical Law and the Origins of Democracy," 155; Markl, *Der Dekalog als Verfassung des Gottesvolkes,* 165.

[17]   Brague, *The Law of God,* 49.

[18]   Ska, "Biblical Law and the Origins of Democracy," 154.

commandment (Deut 5:15); remembering the exodus becomes a central requirement of the command.[19] The reason for this is apparent from another, immediately preceding, addition: "so that your male and female slave may rest as well as you" (Deut 5:14). This seemingly redundant phrase emphasizes the social equality that is restored through the Sabbath rest and is in keeping with Deuteronomy's other expressions of concern for disadvantaged groups that likewise invoke the memory of the exodus (cf. 15:15; 16:12; 24:18, 22).

Second, Moses changes the order of the final prohibitions. While the Exodus Decalogue considers the neighbor's wife to be part of his house (hold) (Exod 20:16–17), Deuteronomy's version gives precedence to the wife and distinguishes "coveting" her (ḥmd) from "desiring" other belongings ('wh; Deut 5:21). It can be argued, of course, that such differences result from different histories of traditions and redactions. Nevertheless, they could have been easily smoothed out. The fact that they were not is likely of hermeneutical significance. In the paradigmatic case of the Decalogue, the Pentateuch preserves an example of variation and refinement in the ethical formulation of norms over time, and thus points to the necessity of development – even for the most highly authorized text, written in stone by the finger of God.[20]

1.4 A MATRIX OF MORALITY

While the literary context of the Pentateuch leaves no doubt about the Decalogue's constitutional significance, much of its reception history has focused on the commandments' moral meaning. Jesus' Sermon on the Mount sets the tone for this development:

> You have heard that it was said to those of ancient times, "You shall not murder"; and "whoever murders shall be liable to judgment." But I say to you that if you are angry with a brother or sister, you will be liable to judgment; and if you insult a brother or sister, you will be liable to the council; and if you say, "You fool," you will be liable to the hell of fire. (Mt 5:21–22)

---

[19]   Motivations are another pedagogical aspect typical of ethics and law in the Hebrew Bible; see Ska, "Biblical Law and the Origins of Democracy," 157.

[20]   E. Otto, "The Study of Law and Ethics in the Hebrew Bible / Old Testament," 607; Dominik Markl, "The Ten Words Revealed and Revised: The Origins of Law and Legal Hermeneutics in the Pentateuch," in *The Decalogue and Its Cultural Influence*, ed. D. Markl, HBM 58 (Sheffield: Sheffield Phoenix, 2017), 13–27.

This exegetical emphasis on ethical generalization expands on a hermeneutical process already inscribed in the Decalogue itself. Jesus extends the prohibition of adultery to merely looking lustfully at a woman, concretizing the prohibition of coveting (Mt 5:27–28). Moving along a similar track, Augustine would later teach that the double commandment – to love God and fellow humans, seen in the gospels as the greatest of all commandments – summarizes the Decalogue (e.g., *Cat. rud.* 41).[21] The Decalogue's purpose – providing an elegantly reduced summary of fundamental norms – is thus taken to its extreme, condensed into one single ethical requirement. Comparing the commandments with the ten strings of the harp (*psalterium*), Augustine recommends to pluck them with love to overcome the vices.[22]

Although Francis of Assisi recommended that the Ten Commandments be kept "simply and without comment" (*simpliciter et sine glossa*), they would soon become the most commentated text in Christianity.[23] Medieval theologians reflected systematically on the status of the laws of the Pentateuch and categorized the Decalogue as moral law (*moralia* as opposed to *caerimonialia* and *iudicialia*) – a category of law usually considered a form of natural law, and thus eternal.[24] This theoretical elevation of the Ten Commandments became practically important in the early modern period, as the Decalogue gradually replaced the Seven Capital Sins as the prevalent moral paradigm.[25]

It was the Reformation, however, that led to the Decalogue's final triumph.[26] Through dissemination in countless catechisms – both those written by reformers such as Luther and Calvin, and those written by

---

[21] Mk 12:28–33; Mt 22:35–40; cf. Lk 10:25–28.

[22] *Sermon 9 (De decem chordis)*, c. 9, n. 13, quoted in L. Smith, *The Ten Commandments: Interpreting the Bible in the Medieval World* (Leiden: Brill, 2014), 46.

[23] Francis of Assisi, *Opuscula sancti patris Francisci Assisiensis*, ed. C. Esser (Grottaferrata: Collegium S. Bonaventurae ad Claras Aquas, 1978), 316, quoted in Smith, *Ten Commandments*, 1.

[24] See Smith, *Ten Commandments*, esp. 2. Most influential became Aquinas (see esp. *Summa theologica, prima secundae*, q. 100, art. 11).

[25] J. Bossy, "Moral Arithmetic: Seven Sins into Ten Commandments," in *Conscience and Casuistry in Early Modern Europe*, ed. E. Leites (Cambridge: Cambridge University Press, 1990), 214–43; D. Markl, "The Decalogue in History. A Preliminary Survey of the Fields and Genres of Its Reception," *ZAR* 18 (2012) 279–93, esp. 281.

[26] On the central role of the Decalogue in the Reformation see J. Willis, *The Reformation of the Decalogue: Religious Identity and the Ten Commandments in England, c.1485–1625*, Cambridge Studies in Early Modern British History (Cambridge: Cambridge University Press, 2017).

counter-reformers such as Canisius – the Ten Commandments became
universally taught in Christian lands and in global missionary contexts.
They were written on church walls, recited in liturgy, learned by heart,
expounded in sermons. They were pedagogically instilled through edifying stories (*exempla*). From the sixteenth century to the twentieth,
"moral manuals" structured according to the Ten Commandments were
used in the training of Roman Catholic clergy.

The reception of the Decalogue in Judaism contrasted with this
elevation in Christianity. Although it had played a major role in the
daily prayers of Second Temple Judaism, the rabbinic sages did not
attribute any special importance to it compared to other parts of the
Torah.[27] Maimonides even declared that a person "who believes there is
in the Torah an essential part and a peripheral one" is a heretic.[28]
Nevertheless, the pervasive role of the Decalogue in Christian discourse
since the Reformation appears to have influenced Jewish iconographic
use of the tablets of the law as a central symbol of Judaism.[29]

The use of the Ten Commandments to represent a synopsis of the
divine will required hermeneutical acrobatics in Christian catechisms
aiming to treat every issue of morality under one of its headings. All
things sexual were discussed under the label of the prohibitions of
adultery and coveting, although the literal meaning of these prohibitions
is specific and restricted. Moreover, as the Decalogue came to function
as a matrix of Christian moral discourse, it also served as the battle-
ground for moral controversies, especially when it contradicted the felt
necessities of a time. How should one explain the prohibition of killing
to soldiers at war, for example? While the Hebrew wording of the
commandment (using the verb *rṣḥ*) prohibits murder and does not as
such relate to killing in war – as Rudolf Kittel pointed out in *The Old
Testament and Our War* – the traditional generalization of the Commandments in Christian moral teaching created unease among a wide
range of commentators and catechists.[30]

[27] A. Oppenheimer, "Removing the Decalogue from the *Shema* and Phylacteries: The
     Historical Implications," in *The Decalogue in Jewish and Christian Tradition*, ed. Y.
     Hoffman and H. G. Reventlow, LHBOTS 509 (New York: T&T Clark, 2011), 97–105.
[28] *Commentary on the Mishnah, Ḥelek*, the eighth article of faith, quoted in G. B. Sarfatti,
     "The Tablets of the Law as a Symbol of Judaism," in *The Ten Commandments in
     History and Tradition*, ed. B.-Z. Segal and G. Levi, Publications of the Perry Foundation
     for Biblical Research (Jerusalem: Magnes, 1990), 383–418, 389–90.
[29] On the iconographic material, see Sarfatti, "The Tablets of the Law."
[30] R. Kittel, *Das Alte Testament und unser Krieg* (Leipzig: Dörffling & Franke, 1916), 43,
     quoted in P. M. Kurtz, "Thou shalt not kill, unless . . .: The Decalogue in a Kaiserreich
     at War," in *The First World War and the Mobilization of Biblical Scholarship*,

Thus Fritz Wilke, professor of Old Testament in Vienna, argued in 1915: "As everything else in ethical life, with killing it also depends not on the act itself but the mindset [*Gesinnung*] from which it springs and on the intention [*Willensrichtung*] that is essentially operative within it."[31] Wilke was but one of many voices that gave eloquently expressed ethical reasons to justify killing in the Great War, seeking to "reconcile unseen principles with seen atrocities."[32] Those who used the Decalogue as an ethical tool to question the practice of war were a minority, but among them was Protestant ethicist Friedrich Siegmund-Schultze, who observed the double address of the Decalogue to the individual and to the people and asked, If the individual was supposed not to kill, why should the people be commanded to do so?[33] As the Great War raged on the battlefields, the Decalogue sparked a war on the field of interpretation.

1.5 AN ICON OF ETHICAL DISCOURSE

The Nietzschean claim that "we" – that is, enlightened thinkers – have killed God implies that there is no room left for divine commandments. In *Human, All Too Human*, Nietzsche explained that

> A prohibition, the reason of which we do not understand or admit, is almost a command, not only for the stiff-necked but for the thirster after knowledge. We at once make an experiment in order to learn *why* the prohibition was made. Moral prohibitions, like those of the Decalogue, are only suited to ages when reason lies vanquished. Nowadays a prohibition like "Thou shalt not kill," "Thou shalt not commit adultery," laid down without reasons, would have an injurious rather than a beneficial effect.[34]

Nietzsche expressed a view common to contemporary European society. Since ethical values and convictions are a personal matter, authoritative claims such as the ones symbolized by the Decalogue provoke doubt and resistance.

---

ed. A. Mein, N. MacDonald, and M. A. Collins, LHBOTS 676 (London: T&T Clark, 2019), 111–34, 126.

[31] Fritz Wilke, *Ist der Krieg sittlich berechtigt?* (Leipzig: Dietrich, 1915), 115, quoted in Kurtz, "Thou shalt not kill, unless," 118.

[32] Kurtz, "Thou shalt not kill, unless," 113.

[33] Kurtz, "Thou shalt not kill, unless," 128.

[34] F. Nietzsche, *Human, All Too Human: A Book for Free Spirits*, trans. A. Harvey (Auckland: Floating Press, 2013), 314 (*The Wanderer and His Shadow*, no. 48).

The atrocities committed during World War II, however, produced a powerful need for unshakable ethical foundations. The Decalogue's iconic power and the dramatic myth of its origins at Sinai lent itself to this need; they were accordingly invoked, for example, in Cecil de Mille's monumental movie *The Ten Commandments* (1956). In 1943, the year of the publication of *The Tablets of the Law* and two years before the foundation of the United Nations, Thomas Mann felt the

> tendency towards some sort of world-organization . . ., and nothing of the sort is possible without a determining dose of secularized Christianity, without a new Bill of Rights, a foundational law of human right and human decency, which guarantees, irrespective of differences between forms of states and governments, a minimum of respect for the Homo Dei in general.[35]

The *Universal Declaration of Human Rights* of 1948 inherited some of the Decalogue's symbolic role as a new charter for human decency. It responded to the collective trauma of World War II and spoke to the moral needs of the twentieth century, but it has faced criticism for being disproportionately dominated by Western worldviews.

The Decalogue stands as an icon of ethical discourse. Although written in stone by the finger of God, it is subject to reinterpretation already by Moses himself. In keeping with its origins and as a matrix of shared morality, it has provided a critical framework for other ethical controversies down the centuries. It remains a cultural classic, raising significant questions for contemporary ethical reflection. What is the source of authority for fundamental ethical issues? Although not all of us have killed our God, we have lost the divine voice as a commonly acceptable source of authority. Yet, the alternatives have proven danger-ous. Absolute political power has revealed itself as a pseudo-religion, prone to extreme violence. The democratic voice of the people is in danger of losing its credibility, as popular majorities are easily manipu-lated. Legal systems devoid of any ethical basis have proven to be apt instruments of political mass violence. What should constitute the

---

[35]   Letter to R. S. Hartman from 7 April 1943, quoted in Assmann, "Mose gegen Hitler," 57: "Die Tendenz zu irgendeiner Art von Welt-Organisation ist unverkennbar vorhanden, und nichts dergleichen ist möglich ohne eine bestimmende Dosis säkularisierten Christentums, ohne eine neue Bill of Rights, ein alle bindendes Grundgesetz des Menschenrechts und Menschenanstandes, das, unabhängig von Unterschieden der Staats- und Regierungsformen, ein Minimum von Respekt vor dem Homo Dei allgemein garantiert."

ethical foundations of law, and how can such foundations be developed in culturally diverse societies?

The Decalogue is deeply ingrained in the fabric of cultures influenced by Judaism and Christianity. It is likely to continue to provoke both conservative approval and Nietzschean resistance.[36] Yet these tablets of stone should be treated as welcome stumbling blocks, facilitating discussion on what should constitute ethical foundations today. In a world that faces global ecological and social crises, how we are to develop a global ethical discourse is a fundamental question. How do we propose to protect and enhance life on our planet? Though the divine voice is lost to us as common ground, perhaps it could be recovered by listening to the voice of humanity.

FURTHER READING

Barton, J. *Ethics in Ancient Israel*. Oxford: Oxford University Press, 2014.

Bossy, J. "Moral Arithmetic: Seven Sins into Ten Commandments." Pages 214–43 in *Conscience and Casuistry in Early Modern Europe*. Edited by E. Leites. Cambridge: Cambridge University Press, 1990.

Brague, R. *The Law of God: The Philosophical History of an Idea*. Trans. L. G. Cochrane. Chicago: University of Chicago Press, 2007.

Buber, M. *Moses: The Revelation and the Covenant*. New York: Harper & Row, 1958.

Kuntz, P. G. *The Ten Commandments in History: Mosaic Paradigms for a Well-Ordered Society*. Grand Rapids: Eerdmans, 2004.

Markl, D. "The Decalogue in History. A Preliminary Survey of the Fields and Genres of Its Reception." *ZAR* 18 (2012) 279–93.

Markl, D. "The Ten Words Revealed and Revised: The Origins of Law and Legal Hermeneutics in the Pentateuch." Pages 13–27 in *The Decalogue and its Cultural Influence*. Edited by D. Markl. HBM 58. Sheffield: Sheffield Phoenix, 2017.

Oppenheimer, A. "Removing the Decalogue from the Shema and Phylacteries: The Historical Implications." Pages 97–105 in *The Decalogue in Jewish and Christian Tradition*. Edited by Y. Hoffman and H. Graf Reventlow. LHBOTS 509. New York: T&T Clark, 2011.

Otto, E. "The Study of Law and Ethics in the Hebrew Bible / Old Testament." Pages 594–621 in *Hebrew Bible / Old Testament. III: From Modernism to Post-Modernism*. Edited by M. Sæbø. Göttingen: Vandenhoeck & Ruprecht, 2015.

---

[36]   For a learned attempt to defend the Decalogue's universal applicability see P. G. Kuntz, *The Ten Commandments in History: Mosaic Paradigms for a Well-Ordered Society* (Grand Rapids: Eerdmans, 2004). Kuntz believed that "the Ten Commandments survive because they are well fitted to the human condition and can be adapted to any stage of cultural development" (214).

Sarfatti, G. B. "The Tablets of the Law as a Symbol of Judaism." Pages 383–418 in *The Ten Commandments in History and Tradition*. Edited by B.-Z. Segal and G. Levi. Publications of the Perry Foundation for Biblical Research. Jerusalem: Magnes, 1990.

Ska, J. L. "Biblical Law and the Origins of Democracy." Pages 146–58 in *The Ten Commandments: The Reciprocity of Faithfulness*. Edited by W. P. Brown. Louisville: John Knox, 2004.

Smith, L. *The Ten Commandments: Interpreting the Bible in the Medieval World*. Leiden: Brill, 2014.

Voegelin, E. *Israel and Revelation*. Baton Rouge: Louisiana State University Press, 1956.

Willis, J. *The Reformation of the Decalogue: Religious Identity and the Ten Commandments in England, c. 1485–1625*. Cambridge Studies in Early Modern British History. Cambridge: Cambridge University Press 2017.

2 The Talionic Principle and Its Calibrations
SANDRA JACOBS

This essay will explore the pathways (or calibrations) of the talionic 'eye for an eye' principle in the Pentateuch from the cultural perspective of the ancient Hebrew scribes. In contemporary doctrine, rabbinic consensus remains characterised by a strident denial of any literal intent of this principle, where it is interpreted exclusively as a monetary fine. This consensus emerged, initially, as a reaction to charges made in the New Testament regarding the excessive literalism of the early Pharisaic sages. With the growth of Christianity and in the wake of the prejudice from the decrees of Hadrian (c. 135 CE), through to the massacres of the crusades – essentially until the present times – the constancy of this denial was inevitable. Leaving the legacy of this reception history aside, how did the principle of 'eye for an eye' attain such prominence in the Hebrew Bible?

2.1 THE ETHICS OF COERCION IN THE PENTATEUCH

Morality and ethics are deeply embedded in their own time and culture, making it inappropriate to impose contemporary ideals on the ancient sources. In the Hebrew Bible – a corpus refined over many centuries prior to its canonisation – the synthesis of law, narrative, wisdom teaching, poetry, and prophetic visions lack the consistency of systematic and philosophical models. Nor is its ethical profile uniform, where it appears as 'fluid and dialogical in character – very much contrary to its popular image,[1] not least because the cosmological world view of the biblical scribes, at least three thousand years away from our own, was so inherently different to our understanding of society now. Thus the integrated genres of law, narrative, and wisdom teachings were also infused with the formal elements of a political covenant, where goodness was conditional and predicated on the optimum fulfilment of divine commands:

---

[1] J. Barton, *Ethics in Ancient Israel* (Oxford: Oxford University Press, 2014), 20.

> I declare to you this day that you shall certainly perish; you shall not long endure on the soil that you are crossing the Jordan to enter and possess. I call heaven and earth to witness against you this day: I have put before you life and death, blessing and curse. Choose life – if you and your offspring would live – by loving the LORD your God, heeding His commands, and holding fast to Him. (Deut 30:15)[2]

Such imperatives defy an altruistic notion of ethics, which is attained when individuals make their own moral judgments, independent of force or coercion. This is exacerbated by the dominance of the talionic principle, which appears in all major collections of law in the Hebrew Bible.[3] Among the issues raised by this principle is the question, Did the talionic principle permit the Israelite male to avenge any physical assault by means of equivalent retaliation? In order to address this, it is necessary to examine the profile of the principle in the legal material, before considering how the principle's retributive pathways (or calibrations) are deployed by other biblical scribes. First, however, a brief account of divine retribution sets the scene.

2.2 THE BELIEF IN DIVINE RETRIBUTION

The integral conviction, widespread throughout the ancient Near East, was that the workings of history were a manifestation of the retributive principle, for which the gods were directly responsible. Thus, a king's correct ordering of his country was essential to secure the divine approval of his reign, together with the most favourable outcomes ("destinies") for him and his people. In this capacity the king's official (and often monumental) formulation of law in scholastic tradition occupied a place of prominence in Mesopotamian intellectual life.

The belief in this principle is apparent, for example, in the epic of Gilgameš, named after a legendary hero who embarked on a quest to locate the secret of immortal life.[4] The action commences as Gilgameš sets out to find Utnapištim, the antediluvian sage and survivor of the flood. Following a series of death-defying escapades, the two meet.

---

[2]   Likewise Exod 15:26; Deut 6:18; 12:25 ; 12:8; 13:19 ; 21:9; 30:18–20b; etc.
[3]   Although often referred to as *lex talionis* (i.e. the law of retaliation) it is formulated as a principle in biblical law. B. S. Jackson, 'The Problem of Exodus XXI 22–25 (*Ius Talionis*)', *VT* 37 (1973): 273–304.
[4]   Versions of this epic are attested in Sumerian (from Ur) in Akkadian (from Assyria, Sultantepe, and Susa, and in a fragment found at the Canaanite site of Tell Megiddo), in Hittite (from Hattusha, modern-day Boghazköi, Asia Minor), and further in Hurrian.

Utnapištim recalls for Gilgameš the aftermath of his ordeal in the ark: upon their safe return to dry land, he and his wife provided thanksgiving offerings to the gods, who descended upon them like flies. Once the gods were sated, the gods Enlil and Ea engaged in conversation.[5] Ea admonished Enlil for his wanton destruction of all humankind, critiquing the loss of innocent lives with the following rebuke:

> You sage of the gods, you hero!
> How could you lack counsel and cause the deluge?
> On him who commits a sin, inflict his crime!
> On him who commits a wrong, inflict [his] wrongdoing!
> Instead of the deluge you caused,
> a lion could arise to diminish the people...
> a wolf could arise to diminish the people...
> famine could happen to slaughter the land...
> Erra could arise to slaughter the land.[6]

At issue is the inappropriate relationship between the crimes committed by the humans and the punishment wrought upon them via the flood. Accordingly Ea insists that less devastating losses would have been preferable, such as those incurred by rampaging wild beasts.

Similar ideas inform the retributive processes reflected in the Hebrew Bible. There, too, is evidence of a belief in a destiny-producing fate ('schicksalentscheidender Tat'), according to which human actions trigger correspondingly good or bad consequences.[7] As Oeming describes it: 'wisdom operates on a principle of analogy, where individual action determines individual fate in a system of connective justice'.[8] Although the extent of this idea in the Hebrew Bible has been vigorously debated, the impact of such convictions upon the historiographical accounts of

---

[5] Enlil was the chief god of the city of Nippur, who personified vital forces driving the cosmic geography, from the surface of the earth up to the vaults of the skies, which directly affected mankind; Ea is the Akkadian name for the Sumerian Enki, god of wisdom, magic, and fresh water, known for his ingenious solutions to dilemmas and for his goodness towards humanity.

[6] Tablet XI, lines 183–189, from A. R. George, *The Babylonian Gilgamesh Epic: Introduction, Critical Edition and Cuneiform Texts: Volume I* (Oxford: Oxford University Press, 2003), 715.

[7] K. Koch, 'Gibt es ein Vergeltungsdogma im Alten Testament?' *ZTK* 52 (1955): 13, 33.

[8] M. Oeming, 'Wisdom as a Central Category in the Book of the Chronicler: The Significance of the Talio Principle in a Sapiential Construction of History' in *Shai-le Sara Japhet: Studies in the Bible, Its Exegesis and Its Language*, ed. M. Bar-Asher, D. Rom-Shiloni, E. Tov, and N. Wazana (Jerusalem: Bialik Institute, 2007), 138, who further suggests that the entire Chronistic history is based upon the sapiential principle of *talio*.

the Hebrew Bible is fascinating. Such connections are more muted in biblical law, where the talionic formulation functioned as a restraint on the excessive use of corporal punishment.

2.3 THE TALIONIC PRINCIPLE IN PENTATEUCHAL LAW

The talionic principle is arguably the most notorious element of biblical law. Dictating precisely tailored, retributive consequences in cases of physical assault by means of its 'life for a life, eye for an eye, tooth for a tooth, hand for a hand' formulations.[9] In the history of scholarship it was long assumed that the principle represents an earlier and primitive stage in the development of criminal law, which gradually gave way to less barbaric punishments. Yet, the fact that monetary fines for assault appear in some of the very earliest legal sources, in both Sumerian and Akkadian collections, indicates that this cannot have been the case.[10] In the Levant, similarly sequenced monetary payments for injuries sustained in an assault appear in two thumb-sized legal fragments from Hazor. These document seven provisions (LHz A§1-5 and B§1-2) relating to the injury of a slave's nose and tooth, together with a penalty for cheek slapping, where penalties range from three to ten shekels. The find is particularly noteworthy because the chemical composition of the tablet is compatible with that of the local clay, suggesting that it may have been inscribed in the vicinity of Hazor and was not necessarily brought into this area from Mesopotamia.

The principle is defined as 'a concept of punishment whereby the prescribed penalty is identical with, or equivalent to, the offense'.[11] Both the qualitative and quantitative limits of punishment are theoretically fixed where the punishment of a guilty assailant would be restricted to the body part which s/he had damaged and also correspond to the exact

---

[9] The two main formulations being the *taḥat* formulation, characterised by the preposition *taḥat* (translated 'for', as in 'an eye *for* an eye'), and the *"ka'asher"* formulation, which utilises the conjunction *ka'asher*, meaning 'as' or 'like', which is attested in Lev 24:19: 'as he has done so shall it be done to him'. See B. S. Jackson, *Wisdom Laws: A Study of the Mishpatim of Exodus 21:1–22:16* (Oxford: Oxford University Press, 2006), 190–206.

[10] See the Laws of Ur-Namma (LU 18–23), where payments for assault are specified for injuries to a man's foot, bone, nose, and tooth and range from two to sixty shekels. See M. T. Roth, *Law Collections from Mesopotamia and Asia Minor* (Atlanta: Scholars, 1997), 190; also the Old Babylonian Laws of Eshnunna (LE 42–47a), in Roth, *Law Collections*, 65–6.

[11] H. Cohn, 'Talion', in *Encyclopaedia Judaica* Vol. 19, ed. M. Berenbaum and F. Skolnik (Detroit: Macmillan, 2007), 463.

number of limbs or organs injured in any given assault. The principle was clearly of major importance for the scribal guilds or schools in ancient Israel, who preserved and transmitted its various versions up until the final stages of the biblical texts' development in the Persian period (539–331 BCE) and beyond, into the period attested by the Temple Scroll from Qumran.[12] All three major collections of law in the Pentateuch (often described as 'codes') use relatively fixed terms, readily identifiable as legal formulations, and present the principle as an integral element of divinely authored law.[13]

Despite their similarities, each of the individual formulation addressed different situations and circumstances and differed accordingly in the details of their formulations. Thus, in the Covenant Code (Exod 20:22–23:19), the talionic principle was applied exclusively to third-party injuries incurred by a pregnant woman in a public brawl (Exod 21:22–25). In the Holiness Code (Lev 17–26), it covered all physical assaults upon men and cattle (Lev 24:17–21), with 'life for life' denoting capital punishment. In the Deuteronomic Code (Deuteronomy 12–26), the principle identified the punishment of a malicious witness who provided false and incriminating testimony against an innocent person in a capital case (Deut 19:16–20). This revision is particularly notable in view of its affinity with the first provision in Hammurabi's laws, which likewise rules: 'If a man accuses another man and charges him with homicide but cannot bring proof against him, his accuser shall be killed'.[14]

These formulations may be further contextualised with regard to the legal authority appropriate to the scribal group or guild responsible for the collection in which it appears. Thus, in the Covenant Code, the talionic formulation appears as one of the *mishpatim* ('rules') presented to the Israelites at the moment of revelation, spoken by God to Moses on Mount Sinai. Representing the word of God, in the narrative continuum of Exodus these *mishpatim* immediately follow on from the Decalogue. The collection assumes the availability of a pre-institutional authority, possibly a group of local elders or tribal heads; the existence of such an authority is implied by the Hebrew phrase $v^e n\bar{a}tan \ biplil\hat{\imath}m$, 'the payment to be based on reckoning' (Exod 21:22). Scholars have

[12]   11Q19, Column LXIII, lines 12–13.
[13]   These collections are not comprehensive, however, nor do they fully represent contemporaneous legal provisions.
[14]   LHI in Roth, *Law Collections*, 81; cf. the Mishnah's ruling that a false witness in a capital case had to be executed, even if the innocent defendant had not been sentenced to death (*Makkot* 1:4).

suggested that this alludes to the potential for third-party moderation, wherein the approval of impartial and independent assessors would ensure that fair compensation was paid.

In the Holiness Code, the principle appears in an account of the blasphemy committed by the son of Shelomith bat Dibri, who is punished by stoning (Lev 24:13–16, 23); thus, 'life for life' is stipulated as the death penalty for homicide. This version covers all instances of physical assault, including that inflicted on livestock, and effectively demonstrates the statutory powers of the priestly leaders to enforce capital punishment. Although it is known that dispute resolution took place in local temples in the Neo-Babylonian period, there is no extra-biblical evidence for such hearings in the Jerusalem temple specifically, even though the Holiness Code appears to presume the legal authority of the priests.

Alternatively, the Deuteronomic scribes stipulate that 'the two parties to the dispute appear before the LORD, before the priests or magistrates in authority at the time'; here, either the priests or the magistrates are able to sentence the malicious witness to death (Deut 19:18). An emphasis on 'justice, justice shall you pursue' (Deut 16:20) affirms the ideal in broad brush strokes, rather than constitutional specifics. Other than the provision for 'magistrates and officials for all your tribes, in all the settlements that the LORD your God is giving you' (Deut 16:18) and the aforementioned prohibition of false testimony, there is almost no practical information in the Deuteronomic material about the workings of a judiciary, let alone its transactional records. The presence of a local court (probably made up of community elders) at the city gate is presumed. In post-biblical literature, the apocryphal tale of Susanna and the Elders provides a striking exemplar of the fulfilment of this law.[15]

For the scribes of the Covenant Code, the talionic formulation was but one of a sequence of provisions modelled on the laws engraved upon King Hammurabi's monumental stele. The stele was discovered in 1901–1902 CE at the ancient Elamite capital of Susa and is now housed at the Musée du Louvre in Paris. Hammurabi (r. 1792–1750 BCE) was the sixth ruler of the First Dynasty of Babylon, defeating powerful rival kingdoms and expanding his empire while developing a complex military bureaucracy to control his newly conquered territories.

---

[15] This tale is known in two Greek recensions, as a continuum of Daniel in LXX; the Theodotion version was canonised by the Roman Catholic Church.

Modelling his reign as one renowned for attaining the apex of divine justice, Hammurabi bequeathed to posterity a law code that remains the most influential and prestigious expression of cuneiform law. His detailed provisions were framed by an explanatory prologue and concluding epilogue in which he proclaimed, 'These are the just decisions which Hammurabi, the able king, has established and thereby has directed the land along the course of truth and the correct way of life'.[16] Affirming his royal appointment as a divine calling, he adds, 'The great gods having chosen me, I am indeed the shepherd who brings peace, whose sceptre is just'.[17] Bible's paradigmatic leaders, particularly Moses and David, are likewise depicted as shepherds tending their flocks. Copies of Hammurabi's stele would have been erected in major city squares and temple courtyards, remaining in prominent public display during his reign and possibly also during those of his son (Samsu-iluna) and later successors. In the twelfth century BCE the stele was taken from the Ebabbar temple in Sippar by the Elamite king Šutruk-Naḫḫunte as highly prized booty, and relocated to his capital city in Susa.

According to Godfrey Driver and John Miles, Hammurabi's laws represented 'a series of amendments and restatements of parts of the law in force when he wrote'.[18] This view is corroborated by contemporaneous legal records, including rescripts. However, it is also clear that these individual stipulations were neither normative nor binding on the local courts in Babylon. Hammurabi's laws entered the professional training curriculum and general scholastic tradition as a model, to be learned and copied in the temples and palaces of ancient Mesopotamia in the centuries that followed. With dozens of duplicates, extracts, and commentaries – including a bilingual Sumerian-Akkadian manuscript, references to the composition in a first-millennium catalogue, and copies preserved in Ashurbanipal's royal library at Nineveh – the collection became a literary classic, remaining in scribal circulation for more than a millennium after Hammurabi's death.

Hammurabi's laws afforded an impressive prototype for the Covenant Code's scribes, who preserved the subject-sequence of these Babylonian provisions in Exodus 20:22-23:19, but customized alternative circumstances and resolutions throughout. The question of how and when this occurred is unknown. David Wright has argued that the

---

[16] Roth, *Law Collections*, lines xlvii 1–8, 133.
[17] Roth, *Law Collections*, 133.
[18] G. R. Driver and J. C. Miles, *The Babylonian Laws: Legal Commentary Vol. I* (Oxford: Clarendon, 1952), 45.

Covenant Code's scribes drew primarily and directly upon the laws of
Hammurabi during the Neo-Assyrian period, between 740 and 640 BCE
concluding that 'the evidence indicates that CC is a creative academic
work, by and large a unitary composition, whose goal is mainly ideological, to stand as a counter-statement to the Assyrian hegemony prevailing at the time of is composition'.[19] His conclusions, however, raise
more questions than answers.

The connection between the texts is nevertheless clear. In addition,
the appropriation of the Babylonian stipulation 'If an *awīlu* should blind
the eye of another *awīlu* of his own rank, they shall blind his eye'[20] is
readily apparent in the formulation of Exodus 21:24 (cf. Lev 24:20; Deut
19:21). The Exodus formulation retains the 'eye for an eye' and 'tooth for a
tooth' elements,[21] with the sequential 'fracture for fracture' distinction
recalled only in Leviticus 24:20. Notably, Babylonian society is presented
as rigidly hierarchical in Hammurabi's laws; even unarticulated social
categories were crucial. In this context, it is especially remarkable to
perceive a community of (by their own account) escaped slaves aligning
themselves with the rulings assigned to the *awīlu*, the most highly ranked
adult male in Hammurabi's cities, rather than with the *muškenu* ('a
member of the commoner class',) or the *warad awīlim* (the '*awīlu*'s slave').

Strikingly, there is no narrative instance in the Hebrew Bible in which
this retributive process is literally applied – no case where both qualitative
and quantitative consequences are imposed identically for physical injuries to eyes, teeth, hands, legs, or feet.[22] This does not, however, signify a
disinterest in retributive justice, where the reworking of the principle in
narrative and historiographic accounts reveals otherwise.

2.4 BEYOND THE LITERAL ('FINITE OR STRICT-SENSE') APPLICATIONS

Despite this absence of finite or strict-sense exemplars, the talionic
principle appears firmly hardwired into the ethical mainframe of the
patriarchal narratives. As Bernard Jackson explains, 'If we ask, then, why
Abraham was tested, the answer would appear to reside in the talionic

---

[19] D. P. Wright, *Inventing God's Law: How the Covenant Code of the Bible Used and
      Revised the Laws of Hammurabi* (Oxford: Oxford University Press, 2009), 346.
[20] LH 196 (Roth, *Law Collections*, 121).
[21] LH 200: 'If an *awīlu* knock the tooth of another *awīlu*, in his own rank, they shall
      knock out his tooth' (Roth, Law Collections, 121).
[22] See S. Jacobs, *The Body as Property: Physical Disfigurement in Biblical Law*. LHBOTS
      582. (London: Bloomsbury, 2014), 134–85.

principle, found elsewhere in the patriarchal narratives (Jacob, the deceiver, deceived): here, Abraham, the tester of God (Genesis 15) is in turn tested by God'.[23] Such consequences were not merely subtle ironies, but communicated confidence in the perfection of divine justice and in God's power to manifest it appropriately. Juxtaposed in these accounts was also the virtue of mercy, which surfaces in response to marginalised figures. Hagar may be thrown out of Abraham's home and left to die of thirst in the wilderness, but God will hear her – and, moreover, he will give her the exact reward that he promised to those who oppressed her: Her son, Ishmael will become 'a great nation' (Gen 21:18). Admittedly, these outcomes were not entirely consistent – nevertheless, such initiatives indicate a keen sensitivity to the effects of human prejudice and a profound desire to redress the effects of such injustice.

The retributive rationale also surfaces in a number of other foundational accounts. Phillip Nel maintains that in Genesis 38 (Tamar and Judah), the book of Ruth, and Judges 13–16 (Samson) 'not only is the organic completeness of the story units determined by a prevailing judicial order, but the story-cycle of Israel's early history is guided by a supreme Providence that could not be divorced from the principle of talion'.[24] The notion is all the more acute in the build-up to the Israelites' dramatic escape from Egypt (Exodus 1–12). The Pharaoh who decrees that 'every boy that is born you shall throw into the Nile' (Exod 1:22) is punished correspondingly: 'In the middle of the night the LORD struck down all the firstborn in the land of Egypt, from the firstborn of Pharaoh who sat on the throne to the firstborn of the captive who was in the dungeon and all the firstborn of the cattle' (Exod 12:29). On the verge of liberation from slavery, Israel's all-powerful blood redeemer avenges the loss of its drowned sons. In these accounts cases, however, retribution was inexact, lacking the quantitative and qualitative criteria inherent in the 'life for a life, eye for an eye' formulations. Here, the total number of the newborn Hebrew boys thrown into the Nile would be clearly outnumbered by all Egypt's firstborn males (not to mention the additional cattle). Nor is there any attempt to provide a qualitative legal

---

[23]   B. Jackson, *Studies in the Semiotics of Biblical Law* (Sheffield: Sheffield Academic, 2000), 241, referring to the testing of Abraham in Gen 22, where he was asked to offer his son Isaac as a burnt offering. This was in response to Gen 15:2, where Abram asks, 'O Lord GOD, what can you give me, seeing that I die childless?' Likewise, in his asking for proof of the promise of land, 'O Lord GOD, how shall I know that I am to possess it?' in Gen 15:8.

[24]   P. J. Nel, 'The Talion Principle in Old Testament Narratives', *JNWSL* 20 (1994): 27.

equivalence. The status of the Hebrews as slaves appears in stark relief
to that of each freeborn Egyptian son and heir – where the incapacity of
the Pharaoh is juxtaposed by the power of the Israelite God.

2.5 REDEPLOYMENT AND REFINEMENT: CALIBRATIONS OF REFLECTIVE AND INSTRUMENTAL TALION

The talionic principle was also creatively deployed – recalibrated, so to
speak – outside of the Pentateuch, in passages that likewise bypass the
qualitative and quantitative fixtures integral to the legal formulations of
this principle. Here the idea of an intrinsic link between a negative act
and an inevitable consequence for its perpetrator was deployed and
refined dramatically by the psalmists, for example, who acknowledged
that 'his mischief will recoil upon his own head; his lawlessness will
come down upon his skull' (Ps 7:17).

Such refinements include the notion of 'reflective talion', in which a
punishment mirrored either the crime or the character flaw of its perpetrator, projecting it back upon their person to their detriment. As
Mary Douglas explains, 'the principle of equivalent retaliation is quite
blatant in the narrative books: Why did Jezebel die by falling out of a
high window? Answer: the false woman built high places for false
gods'.[25] This recalls the psalmist's declaration: 'He who builds a high
threshold invites broken bones' (Ps 17:19b). A further variant appears
also in the account of Absalom's untimely death. According to the
narrator, Absalom's death was a result of his own pride and vanity,
specifically concerning the luxuriance of his own hair – the sheer weight
of which is magnified in vast and unrealistic proportions: 'No one in all
Israel was so admired for his beauty as Absalom; from the sole of his foot
to the crown of his head he was without blemish. When he cut his hair –
he had to have it cut every year for it grew too heavy for him – the hair of
his head weighed two hundred shekels by the royal weight' (2 Sam
14:25–26). Here Absalom's end is brought about by the very object of
his sin: 'Absalom was riding on a mule and as the mule passed under the
tangled branches of a great terebinth, his hair got caught in the terebinth; he was held between heaven and earth as the mule kept going'
(2 Sam 18:9).[26]

A further deployment of the principle has been termed 'instrumental talion'. In these cases, the limb or organ responsible for carrying out

---

[25]   M. Douglas, *Leviticus as Literature* (Oxford: Oxford University Press, 1999), 214.
[26]   Also Mishnah, *Sotah* 1:8.

the crime is cut or injured.[27] Thus Yael Shemesh defines this calibration as 'a punishment of the offending organ'.[28] It is graphically illustrated in Prov 30:17, where 'the eye that mocks a father and disdains the homage due to a mother; the ravens of the brook shall gouge it out; young eagles will devour it'. This recalls earlier Babylonian law, where failure to recognise (see) one's adoptive parents is punishable by plucking out the child's eye.[29]

It is also apparent in Deut 25:11–12: 'If two men get into a fight with one another, and the wife of one intervenes to rescue her husband from the grip of his opponent, by reaching out and by seizing his genitals, you shall cut off her hand; show no pity'. The terms align most closely with Middle Assyrian rather than Babylonian law, but the use of corporal punishment in such a scenario is attested only in case law from Nuzi.[30] There are no precedents for identifying this punishment as symbolic form of female circumcision or cliterodectomy, nor is it appropriate to suggest that 'you shall cut off her hand', was a euphemism for shaving the wife's groin.[31] The amputation of a woman's hand or fingers was a known punishment, however, and appears to have been adapted by the Deuteronomist as a form of instrumental talion in order to allay possibly one of his greatest fears, namely, that a man's participation in the cult could be threatened by a woman (specifically, by another man's wife in a fight).[32] The severity of the prescribed mutilation reflected the heinous nature of the offence; in addition to jeopardising the man's cultic service, the injury might restrict a man's ability to father children. Notably, the law limits its application of the talionic principle to the man's wife, rather than his mother, sister, or other female bystander. As the woman's husband – and also the beneficiary of her intervention   he would be financially responsible for her actions, including liability for restitution arising from her crimes. Talionic punishment could not, therefore, extend to any other woman, since it would have detrimental

[27]   S. Jacobs, 'Instrumental Talion in Deuteronomic Law', *ZABR* 16 (2010): 263–78.
[28]   Y. Shemesh, 'Punishment of the Offending Organ in Biblical Literature', *VT* 55 (2005): 343–65, here 343.
[29]   LH193: 'If the child of [i.e. reared by] a courtier [*mar girseqîm*] or the child of [i.e. reared by] a *sekretu* identifies with his father's house and rejects the father who raised him or the mother who raised him and departs for his father's house, they shall pluck out his eye', Roth, *Law Collections,* 120.
[30]   Jacobs, 'Instrumental Talion', 271–6.
[31]   Jacobs, *The Body as Property,* 154–64.
[32]   Where the provisions in Lev 22:24 and Deut 23:3 prohibited any genitally injured, or castrated, male from entering the wilderness sanctuary and its cult.

(and financial) implications for that woman's husband or father, rather than for the rescued man.

2.6 CONCLUSION

These cases highlight the importance of the talionic principle, beyond its role as a juridical restraint on physical vengeance. To return, then, to the original question: Did the talionic principle permit the adult Israelite male to avenge any physical assault by means of equivalent retaliation? Clearly the restrictive language of each formulation meant that it did not. Moreover, the presentation of each law within a revelatory or juridical context – at Sinai; in court, palace, temple, or city gate; or even in the presence of a local elder – implies that its use was limited to specific authorities exclusively. Though a rhetorically forceful expression of divine resolution, neither the principle nor its formulation in Hebrew Bible grant carte blanche to any individual inclined to employ retaliatory violence in cases of assault. Its legal prominence conveyed the belief that juridical authorities could, in theory, apply the principle to the specific situations described in biblical law, and that such verdicts would reflect the most prestigious conception of justice. For the surviving Judaean authorities in the Persian period, whose monarchies had disappeared in the anonymity of exile, the need to represent their most sacred legal collections as the pinnacle of exemplary justice but also as the stipulated conditions for the fulfilment of their national covenant, was paramount. As such, the principle was never intended to approve individual retaliatory acts. Rather, its preservation in biblical law serves to affirm the supreme rule of Israel's God and his perfect regulation of the juridical sphere, 'on earth as it is in heaven'.[33]

FURTHER READING

Barton, John. *Ethics in Ancient Israel.* Oxford: Oxford University Press, 2014.

Cohn, H. 'Talion'. Page 463 in *Encyclopaedia Judaica: Volume 19.* 2nd ed. Edited by M. Berenbaum and F. Skolnik. Detroit: Macmillan, 2007.

George, A. R. *The Babylonian Gilgamesh Epic: Introduction, Critical Edition and Cuneiform Texts: Volume I.* Oxford: Oxford University Press, 2003.

Jackson, B. S. 'The Problem of Exodus XXI 22–25 (Ius Talionis)'. *VT* 37 (1973): 273–304.

Jackson, B. S. *Studies in the Semiotics of Biblical Law.* JSOTSup 314. Sheffield: Sheffield Academic, 2000.

---

[33]   As Matthew 6:10.

Jackson, B. S. *Wisdom Laws: A Study of the Mishpatim of Exodus 21:1–22:16.* Oxford: Oxford University Press, 2006.

Jacobs, S. 'Instrumental Talion in Deuteronomic Law'. *ZABR* 16 (2010): 263–78.

Jacobs, S. *The Body as Property: Physical Disfigurement in Biblical Law.* LHBOTS 582. London: Bloomsbury, 2014.

Koch, K. 'Gibt es ein Vergeltungsdogma im Alten Testament?' *ZTK* 52 (1955): 1–42.

Nel, P. J. 'The Talion Principle in Old Testament Narratives'. *JNWSL* 20 (1994): 21–9.

Oeming, M. 'Wisdom as a Central Category in the Book of the Chronicler: The Significance of the Talio Principle in a Sapiential Construction of History'. Pages 125–41 in *Shai le-Sara Japhet: Studies in the Bible, Its Exegesis and Its Language.* Edited by M. Bar-Asher, D. Rom-Shiloni, E. Tov and N. Wazana. Jerusalem: Bialik Institute, 2007.

Roth, M. T. *Law Collections from Mesopotamia and Asia Minor.* SBLWAW 6. 2nd ed. Atlanta: Scholars, 1997.

Shemesh, Y. 'Punishment of the Offending Organ in Biblical Literature'. *VT* 55 (2005): 343–65.

Wright, D. P. *Inventing God's Law: How the Covenant Code of the Bible Used and Revised the Laws of Hammurabi.* Oxford: Oxford University Press, 2009.

3 Community Violence in Deuteronomy

CARYN A. REEDER

According to a number of recent interpreters, Deuteronomy represents a humanistic vision, establishing the protection of the economically and socially marginalized as a center of Israel's covenant.[1] The people of Israel have a responsibility to care for the poor, widows and orphans, slaves, and foreigners who are resident in Israelite communities because of both Israel's own story (they were foreign slaves in the land of Egypt) and the character of God (who enacts justice for widows and orphans and loves foreigners).[2] In sharp contrast to this vision, one group does not receive protection: those who worship the gods of the nations.[3] These people are killed without mercy – even if they are Israelite.[4] In perhaps the most horrifying example, if a person's sibling, child, spouse, or dear friend invites the person to worship the gods of the nations, the response must be immediate and absolute. Without pausing for an investigation or public trial, the person must initiate the execution of the offender by stoning: "your own hand shall be first against them to execute them" (13:6–11).

The violence in this law is unsettling, as the history of interpretation shows. Philo, though he ultimately upholds the demands of the law, identifies the execution of a close family member as wicked and impious (*Spec. Laws* 1.312–13, 3.153). In m. Sanh. 7:10, the rabbis add a requirement for witnesses before the execution can be carried out. John Calvin calls the law cruel (*Harmony of the Law* 2.81–82). More recently, interpreters have described this law and Deuteronomy as wholly brutal,

---

[1]   E.g., P. T. Vogt, "Social Justice and the Vision of Deuteronomy," *JETS* 51 (2008): 35–44, esp. 36, 44.

[2]   Deut 5:12–15; 10:17–19; 15:7–18; 23:7–8; 24:17–22; 26:12–15.

[3]   On the conflicting messages of Deuteronomy, see esp. R. D. Nelson, "Herem and the Deuteronomic Social Conscience," in *Deuteronomy and Deuteronomic Literature*, ed. M. Vervenne and J. Lust, BETL 133 (Leuven: Leuven University Press, 1997), 39–54.

[4]   Deut 7:1–6; 13:1–5, 12–18; 17:2–7; 20:16–18.

severe, absolute and abhorrent, draconian, and intolerant of diversity.[5] Such judgments are not entirely foreign to the text itself. Various elements of Deut 13:6–11 draw attention to the ethical dilemma of the execution of a close family member or friend. In this essay, I explore the problem of violence in Deut 13:6–11 through several connected concerns: the development of Israelite identity in Deuteronomy; the function of violence in identity formation; and the potential mitigation of such violence in Deuteronomy and the biblical canon as a whole. This exploration begins with an analysis of Deut 13:6–11.

3.1 THE PROBLEM OF VIOLENCE IN DEUT 13:6–11

The case law in Deut 13:6–11 (7–12 MT) directly addresses a male head-of-house ("you" in the singular), instructing him in the proper response to someone who invites him to worship "other gods" – that is, the gods of non-Israelite peoples. The invitation to worship these other gods conflicts with the demand for loyalty to Yahweh alone (6:4–5 et passim). Therefore, the proper response is execution. The shock of 13:6–11 comes from the expansive descriptions in the list of the persons who offer the invitation: your brother, son of your mother;[6] your son and your daughter; the wife whom you hold to your chest; your friend who is like your own self (13:6).

In Hebrew, the intimacy of these relationships is emphasized by the repetition of the second-person singular pronominal suffix. The extended descriptions of the brother, wife, and friend in Deut 13:6 expand on this intimacy. A full brother receives more love than a half-brother, as in the story of Joseph (Gen 43:29–30; cf. Judg 8:19). Holding a person to one's chest signifies affection for a treasured member of the household (2 Sam 12:3), as well as a representation of sexual intimacy

---

[5] See P. E. Dion, "Deuteronomy 13: The Suppression of Alien Religious Propaganda in Israel during the Late Monarchical Era," in *Law and Ideology in Monarchic Israel*, ed. Baruch Halpern and Deborah W. Hobson, JSOTSup 124 (Sheffield: Sheffield Academic, 1991), 147–216, esp. 206; J. M. Hamilton, "How to Read an Abhorrent Text: Deuteronomy 13 and the Nature of Authority," *HBT* 20 (1998), 12–32, esp. 15; R. L. Cohn, "The Second Coming of Moses: Deuteronomy and the Construction of Israelite Identity," in *The Comity and Grace of Method*, ed. Thomas Ryba, George D. Bond, and Herman Tull (Evanston: Northwestern University Press, 2004), 133–46, esp. 144; and E. Scheffler, "Reflecting on (Non-)Violence in the Book of Deuteronomy in (Old Testament) Canonical Context," *OTE* 27 (2014): 579–96, esp. 583.

[6] In the Hebrew text, the brother is the son of the addressee's mother. The Septuagint and other ancient versions include half-brothers (4Q30 22–23, Syriac, Tg. Ps.-J. Deut 13:7).

(Gen 16:5; 1 Kgs 1:2). The disruption of the relationship between a man and the woman he embraces represents social disintegration in Deut 28:54, 56 and Mic 7:5. A friend like one's own self is elsewhere closer than kin (Prov 18:24), a person who deserves loyalty and aid (2 Sam 16:17). Although the description of the sons and daughters is not expanded, Yahweh's care for Israel is portrayed with a metaphor of a parent's loving care for a child in Deut 1:29–31, 8:3–5, and 32:10–14. The relationship between a parent and child is paradigmatic for affection, attentiveness, and provision for needs, and the failure of parental care is a curse (28:32, 53–57).

Deuteronomy as a whole privileges the household, marking it as the social, economic, and religious center of life.[7] But in Deut 13:8, the expectations provoked by these references to a full brother, child, wife, or close friend are disrupted by a string of prohibitions: "You must not yield to or heed any such persons. Show them no pity or compassion and do not shield them." The addressee, the male head-of-house with a particular responsibility to care for the members of his household and display loyalty in his social bonds, must instead kill his close relation or friend. The use of an infinitive construct and two synonyms for execution in 13:9 emphasize the demand.[8] Moreover, the addressee must initiate the execution with his own hand (13:10).

The violence in this text is appallingly explicit and intimate.[9] Closer examination only heightens its problematic nature. Within this law, there is no due process or public trial. The invitation to worship other gods, given in secret to the male head-of-house, leads immediately and inexorably to the stoning of the family member or friend. The situation suggests an expectation of a police state that extends into the household, with no safety in the most private spaces of the home, even in the embrace of lovers. The authority granted to this male head-of-house also elicits concern for the potential abuse of power. These elements of the law contrast with the establishment of justice and due process and the limitation of patriarchal power elsewhere in Deuteronomy.[10]

---

[7]   Caryn A. Reeder, *The Enemy in the Household: Family Violence in Deuteronomy and Beyond* (Grand Rapids: Baker Academic, 2012), 19–23.

[8]   In the Septuagint, the first reference to execution is instead a public announcement of the offense. The interpretation here follows the Hebrew text.

[9]   See esp. Scheffler, "Reflecting on (Non-)Violence," 586.

[10] Cf. Deut 13:14; 17:4, 6; 19:15–20; 21:15–17; 25:7–10.

3.2 NARRATIVE, LAW, AND THE CONSTRUCTION OF IDENTITY IN DEUTERONOMY

The construction of Israelite identity in Deuteronomy offers an approach to addressing these concerns. Deuteronomy probably dates either to the seventh century BCE (the time of the Neo-Assyrian Empire) or to the postexilic period – two periods marked by extensive contact between the people of Israel and other nations and cultures.[11] The uncertainty of these historical eras is present in the book's framing narrative. As a literary composition, Deuteronomy consists of a series of speeches given by Moses to the people of Israel as they stand on the eastern bank of the Jordan River, ready to cross over and possess the land promised to their ancestors (1:1, 5; 4:44–45:1; 31:1–8). Moses' audience exists in a liminal space between the wanderings in the wilderness and the promised land, between the leadership of Moses and Joshua. In this space, the people of Israel face a choice: obedience, which leads to life, or disobedience, which leads to destruction (30:15–20). The liminality of the narrative setting serves the book's presentation of Israelite identity. With the authority of Moses' own voice, the stories and laws of Deuteronomy offer a vision of an ideal Israel as a community of people who love Yahweh by obeying Yahweh's commands – even as the stories of the people's past and the specter of future disobedience represent the disruption of identity.[12]

The study of identity formation in biblical texts recognizes the concept of identity as a construction. That is, a particular representation of identity offers an interpretation of cultural, religious, legal, social, and economic concerns. With respect to Deuteronomy, Israel's identity is not a reflection of a historical community, but an attempt to establish a communal identity against other possibilities (including the cultural and cultic practices of the time of the book's composition).[13]

---

[11] C. L. Crouch, *Making of Israel: Cultural Diversity in the Southern Levant and the Formation of Ethnic Identity in Deuteronomy*, VTSup 162 (Leiden: Brill, 2014), 2–3 (and throughout) argues persuasively for the historical composition of Deuteronomy in the "long seventh century." K. L. Noll, "Deuteronomistic History or Deuteronomistic Debate? (A Thought Experiment)," *JSOT* 31 (2007): 311–45, esp. 344, places the book in the postexilic period.

[12] On identity formation in Deuteronomy, see K. L. Sparks, *Ethnicity and Identity in Ancient Israel: Prolegomena to the Study of Ethnic Sentiments and Their Expression in the Hebrew Bible* (Winona Lake: Eisenbrauns, 1998), 228–67; Cohn, "Second Coming," 135; L. M. Wills, *Not God's People: Insiders and Outsiders in the Biblical World* (Lanham: Rowman & Littlefield, 2008), 3–4; Reeder, *The Enemy*, 7–8, 18–19; Crouch, *The Making of Israel*, 112–13 and throughout.

[13] See, e.g., Cohn, "Second Coming," 134–5, 144; Crouch, *Making of Israel*, 129–32.

The consistent use of the direct address ("you" in the singular and plural) in Deuteronomy is part of this effort, connecting Moses' audience within the narrative with the audience of the book.[14] Identity is fluid.[15] Distinctive constructions of identity can be present in a synchronous community, and through time constructions of identity shift and change in response to new technologies, political realities, economics, and other forces. Distinctive visions for Israel's identity as a people coexist in the biblical canon, supported with differing interpretations of foundational stories, laws, and traditions. Deuteronomy is one voice among many.

First and foremost, the identity of Israel established in Deuteronomy depends on loyalty to Yahweh: "The LORD your God you shall fear; him you shall serve, and by his name alone you shall swear" (6:13). Yahweh is characterized as just, impartial, loving, faithful, and (importantly, with respect to monotheism) jealous (7:9–10, 10:17–22). Israel's God does not take a visible form, and therefore cannot be represented by human-made idols (4:15–20). Worship is further restricted to the one place God chooses (12:5–27; 14:22–29; 26:1–11). The call to worship (or serve) Yahweh alone, in only the ways Yahweh commands, and in the one place Yahweh chooses, is fundamental to Deuteronomy's construction of Israel's identity (cf. 5:6–10; 6:4–6; 10:14–15; etc.).[16]

The Shema in Deut 6:4–9 and its reiterations in 10:12–22 and 11:18–21 demand wholehearted dedication to Yahweh. Loyalty to Yahweh, expressed with the language of love, requires keeping Yahweh's commands, speaking the commands in the house and on the road, teaching the commands to children, and writing the commands on bodies and buildings. These measures integrate the practices of identity into daily life. More specifically, in Deuteronomy the household provides space for the promulgation of identity through keeping the Sabbath, sacrificing and feasting, and teaching the stories and the covenant to new generations (e.g., 5:12–15; 6:20–25; 12:12, 18; 16:11, 14). The regulation of household life in laws that address parent-child relationships, marriage, and inheritance patterns further indicates the significance of the household for Deuteronomy's construction of Israelite identity (e.g., 5:16; 21:15–21; 22:13–30; 24:1–4). As they speak,

---

[14] See J. G. McConville, "Singular Address in the Deuteronomic Law and the Politics of Legal Administration," *JSOT* 97 (2002): 19–36, esp. 26–9; Chaya Halberstam, "The Art of Biblical Law," *Prooftexts* 27 (2007): 345–64, esp. 355–6, 359.

[15] Cf. Cohn, "Second Coming," 133; Crouch, *Making of Israel*, 94–104.

[16] Cf. Cohn, "Second Coming," 140–1; R. Barrett, *Disloyalty and Destruction: Religion and Politics in Deuteronomy and the Modern World*, LHBOTS 511 (New York: T&T Clark, 2009), 50–4; Crouch, *Making of Israel*, 112–18, 132–7.

live, dwell, and worship together, households embody "Israel." The integration of the commandments into the daily life of households in Deuteronomy makes Israel's identity a household matter.[17]

Israel's identity rests on the fundamental demand for loyalty to Yahweh, and it is practiced in daily life, worship, and obedience to the commandments. In Deuteronomy, Israel is also given a shared past, an origin story that provides a common cultural memory to unify the people.[18] Moses repeatedly calls his audience to remember that they were slaves in Egypt, and God saved them – so they must obey God (e.g., 5:15; 8:2; 15:15; 24:18). When households, including slaves, keep the Sabbath together and celebrate various festivals, they remember this story of salvation (5:12–15; 16:1–12; 26:1–11). The same story also motivates the laws governing the treatment of slaves, foreigners resident in the land, widows, and orphans (15:12–15; 23:7–8; 24:17–22). The reminders of this story and its incorporation into communal life in Deuteronomy develop Israel's identity by providing a common narrative for the people to inhabit.

While Deuteronomy resounds with exhortations to obedience (e.g., 7:12–16; 11:8–9; 27:1; 29:9), the covenant curses and the song of witness at the end of the narrative indicate an expectation of disobedience (28:15–68; 31:16–32:47). The danger of disobedience is itself part of Israel's identity, according to another set of stories Moses tells his audience. Yahweh cared for the people in the wilderness like a parent caring for a child, but Israel rebelled by refusing to trust in God and enter the land, and making and worshiping an idol (1:26–45; 8:1–6; 9:6–21). Israel is stubborn and rebellious (9:6–7, 24; 29:4; 32:4–6). The story of Israel's disobedience provides a warning in Deuteronomy: Israel is its own worst enemy.

3.3 THE ENEMIES OF IDENTITY: OUTSIDERS IN DEUTERONOMY

A key concern in identity formation is the interaction between "self," whether individual or (as in Deuteronomy) communal, and "other."[19] To define a person or community is to some extent a negative process, requiring the definition of what that person or community is not. Identity formation creates insiders and outsiders in order to separate insiders

---

[17]   See further Reeder, *The Enemy*, 19–23, 37–53.
[18]   Cf. Cohn, "Second Coming," 137–8; Crouch, *Making of Israel*, 138–40.
[19]   Sparks, *Ethnicity*, 238–42, 257–60; Wills, *Not God's People*, 3–14.

from outsiders. One tool in the separation of self from others is violence. Wars (especially holy wars), the policing of community members, and the execution or expulsion of people or objects perceived as dangers to identity destroy life and property, but such acts of violence are also productive for communal identity. "Constructive violence" has as its goal the protection of identity from internal and external threats.[20]

Since Israel's identity centers on Yahweh, the identity of the "other" in Deuteronomy is constructed around the worship of "other gods" ('ĕlōhîm 'ăḥērîm), also described as the gods of the nations, whom neither Moses' audience nor their ancestors know (28:64; 32:17). These gods are represented by human-made idols that cannot see or hear – that is, the idols are not living (4:15–20, 28; 7:1–5). This particular description both denigrates the gods worshiped by the nations and elevates Israel, whose God speaks and acts in the world on its behalf (4:32–34). Outsiders to Israel worship their gods in many places, with sacred pillars, stones, trees, and abhorrent practices, again unlike Israel, who worships Yahweh in one place with no images, pillars, trees, or abhorrent practices (e.g., 7:5; 12:2–14, 29–31; 18:9–14).

Outsiders who worship "other gods" are represented by several specific groups and individuals in Deuteronomy. One group, the nations of Canaan, are constructed as a literary foil for the people of Israel.[21] In addition to their sacral practices, the peoples of the land are described as strong and numerous. They live in fortified cities (7:1, 17; 9:1–2; 11:23). The descriptions of the nations reflect positive, desirable attributes of social status and military strength, but these attributes are devalued in Deuteronomy by their contrast with Israel. Israel is a small, weak people, but it has Yahweh on its side, and the strength of Yahweh overcomes the strength of the nations of the land (7:1–2, 17–24; 31:3–5).

Despite the promise of the military defeat of the nations and their dispossession from the land, however, outsiders who worship other gods are a threat to Israel. Israel is not righteous and obedient, the expected contrast to the wickedness of the peoples of the land. Rather, again, Israel is characterized in Deuteronomy as stubborn and rebellious, particularly with respect to the worship of other gods. An assumption of disloyalty and consequent punishment looms over Deuteronomy's stories and laws (cf. 4:25–31; 30:1–5). Idolatry is the fundamental threat to Israel's identity and also Israel's besetting sin (e.g., 4:25–26; 5:6–10;

---

[20]   See Wills, *Not God's People*, 27–30; and on the concept of constructive violence, Reeder, *The Enemy*, 8–9.

[21]   Cf. Sparks, *Ethnicity*, 257–60.

6:13–15; 11:16–17). If Israel gives up its unique identity as Yahweh's people who worship Yahweh alone in the ways and space that Yahweh commands, then Israel becomes the other – a loss of identity that results in devastating punishment (8:19–20).[22]

Outsiders endanger Israel's identity by their presence in Israel's land because of the potential that Israel will learn their worship practices (7:2–4, 16, 25–26; 12:29–31; 20:17–18).[23] Various measures are proposed to protect the identity of Israel from such threats. First, the nations of the land and their cultic practices are eliminated by means of the ban (ḥerem).[24] This process includes killing all the residents of the land – men, women, children, and animals – and destroying their cultic sites (7:1–6, 25–26; 12:2–4; 20:16–18). Second, Israelites who worship other gods or idols are eliminated. A man or woman who worships other gods is stoned to death at the gate of the city, a liminal space that marks the person's identity as an outsider (17:2–7). A prophet or diviner of dreams who calls the people of Israel to worship other gods is executed (13:1–5). If an entire Israelite city worships other gods, that city is treated with the same violence of ḥerem as the nations of the land (13:12–18).

For Deuteronomy, the absolute, total elimination of outsiders from within the land of Israel is a matter of identity. Such acts of violence are preventative, removing these potential temptations to the worship of other gods. These acts of violence are also protective, guarding Israel's apparently fragile identity from threats. The violent destruction of outsiders, whether they be the Canaanite nations or disloyal Israelites, is constructive for Israel's identity. In Deuteronomy, constructive violence guards loyal Israelites and their space against the destruction that comes on outsiders.

3.4 DEUTERONOMY 13:6–11

Deuteronomy's definition of Israelite identity, the distinction between insiders and outsiders, and constructive violence in the service of Israel's identity provide a framework for explaining the execution of a family member or dear friend in 13:6–11. Identity is a key concern in this law, emphasized by its literary context and comparison with the Neo-Assyrian Succession Treaty of Esarhaddon. This law particularizes the

---

[22]   Note also Deut 4:25–29; 6:14–15; 7:3–4; 28:56–61; 29:18–28.
[23]   Crouch, *Making of Israel*, 185–6.
[24]   See Nelson, "Herem," 44–8.

general construction of identity in Deuteronomy. In 13:6–11, individual
Israelites are made responsible for the protection of Israel's identity.

The first two cases in Deuteronomy 13 address threats to Israel's
identity from prophets, diviners of dreams, members of the household,
and close friends. A similar decree in the Neo-Assyrian Succession
Treaty of Esarhaddon helps define the problem. This seventh-century
treaty is broadly comparable with Deuteronomy.[25] Specifically, the
treaty calls on vassals to love Ashurbanipal, being loyal to him in word
and deed (lines 266–268, 385–396; compare Deut 6:5). Disloyalty is
treason. The vassal must report any act or threat of treason, including
those from a prophet, ecstatic, dream interpreter, or member of the
vassal's own family – his brother, son, or daughter. The report should
be accompanied by decisive action, either bringing the guilty party
before Ashurbanipal or killing the traitor and destroying their memory
(lines 73–82, 108–122, 130–146). Treason is part of the vocabulary of
Deuteronomy 13 (sārâ, 13:5). The parallel with the Succession Treaty
clarifies this concern. The worship of other gods is an act of treason
against Yahweh.[26]

Treason in Deuteronomy 13 builds on the delineation of the worship practices of outsiders and insiders in Deuteronomy 12. The nations
of the land worship other gods in many places in the land, using idols,
pillars, poles, and trees as cultic objects; true Israelites must destroy
these places (12:2–7). Insiders in Israel's community worship only
Yahweh in the one place Yahweh chooses, offering sacrifices, tithes,
and more with their children, their slaves, and the Levites who live in
their hometowns (12:8–14, 17–18, 26–27). This section concludes with a
warning against the worship practices of the nations of the land: "Every
abhorrent thing that the LORD hates they have done for their gods"
(12:29–31). The strong negative description reinforces the othering of the
nations of the land. They are dispossessed, destroyed, and hated by God.
To imitate the nations is to give up Israelite identity.

The possibility of the abandonment of Israelite identity continues in
the three case laws of Deuteronomy 13: the prophet or diviner of dreams
who encourages the people to worship other gods; the family member or
close friend who encourage the head-of-house to worship other gods; and

---

[25] Compare, for instance, the covenant curses of Deut 28:15–68 with the Succession
      Treaty, lines 414–668. See further Dion, "Deuteronomy 13," 198–204; B. M. Levinson
      and J. Stackert, "Between the Covenant Code and Esarhaddon's Succession Treaty:
      Deuteronomy 13 and the Composition of Deuteronomy," *Journal of Ancient Judaism*
      3 (2012), 123–40.
[26] Cf. Dion, "Deuteronomy 13," 197; Barrett, *Disloyalty*, 146–50.

the Israelite city that accepts an invitation to worship other gods. The first case incorporates a version of the Shema (Deut 13:3–4; compare 6:4–5). This deliberate reminder of Israel's identity dominates the rest of the chapter, reinforced as it is with references to the origin story narrated in Deuteronomy. Yahweh is the God who saved Israel from slavery in Egypt (13:5, 10). The encouragement to worship other gods is a divine test, as happened to the people in the wilderness (13:3; cf. 8:2, 16). The land and its cities are the gift of God (13:12; cf. 4:1, 6:10–12, 12:29, etc.), and God's compassion on the people fulfills promises to their ancestors (13:17; cf. 4:37, 7:8, etc.). Finally, following a common refrain in Deuteronomy, the Israelites should follow the way of God (13:5; cf. 5:33, 8:6, 10:12, etc.). The three cases in Deuteronomy 13 assume and reinforce Israel's common identity.

The three cases also define non-Israelites. Outsiders are marked by the worship of "other gods," described from the perspective of a loyal Israelite as gods unknown to Moses' audience or their ancestors (13:2, 6, 13). These are the gods of the nations around Israel, not the God of Israel (13:7). The third case holds particularly strong echoes of Deuteronomy's construction of the other. Here, the worship of other gods is abhorrent (13:14), a descriptor more commonly associated with the non-Israelite nations of the land (7:25–26; 12:31; 18:9, 12). Moreover, the city in the third case is utterly annihilated and destroyed, a treatment otherwise reserved for the nations of Canaan (7:1–2; 20:16–18). As in Deut 7:25–26, when the Israelites bring the abhorrent practices of the nations into their own homes, they themselves become abhorrent – they lose their privileged identity and become outsiders. Constructive violence against those who encourage the worship of other gods makes a terrible sense in Deuteronomy; to protect the identity of the people as a whole, the threat represented by the individual prophet, diviner of dreams, family member, friend, or Israelite city is eliminated.

In each case in Deuteronomy 13, the threat comes from inside the community. Prophets and diviners of dreams should be authoritative figures for the community, especially when the signs they promise come true (13:1–2). A city full of Israelites should be a safe space; it is, after all, the gift of God (13:2). And a sibling, child, spouse, or dear friend, someone like "your" very self, should be the ultimate insider. There is, again, an emphasis on the intimacy of the relationship between the male head-of-house and his close kin or friend in 13:6. The expected trustworthiness of these relationships provides the impetus for the string of prohibitions in 13:8. In the case of the prophet or dream diviner, there is only one prohibition, that against listening to the person (13:3), and in the case of the city, the only prohibition is against retaining anything from the city (13:17). By comparison, the list of five prohibited behaviors in 13:8 implicitly indicates the difficulty of treating someone who should be an insider as an outsider.

In Deut 13:6–11, the outsider is, in fact, the ultimate insider. According to Deuteronomy's presentation of household life, family members live together in a house written with the words of the covenant. They recite the words of the covenant in their house and as they walk on the roads together. They celebrate festivals and offer sacrifices together. In this context, the shock of the law is not its violence, which is a standard element in the book's construction of identity. Rather, the shock comes in the revelation of an insider – a close family member or friend – as a traitor, an enemy within the most intimate social circles. In Deut 13:6–11, constructive violence is a requirement even for an individual Israelite approached in secret by a close family member or friend.[27] The individual is given responsibility for maintaining Israel's identity at the expense of personal loyalties, affection, and protective care. This law personalizes the corporate identity of Israel in a jarring, horrifying way.

Self and other, insider and outsider, are carefully delineated in Deuteronomy 13 in the service of Israel's identity. The internal logic of the three cases revolves around constructive violence. Moses' audience within the book is called to be loyal to Yahweh alone. Disloyalty is treason. If an apparent Israelite encourages the people to worship other gods, that person is revealed as an outsider, an enemy in the land (13:17). So, by the logic of identity, the non-Israelite must be removed for the good of the whole (cf. 30:19–20). To protect Israel's corporate identity, the threat of a prophet, dream interpreter, family member or friend, or entire city is eradicated.

3.5 THE ETHICS OF IDENTITY AND CONSTRUCTIVE VIOLENCE

I have argued that there is an internal logic to the violence in Deut 13:6–11. Within Deuteronomy's construction of Israel's identity, loyalty to Yahweh is paramount. The division between insiders and outsiders revolves around their relationship to Yahweh. As such, the stoning of the close family member or friend who invites the addressee to worship

---

[27]   On the issue of individual responsibility, see Dion, "Deuteronomy 13," 162; McConville, "Singular Address," 27–9, 34.

other gods makes sense. Nonetheless, I remain deeply troubled by the demands of this law. To execute someone by stoning is intimate, visible and audible, and brutal.[28] Moreover, for a reader in the twenty-first century, with its celebration of and legal protections for diversity and minority identities, the limitation of allowable identities to one construction is problematic. Explaining the constructive violence in Deuteronomy does not remove its offensiveness.

The problematic nature of Deut 13:6–11 is increased by the consideration of power in the law. The addressee is the male head-of-house, the primary addressee in laws directed to Israelites as individuals and, therefore, a person accorded social, economic, and legal authority within the book's depiction of the Israelite community. The expectations outlined in Deut 13:6–11 give this man absolute authority. In contrast to 13:12–18 and 17:2–7, there is no investigation or requirement for witnesses. The secrecy of the invitation limits such possibilities, of course, but the secrecy also allows for the misuse of the law to rid the household of a troublesome child or unwanted wife. Moreover, the son, daughter, and wife have no explicit rights over the man – what if he secretly invites them to worship other gods? The only potential checks on the male head-of-house come from his brother or dear friend, if the law is taken at face value.

In light of these concerns, is an ethical interpretation of Deut 13:6–11 possible, or even desirable? In the remainder of this essay, I will explore several possible mitigations of the problem of identity and constructive violence in this law and in Deuteronomy as a whole. First, the question of enforceability provides a useful lens for interpretation. Second, recognition of the multiplicity of constructions of identity in Deuteronomy's canonical context and their (limited) reflections in Deuteronomy offers an alternative to the book's apparent intolerance.

First, enforceability. As it is written, the law in Deut 13:6–11 is unenforceable.[29] If the invitation is given in secret, no one else need ever know. The male head-of-house could simply do nothing, allowing the offense to slide. Within Deuteronomy, the law addresses the threat of an outsider infiltrating an Israelite household. But within the structure of the law itself, the prohibitions of pitying, sparing, or concealing the offender suggest that the addressee's response is also a threat. The prohibitions suggest that the law is not about power or violence at all, but about faithfulness and loyalty. In this reading, the extreme

---

[28]   See Scheffler, "Reflecting on (Non-)Violence," 586.
[29]   Cf. Halberstam, "Biblical Law," 347–8, 359.

expectations of the law operate to jolt the audience into a recognition of
the demands of Israelite identity.[30]

Second, multiplicity of identities. Deuteronomy offers one construction of Israel's identity. Some of the other constructions represented in
the biblical canon incorporate Deuteronomy's outsiders into the Israelite community.[31] In Jonah, when the people of Nineveh repent before
God, God forgives them (3:1–10). The book ends with an announcement
of God's care for the people of Nineveh, a population elsewhere characterized as the enemies of the people of God (Jonah 4:11; contrast Nah
1:1–2, Zeph 2:10–13). In Ruth, a Moabite woman, part of a people
excluded from Israel in Deut 23:3–4, expresses loyalty to her Israelite
mother-in-law, her people, and her God. Ruth of Moab becomes the
great-grandmother of King David (Ruth 1:16–17; 4:17). A surprising final
example comes from Joshua, the story of the conquest of the land and
the annihilation of its inhabitants (compare *herem* in 8:26, 10:28, 11:11,
etc., with Deut 7:1–6). In this story, the very first Canaanite the
Israelites meet does not die. Rahab and her household are deliberately
protected from the violence against the nations of the land (note
Josh 6:17), and she and her family live among the Israelites from that
time on (13:25).

Deuteronomy is one voice in a spectrum of identities represented in
the Tanakh. The tolerance and inclusivity expressed by other voices
provide a check on the singularity of Israel's identity in Deuteronomy.
Echoes of the more tolerant or inclusive constructions of identity
are discernable in Deuteronomy in the commandments concerning
strangers or resident foreigners. Because the people of Israel were
strangers in Egypt, they must care for strangers in their own land (Deut
10:19; 24:17–22). There is a distinction between Israelites and strangers
in their midst (cf. 14:21; 23:7–8).[32] However, Yahweh loves the stranger,
and they are allowed to celebrate the Sabbath and some feasts (5:12–15;
10:17–18; 16:9–15; 26:11). These people who, according to the strict
separation of Israelites from all others in Deuteronomy, should be outsiders are instead participants in the Israelite community – and this
despite the fact that their worship practices are never defined.[33]

There is no explanation for the dissonance in the book; it simply
stands. Israel is both the people whose loyalty to Yahweh alone demands

[30]   See further Halberstam, "Biblical Law," 354–6.
[31]   Also noted by Hamilton, "Abhorrent Text," 14–15.
[32]   Cf. Crouch, *Making of Israel*, 211–16, on the foreigner in Deuteronomy.
[33]   See further Crouch, *Making of Israel*, 218–23.

the extermination of any threat to their corporate identity, and at the same time the people whose own story demands care for the outsiders in their midst. Israel's God is both uniquely devoted to the people of Israel and at the same time a God who loves the stranger. In conjunction with the more inclusive representations of Israel's identity elsewhere in the Tanakh, the presence and participation of resident foreigners in the Israelite community offer an alternative to the extermination of all outsiders from Israel.

A final alternative comes with the forgiveness of the people of Israel for disloyalty to God. Again, there is a connection between the story of an individual Israelite who becomes an outsider by virtue of worship of other gods in Deut 13:6–11 and the expectation that the people as a whole will give up their identity by worshiping other gods. The nation is, like the individual, exterminated – treated as the nations of the land, destroyed, and expelled (e.g., 4:25–28; 6:10–15; 7:26; 11:16–17). But when the survivors repent, God forgives them and restores them (4:29–31; 9:18–19, 25–29; 30:1–10). The promise of forgiveness for the stubborn, rebellious nation balances Deuteronomy's extreme monotheism. There is no means for reforming and restoring an individual who worships other gods or invites others to worship other gods. But the model of the nation as a whole at the least suggests the option of forgiveness.

FURTHER READING

Barrett, R. *Disloyalty and Destruction: Religion and Politics in Deuteronomy and the Modern World*. LHBOTS 511. New York: T&T Clark, 2009.

Cohn, R. L. "The Second Coming of Moses: Deuteronomy and the Construction of Israelite Identity." Pages 133–46 in *The Comity and Grace of Method*. Edited by Thomas Ryba, George D. Bond, and Herman Tull. Evanston: Northwestern University Press, 2004.

Crouch, C. L. *The Making of Israel: Cultural Diversity in the Southern Levant and the Formation of Ethnic Identity in Deuteronomy*. VTSup 162. Leiden: Brill, 2014.

Dion, P. E. "Deuteronomy 13: The Suppression of Alien Religious Propaganda in Israel during the Late Monarchical Era." Pages 147–216 in *Law and Ideology in Monarchic Israel*. Edited by Baruch Halpern and Deborah W. Hobson. JSOTSup 124. Sheffield: Sheffield Academic, 1991.

Halberstam, C. "The Art of Biblical Law." *Prooftexts* 27 (2007): 345–64.

Hamilton, J. M. "How to Read an Abhorrent Text: Deuteronomy 13 and the Nature of Authority." *HBT* 20 (1998): 12–32.

Levinson, B. M., and J. Stackert. "Between the Covenant Code and Esarhaddon's Succession Treaty: Deuteronomy 13 and the Composition of Deuteronomy." *Journal of Ancient Judaism* 3 (2012): 123–40.

McConville, J. G. "Singular Address in the Deuteronomic Law and the Politics of Legal Administration." *JSOT* 97 (2002): 19–36.

Nelson, R. D. "Herem and the Deuteronomic Social Conscience." Pages 39–54 in *Deuteronomy and Deuteronomic Literature*. Edited by M. Vervenne and J. Lust. BETL 133. Leuven: Leuven University Press, 1997.

Noll, K. L. "Deuteronomistic History or Deuteronomistic Debate? (A Thought Experiment)." *JSOT* 31 (2007): 311–45.

Reeder, C. A. *The Enemy in the Household: Family Violence in Deuteronomy and Beyond*. Grand Rapids: Baker Academic, 2012.

Scheffler, E.. "Reflecting on (Non-)Violence in the Book of Deuteronomy in (Old Testament) Canonical Context." *OTE* 27 (2014): 579–96.

Sparks, K. L. *Ethnicity and Identity in Ancient Israel: Prolegomena to the Study of Ethnic Sentiments and Their Expression in the Hebrew Bible*. Winona Lake: Eisenbrauns, 1998.

Vogt, P. T. "Social Justice and the Vision of Deuteronomy." *JETS* 51 (2008): 35–44.

Wills, L. M. *Not God's People: Insiders and Outsiders in the Biblical World*. Lanham: Rowman & Littlefield, 2008.

4 The Construction of Gender Roles in the Book of the Covenant and in Deuteronomy

CAROLYN J. PRESSLER

As a very new Hebrew Bible professor working on my dissertation on Deuteronomic family law, I once attended a reception for the great New Testament scholar Krister Stendahl. Someone briefed him well; when he was introduced to me, he murmured, "Women in Deuteronomic law. Not much joy!" Bishop Stendahl's assessment was on target. An analysis of gender norms and biblical law sheds light on the gender ideals and aspirations of certain elite circles of ancient Judahite men, but it does not render an ethical model for folk today. It is, nonetheless, worth undertaking – if only to avoid uncritically passing on abhorrent values. After discussing the nature of biblical legal texts and a brief look at gender and the Decalogue, this essay focuses on how the Covenant Code (C; Exod 20:22–23:33) and Deuteronomic law (D; Deut 12–26) construct gender roles.[1] Analysis of the construction of gender norms in the priestly laws remains for another time.[2]

"Gender" is a contested term. My assumption is that gender is a socially constructed and learned set of behavioral, psychological, and cultural traits assigned to "males" and "females," which are also socially constructed categories. Gender intersects with other social factors, especially class, generation, and ethnicity. The biblical law collections reflect and construct multiple roles for men and for women, but in each, the dominant addressee is the free, landowning "father." Sons, nonlandowning male clients, slaves (freeborn, houseborn,

---

[1] For a fuller discussion see C. Anderson, *Women, Ideology, and Violence: Critical Theory and the Construction of Gender in the Book of the Covenant and the Deuteronomic Law*, JSOTSup 394 (London: T&T Clark, 2004). This article examines the construction of gender roles rather than gender, per se.

[2] On the priestly legislation see N. J. Ruane, *Sacrifice and Gender in Biblical Law* (New York: Cambridge University Press, 2013) and D. W. Rooke (ed.), *Embroidered Garments: Priests and Gender in Biblical Israel* (Sheffield: Sheffield Phoenix, 2009).

purchased Hebrews, or purchased or captured non-Hebrews) and all women are subordinate. Yet, while each biblical legal collection privileges the dominant male, it does so in a different way.

Neither C nor D resembles modern, Western legislation, drafted and enforced by the state. Their relationship to legal practice in ancient Judah is unclear. Although some cases in C and D may stem from trial records, as a whole they reflect legal ideals and assumptions rather than actual legal practice. As such, they reflect particular constructions of Judahite gender norms rather than a clear window on the lived experience of ancient Judahite women and men.

The formulation of these "laws" also differs from modern Western laws. They belong to a broad ancient Southwest Asian legal tradition that began in early Sumer and continued into the fifth century BCE.[3] The ancient legal theorists did not set out abstract principles explicitly, but collected series of concrete cases that illustrated various principles. These examples are not exhaustive, nor are they meant to be interpreted woodenly. They present implicit guidelines; the guidelines, not the specific details of the case, carry the weight of law. Moreover, within series of related cases, the audience is expected to reason from one case to another.[4]

The biblical law collections are also highly selective, reflecting issues particularly pressing to a specific community or their compilers' interests in anomalous or difficult cases. Many basic legal processes or institutions are taken for granted. For example, no biblical legal text defines marriage, nor is there a case identifying who could initiate divorce and under what circumstances.[5] Instead, Deuteronomy includes an idiosyncratic case prohibiting a man who had divorced his wife from remarrying her, if subsequently she had entered into a second marriage with a man who either died or divorced her.

---

[3] Following D. A. Knight, *Law, Power and Justice in Ancient Israel*, LAI (Louisville: Westminster John Knox, 2011), 9 n 2, I use "ancient Southwest Asian" because it more accurately and with fewer colonial overtones describes the territory usually referred to as "ancient Near East."

[4] R. Westbrook, *Studies in Biblical and Cuneiform Law*, Cahiers de la Revue Biblique 26 (Paris: J. Gabalda et Cie, 1988), 6.

[5] I use "marriage" and "to marry" for convenience, though there are no Biblical Hebrew terms for either. See C. Pressler, "The 'Biblical View' of Marriage," in *Engaging the Bible in a Gendered World: An Introduction to Feminist Biblical Interpretation in Honor of Katharine Doob Sakenfeld*, ed. L. Day and C. Pressler (London: Westminster/ John Knox, 2006), 200–11.

4.1 THE DECALOGUE (EXOD 20:2–17; DEUT 5:6–21)

Reflecting on gendering in the Ten Commandments raises issues found throughout the biblical law collections. They reflect deep concern for the stability and integrity of the family; thus, all members of the household as well as livestock and resident aliens observe the Sabbath, a ritual that enhances family solidarity (Exod 20:10; Deut 5:14). Parental authority is resolutely affirmed (Exod 20:12; Deut 5:16) and the prohibition of adultery upholds family boundaries (Exod 20:14; Deut 5:18).

These commandments are not directly aimed at defining or promulgating gender norms, but the family they undergird is the "father's house" (*bêt 'āb*). Its interests are largely the interests of its male head. This is particularly obvious in the prohibition of adultery. In the Hebrew Bible, as throughout ancient Southwest Asian law, adultery is defined unilaterally as sexual intercourse between a betrothed or married woman and a man not her husband. Biblical legislation is not concerned about a betrothed or married man having sex with a woman who is not his wife, as long as it does not violate another man's rights over the woman in question.

This androcentrism is intensified by its audience, who are male, as shown by Moses' command not to "go near a woman" (Exod 19:15), and by the inclusion of the "neighbor's wife" among things not to covet (Exod 20:17). The "you" of the commandments is masculine singular, raising both a pastoral-ethical difficulty and a scholarly puzzle. The pastoral-ethical issue is that women who read these commandments are subsumed under the male pronoun. As Athalya Brenner writes, "the text endows me and my like with hardly any measure of subjectivity."[6]

The academic puzzle is to identify when the grammatically masculine "you" is used inclusively, as can be done in Hebrew. With a number of scholars, I assume that "you" in the Sabbath commandment (Exod 20:10; Deut 5:14) includes the man's wife or wives. Otherwise, male and female minors and slaves are given rest, but the mother is not. This seems unlikely, though some have argued that the mother's tasks are too vital to the running of the household for her to abstain from work.

---

[6] A. Brenner, "An Afterword: The Decalogue, Am I an Addressee?" in *A Feminist Companion to Exodus to Deuteronomy*, ed. A. Brenner (Sheffield: Sheffield Phoenix, 1994), 256.

4.2 THE BOOK OF THE COVENANT

Construction of the "Male" in C

The first section of the Book of the Covenant, the *mišpāṭîm*, (Exod 21:1–22:19) is widely held to be the oldest legal collection in the Hebrew Bible. Like the Decalogue, it assumes that its addressees are adult, landowning, male heads of household. They are the subject of the laws and responsible for enforcing them (see Exod 22:18; 23:2, 6). Other persons come into view as objects, not agents.

Ideal men in C are villagers – a band of neighbors, not autonomous individuals.[7] Living in close proximity, they lend and borrow animals, give animals or goods to one another for safekeeping, and engage in the kinds of conflicts that arise within very small communities. C envisions a group so small that each man knows not only his neighbor, but his neighbors' animals (23:4, 5)! The addressees are relatively well-to-do and have economic control over their households. Thus, when men fighting inadvertently strike a pregnant woman and she miscarries, her husband is compensated (Exod 21:22). Likewise, if a man seduces a young woman, he must compensate her father (Exod 22:16–17). Financial matters arising from conflict between male heads of households dominate the *mišpāṭîm*.

This dominant male "you" is a feisty fellow. C assumes, then seeks to limit, his violence. The aforementioned miscarriage case is one of several laws that address physical altercations. Exodus 21:12–14, 18–19 concern men who strike another free man (or, presumably, woman); Exod 21:15 mandates the death penalty for one who strikes either parent. Exodus 21:20–21, 26–27 set boundaries on a master's violent treatment of his slave.

C's addressee is also religious. C resolves disputes without witness or tangible evidence by having both parties "come before God" (or gods) for judgment or to make a vow (22:8–9; 22:10–11 [Heb 22:9–10]; cf. 21:6). The addressee in the second half of C is more explicitly religious – and more explicitly male. Exodus 23:14–19 commands "you" to observe three annual festivals. Exodus 23:17 requires every Israelite *male* to appear before YHWH; in this instance "you" is clearly gender exclusive.

Not all males in C are dominant. The *son* appears in two cases upholding the authority of the addressee's generation (i.e., the parents).

---

[7] D. J. A. Clines, "Being a Man in the Book of the Covenant," in *Reading the Law: Studies in Honour of Gordon J. Wenham* ed. J. G. McConville and K. Möller (London: T&T Clark, 2007), 3–9.

Striking or cursing one's parent is a capital crime (21:15, 17). Even if they are subordinate, however, sons are not chattel. The case of a habitually goring ox treats free adults and free minors in the same way, male or female. As in the case of an adult killed by the ox, the death of a son means the ox is stoned and its negligent owner must die or ransom his life. Thus, free sons (i.e., male minors in the household, not necessarily the dominant man's biological sons) are persons (21:31).

Enslaved males and females are both human beings and property. If the habitually goring ox kills a *slave*, it is stoned; vis-à-vis the ox, then, the male or female slave is a human being. Yet, unlike the case of a free person gored to death, the ox's owner is required to pay a fine, not a ransom. Vis-à-vis other human beings, then, the slave is property. The same dual status underlies the twin cases dealing with a master who beats his slave to death (21:20–21). If the slave dies immediately, the master is punished, suggesting the slave's personhood. But if the slave survives for a while the master is not liable, because "the slave is the owner's property." Cases that mandate a male or female slave be freed if the master's beating permanently injures him or her also recognize these persons' humanity, despite their status as property (21:26–27).

The Construction of "Female" in C

C offers few explicit glimpses of women or girls. Where they do appear, C treats them as it does minor or enslaved males; that is, as objects, not subjects. Some scholars therefore assert that biblical law treats women as property,[8] but the evidence of C suggests that, while subordinate to the male head of their household, women's gender does not make them chattel. In C, as elsewhere in biblical law, gender intersects with generation and class; C does not deal with "women" per se, but with wives, mothers, daughters, widows, and slave women.

Two cases contrasting male and female Hebrews forced by poverty into slavery illustrate C's construction of the *wife*. The first concerns how to treat a Hebrew man whom the addressee has purchased as a slave: At the end of six years, he must set the man free (Exod 21:2). But a daughter sold as an *'āmāh* does not go free as do the (masculine plural) slaves (21:7–11). The explicit contrast in C, together with the pointed inclusion of the Hebrew woman in Deuteronomy's revision (Deut 15:12–18) has garnered a great deal of attention. Many take D's revision as evidence that Deuteronomy sought to improve the status of women.

---

[8]   *s.v.* "Woman," *Anchor Bible Dictionary*.

Elsewhere, I have argued that the difference is narrower than often understood. Exodus 21:7–11 makes clear that the daughter is sold as a slave wife for the purchaser or for his son. This purpose would be frustrated were she released. It seems plausible that the drafters of the Exodus case imagined that Hebrew women who sold themselves as slaves in order to survive or who were distrained as debt slaves, rather than sold as slave wives, would be released under the provision of 21:2. Perhaps D held that a woman could not be both a wife and a slave. Comparison of the Exodus and Deuteronomic laws provides little support for the thesis that C viewed women as property, or that D sought sweeping improvements in their status.[9]

These laws do, however, contribute to the construction of gendered norms, insofar as the woman's status depends on her relationship to the dominant male. If the enslaved man was married before entering into slavery, his wife follows him into bondage; when he is released, she follows him out (21:3). If the master had given the slave a wife, she and her children remain the master's property when the enslaved man is released (21:4). Sub-cases in the case of a daughter sold as a slave wife seek to establish that she had rights. The master must accord her food, clothing, and either oil or conjugal rights (21:10). If he fails to do so, he must let her go free; he may not sell her. A fortiori, neither could a man sell his free wife.[10] Though there has been a tendency to confuse "subordinate" or "dependent" with "property," a free wife is not chattel. The aforementioned miscarriage case affirms this. If the woman dies as a result of the blow, the punishment is "life for life" (21:23). While C mandates payment for destruction or theft of property, the destruction or theft of a person is a capital offense.[11]

Exodus 21:7 indicates that a father could sell his *daughter*, but this is an expression of generational authority, rather than gendered authority. In ancient Israel, as in the surrounding nations, mothers as well as fathers had the (dubious) right to sell or surrender their children into slavery.[12] The case of the seduced virgin also underscores

[9] C. Pressler, "Wives and Daughters, Bond and Free: Views of Women in the Slave Laws of Exodus 21:2–11," in *Gender and Law in the Hebrew Bible and the Ancient Near East*, ed. V. H. Matthews, B. M. Levinson, and T. Frymer-Kensky (London: T&T Clark, 1998), 147–72.
[10] Pressler, "Wives and Daughters," 161.
[11] Exod 21:12, 14, 16; cf. 21:28–32.
[12] Cf. 2 Kgs 4:1; Neh 5:5. On this practice at Nippur, see M. Dandamaev, *Slavery in Babylon*, trans. V. Powell, rev. ed. (DeKalb: Northern Illinois University Press, 1984), 170–1.

that C constructs daughters as subordinate to the father (22:16–17 [Heb 22:15–16]). If a man seduces an unbetrothed girl, he must pay her father the customary bride-wealth for a young woman who has never been married. To be clear, bride-wealth (Hebrew *mōhar*; NRSV "bride-price") is not a purchase price. In ancient Israel, as in surrounding cultures, betrothal involved a negotiated exchange of goods. The groom or his family contributed the bride-wealth and the bride's family contributed the dowry (which might be larger than the bride-wealth). Apparently, a groom would pay less (or no) bride-wealth for a girl who was no longer virgin. The case thus constructs the seduction of an unbetrothed girl as a financial injury to her father, whom the seducer must compensate. The father also determines whether the seducer must marry his daughter; the wishes of the daughter or her mother are ignored.

In C, as in the Decalogue, generation can trump gender. The *mother* (probably the father's primary wife) has authority over the sons and daughters (21:15, 17). Despite the gravity with which C views striking or cursing either parent, however, C does not construct the mother's authority as completely comparable to the father's. The father, not the mother, determines whether her daughter will marry the man who seduced her. In the miscarriage case, the mother does not own her reproductive capacity (21:22). Not she but her husband determines and receives compensation.

Exodus 22:22–24 prohibits abusing a *widow*. The case, grouping her with the resident alien and the fatherless child, is first of all a matter of class. The propertied, male "you" is not to abuse any vulnerable, impoverished persons. That vulnerable classes include widows assumes the dependence of women on male heads of household.

Except for the case of the daughter sold to become a slave wife, C deals with male and female *slaves* with notable parity. A man who beats his male or female slave so badly that he or she dies immediately is to be punished (21:20). A master who beats his male or female slave badly enough to permanently injure him or her must let the slave go free. The owner of a persistently goring ox who kills a female slave must pay her master thirty shekels, the same as if the victim were a male slave (21:32).

4.3 THE DEUTERONOMIC LAWS

The narrative overlay of the Deuteronomic laws sets them just prior to Israel's entrance into its land. Historically, the earliest iteration of the book dates no earlier than the reign of Josiah (r. 640–609). There is widespread agreement that the Deuteronomic authors were familiar with the Book of the Covenant, which they revised to suit their agenda. D stresses the unity of Israel and the exclusive loyalty to YHWH and YHWH's covenant, required of all Israelites. All are responsible for carrying out Israel's covenantal obligations. In contrast to C, therefore, the framework of D includes women, children, resident aliens, and slaves as addressees. The account of the covenantal renewal ceremony explicitly identifies women among the participants (Deut 29:10–11; see also 31:12).

The rhetoric in which a number of Deuteronomic cases are couched similarly stresses inclusivity. Celebrations of cultic meals "before YHWH" include not only "you" – the householder and presumably his wife – but also their sons and daughters, their male and female slaves, and the Levites (12:12, 18; 16:11, 14). Where C depicts members of the community as "neighbors," D speaks of Israelites as both neighbors and "brothers." In C, only the male head of a household counts as a "neighbor," whereas Deut 15:12 explicitly includes the Hebrew woman as well as the Hebrew man as "your brother."

Moreover, unlike C, D constructs women as agents as well as objects. Again, daughters, female slaves, widows (16:11), and presumably wives and mothers participate in sacrificial meals. The inclusion of wives and daughters among potential apostates (17:2) who might attempt to lead husbands and fathers into idolatrous worship also constructs them as possessing personal religious agency. Moreover, D constructs women as having legal agency. This is seen not only by their inclusion in the covenant renewal ceremony, but also in cases in which women present evidence or perform legally significant acts (21:18–21; 22:15; 25:7–10).

That women are explicitly named in the Deuteronomistic description of the covenant community offers a sharp contrast to the all-male community envisioned by Exod 19:15. It does not, however, suggest that D promulgated gender equality. In the history of interpretation there has been a tendency to confuse "inclusive" with "egalitarian" and "agency" with "equality." Despite popular usage, "inclusive" and "egalitarian" are not interchangeable. Deuteronomy 29:9–14 sets out both the inclusive nature of the Deuteronomists' vision and its hierarchical structure. It lists tribal leaders, then elders and officials, and then the rest of the Israelite men, followed by children and women, resident aliens, and finally slaves. That *all* are to participate in the covenantal community does not mean that women received "equal cultic rights" in the Deuteronomic "ideal society," "together without any social distinction."[13]

Similarly, while D constructs females in various roles as religious and legal agents, it also constructs them as subordinate to male heads of household and male leaders of their city (the elders; 21:19; 22:18, 21) and nation (23:2; 17:8–18:8). This is perhaps clearest in the Deuteronomic sexual offense laws. As they construct gender, neither a wife/mother nor a daughter has bodily or sexual integrity. Deuteronomy 22:13–29 comprises a tightly knit series of cases that together define adultery. The cases revolve around two factors: marital status, which defines the gravity of the offense, and the girl or woman's consent, which indicates only whether she is herself guilty. Terminology underscores her subordinate status. Normally, the Hebrew Bible uses the term 'iššah for both "woman" and "wife," but Deut 22:22 refers to the wife as b^e'ūlat-ba'al, "mastered by a master." Neither women's inclusion nor their agency in D implies equality.

The Construction of "Male" in D

As in C, gender is constructed by D as male dominance and female subordination. Again, the dominant male is a relatively well-to-do, landowning head of household, albeit living in an urban rather than a rural setting. D shows great anxiety that this dominant male must control "his" females' sexuality. This control demonstrates the stability and order of his household, a matter of great importance in Israel's honor-shame culture.[14]

Such anxiety is also apparent in the effort D expends establishing an expanded definition of adultery. Deuteronomy 22:20–21 extends a man's exclusive claim to his wife's sexuality into the past. If she is not a virgin when she marries him, the young woman is to be stoned to death. In the case of Levirate marriage, the husband's claim extends even beyond his death (25:5–10). Numerous studies, including my own, have described

---

[13] E. Otto, "False Weights in the Scales of Biblical Justice? Different Views of Women from Patriarchal Hierarchy to Religious Equality in Deuteronomy," in *Gender and Law in the Hebrew Bible and the Ancient Near East*, ed. V. H. Matthews, B. M. Levinson, and T. Frymer-Kensky (London: T&T Clark, 1998), 143–4.

[14] V. Matthews, "Honor and Shame in Gender-Related Legal Situations in the Hebrew Bible," in *Gender and Law in the Hebrew Bible and the Ancient Near East*, ed. V. H. Matthews, B. M. Levinson, and T. Frymer-Kensky (London: T&T Clark, 1998), 97–112. See also T. Frymer-Kensky, "Virginity in the Bible," in *Gender and Law in the Hebrew Bible and the Ancient Near East*, ed. V. H. Matthews, B. M. Levinson, and T. Frymer-Kensky (London: T&T Clark, 1998), 84–5.

the wife's sexuality as her husband's property. Yet, while D constructs the daughter's sexuality as her father's property, it constructs the wife's sexuality as *more* than her husband's property; rather, it is integral to his very person. In biblical law, only crimes against a person (kidnapping or murder) are capital; property crimes are not. The penalty for adultery, according to pentateuchal laws, is death. The incest law suggests a similar principle: for a man to marry his father's wife is to "uncover his *father's* skirt" (22:30 [Heb 23:1], my translation; cf. Lev 18:7, 8, 10, 13, 16).

In D, the dominant male is virile, fathering sons who inherit his property and thereby establish his "name." The Levirate law (25:5-10) rules that, if a man dies with no sons, his brother is to marry his widow. By a legal fiction, their firstborn son counts as the son of the deceased, inheriting the dead man's share of the family's land.

Probably because fathering a son is so important, D views intact male genitalia as the *sine qua non* of full participation in Israel's life. Deuteronomy 23:1 [Heb 23:2] rules that "No one whose testicles are crushed or whose penis is cut off" may participate in "the assembly of the LORD." Deut 25:11-12 also reflects and promulgates the sacrosanct character of male genitalia: If a woman defends her husband in a fight by grabbing his opponent's genitals, her hand is to be cut off. This is the only judgment involving physical mutilation in the whole of the Bible.[15] For a woman to come to her husband's defense would be considered an extremely extenuating circumstance; the uniqueness and severity of the judgment underline the gravity of violating a man's sexual organs.[16]

While C accepts but seeks to limit the dominant male's aggression, D constructs and lauds him as an aggressor and a warrior. D's historical review (chs 1-3), its war laws (20:1-18), and the law of the captured bride (21:10-14) all depict male violence. Harold Washington makes a compelling case that violence plays a constitutive role in D's construction of "maleness." Correspondingly, D constructs "female" as the object of violence.[17]

In keeping with other biblical texts, D assumes that Judahite society is patrilineal. The Levirate law attests to the importance of a *son* to

---

[15]   I take "eye for an eye" (Exod 21:23-25, etc.) nonliterally.

[16]   See C. Pressler, "Sexual Violence in Deuteronomic Law," in *Feminist Companion to Exodus to Deuteronomy*, ed. A. Brenner (Sheffield: Sheffield Academic, 1994), 102-12.

[17]   H. Washington, "'Lest He Die in Battle and Another Man Take Her': Violence and the Construction of Gender in the Laws of Deuteronomy 20-22," in *Gender and Law in the Hebrew Bible and the Ancient Near East*, ed. V. H. Matthews, B. M. Levinson, and T. Frymer-Kensky (London: T&T Clark, 1998), 185-213.

inherit; its gender-specific wording makes clear that, in D, daughters do not establish their father's name.[18] The law of primogeniture, which protects the inheritance rights of the firstborn son (21:15–17), likewise reflects and reinforces the patrilineal character of ancient Israelite society.

The law of primogeniture (21:15–17) also seeks to prohibit the father from assigning the rights of his firstborn son to a younger son; the father's authority over members of his household is not unlimited. The next law, however, affirms the authority of both father and mother over their sons (21:18–21).[19]

The Construction of "Female" in D

Like C, Deuteronomy constructs "woman" as a subordinate whose legal status is determined by her relationship to the male head of household. Ideally, a female is either a daughter under the authority of her father or a wife and mother under the authority of her husband. Females come into view not as women, but as wives, daughters, mothers, widows, and slaves.

Again, D constructs female sexuality, especially that of a *wife*, as a source of anxiety and as a threat to the boundaries of the family and harmony of the community. The wife is responsible for safeguarding her husband's honor by reserving her sexuality for him. The husband has no reciprocal obligation; unless a husband violates the rights of another man, he is free to have sex with women other than his wife or wives.[20] Perhaps surprisingly, D also constructs the wife's sexuality as a source of pleasure; Deut 24:5 exempts a newly married man from military service for a year, "to give happiness to the woman he has married" (JPS).

The wife's sexuality belongs to her husband, but she is not thereby his property. The law of the slave wife in Exod 21:2–11 has a functional parallel in Deut 21:10–14, which concerns a woman taken captive in battle whom an Israelite man wishes to marry. The main case provides a way for him to do so. A sub-case rules that, having married her, he may not sell her.[21]

---

[18] Contrast Num 27:1–11.

[19] T. M. Willis, *The Elders of the City: A Study of the Elders-Laws in Deuteronomy*, SBLMS 55 (Atlanta: Society of Biblical Literature, 2001).

[20] The legal code of Minnesota, where I live, likewise defines adultery unilaterally as a violation of a husband's exclusive rights to his wife's sexuality, not of a wife's rights to her husband's.

[21] As Washington, "'Lest He Die,'" 207, ably argues, Deut 21:10–14 codifies and thus seeks to legitimize rape: the woman is captured, subjected to degrading rituals, and forcibly married to her enemy.

Arguing from lesser to greater, a man who contracted for his wife in a more typical way cannot sell her either.

In certain circumstances, D constructs the wife as competent to testify in court and to make legally significant actions. In the Levirate law (25:5–10), a deceased man's wife rejected by her brother-in-law is to publicly humiliate him: drawing off his sandal, spitting in his face, and declaring that "this is what is done to the man who does not build up his brother's house." Those acts have legal import, freeing the woman from the obligation to marry her husband's brother. The passage also contributes to D's construction of the wife as, above all, the mother of her husband's sons.

As in C, gender and generation intersect in D's construction of the role of *mother*. She, along with the father, is to be honored and obeyed. This is seen not only in the Decalogue (5:16), but also in the law of the rebellious son, which seeks to curtail filial disobedience to mother as well as father (21:18–21). The case also contributes to D's construction of women as legally competent, at least in some roles. Both parents bring the son to the elders to be tried. *Both* testify. Similarly, the mother accompanies the father to court in the case of the spurned bride (22:13–21) and, with him, presents evidence. In this case, involving two separate households, however, she does not speak.

The same case constructs the *daughter's* primary responsibility as preserving her virginity until she is betrothed. If she fails, she dishonors her father and his household and is to be stoned to death at the door of her father's house; this indicates the gravity of the girl's "crime" and highlights her father's failure to maintain control in his household. The case also suggest that married women maintained ties with their natal families; cross-cultural studies suggest this is a key factor in a wife's status and treatment.

That D, like C, constructs a daughter's sexuality as an economic asset for her father is clear in the law of the violated unbetrothed girl. The violator must pay the father fifty shekels – presumably a fixed amount for the bride-wealth – and must marry her, with no option of divorce. The wording supports the traditional interpretation that D's case deals with rape, while its parallel in Exod 22:16–17 [Heb 22:15–16] concerns seduction.[22] The cases' resolutions do not imply that rape is more serious than seduction. That is, D constructs the daughter's will as legally immaterial; her sexuality belongs to her father. D's resolution,

---

[22]   C. Pressler, *The View of Women Found in the Deuteronomic Family Laws*, BZAW 216 (Berlin: de Gruyter, 1993), 32–9.

imposing marriage with no possibility of divorce, similarly disregards her will.

Elsewhere D constructs the daughter as not only a threat to the family but also a valued member of it. She comes into view as a member of the household that partakes of sacrificial meals (12:12, 18; 16:11, 14) and is grouped with the son among those whom the father may not shield should they try to persuade him to commit apostasy (13:6). The law would not include daughters if they had no voice and no influence on their fathers. Two of the Deuteronomic curses aver that covenant breakers will watch their sons and daughters dragged away into exile (28:32, 41). These curses construct these daughters as cherished; otherwise, they would be meaningless.

Women outside the Male-Headed Household

D refers to three groups of women who fall outside the male-headed household: divorced women, widows, and prostituted women. D refers to divorce in three cases. Deuteronomy 24:1–4 prohibits a man from remarrying a woman whom he had divorced if she had subsequently entered into a second marriage, but then was either divorced again or widowed. Twice D prohibits a man from divorcing a wife whom he has wronged (22:19, the case of the slandered bride, and 22:29, the rape of a young woman who has never been betrothed). All three cases assume and inscribe that the man, not the woman, initiates divorce.[23]

It is unclear when a man could divorce his wife. Deuteronomy 24:1 makes a rare mention of grounds for divorce: "she does not please him because he finds something objectionable about her." Hillel and Shimmai, rabbis of the first century CE, famously debated the meaning of the phrase. Shimmai, focusing on "something objectionable," concluded that the wife's unchastity was the only permissible grounds for divorce; Hillel, focusing on "she does not please him," argued that the husband could divorce her for much slighter reasons. If we knew what the verse meant, it would shed light on D's construction of the divorced woman. Shimmai's strict position would suggest that D sought to protect the wife from divorce, while constructing the divorcee as unchaste and, hence, reprehensible. Unfortunately, the crux remains unresolved. Deuteronomy 22:19, 29 may indicate more strongly that D assumed or favored men being able to divorce an unwanted wife easily. It is unlikely that the prohibition against divorcing the wronged woman would apply in cases of adultery; the

---

[23]   The Elephantine papyri show that in Persian-period Jewish colonies in Egypt the wife could also initiate divorce.

prohibitions would be unnecessary if the man could not ordinarily divorce his wife over lesser matters.[24] Nonetheless, the phrase "she has been defiled" (24:4) constructs the divorcee as in some way impure.

D's divorcee does merit some protection. References to "a certificate of divorce" (24:1, 3) were probably intended to safeguard the divorced woman and any man she might subsequently marry from accusations of adultery. The language of Deut 24:2 hints that D's divorcee has some agency. For D, as for other biblical and comparative Southwest Asian texts, a woman is an object, not a subject, of her first marriage – yet, Deut 24:2 makes the divorced woman the subject: "She leaves his house and goes and becomes the wife of second man." She chooses, and is therefore a subject in, her second marriage.

In patrilineal cultures a widow ('almanah) holds a socially anomalous and economically precarious position. Although both biblical and extrabiblical texts depict widows possessing or at least managing land, pentateuchal laws make no mention of women inheriting property. D groups the widow with the resident alien and the fatherless as indigent persons, commending them to the generosity of D's relatively prosperous addressees (see 14:28–29; 16:11, 14; 24:19–21), whom it prohibits from taking a widow's garment in pledge (24:17).

D alludes to prostituted women only once, prohibiting using the wages of prostitution as temple gifts (23:18 [Heb 23:19]).[25] Presumably it aims to protect the purity of the temple by keeping "dirty money" away; it thus constructs prostituted girls and women, along with their money, as unclean. Like much modern interpretation, it falsely assumes that prostitution results from immoral choices. In fact, then and now, girls and women (and boys and men) who trade sex most often do so as a survival strategy, selling their bodies to feed themselves or their children. Other times, then and now, sex-trafficking is out-and-out slavery.[26]

---

[24]   C. Pressler, "Deuteronomy," in *Women's Bible Commentary* (Louisville: Westminster John Knox, 2012), 99.

[25]   Deut 23:17 [Heb 23:18], prohibits Israelite women from becoming *qedeshah*, traditionally understood as "temple prostitute." Recent scholarship has raised questions about the existence of sacred prostitution in either Israel or the surrounding nations. The term seems to refer, rather, to some sort of temple functionary.

[26]   For over a decade, I have volunteered at a center in Minneapolis that seeks to provide healing space for prostituted girls and women. As I have noted elsewhere, "Minneapolis is the thirteenth largest center of human trafficking in the United States. The average age at which its young victims enter—or are forced—into the sex trade is between 12 and 13. The young women and boys caught up in it often recount experiences of kidnapping, gang rape, and threats against their lives or the

4.4 ETHICAL REFLECTION

I began this essay by asserting that biblical law "does not render an ethical model for modern (and postmodern) folk." As I – a liberal, biblically engaged Christian – understand it, the social norms encoded in biblical laws are not binding on us.

I believe Israel's sacred traditions reflect genuine encounters with God, filtered through the social, political, and familial structures of ancient Judah, its historical upheavals, and the finitude of the laws' drafters. Put bluntly: Judah did not always hear rightly. When it comes to gender equality, the urban elite males who drafted and edited the pentateuchal laws got much of it wrong. Moreover, postindustrial Western society stands at an almost unfathomable distance from the preindustrial, agrarian, tribal Judahite society from which the Hebrew Scriptures emerged. Furthermore, often either the wording or the rationale of a biblical case eludes us; ethical judgments that rely on proof texts are accordingly tenuous.

What, then, do we do with such texts? The Hebrew Bible is the distillation of centuries of Israelite dialogue about who God is, how God acts, and what God expects. As we interpret, we enter that dialogue. As in any cross-cultural conversation, we first listen carefully to the laws in their cultural contexts. Scholarly methodologies are ways of listening with care to what ancient voices are saying.

We must also listen critically. Not all of these voices align with the deepest theological and ethical values of one's faith community. We may use those values – forged in part through encounters with the biblical text – to critique the constructions of gender in biblical laws and in our own culture. The biblical legal collections themselves provide warrant for critique and reformulation of our sacred traditions. As has long been recognized, the center of the Deuteronomy is the Shema, the affirmation that YHWH alone is God, and the command to love God with all of one's heart, soul, and might (Deut 6:4–5).[27] Next most important is the Decalogue, understood as the stipulations of God's

lives of their families" (Pressler, "Deuteronomy," 99). There is dirty money involved: the millions made by pimps and organized criminals who exploit people's dire poverty and make it nearly impossible for sex workers to break free. Sex workers who operate independently are a minority.

[27] For a helpful exposition of the centrality of the Shema, see P. D. Miller, Jr., "The Most Important Word: The Yoke of the Kingdom," *Iliff Review* 4 (1984): 17–29.

covenant with Israel. The Decalogue is set apart narratively as direct revelation, found twice in the Pentateuch (Exod 20; Deut 5), and is alluded to in all three sections of the canon.[28] The stipulations in D and C spell out these commandments' meaning in particular times and places: D includes cases drawn from C, but adapts them to fit a later, urban context. They thus spell out what their drafters and redactors believed it meant to love God and live in covenantal relationship with one another *in their own time*. The Shema and Decalogue endure, but the remaining laws are dynamic.

As we dialogue with these ancient voices, we do well also to listen for insights from those who, standing at a great distance from us, see what we cannot see. The dynamism of sacred traditions is one such profound insight. Even more important is D's recognition that the center of faithful ethical thought is wholehearted love of God. Neither Deuteronomy nor Exodus leave the nature of that God undefined. YHWH is a God who liberates and who calls those liberated into just relationship. Both C and D insist that loving God involves the whole of communal and personal life. We may not find their gender hierarchies authoritative for our times yet may still acknowledge that how we understand gender and how we relate to one another in our varying genders is a matter of faithfulness to the liberating God.

Deuteronomy 6:20 reads: "When your children ask you in time to come, "What is the meaning of the decrees and the statutes and the ordinances that the LORD our God has commanded you?" One might expect the answer to be, "You must obey the commandments to keep covenant with God, lest you be judged." Instead, the text instructs the people to "say to your children, 'We were Pharaoh's slaves in Egypt, but the LORD brought us out of Egypt with a mighty hand.'" The meaning of biblical law is thus, "God freed us." The paragraph continues: "Then the LORD commanded us to observe all these statutes, to fear the LORD our God, for our lasting good, so as to keep us alive, as is now the case." This declaration provides a clear governing rubric: The law is meant "for our lasting good . . . to keep us alive." If a law no longer achieves this purpose, we must imitate the dynamism of the biblical legal tradition and change it, in order to keep *all* of us – all genders, all ages, all races, and all classes of persons – alive.

---

[28] See P. D. Miller, Jr., "The Place of the Decalogue in the Old Testament and Its Law," *Int* 43 (1989): 229–42.

FURTHER READING

Anderson, C. B. *Women, Ideology, and Violence: Critical Theory and the Construction of Gender in the Book of the Covenant and the Deuteronomic Law.* JSOTSup 394. London: T&T Clark, 2004.

Clines, D. J. A. "Being a Man in the Book of the Covenant." Pages 3–9 in *Reading the Law: Studies in Honour of Gordon J. Wenham.* Edited by J. G. McConville and K. Möller. London: T&T Clark, 2007.

Knight, D. A. *Law, Power, and Justice in Ancient Israel.* 1st ed. Library of Ancient Israel. Louisville: Westminster John Knox, 2011.

Matthews, V. H., B. M. Levinson, and T. S. Frymer-Kensky, eds. *Gender and Law in the Hebrew Bible and the Ancient Near East.* JSOTSup 262. London: T&T Clark, 2004.

Morrow, W. S. *An Introduction to Biblical Law.* Grand Rapids: Eerdmans, 2017.

Pressler, C. *The View of Women Found in the Deuteronomic Family Laws.* BZAW 216. Berlin: de Gruyter, 1993.

Westbrook, R. *Studies in Biblical and Cuneiform Law.* Cahiers de la Revue Biblique 26. Paris: J. Gabalda et Cie, 1988.

5 Economics and the Law

ALBINO BARRERA

Care for the poor has been widely viewed as a defining characteristic feature of Hebrew ethics. There is a wealth of normative prescriptions across the law, the prophets, and the wisdom writings on the proper treatment of the marginalized and the vulnerable. Economic morality is not a peripheral concern in the Hebrew Scriptures. This essay considers the law's teachings on economic life. Economic norms are found in the Decalogue (Exod 20:2–17; Deut 5:6–21), the Covenant Code (Exod 20:22–23:33), the Deuteronomic Code (Deuteronomy 12–26), and the Holiness Code (Leviticus 17–26). These laws are an expression of God's moral will and articulate ideals on how Israel should live as the chosen people of God – but these laws, including the prescriptions on economic life, should not be taken as descriptions of the nation's actual practice.

5.1 HEBREW ECONOMIC IMPERATIVES

The law's economic norms include the proper treatment of persons, property, and animals and the proper discharge of cultic obligations. The chosen people of God were to be truthful in their speech and conduct, impartial in their judgment (Exod 23:1–3, 6–7, 8; Deut 19:14; 21:15–17; 24:14–15; 25:13–16; Lev 19:11, 15, 35–37), and immune to bribes (Exod 23:8; Deut 16:18–20). As in contemporary torts, the Hebrews were held responsible for the injury they inflicted on others or their properties through negligence or recklessness (Exod 21:18–19, 22–36; 22:4–7, 13–16; Deut 22:8; Lev 24:17–21) or through their dishonest behavior (Exod 22:1–4, 9–12; Deut 22:13–19). Restitutionary justice was paramount. They were to be respectful of others' property (Deut 23:24–25). They were bound by the duty to care for animals and plants and to prevent harm to these creatures (Exod 23:4–5; Deut 20:19–20; 22:1–4; 22:6–7; 25:4). Land, too, was to be cared for, allowed to rejuvenate, and left fallow every seventh year (Lev 25:1–7). They were to be prompt in offering the requisite cultic sacrifices, the firstfruits of their harvest and firstlings, in gratitude to the LORD and in support of the Levites (Exod 22:29–30; 23:15–17, 19; Deut 14:22–27; cf. Numbers 18; Deut 12:5–7, 10–12, 17–19; 15:19–20; 16:9–12, 3–15, 16–17; 17:1; 18:1–4, 8; 26:12–15; Lev 19:23–24; 22:20–25; 23:9–14). They were not to value anything or anyone more than God (Exod 20:23).

The vast majority of these economic norms pertain to the proper treatment of other people, especially the distressed in their midst. Some have suggested that these admonitions can be differentiated: (1) the laws that provided a safety net to the chronically poor and (2) the norms that sought to restore the temporarily poor.[1] The permanently poor were the widows, aliens, orphans, and slaves. Since these people did not have access to land of their own, the law acted to ensure that they were properly provisioned. Thus, there were extensive protections concerning the proper treatment of slaves (Exod 21:1–2, 7–11; Deut 15:12–14; 20:11, 14; 21:10–14; 23:15–16; 25:1–3), the strangers (Exod 22:21; Lev 19:9–10, 33–34; 24:22), and the disabled (Lev 19:14). Cultic offerings and festival meals and offerings were to be shared with widows, strangers, slaves, and orphans (Deut 12:17–19; 16:9–12, 3–15; 26:1–11). The poor had gleaning privileges both at harvest time (Deut 24:19–22; Lev 19:9–10; 23:22) and during the Sabbath fallow (Exod 23:10–11; Lev 25:1–7). The Sabbath, the Day of Atonement (Lev 23:31–32), and the Feast of Booths (Lev 23:33–38) ensured that rest was afforded to those who would have otherwise had to work unceasingly, including slaves, servants, strangers, and even farm animals (Exod 23:12; Lev 23:3). Tithes were set aside every third year for the poor (Deut 14:28–29; 26:12). These measures ensured that those who did not own land were nevertheless adequately provisioned.

The second set of norms pertaining to the poor assisted the temporarily poor, that is, those who had fallen prey to the chance and contingencies of economic life. Thus, the law codes have extensive debt legislation, from the mandatory provision of loans to distressed neighbors (Deut 15:7–11), to forgoing the charging of any interest (Deut 23:19), to tight restrictions on securing collateral for such loans (Exod 22:26–27; Deut 24:6, 10–11, 12, 17), to debt forgiveness (Deut 15:1–2). Slaves were to be freed after six years of service (Exod 21:1–2). Upon their manumission, they were not to leave empty-handed but were to be generously furnished with supplies by the master (Deut 15:12–14), so that they might not fall back into debt and subsequent re-enslavement. Ancestral

[1]   N. Lohfink, "Poverty in the Laws of the Ancient Near East and of the Bible," *TS* 52 (1991): 43–7.

lands were to be returned to the original families that had received these as their heritage from the LORD (Lev 25:8–16). Those who had fallen on hard times and were selling themselves as slaves were to be accepted instead as tenants or hired hands and not bought as slaves (Lev 25:35, 39–43). Food was not to be sold at a profit to the impoverished, nor should the latter be charged interest for money or food loans (Lev 25:36–37). Day laborers were to be paid their wages promptly and in full (Deut 24:14–15; Lev 19:13). These provisions from the law codes were designed to assist those who had fallen on hard times and to restore them as independent landholding families, able to provide for their own needs.

Given the extensive and overlapping provisions of the law codes on the proper treatment of widows, aliens, orphans, and slaves, it is not surprising that care for the poor is a distinctive, defining characteristic of Hebrew social ethics. The law is clear and emphatic that there ought to be no poor among the chosen people of God because of their mutual solicitude (Deut 15:4–5).

5.2 SOCIOHISTORICAL ECONOMIC CONTEXT

Many of the aforesaid imperatives are demanding. Take the case of the extensive laws dealing with lending to one's neighbor in distress. The moral obligation to lend what little surplus one might have could mean lending away the family's safety cushion. If the lender suffers a subsequent crop failure, the family will be in exactly the same plight as the needy neighbor in having to borrow from others. In other words, lending one's surplus is quite an unselfish act, insofar as one puts oneself and one's own family at risk for others. One embraces risk for the sake of the neighbor in need. One makes one's own loved ones vulnerable in order to help a neighbor in distress. Why were Israelites willing to do this for one another? The sociohistorical economic context shows us that such assistance may not have been motivated by altruism alone.

Some of the aforesaid laws are believed to date all the way back to the pre-monarchic, nomadic period, as common-law practices that were then codified when Israel finally settled into agriculture. Nomadic life was precarious and uncertain at best. Many dangers lurked, from the constant threat of predation from roving bandits, to the unpredictable harshness of the environment, to the chronic insufficiency of food, to the unceasing need to move, to the perennial threat of disease wiping out their livestock. Thus, the extended family clan was essential for the individual's survival and protection.

Windfall wealth was widely shared with one's kin and neighbors and not necessarily for unselfish reasons. Sharing was a rational way of holding onto wealth. After all, today's wealth could be lost in the blink of an eye to theft, raiding parties, bad weather, or disease. The best way of holding on to wealth was to share it with others; by building goodwill and deepening one's relationship with kin and neighbors, one could be assured of sharing in the latter's own good fortune at some point in the future. Sharing became a mechanism for converting one form of wealth (property, money) into another form of wealth (goodwill). One could view it as an intertemporal means of saving or of smoothing out one's consumption over time.[2] By readily and generously extending assistance to kin or neighbors who had fallen on hard times (e.g., lending without interest), one could be assured of reciprocal assistance from such kin and neighbors in one's own moment of need in the future. Generosity and sharing were not only forms of holding onto wealth but very important forms of insurance against the uncertainties of nomadic life. In modern economic language, it constitutes a risk-mitigation strategy.

Danger and uncertainty also turned out to be characteristic features of Israel's life in settled agriculture. Unlike the fertile plains of the Philistines, the highlands where Israel settled posed numerous challenges for farming. Sufficient rain at the right time during the planting season was critical. Moreover, saving and storing water required innovative practices, such as digging and waterproofing cisterns. There was need to terrace the hillsides, to slow down the runoff of rainwater and to enable level farming. Besides the enormous initial investment of labor in cutting the hillside for such terracing, there was a constant need for maintenance work. On top of all these demands, there were the vagaries of weather and the recurrent specter of crop failure. Agriculture, by its nature, is fraught with chance and contingencies. Being in the highlands compounded these risks even further.

Again, family was key to survival. Kin and neighbors provided the collective labor needed to construct and maintain the cisterns and the terracing. Kin and neighbors provided one another with assistance in the face of crop failures. Even should crop failures hit entire communities and family clans, nearby communities and family clans extended

---

[2] W. Schottroff, "The Prophet Amos: A Socio-Historical Assessment of His Ministry," in *God of the Lowly: Socio-Historical Interpretations of the Bible*, ed. L. Schottroff and W. Steggemann (Maryknoll: Orbis, 1984). 37. See also M. Mauss, *The Gift: The Form and Reason for Exchange in Archaic Societies* (New York: W.W. Norton, 2000).

assistance to one another, with the expectation that they in their own moment of need would receive the same kind of assistance.[3]

In addition to the vagaries of the weather and soil conditions, common folk were saddled further with heavy exactions from extractive regimes, both local elites and the neighboring empires. This rendered their daily lives even more precarious and made a strategy of mutual assistance even more important.[4]

There is a second important sociohistorical context behind these laws. These codified common-law practices were not merely a formalization of what was standard practice or even an adaptation of ancient Near Eastern practices. Israel's laws were grounded in and drew their power from its unique history.[5] We see this vividly in the motive clauses (e.g., Lev 25:38, 42, 55).[6] While Israel's economic imperatives were exacting – even sacrificial – in the obligations they imposed, the LORD was quick to remind Israel of the signal, unmerited favors it had itself received in its liberation from slavery in Egypt. Many of these motive clauses are appended to norms pertaining to the proper care of the poor: giving servants and slaves Sabbath rest (Deut 5:13–15); generously provisioning freed slaves (Deut 15:12–15); sharing cultic offerings with the distressed (Deut 16:12); letting the poor glean on one's land (Deut 24:19–22); not exploiting the weak (Deut 24:17); acting honestly in commercial transactions (Lev 19:35–37); properly treating aliens (Lev 19:33); lending without interest (Lev 25:35–38); not enslaving the insolvent but welcoming them in one's household as tenants or as hired hands (Lev 25:39–43); and releasing all who are in bondage in the Year of the Jubilee (Lev 25:54). Common to all is a reminder that the LORD was not asking much – only that Israel extend to others the same favors that

---

[3]   See M. Chaney, "Systematic Study of the Israelite Monarchy," *Semeia* 37 (1986): 3–76; D. Hopkins, "The Dynamics of Agriculture in Monarchial Israel," *Society of Biblical Literature Seminar Papers* 22 (1983):177–202; D. Hopkins, "Life on the Land: The Subsistence Struggles of Early Israel," *BA* 50 (1987):178–91; D. Hopkins, "Bare Bones: Putting Flesh on the Economics of Ancient Israel," in *The Origins of the Ancient Israelite States*, ed. V. Fritz and P. R. Davies (Sheffield: Sheffield Academic, 1996).

[4]   For recent expositions on the challenging living conditions and the political economy of Biblical Israel, see R. Boer, *The Sacred Economy of Ancient Israel* (Louisville: Westminster John Knox, 2015) and S. Adams, *Social and Economic Life in Second Temple Judea* (Louisville: Westminster John Knox, 2014).

[5]   Lohfink, "Poverty in the Laws of the Ancient Near East," 40–2.

[6]   For an exposition on motive clauses, see B. Gemser, "The Importance of the Motive Clause in Old Testament Law," in *Congress Volume, Copenhagen*, VTSup 1 (Leiden: Brill, 1953), 50–66 and P. Doron, "Motive Clauses in the Laws of Deuteronomy: Their Forms, Functions and Contents," *HAR* 2 (1978): 61–77.

it had received from God in its own moment of need.[7] These motive clauses have been viewed as soteriological, because God's saving act in the exodus becomes the basis for Israel's economic duties.

In sum, the laws on proper economic conduct in the Hebrew Scriptures did not arise in a vacuum. Empathy with the poor and the distressed may in fact be a reflection of Israel's appreciation of the need to extend to others God's loving kindness that Israel had itself experienced in its own moment of need. The generous mutual assistance called for by the law may in fact be, at the very least, a rational strategy for mutual survival. Generosity and sharing served as important ancient forms of insurance. Laws about caring for aliens, widows, and orphans, such as not charging interest from the poor (Exod 22:25), not taking the cloak of the destitute as a loan collateral (Exod 22:26–27), and leaving to the poor the produce of the land during the Sabbath fallow (Exod 23:11), may antedate the formation of Israel.[8]

5.3 CONTEMPORARY RELEVANCE AND APPLICATION

The Hebrew economic norms emerged from a socioeconomic context that is radically different from ours today. Nevertheless, they are applicable to our contemporary economy because of their underlying rationale.[9]

Poverty Traps and Adverse Pecuniary Externalities

There were both practical reasons for and theological significance attached to mandatory lending, lending without interest, debt forgiveness, slave manumission, the return of ancestral land to its original family, gleaning privileges, the shared festival meals, the tri-annual poor tithing, and the provisioning of freed slaves. These were meant to provide a cushion for life's unexpected misfortunes, for both the chronically poor and the temporarily poor. For the chronically poor, these measures ensured that they were properly provisioned. For those who had fallen on hard times, these laws were supposed to offer a fresh beginning.

In both cases, these admonitions speak a message of hope – that those who had been adversely affected by life's chance and contingencies

---

[7] Gemser, "The Importance of the Motive Clause," 60.

[8] H. E. von Waldow, "Social Responsibility and Social Structure in Early Israel," *CBQ* 32 (1970): 184–5 and Lohfink, "Poverty in the Laws of the Ancient Near East," 39–40.

[9] For the hermeneutical rules of purpose and analogy, see C. Cosgrove, *Appealing to Scripture in Moral Debate: Five Hermeneutical Rules*, (Grand Rapids: Eerdmans, 2002). For other applications, see A. Levine, *Oxford Handbook of Judaism and Economics* (Oxford: Oxford University Press, 2010).

would be cared for or might start anew. Indeed, these laws may have been the means of ensuring that there would be no poor in Israel (Deut 15:4), despite the intrinsic risks and uncertainties of ancient economic life.

This vision of an economy of hope – an economy of second chances – continues to capture the imagination of people in our own day. For example, Jubilee 2000 was a global grassroots coalition of civil and religious groups, inspired by Leviticus 25, who lobbied governments and financial institutions for debt forgiveness for developing countries in celebration of the turn of the millennium.[10] Despite resistance from powerful quarters of the economy, the G-8 eventually acceded to debt forgiveness for highly indebted poor countries.

However, this one-off debt forgiveness merely scratches the surface of the full contribution that these Hebrew laws can yet make in the modern economy. Like biblical Israel, we have our share of people who are chronically or temporarily poor. The most severe form of poverty, "ultrapoverty," includes the poorest of the poor, who do not generally benefit from public antipoverty programs and are unable to participate successfully in the marketplace given their chronic poor health, their lack of skills, and their limited social network. These are people caught in a poverty trap with little prospect for relief and improvement in life. They are born ultrapoor, and they will most likely die ultrapoor.[11] It is an indictment on the rest of humanity that in this age of great affluence and stunning technical-scientific achievements there are hundreds of millions of people in destitution, barely keeping body and soul alive, with no access to clean water or sanitation. That there are people who live in such conditions is evidence of our collective moral failure – just as it was in Israel, where there were supposed to be no poor (Deut 15:4). The economy of the ultrapoor is not an economy of hope, but an economy of despair and suffering, bereft of any optimism for the future.[12]

---

[10]   A. Pettifor, "The Jubilee 2000 Campaign: A Brief Overview," in *Sovereign Debt at the Crossroads: Challenges and Proposals for Resolving the Third World Debt Crisis*, ed. C. Jochnick and F. Preston (Oxford: Oxford University Press, 2006), 297–318.

[11]   For an exposition on the ultra-poor, see A. Ahmed, R. Vargas Hill, L. Smith, D. Wiesmann, and T. Frankenberger, *The World's Most Deprived: Characteristics and Causes of Extreme Poverty and Hunger*, 2020 Discussion Paper no. 43 (Washington, DC: International Food Policy Research Institute, 2007).

[12]   For a first-hand account by the poor of their plight and their helplessness, see D. Naraya, R. Patel, K. Schafft, A. Rademacher, and S. Koch-Schulte, *Voices of the Poor: Can Anyone Hear Us?* (Oxford: Oxford University Press, 2000).

Unintended destitution is the most immediate application and relevance of Hebrew economic ethics for our own day.

Israel's economy of hope resonates today for a second reason. The market is touted for its ability to produce the right goods and services, at the right time, at the right place, and in the right quantity and quality, producing and delivering these with the right methods and inputs. There is no other social institution to date that can match the market for its capacity to achieve allocative efficiency. Constant and speedy price adjustments lie at the root of the marketplace's unique ability to orchestrate such a difficult accomplishment. Unfortunately, these efficiencies create harmful unintended consequences. Cheap imports, for example, increase the real incomes of consumers and free up resources for higher-paying economic activities, such as work in the information technology sector. Unfortunately, they also lead to the loss of domestic manufacturing jobs. The people who worked in these jobs are often not the same people who will be capable of filling the new higher-value-added jobs in information technology. This is an instance of what is called adverse pecuniary externalities, which are often left unaddressed. Social safety nets such as unemployment insurance or trade-adjustment assistance programs are limited in their scope, duration, and effectiveness. People are often left to bear the market's harmful unintended consequences on their own. The biblical principles of mutual assistance and of providing new beginnings for people who have fallen prey to the economy's chance and contingencies are tailor-made for this contemporary problem.

Erosion of Civic Spirit of Mutual Assistance

The principle of subsidiarity calls on higher bodies (e.g., government) not to arrogate for themselves functions that lower bodies and individuals are able to do for themselves, while acknowledging that these higher bodies have a moral obligation to intervene or assist when lower bodies and individuals are not able to function for the common good.[13] Although this principle is not explicitly articulated in the Hebrew Scriptures, we nevertheless find its spirit in operation in the economic laws. Observe that there were no enforcement mechanisms for these economic imperatives. Compliance flowed from the heart. Moreover, note how these economic admonitions were not reserved for the temple, priests, or royal officials alone. Rather, they were addressed to everyone, by virtue of being numbered among the chosen people of God. Everyone

---

[13] Pius XI, *Quadragesimo Anno* (Boston: Daughters of St. Paul, 1931).

had a contribution to make in bringing about a nation where there were
to be no poor (Deut 15:4), whether through tithing, shared cultic offerings, or lending to a neighbor in distress. Everyone was to fulfill these
obligations according to his or her means, no matter how modest.
Conscience and accountability before God became the enforcement
mechanism.

This spirit of subsidiarity is urgently needed in the modern era. In
the ancient Near East, family membership was key to survival. It was
the family that provided the safety net and protection for its members
against the vicissitudes of life and the predation of others. Given such
close and tightly knit family groupings, individuals did their share in
building up the clan from which they derived benefits and to which they
contributed.

Today, citizenship has replaced family membership as the key to
survival. In the developed world, the public social safety net has
replaced what used to be provided by families (e.g., elder and child
care). To be sure, public social safety nets are vital, especially for the
ultrapoor. Nevertheless, public programs also come with dangers. In
particular, they can dull people's sense of personal and familial responsibility. Government largesse may crowd out private effort and, by
extension, weaken civic spirit and civil society. It is the classic
problem in which people hide in the anonymity of the group and cut
back on their personal contribution, fearing that others will ride on
their efforts.[14]

The invitation to every Hebrew to internalize these divine economic imperatives and to provide assistance according to his or her
own means is an invitation extended to everyone today. It is the call
to provide mutual assistance and not to rely on government as the first
recourse.

Assistance to Others as Supererogatory or a Demand of Justice?

How much are we obligated to give of our time, talent, and treasure in
assisting our neighbor? There is no consensus on this question. The
Christian Gospels provide a range of options, from outright voluntary
poverty through total radical divestment (Matt 19:16–22), all the way to
the use of properties and wealth in support of the preaching of the
Gospel (Luke 8:1–3). St Paul urged the Corinthians to give to his collection for the poor in Jerusalem, but not to the point of impoverishing

---

[14]   G. Hardin, "The Tragedy of the Commons," *Science* 162 (1968): 1243–8.

themselves (2 Cor 8:13). The Patristic Fathers were adamant that alms-giving was merely giving to the poor what properly belonged to them. Many go so far as to claim that idle wealth is theft from the poor.[15] Thomas Aquinas suggested that what one did not need to preserve one's family's social standing was superfluous and ought to be used for the welfare of others, especially the poor.[16] John XXIII measured superfluity according to the relative unmet needs of one's neighbor.[17] In sum, is almsgiving or assistance to a neighbor in distress supererogatory or a duty of justice?

This not an idle musing, as evidenced by the debates within and across nations on how much aid to extend to poor countries. Few have reached the goal of giving at least 0.7 percent of gross domestic product as overseas assistance to poor nations. Moreover, there is disagreement on whether foreign aid is helpful or injurious to poor nations.[18]

In the absence of a universally accepted standard, such questions ultimately become a matter of prudential judgment or conscience at both the personal and collective level. The motive clauses of the Hebrew economic laws are helpful in this regard. Just as the motive clauses of the Hebrew economic imperatives reminded Israel that it was merely being asked to extend to others the same favors that it had received in its own moment of need, they serve as a reminder for us today that we are merely invited to extend to others what we have received as blessings and graces from God. Were it not for the grace of God, by accident of birth or geography we might be dependent on the goodwill and kindness of other people. Thus, our acts of kindness may in fact be a demand of justice rather than of charity. They are not supererogatory but obliga-tory. In the event of doubt as to whether we have given enough, it is better in light of these motive clauses to be forward-leaning on the side of generosity and give what we ourselves have received for free (Matt 10:8). For non-believers, this is a matter of reciprocity or paying forward others' benefactions to them. For believers, it is a matter of

---

[15] P. Phan, *Social Thought*, Message of the Fathers of the Church 20 (Delaware: Michael Glazier, 1984): 37–41.

[16] T. Aquinas, *Summa Theologica*, trans. Fathers of the English Dominican Province, 3 vol. (New York: Benzinger Brothers Aquinas, 1947–1948: II–II Q. 32, article 6, answer); cf. Leo XIII, *Rerum Novarum* (Vatican, 1891): #22.

[17] Vatican Council II, *Gaudium et Spes* (Rome: Vatican, 1965): Part II, Chapter 3, footnote 10.

[18] See J. Sachs, "The Case for Aid," *Foreign Policy* (January 21, 2014); W. Easterly, *The White Man's Burden: Why the West's Efforts to Aid the Rest Have Done So Much Ill and So Little Good* (New York: Penguin, 2006).

sharing with others the unmerited divine graces they had the good fortune of receiving.

Responsibility and Collective Action

A clear pattern in Hebrew economic ethics is the Deuteronomic doctrine of divine retribution or just deserts. We see this vividly in Deut 15:4, in which the LORD tells Israel that there will be no poor in its midst – but only if it lives up to the laws. We find the same point reiterated in Deut 15:5–6 and 26:16–19. Deuteronomy 28–30 picks up the same theme, dwelling on the blessings that will come upon the nation if it lives up to its economic obligations and the disasters that will befall it with disobedience. This link between material prosperity and observance of these economic imperatives applies just as well at the personal level. Thus, the Deuteronomist carefully outlines the rewards and the good life that those who observe the economic statutes will enjoy in their lifetime (Deut 12:28; 15:7–11, 18; 16:18–20; 23:19–20; 24:19). Indeed, our economic choices are consequential.

In the sojourn through the desert, Israel lived without undue care because it was provisioned by God with manna. God could have done similarly after Israel had settled in the promised land. The almighty Creator of the heavens and the earth could have let Israel settle in the land flowing with milk and honey without undue care. But God chose not to do for Israel what Israel could and should do. Israel had to build the nation. Israel had to work toward the prosperity it longed for. Israel had to labor to turn the promised land into a land flowing with milk and honey. Everyone was to do his or her share. Thus, we read tort laws in which a person was to take responsibility for the loss of life or damage to property on account of negligence. We see family members taking responsibility for one another in serving as a *go'el* (redeemer), liberating kin who had been sold into slavery or retrieving ancestral land that had been alienated from the family (Lev 25:47–55). The cultic laws emphasize how eleven tribes were to support their Levite brethren in their service to the LORD with the offerings of their firstfruits, sacrifices, and tithes. In other words, everyone was to take responsibility in maintaining and supporting worship and the socioeconomic life of the nation. This is the scholastic principle of general-legal justice at work, in which people supported the common good according to their means.[19]

---

[19]   Aquinas, *Summa Theologica*, II–II Q. 58, article 6, answer.

It is the same dynamic in the modern era. A critical lesson that reverberates down to our own day is that we are individually and collectively responsible for the quality and the character of our community. Our community (or lack thereof) is a function of what we make of it. The quip in data processing is apt in this regard: "Garbage in, garbage out." We get what we put in. We get the community that we deserve. Biblical economic ethics underscores God's gift of material abundance to humanity. But it is conditional on our moral choices. The Deuteronomic doctrine of divine retribution highlights the real impact of human freedom and the need for us to take responsibility for our obligations. God's gift of conditional prosperity is very much in effect today. Unfortunately, it also sheds light on the true nature of ultrapoverty and poverty traps in our midst – evidence of our individual and collective moral failure to live up to our obligation of mutual assistance.

Proprietary Attitudes Concerning Economic Accomplishments

The Industrial Revolution inaugurated an era of mass production and mass consumption. It enabled ordinary people to consume goods and services that in the ancient and feudal eras were reserved only for the elite and the wealthy. The Internet-microelectronic revolution built on this and inaugurated in its own turn an era of mass affluence.

This economic success and plenty are fraught with danger. In particular, the marketplace can generate and impress its own values of consumerism, materialism, and secularism on unsuspecting economic agents. More is better. Material wealth is the yardstick of success. Nothing is awry with self-indulgent consumption because one has earned it. Consumer sovereignty backed up by purchasing power is near absolute. Prosperous market participants are self-made people who created opportunities for themselves.

Such values only serve to accentuate the contemporary relevance of Lev 25:23–28. The Israelites cannot sell land in perpetuity because they did not own the land to begin with. The land belongs to the LORD alone. It had merely been entrusted to Israel for its care and upkeep. By extension, there is nothing that humanity enjoys that does not belong to God – not their properties, their wealth, or even their accomplishments. Humans do not even own that which is most intrinsic to them – their human dignity. Rather, they owe their human dignity to God. Nothing escapes the absolute sovereignty of God, for all are mere creatures. Leviticus 25:23 is particularly apt for our times because it is a stark reminder that stewardship rather than a proprietary attitude is the proper human posture vis-à-vis economic accomplishments or possessions.

5.4 TO WHAT END DO WE EXERCISE OUR MORAL AGENCY?

The Hebrew economic imperatives are undoubtedly exacting. They demand self-giving and self-sacrifice for the sake of the poor and the distressed. Leviticus 19:2 and 20:7–8 are clear as to what end the chosen people were to act in such a fashion – to be holy as God is holy. At the end of a list of challenging admonitions, the priestly writer ends with a simple rationale for why Israel ought to live up to these duties. It is to emulate God in the way God is, to the extent humanly possible.

We face the same set of demanding economic imperatives today. It is still the same rationale. Far from being disheartened or cowed by the difficulty of the laws' demands, we are to rejoice at being invited to live up to these obligations. Not only do they allow us to experience the joy of caring for one another, but they also show us a pathway to being holy as God is holy, to the extent humanly possible. God asks much from us because God thinks highly of us. Even more exciting, it is a concrete way of loving God with our whole heart, soul, and strength (Deut 6:5). Lest we think that we are self-made in reaching such holiness (Pelagianism), we remember that even such holiness and righteousness are gifts from the God of Abraham, Isaac, and Jacob (Isa 45:22–25; 61:10).

FURTHER READING

Ahmed, A. R. Vargas Hill, L. Smith, D. Wiesmann, and T. Frankenberger, *The World's Most Deprived: Characteristics and Causes of Extreme Poverty and Hunger*. 2020 Discussion Paper no. 43. Washington, DC: International Food Policy Research Institute, 2007.

Aquinas, T. *Summa Theologica*. Translated by Fathers of the English Dominican Province. 3 vols. New York: Benzinger Brothers Aquinas, 1947–1948.

Gemser, B. "The Importance of the Motive Clause in Old Testament Law." Pages 50–66 in *Congress Volume, Copenhagen*, VTSup 1 Leiden: Brill, 1953.

Hardin, G. "The Tragedy of the Commons," *Science* 162 (1968): 1243–8.

Lohfink, N. "Poverty in the Laws of the Ancient Near East and of the Bible," *TS* 52 (1991): 34–50.

Pettifor, A. "The Jubilee 2000 Campaign: A Brief Overview," in *Sovereign Debt at the Crossroads: Challenges and Proposals for Resolving the Third World Debt Crisis*. Edited by C. Jochnich and F. Preston. Oxford: Oxford University Press, 2006.

Phan, P. *Social Thought*. Message of the Fathers of the Church 20. Delaware: Michael Glazier, 1984.

Pius XI. *Quadragesimo Anno*. Boston: Daughters of St. Paul, 1931.

Schottroff, W. "The Prophet Amos: A Socio-Historical Assessment of His Ministry," in *God of the Lowly: Socio-Historical Interpretations of the Bible.* Edited by L. Schottroff and W. Steggemann. Maryknoll: Orbis, 1984.
von Waldow, H. E. "Social Responsibility and Social Structure in Early Israel," *Catholic Biblical Quarterly* 32 (1970): 182–204.

Part II

Narrative Ethics

6 Creation Ethics in Genesis

MATTHEW RICHARD SCHLIMM

Genesis 1–11 introduces not only Genesis but the Bible as a whole. With remarkable realism, these chapters present manifold challenges to ethical living. They suggest that humanity does not operate in an overwhelmingly positive moral space. Instead, human beings face a variety of challenges. Humanity is not necessarily damned to lives of immorality, but praiseworthy people are rare, and temptations are great. While creating a thirst for upright behavior, the text explains the difficulty of doing the right thing. This emphasis on moral difficulty has important resonances with both its earliest and its most recent readers.

A word about each of these audiences is in order. While dating biblical texts is notoriously complex, it is fruitful to examine the reception of Genesis 1–11 among readers in the second half of the sixth century BCE, a time when the memories of exile and Jerusalem's destruction were still relatively fresh in readers' minds.[1] Scholars differ in their accounts of what life was like for people during this period. A mediating position recognizes that while many people found ways to move forward with their lives, a great number wrestled with profound questions after facing the loss of life, home, land, honor, institutions, and theologies in the preceding decades. As the Jewish people sought to rebuild and make sense of their new lives, competing ideas arose about who they were and how they should act, leading to internal divisions. Externally, they faced challenges from neighboring peoples like the Edomites/Idumeans, who cheered Jerusalem's fall, as well as the superpowers to whom they needed to make necessary homages. In this period

---

[1] Cf. M. S. Smith, *The Genesis of Good and Evil: The Fall(out) and Original Sin in the Bible* (Louisville: Westminster John Knox, 2019), 47; K. Schmid, "Creation," trans. P. Altmann, in *The Oxford Encyclopedia of the Bible and Theology*, ed. S. E. Balentine (Oxford: Oxford University Press, 2015), 1.166–76, here 1.168. The text itself presents something like exile as a common divine punishment (3:22–24; 4:12–16), and it critiques Babylon/Babel (11:1–9).

of immense challenge, Genesis 1–11 grounded readers in origin stories and provided ethical guidance.

Although modern people read the Bible in a different light, it can continue to function as a constructive dialogue partner for ethics. Granted, the Bible does not *necessarily* function in ethically helpful ways. Two of the Christian gospels purport that even the devil himself can cite scripture for his own ends (Matt 4:1–11; Luke 4:1–13). With a text like Genesis 1–11, people can condone exploitation of the earth on the basis of 1:28 or the promulgation of patriarchy on the basis of 3:16. However, using the Bible for these unethical ends is not the only possible way of reading the text. This essay focuses on how the Bible can be a force for good in the world.

This essay's organization draws on the work of literary critic Kenneth Burke, who advocated analyzing human behavior as though it were a dramatic play. It focuses on five key elements (often referred to as the Burkean pentad): "what was done (act), when or where it was done (scene), who did it (agent), how [the agent] did it (agency), and why (purpose)."[2] The academic field of rhetorical criticism has developed an entire subfield using this five-point heuristic. Mutatis mutandis, the field of biblical ethics can build on Burke's insights to understand the range of ethical content in biblical texts.

6.1 SCENE: THE MORAL SPACE OF GENESIS 1–11

The first two chapters of Genesis present a world that is thoroughly good. With refrains and rhythmic precision, the first creation account stresses seven times that God creates order and what is "good" ($t\hat{o}b$; 1:4, 10, 12, 18, 21, 25, 31).[3] While the second creation story has a very different style than the first, it too presents God creating a good world. Humanity inhabits a garden – the type of land most precious to the text's earliest readers. "Eden" means "delight." It contains not only "every tree that is pleasant to the sight and good for food" but also "the tree of life" (2:9). There is no shame, suffering, or death.

The events of Genesis 3 transform not only humanity's ability to remain within the garden but also the good nature of the earth itself, which receives God's curse (3:17–19; cf. 4:12). Serving as God's agent of

---

[2]   K. Burke, *A Grammar of Motives* (Berkeley: University of California Press, 1969), xv.

[3]   For more on this order and precision, see G. J. Wenham, *Rethinking Genesis 1–11: Gateway to the Bible*, Didsbury Lecture Series (Eugene: Cascade, 2015), 4–6.

justice, the ground reacts to humanity's transgressions.[4] The earth becomes a graveyard, as the reality of death replaces the possibility of eternal life (3:19; 4:8–10). God's commands remain in force, but obedience now entails suffering: Being fruitful (1:28) now means tremendous pain (3:16), and working the earth (2:15) becomes a matter of suffering atop a thorn-covered and cursed soil until one returns to the ground (3:17–19). Such conditions endure even today.[5]

Why does the text bother describing a world that is good, only to present humanity as forced onto a less than ideal space? First, many biblical voices express that the world should be better than it is (e.g., Isa 5:7; 8:21). By presenting a good world that is then lost, Genesis 1–11 participates in broader biblical traditions about humanity and creation falling short of high ideals. Second, the text upholds God's goodness. If God originally created a world of hardship, suffering, and death, then readers would have reasons to question God's goodness. By presenting God as creating a good world that humans subsequently shape for the worse, God no longer bears sole responsibility for the difficulties of life. Humankind has played a role in its own fate. Third, the conviction that evil deeds lead to disastrous consequences runs throughout the Bible (e.g., Deut 31:29). This conviction is balanced, however, by the idea that ethical actions do not always correspond to one's fate (e.g., Eccl 2:14). By presenting a good world that is distorted, Genesis 1–11 allows readers to conceptualize creation as having moral dimensions even if their experience of moral consequences does not rigidly correspond to ethical expectations. Finally, the loss of a good world would have certainly resonated with sixth-century audiences, who had relatively recently had their land destroyed. By describing the world's distortion, Genesis 1–11 validated the experiences of people who had suffered immeasurable losses.

Not every modern reader can relate to the loss of a good world as extensively as the text's earliest readers. Nevertheless, many people today sense that the world should be better than it is. Amid a landscape of empty promises made by politicians, marketing campaigns, and modernity itself, people long for a better life. Even with modern-day comforts, life remains stressful. Despite incredible medical advances, death

---

[4] E. F. Davis, "Learning Our Place: The Agrarian Perspective of the Bible," *WW* 29 (2009): 109–20, here 114; M. Jørstad, "The Ground That Opened Its Mouth: The Ground's Response to Human Violence in Genesis 4," *JBL* 135 (2016): 705–15, here 711–13.

[5] While God promises in 8:21 not to bring additional curses on the ground, previous ones endure (Jørstad, "Ground," 714n23).

haunts us all. The earth remains a challenging place, with many threats, limited resources, and the potential for tragedy. A first step toward moral responsibility is recognizing the limitations we face. The ethical task needs to focus less on merely doing good and more on doing good amid a world of limitations where upright behavior entails difficulty.

6.2 AGENTS: THE ETHICAL ANTHROPOLOGY OF GENESIS 1–11

Genesis 1–11 warns human beings against seeing themselves too highly or too lowly. Although some interpreters claim human beings are the crowning achievement of the first creation story,[6] the text says that humans and other animals were created on the same day (1:24–31). When God blesses humanity and tells them to be fruitful (1:28), God is merely repeating what happened with fish and birds (1:22). Furthermore, God creates human beings on neither the first day nor the seventh day. The Sabbath, not humanity, is the only part of creation that God sanctifies (2:3).

The second creation story emphasizes that humans are made from dirt, and their return to dirt is guaranteed (2:7; 3:19). God creates animals in a way similar to humans (2:7, 19).[7] In what Mark Brett calls "a cutting humiliation," the humans are tricked by a reptile.[8] The broader text reinforces the idea that humans are not divine: When humanity both has access to immortality and knows good and evil, God decides to remove them from the tree of life (3:22–24). God makes the Bible's first covenant with both humans and nonhuman animals (9:9–12). In Genesis 11:1–9, God does not allow humanity to obtain Godlike power to do anything (11:6), counteracting a people that wants to make a name for itself (11:4).[9]

On the whole, Genesis 1–11 suggests that human beings have a natural affinity for evil. Although Genesis 3 may not speak explicitly about "original sin," it does present the very first humans – whose names mean "Humanity" and "Life" – as disobeying their creator and disregarding

---

[6] Wenham, *Rethinking*, 10, 16.

[7] M. G. Brett, *Genesis: Procreation and the Politics of Identity*, Old Testament Readings (London: Routledge, 2000), 30–1.

[8] Brett, *Genesis*, 33.

[9] G. West observes and critiques how Gen 11:1–9 was used to justify apartheid in South Africa (*Genesis*, People's Bible Commentary [Oxford: Bible Reading Fellowship, 2006], 79).

strong divine warnings (2:17; 3:6).[10] In a story that has multiple points of continuity with Genesis 2–3, Genesis 4:1–16 presents Cain as welcoming death into the world when he kills his own brother. Genesis never speaks explicitly about individuals inheriting a sinful nature, but the severity of bloodshed with Cain's descendant Lamech suggests that violence has become fruitful and multiplied (4:23–24).[11] By 6:11–13, violence has "filled" the earth.[12] In this context, readers find the most explicit statement about human nature,[13] and it is damning enough to warrant God's flooding the entire world: "The Lord saw that the wickedness of human-kind was great in the earth, and that every inclination of the thoughts of their hearts was only evil continually" (6:5). Yet, not even a worldwide bath is able to wash away human evil, as 8:21 and 9:20–27 make clear.

While Genesis 1–11 thus gives people many reasons to exercise humility, this section of the book is about more than human shortcomings. It talks about three people who win God's approval: Abel (4:4), Enoch (5:22–24), and Noah (6:8–9; 7:5).[14] These examples are rare, given that Genesis 1–11 names approximately ninety individuals in all. Nevertheless, their presence within the text opens the possibility of human beings doing more than continuing a downward spiral into evil.

In addition to pointing to a few godly people, the text boldly claims that all human beings possess the very image of God (1:26–28; 9:6; cf. 5:1–2). In an important study, Richard Middleton builds on the work of others to show how the literature of the ancient Near East uses the phrase "image of God" almost exclusively to talk about rulers and elites. In Genesis, however, this royal phrase is democratized, applied to every-one.[15] As bearers of the divine image, human life is sacred and should not be taken (9:5–6). These points about the intrinsic value of all human beings are reinforced by Genesis 2:7, which says that God created humanity first out of all living creatures, endowing the human creature with God's own breath. Later portions of Genesis 1–11 move in similar directions. As Amanda Mbuvi points out, God's covenant with "every living creature" in 9:12 precludes "anyone from occupying the position

[10] Cf. Jørstad, "Ground," 707.
[11] L. Alonso-Schökel, ¿Dónde está tu hermano? Textos de fraternidad en el libro del Génesis, Tesis y Monografías 19 (Valencia: Institución San Jerónimo para la Investigación Bíblica, 1985), 323.
[12] West, Genesis, 57.
[13] Smith, Genesis, 76.
[14] Smith, Genesis, 84–5.
[15] J. R. Middleton, The Liberating Image: The Imago Dei in Genesis 1 (Grand Rapids: Brazos, 2005), 121, 204. See also Brett, Genesis, 28.

of outsider. Every living being stands in covenantal relationship to God."[16] Moreover, the genealogies of Genesis 1–11 suggest that human beings should see each other as part of a broader interrelated family.[17]

In a truly remarkable move, parts of Genesis affirm the equal worth of male and female.[18] Rather than presenting woman as less than man, both share in the divine image (1:27; cf. 5:1–2). Rather than strongly differentiating male from female, Genesis 2:23 emphasizes how similar man and woman are: The first human words in the Bible are, "This at last is bone of my bones and flesh of my flesh." These two are able to become "one flesh" (2:24). The woman is called a "helper" (2:18–20), but this title does not suggest she is inferior; it often refers to God (e.g., Deut 33:29). Although patriarchy enters the picture in 3:16, the text suggests it is problematic by naming it alongside curses, suffering, and death.

In the second half of the sixth century, the messages of Genesis 1–11 would have had important resonances. As in other periods of biblical history, life expectancy was roughly half what it is in the modern world. The death-bound nature of humanity would have been all too apparent, especially when recent decades had involved catastrophic war. Understanding humanity to have a strong proclivity toward evil would have helped people make sense of not only the treatment they received from their enemies, but also why previous generations had committed the sins that led to exile. By not thinking too highly of themselves, people in this period would have found ways to avoid confrontations with overlords as well as ways through the threat of internal division. At the same time, finding value in oneself and others would have been essential for survival amid trying times. A text envisioning gender equality while problematizing patriarchy had the potential to unite men and women facing splintering factions and widespread patriarchy.

In the modern world, an awareness of human fallibility can lead to humility and an urgency to safeguard against temptation. The text's emphasis on the image of God counteracts hatred of both others and oneself. The text's teachings on gender uphold ideals of equality in a world where fundamental gender inequalities persist. Furthermore, as the limitations of gender binarism become increasingly apparent, readers can highlight that a foundational text like Genesis 2:23

---

[16]   A. B. Mbuvi, *Belonging in Genesis: Biblical Israel and the Politics of Identity Formation* (Waco: Baylor University Press, 2016), 145.

[17]   Mbuvi, *Belonging*, 49, 67, 92–3. On racism and the curse of Ham, see Mbuvi's excellent treatment in Ch. 5, esp. pp. 70–5, and West, *Genesis*, 71, 73.

[18]   Middleton, *Liberating*, 204–7.

does little to differentiate male and female, but rather affirms how alike they are.

6.3 ACTS: WHAT THE ETHICAL LIFE ENTAILS

Genesis 1–11 places its highest ethical emphases on (1) helping life flourish; (2) exercising restraint in consumption; and (3) avoiding violence.

The Flourishing of Life

In both Genesis 1 and 9, God blesses humanity and immediately commands that they "be fruitful and multiply, and fill the earth" (1:28; 9:1, 7). Foundational to these commands is the idea that life should flourish. When God issues these commands in 1:28, God also tells the people to "subdue" (*kbš) the earth and "have dominion" (*rdh) over all animals. Many exegetes worry that these verbs give permission for violence and exploitation. However, these expectations occur in the context of God making humanity in the image of God, suggesting that whatever subduing and dominion may entail, human beings should follow God's example by creating order that is conducive to the flourishing of life, resulting in what can unambiguously be called "good."[19]

The second account of creation also emphasizes the role of humanity in helping life flourish. The focus here is especially on vegetation and the soil. The NRSV says that humanity's job is to "till" *ʿbd and "keep" (*šmr) the garden (2:15; cf. 2:5). The Hebrew words normally mean "serve" and "protect," respectively.[20] They carry reverential overtones, describing divine worship (e.g., Exod 10:24) and keeping God's commandments (e.g., Exod 20:6). In light of these responsibilities, as well as the emphasis on the earthling ('ādām) being made from the earth ('ădāmâ) in 2:7, a core point of the text is that humans live in a symbiotic relationship with the land.[21] As Mbuvi points out, "Genesis specifies that wholeness involves humans in relationship with land."[22]

In Genesis 3, consuming the fruit is a violation of the creator's intention for creation. The world suffers after humanity misuses it.

---

[19] Cf. Davis, "Learning," 112; W. P. Brown, *The Ethos of the Cosmos: The Genesis of Moral Imagination in the Bible* (Grand Rapids: Eerdmans, 1999), 45–6; T. E. Fretheim, *God and World in the Old Testament: A Relational Theology of Creation* (Nashville: Abingdon, 2005), 48–53; Middleton, *Liberating*, 287–97.

[20] Davis, "Learning," 112.

[21] Cf. Davis, "Learning," 110, 112; Jørstad, "Ground," 706.

[22] Mbuvi, *Belonging*, 58; cf. Brown, *Ethos*, 138.

The earth becomes cursed, covered with thorns and thistles, and the abode of the dead (3:17–19).[23]

In Genesis 4, Cain takes his brother to a field where Cain, as the story's farmer, should have brought forth life. Instead, Cain brings forth death. In response to Cain's profoundly anticreational act of violence, the soil stops functioning in life-giving ways (4:11–12).

God gives Noah a series of commands in 6:14–17:4, 8:16–17. While they all refer to a one-time event, they all relate to the broader category of caring for the earth's creatures and helping animal life to flourish amid catastrophic disaster.

Caring for the world is an overarching moral imperative of Genesis 1–11. For readers in the sixth century, caring for the earth was necessary for survival. Only by serving the soil did it produce the sustenance necessary to survive. Readers today face ecological crises largely unimaginable among the text's earliest readers. At the same time, caring for the earth remains necessary for survival. The divine mandates to ensure the flourishing of life and to serve and protect the soil remain as relevant as ever. The earth needs people like Noah, who will uphold the highest ethical ideals and play key roles in preserving life amid rising sea levels.

Restrain in Consumption

In Gen 2:16–17, God urges humanity to eat from any tree of the garden, except the tree of the knowledge of good and evil. In Gen 3:6, the couple casts off restraint, consuming what they do not need.[24] They eat what is said to be deadly. They feed themselves more than necessary, swallowing what is harmful. They use creation in a way that violates how the creator insisted it function.

By Genesis 9, the luxurious garden is a thing of the past. Nevertheless, God issues a commandment very similar to the earlier one: Humanity can eat anything (2:16; 9:3) except one particular food (2:17; 9:4). The prohibition this time is not fruit but "flesh with its life, that is, its blood" (9:4). While some modern readers might wish to classify the second prohibition less as a matter of ethics and more of a matter of ritual purity, the text itself makes no such distinction, moving directly from this topic to forbidding murder (9:5–6).

---

23 Cf. Fretheim, *God*, 80.
24 Davis, "Learning," 115.

Through repetition, Genesis 1–11 suggests that what humans eat are matters of highest importance to their conduct.[25] Most early readers of this text would agree. A variety of biblical texts suggest that dietary restraint constituted a key means by which Jewish peoples ordered their lives and maintained their identities. In modern times, these texts invite readers to consider the ethics of their diets, particularly regarding the ethics of food production, distribution, and consumption. The text emphasizes that casting aside restraint and engaging in overconsumption can damage both eaters and the world itself.

Violence

Unlike other ancient creation stories that portray violence as a fundamental feature of the divine life (e.g., *Enuma Elish*), Genesis 1–2 gives violence scant attention.[26] Only outside the garden, amid the concrete realities of the present world, does bloodshed erupt in the most insidious of ways.[27] Death appears as one brother takes the life of another. Beforehand God seeks to prevent this murder (4:6–7), and afterward God has severe punishments for Cain (4:11–16). Lamech, one of Cain's descendants, brags of killing a child (4:23; the NRSV says he killed "a young man," but "child" is the most common way to translate the Hebrew noun *yeled*). Lamech even boasts of having an appetite for vengeance that rivals that of God (4:24; cf. 4:15).[28] By the time of Noah, humanity is described as entrenched in evil – and the one specific expression of evil named in that context is violence, which is referenced twice (6:11, 13). After Noah's family survives the worldwide destruction, God gives them a surprisingly small list of instructions, including never to kill human beings (9:5–6).

The second half of the sixth century was a time of immense internal and external struggle. Internally, the Jewish people faced deep divisions as competing ideas arose about how to define their identity. Externally, they faced a host of challenges from both encroaching neighboring peoples and imperial powers whom they needed to placate. Amid such pressures, oppressed people can quickly turn against each other. In this context, Genesis 1–11 makes clear that violence is not an acceptable course of action. This message continues to have resonances today,

---

[25]   Davis, "Learning," 114.
[26]   Brett, *Genesis*, 25; Wenham, *Rethinking*, 12; Middleton, *Liberating*, 263–9.
[27]   Alonso-Schökel, *Dónde*, 34.
[28]   Alonso-Schökel, *Dónde*, 323.

particularly when technological "advances" have made it possible to commit violence on scales never before possible.

6.4 AGENCY: HOW IMMORAL BEHAVIOR IS ACHIEVED

Rather than focusing on the righteous, Genesis 1–11 gives its greatest attention to individuals who make problematic decisions. As it does this, the text frequently focuses on the interior factors – motives, emotions, dispositions – that lead to their actions.

How Forbidden Fruit Was Consumed

When the first couple disobeys God's command, the normally concise narrative slows down, shares a conversation, and details the thought process leading toward consumption. The conversation between the woman and snake raises doubts about the consequences God has outlined (3:1–5). With that doubt lingering in the air, the text explains several judgments that combine to result in consumption (3:6). First, the tree looks "good [ṭôb] for food." Second, it is "a delight [ta'ăwâ] to the eyes." Third, it is "desired [neḥmād] to make one wise [lĕhaśkîl]." Remarkably, there is nothing intrinsically bad about any of these three reasons for eating the fruit. The other trees of the garden are also "good [ṭôb] for food" and "desired [neḥmād]" (2:9). The word "delight [ta'ăwâ]" is elsewhere ascribed to the righteous who receive God's favor (e.g., Prov 10:24). The word for "make one wise [lĕhaśkîl]" can describe the blessings God gives for obedience (Deut 29:8[9]; Josh 1:8). As many commentators note, consumption even allows the first couple to grow in knowledge, which is normally a good thing in the Bible.[29]

Yet, consuming this fruit violates God's orders in 2:17. It leads to curses, suffering, patriarchy, and eventually entombment (3:14–19). Why does the text give genuinely compelling reasons for consuming the fruit when it comes with disastrous results? First, the text presents the temptation to disobey God as truly attractive.[30] One can easily find reasons to go against God's stated will. Second, the text makes clear that human judgment alone is insufficient to avoid suffering. Especially when God's commands are laid aside, tragic outcomes can result from seemingly sound decisions. Third, the text suggests that humanity can make advances while simultaneously ending up in a worse condition. Here, the humans grow in maturity, gain knowledge of good and evil,

---

[29]   Smith, *Genesis*, 38–9.
[30]   Brown, *Ethos*, 148.

and become morally accountable agents.[31] At the same time, they become expelled from the garden, lose immortality, experience patriarchy, and face suffering in trying to reproduce and find sustenance. A step forward in knowledge comes with tragic consequences.

How Death Entered the Earth

Outside the garden, a murder takes place. While the setting of Genesis 4 is obviously different than that of Genesis 2–3, a number of parallels suggests that Genesis 4 recapitulates Genesis 2–3. In each case, God gives a warning (2:17; 4:7) that humans fail to heed (3:6–7; 4:8). Both stories focus on death (2:17; 3:3–4, 19; 4:8). God repeatedly interrogates the subjects, asking both, "Where…?" (3:9; 4:9) and "What have you done?" (3:13; 4:10). Next, God issues punishments that include curses (3:14–19; 4:11–12) – particularly those concerning the ground (3:17, 19; 4:11–12) – and expulsions east of Eden (3:24; 4:16). Whether through leather clothes or a mysterious sign, God exercises some level of care for the punished humans (3:21; 4:15).[32]

In Genesis 3, readers learn nothing of what the fruit tasted like, its color, or its texture. The focus is on what leads to disobeying God and its consequences. In Genesis 4, readers learn very little of how Cain kills his brother. The focus again is on what leads to disobeying God and its consequences. For reasons that the text never fully explains, God shows favor to Abel's offering but not to Cain's (4:3–5a). Cain becomes very angry (4:5b). In the Hebrew Bible, anger is prototypically caused by the perception of injustice.[33] Here, the perceived injustice appears to be that God's favor eludes Cain. Approximately one-third of the verses mentioning jealousy in the Hebrew Bible also mention anger.[34] So, it may not be coincidental that Cain's Hebrew name (qayin) sounds similar to the Hebrew word for jealousy (qin'â). The text implies that Cain is jealous of Abel's receiving God's favor.

Although Cain's sacrifice merited little divine attention, his emotions cause direct divine intervention. God speaks to Cain. The conversation makes clear that anger is not a sin in itself: Cain can still do what is right (4:7a). However, Cain's emotional state has placed him in imminent danger near the doorway to sin (4:7b). As soon as God's word ends,

---

[31] Smith, *Genesis*, 38–9; Schmid, "Creation," 171. Cf. Deut 1:39, Isa 7:14–16, 1QSa 1:10–11.

[32] M. R. Schlimm, *From Fratricide to Forgiveness: The Language and Ethics of Anger in Genesis*, Siphrut 7 (Winona Lake: Eisenbrauns, 2011), 139–40; Jørstad, "Ground," 706.

[33] Schlimm, *From Fratricide to Forgiveness*, 53–6.

[34] Schlimm, *From Fratricide to Forgiveness*, 65–7.

Cain invites Abel to the field where the younger is slaughtered (4:8).
God's judgment comes quickly, cursing Cain away from the ground,
which will no longer give its strength to Cain, who must become an
exile and a refugee (4:11–16).

By presenting anger as the reason death enters the world, Genesis
joins several ancient texts that present anger as an ethical matter of
highest significance. Aristotle and Seneca, for example, devote considerable time to this emotion, the latter arguing that it has done more to
threaten humanity than even the deadliest plague (*Ira* 1.1–2). Although
Genesis is no philosophical treatise, it does name anger as an ethical
matter of foremost importance. As the book unfolds, every patriarch and
many matriarchs will have significant encounters with jealousy and
anger on implicit or explicit levels (13:7–8; 16:4–6; 21:9–10; 26:14–22;
27:41–45; 30:1–4; 31:35–32:1[31:35–55]; 34:7; 37:11; 39:17–20; 40:1–3;
41:10; 44:18; 45:5, 24; 49:6–7), until at last Joseph and his brothers find
reconciliation after many anger-filled episodes that have left no one free
of guilt (50:15–21). By including so many anger-filled episodes between
Cain and Joseph with varying outcomes, Genesis provides readers with a
moral guide about how anger can unfold in their own lives.[35]

How Humanity Became Wicked and Violent

When God decides to destroy all of creation besides the creatures aboard
the ark, the text speaks generically of wickedness (6:5) and specifically of
violence (*ḥāmās*, 6:11, 13). As with Genesis 3 and 4, the text turns to the
interior life of human beings. Genesis 6:5 says that God saw that "every
inclination of the thoughts of [humanity's] hearts was only evil continually." The Hebrew here translated "inclination of the thoughts" (*yēṣer
maḥšĕbōt*) comes from the semantic field of craftsmanship, suggesting
that human beings inwardly craft their evil before it arises outwardly.[36]
This inner evil is not cleansed by the worldwide flood, as 8:21
makes clear.

Resonances among Readers

Most characters in Genesis 1–11 face horrible repercussions because of
their actions. These negative outcomes create in readers a desire for
alternatives. Because the narrative consistently suggests that problematic actions begin with inner thoughts, emotions, and dispositions, the
text calls readers to reflect on their interior lives. Specifically, Genesis 4

[35]   Schlimm, *From Fratricide to Forgiveness*, esp. Part 3.
[36]   Smith, *Genesis*, 76–7.

provided an important cautionary tale during the second half of the sixth century. Emotions like anger and jealousy were probably quite common among minority communities facing imperial pressures and inner divisions. They needed careful attention to prevent tragic outcomes.

For the modern world, with its insatiable hunger for knowledge, Genesis 3 suggests that the consequences of gaining knowledge may be more severe than anyone has anticipated. The modern age has brought unprecedented knowledge, especially in the sciences. Sadly, this newfound knowledge has led to newfound methods of violence through chemical warfare, atomic and nuclear bombs, and drones. Meanwhile, the internet has given individuals unprecedented access to knowledge but has also led to a host of problems, including widespread pornography, misinformation, political polarization, and cybercrimes. Although many use social media to feel "connected," they also admit to feeling deep-seated inadequacies and loneliness in the information age. Like the tree of the knowledge of good and evil, modernity has unlocked the doors to unprecedented knowledge, but these advances have also brought unforeseen problems.

6.5 PURPOSE: WHY PURSUE THE ETHICAL LIFE?

Genesis 1–11 points to three key motivations for ethical behavior. First, God commands it. Second, ethical behavior is part of imitating God. Third, ethical behavior entails good consequences.

Divine Orders

Throughout the Hebrew Bible, one of the most basic and pervasive reasons for engaging in ethical behavior is that God commands it.[37] Genesis 1–11 participates in this broader biblical tradition by presenting God both as commanding ethical behavior and as a deity worth obeying.

In Genesis 1–11, God issues commands governing human conduct, often giving them more than once. God orders humanity to "be fruitful and multiply, and fill the earth" (1:28, 9:1, 7). God commands human beings to eat from everything with a single exception (2:16–17; 9:3–4). God forbids killing others, warning of punishment (4:6–7; 9:5–6).

The text also gives readers reasons to abide by God's particular commands. God is presented on the Bible's first page as the universe's creator and thus its ultimate being. Furthermore, the chief concern of

[37] J. Barton, *Understanding Old Testament Ethics: Approaches and Explorations* (Louisville: Westminster John Knox, 2003), 47–8.

this creator is goodness (1:4, 10, 12, 18, 21, 25, 31). While the world changes dramatically in Genesis 3, God remains concerned with ethical goodness, intervening when temptation is present (4:6–7), experiencing heartbreak over evil (6:5–7; 11–13), and reacting to violence by beginning anew with someone who has integrity (6:8–9, 13–22; 7:1–4). This God is an ethical force to be reckoned with.

Imitating God

Genesis 1–11 joins the broader biblical tradition in encouraging the imitation of God (e.g., Lev 19:2),[38] though it also contains some qualifications. While there is much debate about what exactly the *imago dei* entails, the immediate context suggests that human beings should imitate God in governing creation to bring about good.[39] Genesis 2:2–3 lays a framework for humanity to imitate God by Sabbath-keeping. Enoch and Noah are described as walking with God, which certainly entails imitation (5:22, 24; 6:9).[40]

At the same time, Genesis 1–11 limits the degree to which humanity should participate in the *imitatio dei*. When human beings become like God by both being able to live forever and knowing good and evil, God removes them from the tree of life (3:22–24). Genesis 6:1–4 is open to many interpretations, but 6:3 appears to communicate God's desire to differentiate the human and divine. In Genesis 11:1–9, God seeks to prevent humanity from obtaining a Godlike power to do anything (esp. 11:6). While imitating God can lead to ethical behavior, seeking to be like God can also bring pride. Genesis makes clear that human creatures are not God's equals.[41]

Consequences

Like other parts of the Bible (e.g., Deut 28), Genesis 1–11 emphasizes that consequences provide a key motivator for engaging in ethical behavior and avoiding unethical conduct. In Genesis 1–11 the results of disobeying God are catastrophic. Frequently, punishments resemble exile. After God makes a curse involving the ground (Gen 3:17; 4:11; cf. Deut 28:18–24), God forces both the first couple and Cain away from their homes (3:22–24; 4:12–16; cf. Deut 28:33–36). Similarly, the

---

38   Barton, *Understanding*, 50–4.
39   Wenham, *Rethinking*, 15; Middleton, *Liberating*, 43–90.
40   Barton, *Understanding*, 53.
41   Schmid, "Creation," 170.

builders at Babylon/Babel are "scattered" across the earth (11:8–9; cf. Deut 28:64).

As has been commonly recognized, the defeat of Jerusalem would have provoked a crisis of faith: Nationalistic theology about the inviolability of Zion would have appeared inadequate, while Babylonian theologies about the all-surpassing power of Marduk would have appeared attractive. By presenting God as one who sends people into exile as a result of their actions, Genesis joins prophetic writings in assisting early readers to make sense of their fate and defeat by imperial powers. God's goodness could be affirmed; conversion to another religion was unnecessary. The ethical dimensions of religion were underscored.

The text also invites readers today to consider the long-term consequences of ethical and unethical living. Naturally, one should not assume that all suffering is caused by a person's moral failings. At the same time, on individual, societal, and planetary levels, one's actions have profound consequences. Genesis 1–11 invites readers to consider the ways that ethical decisions reverberate into the future.

6.6 CONCLUSION

Genesis 1–11 presents the world as filled with challenges and asserts that humanity struggles immensely with evil's attractiveness. Providing ethics for a world of limitations, it teaches readers to reflect deeply on inner thoughts, emotions, and inclinations. It warns of the potential for violence to erupt even within families, and it inspires humanity to see its own value, the value of others, and the value of life in all of God's creation. It explains that the ethical life is part of obeying a good God, imitating God, and avoiding tragic outcomes.

FURTHER READING

Alonso-Schökel, L. ¿Dónde está tu hermano? Textos de fraternidad en el libro del Génesis. Tesis y Monografías 19. Valencia: Institución San Jerónimo para la Investigación Bíblica, 1985.

Barton, J. Understanding Old Testament Ethics: Approaches and Explorations. Louisville: Westminster John Knox, 2003.

Brett, M. G. Genesis: Procreation and the Politics of Identity. Old Testament Readings. London: Routledge, 2000.

Brown, W. P. The Ethos of the Cosmos: The Genesis of Moral Imagination in the Bible. Grand Rapids: Eerdmans, 1999.

Burke, K. A Grammar of Motives. Berkeley: University of California Press, 1969.

Davis, E. F. "Learning Our Place: The Agrarian Perspective of the Bible." *Word and World* 29 (2009): 109–20.

Fretheim, T. E. *God and World in the Old Testament: A Relational Theology of Creation*. Nashville: Abingdon, 2005.

Jørstad, M. "The Ground That Opened Its Mouth: The Ground's Response to Human Violence in Genesis 4." *JBL* 135 (2016): 705–15.

Mbuvi, A. B. *Belonging in Genesis: Biblical Israel and the Politics of Identity Formation*. Waco: Baylor University Press, 2016.

Middleton, J. R. *The Liberating Image: The Imago Dei in Genesis 1*. Grand Rapids: Brazos, 2005.

Schlimm, M. R. *From Fratricide to Forgiveness: The Language and Ethics of Anger in Genesis*. Siphrut 7. Winona Lake: Eisenbrauns, 2011.

Schmid, K. "Creation." Translated by Peter Altmann. Pages 166–76 in vol. 1 of *The Oxford Encyclopedia of the Bible and Theology*. Edited by S. E. Balentine. Oxford: Oxford University Press, 2015.

Smith, M. S. *The Genesis of Good and Evil: The Fall(out) and Original Sin in the Bible*. Louisville: Westminster John Knox, 2019.

Wenham, G. J. *Rethinking Genesis 1–11: Gateway to the Bible*. Didsbury Lecture Series. Eugene: Cascade, 2015.

West, G. *Genesis*. People's Bible Commentary. Oxford: Bible Reading Fellowship, 2006.

7 Migrant Ethics in the Jacob Narratives

C. A. STRINE

I am the wrong person to write this essay. I should have recognized this earlier and suggested another author. I did not. Drafting what follows, I became keenly aware that exploring the ethical aspects of the Jacob narrative necessitates a deeper and probably more personal comprehension of marginalization than I have from my current experience.

Lest other elements of this essay obscure this point, I state it plainly here. I will return to it in the final section of the essay, where I consider its wider implications for the study of ethics and the Hebrew Bible. Not to put too fine a point on things, I believe this is a matter every editor, author, and reader of work in this area must grapple with and address.

*

The story of Jacob presents a conundrum for those exploring the intersection of ethics and the Hebrew Bible. The younger of two sons, Jacob, obtains the inheritance and blessing of the firstborn through deceit and trickery. Compelled to deal with his domineering uncle, Laban, Jacob resorts to duplicity again. Nevertheless, Genesis consistently affirms his status as the third elect patriarch. Elsewhere in the Hebrew Bible, authors venerate Jacob as the eponymous ancestor of Israel. Never does this anthology disown his behavior.

What does one do with a problematic character, who exhibits behavioral tendencies not amenable to most ethical systems, and yet remains not just a role model but the eponymous role model of the ancient society from which these ethical formulations emerge? How might Jacob fit into an ethical model that includes the Hebrew Bible as a key input? Some abdicate on the question. A narrative contains too much ambiguity to offer a basis for drawing ethical principles or perspectives, they say. The requirement to discern authorial perspective in order to identify the ethical views of such a text is too difficult – indeed, it is an impossible hermeneutical task.

No doubt, it is a challenging one. In *Story as Torah*, however, Gordon Wenham argues that the effort to read narratives for ethical insight is necessary, despite its difficulty. Narrative, he argues, sketches ethical virtues; legal material addresses only the minimum expectations of ethical conduct.[1] Through their development of rounded characters, narratives explore ideals of ethical conduct in a way that legal discourses cannot.

Even so, the task remains complex. A plethora of views as to which ethical ideas a story seeks to communicate may still arise with even the most superficially straightforward tale – and some problematic passages escape consensus entirely. Wenham's discussion of Genesis 34, the disturbing episode of Dinah's rape and forced marriage, illustrates the point well.[2] Indeed, one could be forgiven for giving up the enterprise of reading the Jacob story for ethical ideas altogether.

On the other hand, one might need to read the story differently.

Consider this atypical summary of the ancestral narratives (Genesis 12–36). The story begins with Abraham, who migrates to Canaan.[3] On arrival, famine forces Abraham and Sarah to flee to Egypt (12:10–13:1), where she enters into a form of sex work in order to provide for their safety and financial needs. Sarah and Abraham return to Canaan, where their son Isaac is also compelled to migrate by a famine (26:1). Isaac remains in Canaan, yet Rebekah, Isaac's wife, must also engage in sex work to ensure their survival.[4] Isaac's son Jacob grows up in Canaan, but spends his early adulthood as an asylum seeker, avoiding the aggression of his brother Esau by taking refuge with family in Mesopotamia. After twenty years, Jacob returns to Canaan to find a transformed, unrecognizable society. Esau's willingness to reconcile symbolizes this massive change. Jacob's inability to understand it exemplifies his reverse culture shock.

One might describe all these characters in the terms employed by the United Nations High Commissioner for Refugees: Abraham and Sarah are environmentally induced externally displaced persons; Isaac

---

[1] G. Wenham, *Story as Torah: Reading the Old Testament Ethically* (Edinburgh: T&T Clark, 2000).

[2] Wenham, *Story as Torah*, 109–19.

[3] I shall use "Abraham" throughout, though the first patriarch's name is "Abram" until it is changed by YHWH in Gen 17:5.

[4] See C. A. Strine, "Sister Save Us: The Matriarchs as Breadwinners and Their Threat to Patriarchy in the Ancestral Narrative," in *Women and Exilic Identity in the Hebrew Bible*, ed. M. Halvorson-Taylor and K. Southwood (London: Bloomsbury T&T Clark, 2018), 53–66.

and Rebekah are environmentally induced internally displaced persons; Sarah and Rebekah both engage in sex work to provide for their involuntary migrant families; and Jacob is an asylum seeker who subsequently repatriates by choice. The ancestors are all involuntary migrants.[5]

Although this summary makes clear that Genesis 12–50 lends itself to interpretation through the lens of involuntary migration, attempts to explore the ethics of the ancestral narrative have thus far failed to take this aspect of the narrative on board. The lacuna no doubt derives from the relative youth of forced migration studies: although some trace its origin to a 1951 United Nations convention relating to the status of refugees,[6] most place it in the early 1980s.[7] Still in its infancy, the field has only recently begun to deliver findings that can be used in other disciplines.

Taking up these findings, this essay reads the Jacob narrative as a narrative about involuntary migration. It does so because this generates a clearer view of the way that the text presents Jacob as an ethical paradigm for subaltern persons. Jacob's identity as a marginalized person thus unlocks the ethical perspective of the text and explains why its content has caused concern among modern Western scholars. The Jacob narrative destabilizes Genesis' use in the production of ethical norms, insofar as the latter enterprise remains bound up with imperial structures that contribute to oppression. In short, the way the Jacob story advocates for involuntary migrants necessitates a different approach: one that facilitates an ethics of liberation.

7.1 JACOB THE INVOLUNTARY MIGRANT (GEN 25:19–29:14A)

The Jacob narrative begins with a description of a struggle between Esau and Jacob that culminates in conflict about the family birthright (25:27–34).[8] After an interruption dealing with Isaac and Rebekah's

---

[5] For further details on the UNHCR approach, see their annual global report; the most recent, from 2017, is available at http://reporting.unhcr.org/sites/default/files/gr2017/pdf/GR2017_English_Full_lowres.pdf (accessed September 19, 2019).

[6] R. Black, "Fifty Years of Refugee Studies: From Theory to Policy," *International Migration Review* 35 1 (2001): 57–78; for the United Nations document see www.unhcr.org/pages/49da0e466.html (accessed February 23, 2017).

[7] D. Chatty, "Anthropology and Forced Migration," in *The Oxford Handbook of Refugee and Forced Migration Studies*, ed. E. Fiddian-Qasmiyeh et al. (Oxford: Oxford University Press, 2014), 74–80.

[8] A more detailed version of the material in this section appears in C. A. Strine "Your Name Shall No Longer Be Jacob, but Refugee: Insights into Gen 25:19–33:20 from

involuntary move to Gerar, the conflict returns with Rebekah and Jacob's ruse to gain the patriarchal blessing for Jacob.

The ploy prompts Esau to ponder murdering Jacob. Rebekah counsels Jacob to flee Canaan, where he might find safety with Laban. She recommends that Jacob seek asylum and become a refugee, that is, assume the status of "someone who has been forced to flee his or her country because of persecution, war, or violence,"[9] and "cannot return home or [is] afraid to do so."[10] Rebekah facilitates Jacob's departure by expressing to Isaac her disgust at the idea that Jacob might marry a Canaanite woman (27:46–28:5).[11] For an involuntary migrant, this is logical: asylum seekers and refugees – like all manner of marginalized people – see their claims succeed far more often when a qualified person takes them forward.[12] Today, this generally means legal counsel; in antiquity, it meant an influential person with the social status to influence a powerful person (e.g., Nathan, who had influence with David). Jacob relies upon his mother. This is unsurprising; research indicates that "the *only* person a man can *really* trust is the one person who will not stand to gain by his death. This person is neither his wife nor his children; it is his mother."[13] Rebekah is a powerful figure in this narrative,[14] far more than "a simple housewife."[15] She knows well that

Involuntary Migration Studies" in *Scripture in Social Discourse: Social Scientific Perspectives on Early Jewish and Christian Writings*, ed. C. Strine, T. Klutz, and J. Keady (London: Bloomsbury T&T Clark, 2018), 51–69. Thanks to Bloomsbury T&T Clark for permission to reuse some of that material here.

9   www.unrefugees.org/site/c.lfIQKSOwFqG/b.4950731/k.A894/What_is_a_refugee.htm (accessed February 23, 2017); cf. Article 1, 1951 Convention Relating to the Status of Refugees, which says "owing to a well-founded fear of being persecuted for reasons of race, religion, nationality, membership of a particular social group, or political opinion, is outside the country of his nationality, and is unable to or, owing to such fear, is unwilling to avail himself of the protection of that country."

10   www.unrefugees.org/site/c.lfIQKSOwFqG/b.4950731/k.A894/What_is_a_refugee.htm (accessed February 23, 2017).

11   On diachronic issues, see Strine, "Your Name Shall No Longer Be Jacob," 60–6.

12   See E. Acer, "Making a Difference: A Legacy of Pro Bono Representation," *Journal of Refugee Studies* 17 (2004): 347–66, and K. Bianchini, "Legal Aid for Asylum Seekers: Progress and Challenges in Italy," *Journal of Refugee Studies* 24 (2011): 390–410, for discussion and further references.

13   E. Voutira and B. E. Harrell-Bond, "In Search of the Locus of Trust: The Social World of the Refugee Camp," in *Mistrusting Refugees*, ed. E. V. Daniel and J. C. Knudsen (Berkeley: University of California Press, 1995), 208.

14   M. Brett, *Genesis: Procreation and the Politics of Identity* (London: Routledge, 2000), 88–9.

15   J. E. Anderson, *Jacob and the Divine Trickster: A Theology of Deception and YHWH's Fidelity to the Ancestral Promise in Jacob Cycle* (Winona Lake: Eisenbrauns, 2011), 70.

Isaac's own life was shaped by endogamous marriage – she is his wife for just that reason! She also knows his distrust for the local population, because she accompanied him among the men of Gerar during the recent famine (cf. Genesis 26). Rebekah, much like a modern legal advocate, persuades Isaac to allow Jacob's departure.

As Jacob sets out for Canaan (28:10), he spends a night in the place that he will name Bethel. Jacob's vow is critical to his experience there:

> If God will be with me, and will keep me in this way that I go, and will give me bread to eat and clothing to wear, *so that I come again to my father's house in peace* – then YHWH shall be my God, and this stone, which I have set up as a pillar, shall be God's house; and of all that you give me, I will surely give one-tenth to you. (28:20b–22)

The scene conveys the hopes and fears of an involuntary migrant fleeing mortal danger by traveling into an unknown place, without assurance things will be better there.

7.2 JACOB THE REFUGEE (GEN 29:14B–32:1)

When Jacob finally reaches Laban, he explains what has prompted his departure from Canaan (Gen 29:13b). Laban declares his willingness to protect Jacob by calling him "my bone and my flesh" (29:14a). Recognizing him as family, Laban grants Jacob an ancient form of asylum.

Laban and Jacob's relationship is not an equal one. After a month of service, "Laban said to Jacob, 'Because you are my kinsman, should you therefore serve me for nothing?'" (29:15a). The text leaves Laban's motivation ambiguous. Wenham concludes that the extraordinarily large commitment Jacob makes for Rachel suggests that he will pay handsomely for her.[16] From the perspective of involuntary migration, however, one may add that Jacob's extended commitment effectively assures him of Laban's extended protection. Though seven years constitutes an extraordinarily long term of service for a bride, it assures Jacob of protection against Esau's violent retribution.

Jacob's "refugee status" illuminates the power dynamics at play in the narrative. In today's world, asylum seekers in the United Kingdom live in constant fear of deportation. Even after receiving refugee status, involuntary migrants live not as citizens but on time-limited and

---

[16]   G. J. Wenham, *Genesis 16–50* (Nashville: Thomas Nelson, 2000), 235.

revocable visas. Without being anachronistic, one can see how in both
situations the one granting protection possesses tremendous power
overs the asylum seeker. As long as the threat of expulsion exists, so
does an asymmetric power relationship.

This dynamic explains Laban's duplicitous behavior. When Laban
takes advantage of Jacob's status as a refugee, Jacob has little recourse.
"Benevolent" Laban, remarks Gerhard von Rad, is "a master of
deceit":[17] Though Laban agrees that seven years of service from Jacob
will warrant a daughter in marriage (29:19), without warning or regret he
gives Jacob the older, unwanted daughter, Leah. "Laban said, 'This is not
done in our country – giving the younger before the firstborn. Complete
the week of this one, and we will give you the other also in return *for
serving me another seven years'*" (29:26–27). Claus Westermann
remarks: "Jacob agrees; he has no option."[18]

Westermann is correct, but fails to notice the significance of Jacob's
migrant status. Jacob is, like all refugees, in a subordinate position:
marginalized, disempowered, and circumscribed in his ability to pursue
his rights for fear of expulsion. Laban's dismissive comment that "it is
not done thus in *our* place" (29:26a) reflects Jacob's status as an outsider.
Jacob's options are severely limited. It is hard to avoid the conclusion
that Jacob accepts Laban's one-sided offer to serve another seven years
for Rachel without resistance or negotiation as a consequence of their
asymmetric power relationship.

After those additional seven years, Jacob expresses his desire to
leave (30:25). Laban refuses, suggesting instead that Jacob specify
another "wage." This is far from generosity; Westermann explains this
is "a rejection of Jacob's request."[19] Laban imitates a loving father, but
leverages his power to compel Jacob into further service.

Most commentators interpret the confusing set of statements
between Laban and Jacob in Gen 30:25–34 through their kinship;[20] it is
more helpful to examine it through migration studies. Jacob expresses
the desire to live on his own, to manage his own affairs, and to be treated
as a fully capable agent (30:25–26, 30b). These desires are common to
involuntary migrants, who prefer to self-settle and to survive by their

---

[17]   G. von Rad, *Genesis: A Commentary*, trans. J. H. Marks (London: SCM, 1961), 292.
[18]   C. Westermann, *Genesis 12–36: A Commentary*, trans. J. K. Scullion S. J.
       (Minneapolis: Augsburg, 1985), 467.
[19]   Westermann, *Genesis 12–36*, 481.
[20]   For example, B. T. Arnold, *Genesis* (Cambridge: Cambridge University Press, 2009),
       271–2.

own agency.[21] When Laban refuses Jacob's request (30:31a), Jacob employs Laban's paternalistic language against him, utilizing it to construct a ruse whereby he will acquire the majority of Laban's livestock.

James C. Scott has demonstrated that subaltern groups frequently resist and deceive dominant groups in their daily practices, asserting their rights through disguised behaviors that push the established boundaries of obedience without breaking them so blatantly as to provoke punitive measures.[22] Scott's observation that subaltern groups employ dominant powers' "paternalist flourishes about care, feeding, [and] housing"[23] to formulate requests that suit their needs explains Jacob's behavior. Indeed, Laban's disingenuous rhetoric gives Jacob an opportunity to resist, capitalizing upon Laban's rhetoric to achieve his aim of autonomy. Jacob's final conversation with Laban states the dynamic explicitly, as Jacob confesses, "I was afraid because I thought you would take your daughters from me by force" (31:31).

Once outside of Laban's home and protection, however, Jacob is unafraid to assert his rights and is even accusatory. No longer a refugee dependent upon a protective power, Jacob negotiates a preferential agreement with Laban that liberates him from his longtime oppressor.

7.3 JACOB THE RETURN MIGRANT (GEN 32:2–33:20)

The narrative then pivots toward Canaan. Jacob's demeanor changes as he contemplates returning "home": he dreads meeting Esau. Preparing to cross the Jordan, Jacob struggles with a divine being (Genesis 32). Afterward, Jacob proclaims, "I have seen God face to face yet my life has continued" (32:31) – the exclamation of a traumatized involuntary

---

[21]   See B. E. Harrell-Bond, *Imposing Aid: Emergency Assistance to Refugees* (Oxford: Oxford University Press, 1986), Liisa H. Malkki, *Purity and Exile: Violence, Memory and National Cosmology Among Hutu Refugees in Tanzania* (Chicago: University of Chicago Press, 1995), and the synthesis in E. Colson, "Forced Migration and the Anthropological Response," *Journal of Refugee Studies* 16 (2003), 7–10; for an anecdotal overview, compare the recent lecture by Jeff Crisp at the Refugee Studies Centre in Oxford: www.rsc.ox.ac.uk/news/in-search-of-solutions-refugees-are-doing-it-for-themselves-refugee-voices-opening-plenary-jeff-crisp (accessed February 23, 2017).

[22]   J. C. Scott, *Weapons of the Weak: Everyday Forms of Peasant Resistance* (New Haven: Yale University Press, 1985); J. C. Scott, *Domination and the Arts of Resistance: Hidden Transcripts* (New Haven: Yale University Press, 1990), 110–25.

[23]   Scott, *Domination*, 18.

migrant, declaring that "if I can deal with this, I can deal with anything."[24]

When Jacob encounters Esau, he remarks – in an explicit echo of 32:31 – that "to see your face is like seeing the face of God, since you have received me with such favor"[25] (33:10). Jacob is astonished that Esau does not attack him, just as he was at surviving his melee with God. Jacob's return "home" disorients him; nothing resembles his memories or expectations. Esau confuses Jacob by seeking reconciliation, not revenge; thus Jacob faces yet another new place with yet another unfamiliar host. Laban appeared benevolent before oppressing him, will Esau behave similarly?

Jacob accordingly responds to Esau using the same strategies he employed with Laban. He offers a huge, apparently unnecessary payment (33:1–11; cf. 29:15–20) and treats the offer of assistance with suspicion. Jacob recognizes the generosity (compare 30:31 and 33:15), but refuses to accept. With Laban, this strategy opened the way to regaining his autonomy; with Esau, it preserves his autonomy from someone he does not trust. Though the circumstances might appear quite different, they are alarmingly similar to an involuntary migrant.[26]

The final episode in the Jacob narrative describes Shechem's appalling rape of Dinah. Jacob is largely absent – an aspect of the story that makes it possible to regard Jacob as an example of ethical dereliction, not virtue. Simeon and Levi are the protagonists, responding to Shechem's vile act with a deceitful scheme that enables them to debilitate the Shechemites and then kill them. When Jacob finally appears (34:30) he makes a solipsistic statement lamenting the trouble Simeon and Levi have caused, by making him abhorrent to other communities living in Canaan. This response derives directly from Jacob's migrant identity. The patriarch expresses a legitimate fear of his hosts, who may not welcome his presence, together with his frustration that his sons' conduct has increased the likelihood that these hosts will harass him. To understand the ethical ramifications of Jacob's statement requires recognizing the context provided by his series of traumatic migratory experiences, rather than abstract ethical reflection. That is the unmistakable lesson of this exegesis.

---

[24] Cf. Anderson, *Jacob and the Divine Trickster*, 160–9.

[25] So JPS; cf. Westermann, *Genesis 12–36*, 522–3.

[26] See K. Southwood, *Ethnicity and the Mixed Marriage Crisis in Ezra 9–10: An Anthropological Approach* (Oxford: Oxford University Press, 2012), for a detailed discussion of this phenomenon. For the social scientific research, see pages 49–56.

7.4 FROM TRICKSTER TO THE ETHICS OF LIBERATION

When Wenham analyzes the Jacob narrative ethically, he brackets the Dinah episode and intimates that it is especially problematic. "Sometimes the stories of Genesis show the patriarchs acting in exemplary fashion," he remarks, but sometimes "they fall very far short" of a "lofty ideal of human behavior."[27] Wenham's assessment feels more realistic after his discussion of Genesis 34, when he observes that "no one comes out of this episode very creditably on the Israelite side,"[28] because they abide by neither the legal material one finds elsewhere in the Hebrew Bible nor the "lofty ideal" Wenham struggles to find elsewhere in Genesis. Jacob repeatedly acts deceitfully, sometimes avoids making decisions with ethical implications, and fixates on personal problems when deeply troubling issues are distressing his children – none of which comports with the modern Western sort of ethic Wenham seeks to identify in Genesis.[29]

Other scholars grant these features of Jacob's conduct more weight. Susan Niditch's influential analysis outlines the ways in which Jacob represents a classic trickster, but contends that the schemes Jacob employs against both Esau and Laban preclude him from being a positive role model. "Tales of the trickster Jacob are, indeed, central to Israelite identity and self-image," but this is "an identity with which the prophet Hosea is none too comfortable (Hos 12:4–6)."[30] For Niditch, it is only Jacob's encounter with the divine being in Genesis 32 that finally transforms him into a reputable character worthy of emulation: a "generous reconciliatory," seeking to outperform his brother "in offers of peace and friendship."[31] While Niditch more honestly confronts the problems that Jacob presents, she still attempts to redeem Jacob to a modern Western ethic, and fails to account for his lies to Esau in their final encounter (33:12–17).

Niditch distinguishes tricksters (e.g., Jacob) from wise men (e.g., Joseph), contrasting tricksters as antiestablishment figures with wise men as establishment figures; Daniel Smith-Christopher asks whether

[27] Wenham, *Story as Torah*, 107.
[28] Wenham, *Story as Torah*, 119.
[29] Wenham, *Story as Torah*, 151–5.
[30] S. Niditch, *Underdogs and Tricksters: A Prelude to Biblical Folklore* (San Francisco: Harper & Row, 1987), 117. One must note that Niditch's reading of Hos 12:4–6 as an indictment of Jacob is debatable, both in the view that it comments upon Jacob as an individual and also that it is a negative assessment of his conduct.
[31] Niditch, *Underdogs and Tricksters*, 117.

this contrast is correct.[32] "What would happen," he wonders, if one read wisdom texts as "also a product of the social circumstances of exilic subordination?"[33] Smith-Christopher concludes that Proverbs, Ecclesiastes, and Daniel also exhibit the "ethics of the trickster, with its definite lack of respect for establishment ethics."[34] His rereading accentuates "a nonviolence of radical doubt and irreverence to the self-proclaimed state power and piety, a nonviolence based on the fact that God's plans are centered on the people of God, and the nation-state is not the center of the universe."[35] He identifies a fusion of these traits in "the figure of a wise trickster in the court of the conqueror,"[36] dissolving the demarcation between the proestablishment ethics of the wise man and the subaltern trickster. Instead, all these texts represent and support a "subcultural ethics" that emerges from the social circumstances of exilic subordination and extols the subaltern's ability to successfully navigate problematic circumstances[37] – epitomized in a willingness to use falsehood and deception to survive. Smith-Christopher's discomfort is plain:

> Am I suggesting that diaspora trickery and self-interested cleverness are positive virtues of the exilic experience? It is a complex question, of course. The irreverence toward the state and the advice to keep one's wits in relation to the state are quite simply the practical wisdom of the Diaspora. Such wisdom does not believe in the myths of the state.[38]

Does all this challenge the concept of the state – or does it challenge modern Western ethical norms? Smith-Christopher's unease with Jacob's ethical conduct – whether one should view deceit as an ethical virtue – suggests a disjuncture in the ethical realm, not the political.

John E. Anderson heightens the tension by asking whether even YHWH, Jacob's divine patron, engages in tricksterism.[39] Anderson argues that Jacob's deceptions of Esau are responses to ambiguity in the divine oracle about the boys' future (25:23) and therefore necessary

---

[32] D. Smith-Christopher, *Biblical Theology of Exile* (Minneapolis: Augsburg Fortress, 2002), 164–6; cf. S. Niditch, *A Prelude to Biblical Folklore: Underdogs and Tricksters* (Urbana: University of Illinois Press, 2000).
[33] Smith-Christopher, *Biblical Theology of Exile*, 167.
[34] Smith-Christopher, *Biblical Theology of Exile*, 164.
[35] Smith-Christopher, *Biblical Theology of Exile*, 188.
[36] Smith-Christopher, *Biblical Theology of Exile*, 187.
[37] Smith-Christopher, *Biblical Theology of Exile*, 167.
[38] Smith-Christopher, *Biblical Theology of Exile*, 188.
[39] Anderson, *Jacob and the Divine Trickster*.

in order to bring the oracle to fruition. "God appears deeply involved in Jacob's deceptions," he observes, "all with the intent of carrying forward the ancestral promise."[40] Anderson concludes that "God the trickster selects Jacob because it is he, not Esau, who is a trickster from the very beginning."[41] Moreover, YHWH not only tolerates Jacob's tricksterism but embraces it:

> there is a certain level of destabilization that accompanies this portrait of YHWH as trickster. This God has subversive tendencies... God is a God of inversion who is not circumscribed by the strictures imposed by the various power brokers of the narrative... One may surmise that a trickster God would have been attractive to ancient Israel for this very reason; one has less use for a trickster God if one is in a position of power and authority.[42]

Anderson comes closest to embracing the disruptive nature of the Jacob narrative's ethics – but still mitigates his deceit. It is tolerable only so long as it serves God's covenant: "Divine deception is the vehicle that will lead to the renewal of Israel and the flourishing of the covenant relationship."[43] Indeed, Anderson's unease manifests in his final statement:

> This divine unscrupulousness, *while not entirely benign*, is the mechanism by which YHWH tenaciously works towards the divine purpose... In the Jacob cycle, therefore, one observes not an aberrant, devious God but a divine trickster who will go to any lengths for the sake of the ancestral promise.[44]

Like Wenham, Niditch, and Smith-Christopher, Anderson assuages his discomfort by precluding deceit from forming a generally applicable ethical principle.

*

These scholars' hesitation contrasts dramatically with the succinct, unencumbered insight of one involuntary migrant: "To be a refugee

[40]   Anderson, *Jacob and the Divine Trickster*, 33.
[41]   Anderson, *Jacob and the Divine Trickster*, 86.
[42]   Anderson, *Jacob and the Divine Trickster*, 176.
[43]   Anderson, *Jacob and the Divine Trickster*, 185.
[44]   Anderson, *Jacob and the Divine Trickster*, 188. Emphasis added.

means to learn to lie."[45] What is it about the experience of involuntary migration that eliminates any reluctance to state this plainly and to embrace its ethical ramifications? In short, deceptive actions constitute one of very few survival mechanisms available to people with a legitimate fear for their life and living in an asymmetric power relationship with a foreign host. The conditions of subaltern existence, not deficient understanding of modern Western morality, frame the role of dishonesty in this ethical realm.

When one accepts the overwhelming evidence that the Jacob narrative can and should be read as a depiction of an involuntary migrant living in this kind of subaltern context, the ethical implications of its *human and divine* protagonists' deception transform radically. Dishonesty and duplicity cannot be scrutinized from a dominant perspective; doing so ignores the setting of the implied author and the main characters of the text. Even though Wenham argues adamantly for attention to implied authors in *Story as Torah*, his analysis of Jacob fails to do so, and this explains much of his unease with the narrative. Perhaps this is also why Smith-Christopher, who apprehends the "diasporic" character of the Hebrew Bible, comes closest to sanctioning the trickster conduct that Jacob exemplifies.

The Jacob narrative illustrates the deep fissures between the ethics of the Hebrew Bible and modern Western ethics. As a subaltern text, it espouses an ethical system intended for a colonized community. It cannot be comfortably integrated with modern Western ethics because it is fundamentally at odds with the imperial concerns that characterize modern Western ethical thinking.

7.5 ISRAEL AS ETHICAL PRINCIPLE

Paulo Freire, author of the landmark *Pedagogy of the Oppressed*,[46] offers guidance for navigating this problem. Although Freire addresses education, not ethics, the formulation of ethical virtues aims to create a paradigm for action that can be disseminated to others and thus strongly resembles an educational curriculum. Insights on the imperial nature of education from Freire are, then, illuminating.

Freire employs critical theory to critique existing structures, to develop normative responses that promote liberation for oppressed

---

[45] Voutira and Harrell-Bond, "In Search," 216. See Smith-Christopher, *Biblical Theology of Exile*, 167, for his view on this quote.

[46] P. Freire, *Pedagogy of the Oppressed*, trans. M. B. Ramos (London: Penguin, 2017).

groups, and to identify the mechanisms by which this might be accomplished. What emerges is a recognition that education plays a crucial role in inscribing and reinscribing imperial models of thought upon subaltern groups in ways that impede liberation. Combating this culture of imperialism requires a learning context that enables the powerless to change the circumstances that perpetuate their experience of injustice and marginalization.

In order to liberate themselves, the oppressed must expel "the myths created and developed in the old order."[47] The exegetical discussion above accomplishes this, at least in part, by demonstrating that the Jacob narrative speaks from the perspective of an involuntary migrant. The involuntary migrant perspective suffuses everything about the narrative from beginning to end. One cannot and therefore should not absorb the Jacob narrative into a modern Western ethical myth. Rather, the foregoing exegesis demands the adoption of a subaltern perspective; it demonstrates that the Jacob story reflects a subaltern community from the ancient world processing its lived experience and articulating its ethical ideals.

Once one acknowledges this, the problematic nature of the narrative's appropriation for Western ethical thought comes into stark relief. Wenham, Niditch, Smith-Christopher, and Anderson all recognize that there is a point at which the modern Western ethical myth collides with the subaltern liberationist ethos of the Jacob narrative. Freire would be unsurprised. Those associated with imperial power routinely domesticate liberationist messages – consciously or subconsciously – to support the status quo. Freire states Western interpreters' problem: they read a text's ethical content in a way that presumes their own preexisting ideas as the model of good ethical thinking. The oppressor thus portrays any differing ethical perspective as deficient – as reflective of a community that must make "progress" toward its own sophisticated and enlightened ethical myth.[48] Wenham illustrates this flaw: He is able to maintain his claim that Genesis advocates a "lofty ideal" indistinguishable from a modern Western ethic only by sometimes endorsing and sometimes disavowing Jacob's behavior. Freire could not construct a better example: The subaltern perspective of the Jacob story can only be harmonized with Western imperially oriented ethics by deforming it.

Apprehending the subaltern viewpoint of the Jacob narrative requires that scholars situated in a dominant sociopolitical context or

---

[47] Freire, *Pedagogy*, 29.
[48] Freire, *Pedagogy*, 125–35.

lived experience disqualify themselves from the enterprise of analyzing its ethics. Freire writes:

> If what characterizes the oppressed is their subordination to the consciousness of the master, as Hegel affirms, true solidarity with the oppressed means fighting at their side to transform the objective reality which has made them these "beings for another." *The oppressor is solidary with the oppressed only when he stops regarding the oppressed as an abstract category and sees them as persons who have been unjustly dealt with, deprived of their voice, cheated in the sale of their labor* – when he stops making pious, sentimental, and individualistic gestures and risks an act of love. True solidarity is found only in the plenitude of this act of love, it its existentiality, in its praxis.[49]

Elsewhere, Freire explains that the oppressor cannot redress the problem; attempting to do so amounts to "paternalistic treatment of the oppressed, all the while holding them fast in a position of dependence."[50] Instead, "the oppressed must be their own example in the struggle for their redemption."[51] Jacob – the involuntary migrant renamed Israel because he struggles against God and man and succeeds (32:28) – exemplifies the ethics of the subaltern trickster: His liberating power, his model of struggle, must be given up for ethical analysis to those not enmeshed in the Western imperial context.

Freire reminds his reader that "acts which prevent the restoration of the oppressive regime cannot be compared with those which create and maintain it, cannot be compared with those by which a few men and women deny the majority their right to be human."[52] If Jacob's actions as a marginalized involuntary migrant do not comport with our abstract ethical formulations, it licenses us neither to disregard them nor to deform them so that they do. When an involuntary migrant observes that "to be a refugee means to learn to lie," one's discomfort may or may not be related to the ethical questions this statement raises. The oppressor cannot pass judgment – for the modern Western ethical myth arises from an imperial perspective that incapacitates such judgment. Only someone with a subaltern or marginalized context, operating with

---

[49]   Freire, *Pedagogy*, 23–4. Emphasis added.
[50]   Freire, *Pedagogy*, 23.
[51]   Freire, *Pedagogy*, 28.
[52]   Freire, *Pedagogy*, 31.

the presuppositions and perspective of the subaltern, can explore these matters openly and productively.

*

I opened this essay by declaring my unsuitability to write it. I did so because I am tainted by the Western imperial perspective and the ethical myths imbedded within its thinking and my experience. Like those I have critiqued, I am encumbered with presuppositions at odds with the ethical perspective of the Jacob narrative. No amount of effort will release me from them.

I want to understand how Genesis 25–34 might be used ethically. But if I attempt to do so, I would unavoidably warp it – indeed, in ways I cannot apprehend because of my own positionality. Freire teaches me that if I want to understand the Jacob narrative's disposition and release its liberating potential, I must recognize my own inadequacy. Take Jacob's propensity to lie: My efforts to analyze its ethical intent will always be inflected by my larger modern, Western, and inextricably imperial ethical framework, no matter how diligently I endeavor to explore this matter from another point of view.

My only recourse is to accept my limitation, to highlight the limitations of myself and others, and to do what I can to promote those unhindered by such circumstances to do this work on the Jacob narrative. Rather than make an argument about how we should employ the Jacob narrative in ethical thinking, I must argue instead for the necessity that those from minority and marginalized perspectives do so. To heed Freire, I must stand aside. I should have known that before I wrote this essay. I did not. Perhaps my belated discovery can encourage others to recognize this issue too.

FURTHER READING

Anderson, J. E. *Jacob and the Divine Trickster: A Theology of Deception and YHWH's Fidelity to the Ancestral Promise in Jacob Cycle*. Winona Lake: Eisenbrauns, 2011.

Brett, M. G. *Genesis: Procreation and the Politics of Identity*. London: Routledge, 2000.

Chatty, D. "Anthropology and Forced Migration." Pages 74–80 in *The Oxford Handbook of Refugee and Forced Migration Studies*. Edited by E. Fiddian-Qasmiyeh et al. Oxford: Oxford University Press, 2014, 74–80.

Freire, P. *Pedagogy of the Oppressed*. Translated by M. B. Ramos. London: Penguin, 2017.

Harrell-Bond, B. E. *Imposing Aid: Emergency Assistance to Refugees*. Oxford: Oxford University Press, 1986.

Malkki, L. H. *Purity and Exile: Violence, Memory and National Cosmology among Hutu Refugees in Tanzania*. Chicago: University of Chicago Press, 1995.

Niditch, S. *Underdogs and Tricksters: A Prelude to Biblical Folklore*. San Francisco: Harper & Row, 1987.

Scott, J. C. *Weapons of the Weak: Everyday Forms of Peasant Resistance*. New Haven: Yale University Press, 1985.

Scott, J. C. *Domination and the Arts of Resistance: Hidden Transcripts*. New Haven: Yale University Press, 1990.

Smith-Christopher, D. *Biblical Theology of Exile*. Minneapolis: Augsburg Fortress, 2002.

Southwood, K. *Ethnicity and the Mixed Marriage Crisis in Ezra 9–10: An Anthropological Approach*. Oxford: Oxford University Press, 2012.

Strine, C. A. "Sister Save Us: The Matriarchs as Breadwinners and Their Threat to Patriarchy in the Ancestral Narrative." Pages 53–66 in *Women and Exilic Identity in the Hebrew Bible*. Edited by M. Halvorson-Taylor and K. Southwood. London: Bloomsbury T&T Clark, 2018.

Strine, C. A. "Your Name Shall No Longer Be Jacob, but Refugee: Insights into Gen 25:19–33:20 from Involuntary Migration Studies." Pages 51–69 in *Scripture in Social Discourse: Social Scientific Perspectives on Early Jewish and Christian Writings*. Edited by C. Strine, T. Klutz, and J. Keady. London: Bloomsbury T&T Clark, 2018.

Voutira, E., and B. E. Harrell-Bond. "In Search of the Locus of Trust: The Social World of the Refugee Camp." In *Mistrusting Refugees*. Edited by E. V. Daniel and J. C. Knudsen. Berkley: University of California Press, 1995.

Wenham, G. J. *Story as Torah: Reading the Old Testament Ethically*. Edinburgh: T&T Clark, 2000.

8 Settler Mandates and the Book of Joshua

MARK G. BRETT

The book of Joshua presents a multitude of ethical quandaries, both ancient and modern. After identifying some of the key questions about the text and its composition, our discussion will trace the distinctive kinds of influence that this book has exercised in a number of Jewish and Christian traditions. All of these elements will then figure in concluding reflections on how the book of Joshua may, and may not, help us to reflect on the legacies of imperialism and colonialism.

8.1 QUESTIONS ARISING FROM THE NARRATIVES

The book begins with the children of Israel poised at the Jordan River, about to cross into a land that has been promised 'to Moses' (1:3; cf. 11:23). We read that the land can only be taken into Israel's possession if the law of Moses is observed in every detail, yet this same land is also seen as a gift sworn to the ancestors (1:6; cf. 21:43). The promises of land in Genesis did not come with conditions attached, however, so the settlement traditions in Joshua are assuming obligations expounded in the books of Exodus through Deuteronomy. Consequently, the Israelites poised at the Jordan were not really in a position to choose their ethical framework; they were born into it. They are thrust into a theological tension between gift and obligation, and beyond such generalised theological tensions, the details of the texts are yet more complicated.

For example, we find differing perspectives on the extent of the promised land and even some disagreement on the name of the divinity who provides it. In Gen 17:8, El Shaddai promises 'the land of Canaan', which implies a limited Levantine territory. This version of the story appears to be linked with Exod 6:2–3, which claims that the ancestors did not know the name YHWH but only the name El Shaddai. In Gen 15:7–18, however, it is precisely YHWH who promises Abram all the land 'from the river of Egypt to the great river, the river Euphrates', the empire-wide imagination that appears in Josh 1:4. Yet according to

the details provided in the subsequent narratives in Joshua, the conquered territories fall mainly within the kingdoms of Israel and Judah,
excluding the coastlands, with significant cities not taken, including
Jerusalem (15:63). It is therefore puzzling to find that the conquered land
is sometimes presented hyperbolically as 'all the land' promised to
Moses or sworn to the ancestors. Even if these plenary claims should
be seen as the standard rhetoric of ancient conquest accounts, commonly found in royal ideologies, the hyperbole stands in clear tension
with the detailed lists of lands not taken. Imperial ideology is not greatly
interested in failed conquests.

Israel's key ethical challenge in the book of Joshua is framed at the
outset as a call to comply with Mosaic law. There is no critical reflection
within the book of Joshua itself on the reasons why it might be possible
to take land and resources belonging to other peoples; it is simply a
matter of divine command. In other books, some reasons are provided,
notably in Gen 15:16, where it is presumed that the accumulated
'iniquity of the Amorites' provides sufficient justification for dispossession. The moral calculus here assumes the validity of intergenerational
punishment, which is accepted in some biblical texts and rejected in
others.[1] Considered within the larger context of the canon, then, this
intergenerational reasoning is not entirely satisfactory.

The primary framework for divine commands in Joshua is usually
understood to be the law of Moses, but in a few cases, YHWH issues
commands directly to Joshua that do not actually conform to Mosaic
law. For example, the animals are spared in Ai (Josh 8:27; cf. 11:9, 14),
contravening the law in Deut 20:16. Hence, not all the divine commands
at issue in the interpretation of Joshua can be organised into a coherent
whole; there is evidently an unfolding debate within the biblical canon
about how to construe the content of the divine promises and commands. We cannot understand the significance of the settler mandates
within the book of Joshua without an appreciation of this diversity.

8.2 MULTIPLE VOICES IN JOSHUA

The conquest narratives have clearly been edited by scribes who are
familiar with the book of Deuteronomy, and it is often assumed that
this editing began in the seventh century BCE, particularly around the

---

[1]   B. M. Levinson, 'The Reworking of the Principle of Transgenerational Punishment', in
      Legal Revision and Religious Renewal in Ancient Israel (Cambridge: Cambridge
      University Press, 2008), 57–88.

time of King Josiah's reign in Judah (640–609). Having experienced a series of Assyrian invasions, these 'Deuteronomic' writers seem to have mimicked the Assyrian royal ideology, both in the shaping of conquest narratives in Joshua and in the treaty language of Deuteronomy.[2]

This mimicry cannot be understood as a capitulation to imperial ideology or a failure of theological imagination, but neither is it a direct confrontation with Assyrian power. Instead, there is evidence of subtle interactions with imperial literature precisely in order to assert the sovereignty of Israel's own God. This would have had a powerful relevance when, having destroyed the northern kingdom, the Assyrians advanced to the south and rendered King Manasseh (r. 687–642) one of their many vassals. But on a closer reading of Joshua, not all the narratives can be understood as Judean responses to Assyrian incursions, and not all of the details can be related straightforwardly to Deuteronomy.

To begin with, there is evidence of some earlier material that depicts Joshua as a charismatic warrior from the north, directly receiving divine commands from YHWH. He engages in battles with particular kings, rather than with the whole people groups envisaged in Deuteronomy. In Josh 11:1–5, for example, we find that Joshua attacked an army marshalled by the kings of northern cities – Hazor, Madon, Shimron, and Achshaph – before the text turns to talk more generally in ethnic terms about Canaanites, Amorites, Hittites, Perizzites, Jebusites, and Hivites, in the way that Deuteronomy does. In 11:6, Joshua is commanded directly by YHWH only to hamstring horses and burn chariots. This might well reflect an older narrator's view of an Ephraimite leader who acts without a mediating legal tradition. The subsequent portraits of Joshua see him as an exponent of Mosaic Torah, including Josh 11:11–15.

In this vein, Daniel Fleming has argued that Josh 8:3–29 was initially conceived in local northern tradition, and only subsequently drawn into the southern conquest narratives, after the fall of the northern kingdom. In the earlier narrative core of Joshua 8, the character of Joshua conducts a local YHWH war against Ai. According to Fleming's hypothesis, 'Ai would have no larger identity or association; it is never called Canaanite or the like'.[3] Instead of seeing the attack on Ai as colonial violence exercised by an invading nation, Fleming sees it as a relatively local conflict, and possibly intra-indigenous. The ḥērem tradition of warfare is

[2] T. Römer, *The So-Called Deuteronomistic History: A Sociological, Historical and Literary Introduction* (London: T&T Clark International, 2005), 67–90.
[3] D. E. Fleming, *The Legacy of Israel in Judah's Bible: History, Politics and the Reinscribing of Tradition* (Cambridge: Cambridge University Press, 2012), 140–1.

older than the seventh century and can be distinguished from the imperial Assyrian genres mimicked in Deuteronomy.[4] An Ephraimite charismatic leader might have known of the *ḥērem* before it was reconfigured within Deuteronomy as rules of engagement for all the territories of Israel and Judah. In short, it is very unlikely that the conquest tradition was entirely invented by Deuteronomistic scribes.

At some points, the text assumes the laws in Deuteronomy while also contesting them. Surprisingly, it is only the Jericho narrative that explicitly presents a comprehensive 'devotion to the ban (*ḥērem*)', which includes the slaughter of animals along with the people of the city, matching Deut 20:15–17. Yet even in this most extreme observance of the Mosaic rule of engagement in Josh 6:21–25, a Canaanite woman and her family are spared, contrary to the law (cf. Deut 7:1–2). The reasons for Rahab's survival are provided in Joshua 2, where her collaboration with Israel's spies includes her submission to Israel's God (2:9). Joachim Krause has suggested that it would have been a 'sheer provocation' to give prominence to a Canaanite prostitute like Rahab – 'the incarnate stereotype of the peoples of the land as entertained in Deuteronomistic circles'.[5] Her example constitutes a counter-narrative, or narrative jurisprudence, which demonstrates why exceptions to Deuteronomic law might actually be acceptable for Yahwist reasons.

In the case of Joshua 8, the animals are spared at Ai following a divine command to Joshua, though this provision does not conform with the law of Moses. In Joshua 9, the Gibeonites survive the ban by securing a covenant before it is discovered that they are native to the area; Joshua then has to decide whether to follow the Mosaic law or to keep the freshly made covenant. The Gibeonite (or 'Hivite') tricksters manage to circumvent the *ḥērem* law by exploiting the distinction in Deut 20:10–18 between 'near' and 'far' cities; they claim to come from a 'far' country. The Gibeonites survive, and then become 'hewers of wood and drawers of water for the congregation and for the altar of YHWH' (9:27).

One could conclude that Deuteronomy's ideal of national uniformity is not so much assumed as interrogated in Joshua 6–12. Evidently, the conquest narratives have been thoroughly edited by scribes who are responding critically to Deuteronomic law – and it is not at all clear that they are affirming a new national capital in Jerusalem after the fall

---

[4]   See especially L. A. S. Monroe, 'Israelite, Moabite and Sabaean War–ḥerem Traditions and the Forging of National Identity: Reconsidering the Sabaean Text RES 3945 in Light of Biblical and Moabite Evidence', *VT* 57 (2007): 318–341.

[5]   J. J. Krause, 'Hexateuchal Redaction in Joshua', *HeBAI* 6 (2017): 181–202, 186.

of the northern kingdom. Instead of supporting a Judean king or insisting on the legitimate worship of YHWH at only one place in the south (cf. Deut 12:13–19), the northern profile of Joshua as an Ephraimite leader continues to play a significant role. This is especially clear in the second half of the book, which shows evidence of a priestly reinterpretation of the settlement traditions, but this is also clear in Josh 8:30–35, where a covenant ceremony is associated with Mt Ebal and Mt Gerizim.

According to Josh 11:23, the 'whole land' had been taken into possession by Israel and allocated to the tribes by Joshua alone. But in Joshua 13–21 the management of land allocations is shared with Eleazar (Josh 14:1; 17:4; 19:51; 21:1), the senior priest whose leadership is not mentioned in the first part of Joshua. In Josh 19:51 and 21:2, Eleazar and Joshua decide on land allocations at 'the tent of meeting' in Shiloh (cf. 18:1).[6] The idea that Eleazar would share power with Joshua is foreshadowed in Num 34:17, but not in Deuteronomy. The land allocations in Joshua 13–21 then conclude with the reiteration in Josh 21:43–45 that the 'whole land' was taken, including Israelite land, providing a priestly 'bookend' to the same wording in Josh 11:23.[7]

We can conclude not just that the book of Joshua has been edited from a priestly perspective, but that this particular priestly perspective is linked with a defence of northern Yahwism. When the legitimacy of an altar built by trans-Jordanian tribes is questioned in Joshua 22, it is defended on the grounds that it is only a 'witness' to authentic Yahwism and not intended to replace 'the altar of YHWH our God that is before his tabernacle' (22:29). In the narrative context of Joshua, the most likely location of this altar is Shiloh, in Ephraimite country. The overriding concern in Joshua 22 is that the Yahwist credentials of peripheral kinship groups in the trans-Jordan might be denigrated by those who live centrally in the west bank (22:24–25).

The same kind of concern seems to lie behind the account of the covenant ceremony in the final chapter of the book. Strikingly, Josh

---

[6]   In sharp contrast with priestly literature in the Pentateuch, the tent of meeting is referred to only once in Deuteronomy (31:14). Eleazar is briefly acknowledged in Deut 10:8 as the successor of Aaron.

[7]   There are many reasons to suspect that the 'priestly' traditions of Numbers and Joshua present a model of priestly ethics different from those found in Genesis through Leviticus, which have no theology of conquest. See, e.g., R. Achenbach, 'Divine Warfare and YHWH's Wars: Religious Ideologies of War in the Ancient Near East and in the Old Testament', in *The Ancient Near East in the 12th–10th Centuries BCE: Culture and History*, ed. G. Galil et al., AOAT 392 (Münster: Ugarit-Verlag, 2012), 1–26.

24:25-26 mentions the oak in Shechem as part of the sacred site, invoking the memory of Abram's encounter with YHWH at the very same tree in Gen 12:6-7. The chapter then goes on to memorialise all the leaders buried in Ephraimite county: Joseph, Joshua, and Eleazar (Josh 24:29-33). In short, the social vision in Joshua 24 is pan-Israelite and implicitly resists any suggestion that legitimate Yahwism belongs only in the south – a view that emerged very clearly in the books of Ezra and Nehemiah during the time of Persian administration. The ceremony in Josh 8:30-35 serves a similar function, implicitly acknowledging the temple that was built on Mt Gerizim during the Persian period.[8]

8.3 HISTORIES OF INFLUENCE

The New Testament takes remarkably little interest in Joshua. Acts 7:45 mentions him in passing, and Heb 4:8 criticises the claim that he actually gave the people rest, in spite of the emphasis on rest in the book of Joshua itself. Most intriguing in the letter to the Hebrews, however, is the implication that the faith of Rahab in Jericho is more memorable than Joshua's (11:31). Rahab is also remembered in Matthew's genealogy as the mother of Boaz (Matt 1:5), and she therefore takes her place in the lineage of Jesus. The theological inversion implied by this Canaanite inclusion in Matthew 1 is no doubt linked thematically to Jesus' encounter with the Canaanite woman in Matt 15:21-28.

The traditional Christian allegory that connects Joshua and Jesus, making much of their shared name in Greek and Latin, begins in the second century CE and arguably finds its most detailed expression in the homilies of Origen.[9] This early homiletical logic could turn Joshua into Jesus, transforming ancient conquest narratives into spiritual challenges shared by all believers in every time and place. For more a millennium, these were the dominant appropriations of Joshua in Christian tradition.

Even when St Augustine was moved to create a Christian theory of 'just war' in the fifth century, he sidelined the waging of war in ancient Canaan, apparently because the justice of war needed to be based on universalisable reasons. At most, reflecting on King Sihon's denial of a right to travel in Num 21:22-55, Augustine concluded that there is a

---

[8] C. Nihan, 'The Torah between Samaria and Judah: Shechem and Gerizim in Deuteronomy and Joshua', in *The Pentateuch as Torah*, ed. G. N. Knoppers and B. M. Levinson (Winona Lake: Eisenbrauns, 2007), 187-223.

[9] For an overview of early Christian interpretations, see Z. Farber, *Images of Joshua in the Bible and their Reception*, BZAW 457 (Berlin: de Gruyter, 2016), 276-365.

universal right to 'harmless passage' that should be granted by all reasonable societies (*Questions on the Heptateuch* IV, 44). This articulation of a 'right to travel' was to play a role in later defences of Christian exploration, ambiguously positioned between economic and religious ambitions. But even after the possibility of war was grafted on to Christian tradition, having been absent from the first few centuries, this new defence of violence was not often associated with emulations of warfare in Canaan. It was not until the twelfth century that Joshua began to be invoked as a model for the crusades.[10]

The conquest of Canaan also figured as a precedent for Catholic expansion in the fifteenth and sixteenth centuries, although at the outset Christopher Columbus was more directly influenced by the universal dominion envisaged in the prophecies of Isaiah.[11] Papal authority aspired to control the whole earth, and Catholic monarchs were regarded as divine viceroys wherever new worlds were 'discovered'. Although the obvious abuses committed by the *conquistadors* were enumerated in famous defences of Indigenous rights, such as those provided by Bartolomé de Las Casas (1484–1566) and Francisco de Vitoria (1483–1546), anti-conquest ethics could also serve in the end to legitimise colonial expansions.[12]

In the North American context, the strongest defence of Indigenous rights came from Roger Williams, a co-founder of the first Baptist church in the colonies in 1638. Williams was expelled from Massachusetts Bay in part for questioning the authority of the English Crown to license colonial settlements; accordingly, the settlement on Rhode Island was secured by agreement with the Narragansett Indians. Williams denied Christendom's doctrine of discovery in the clearest possible terms, condemning it as a 'solemne publick lye' by means of which 'Christian kings (so calld) are invested with Right by virtue of their Christianitie to take and give away the Lands and Countries of other men'.[13] His hermeneutical arguments reversed the common Puritan vision that saw

[10] C. Hofreiter, *Making Sense of Old Testament Genocide: Christian Interpretations of Herem Passages* (Oxford: Oxford University Press, 2018), esp. 160–212, 'Violent Readings', on the crusades and the Catholic expropriation of Latin America.

[11] J.-P. Ruiz, *Readings from the Edges: The Bible and People on the Move* (Maryknoll: Orbis, 2011), 123–35.

[12] For example, Vitoria famously defended the Spanish rights to travel, to trade, and to convert the local population to Christianity, while rejecting papal jurisdiction over land in the new world and by affirming the property rights of the Indians. See B. Tierney, *The Idea of Natural Rights* (Atlanta: Scholars, 1997), 265–71.

[13] R. Williams, *The Bloody Tenent yet More Bloody* (Bedford: Applewood, [1652] 2009), 276.

New England as a New Israel, arguing instead that the best political model for Gentile governments came from the Persian administration of Cyrus and Artaxerxes, not the laws and histories of Israel. According to Williams, it was the Persians who allowed for a diversity of ancestral laws within their empire.

In the seventeenth century, political arguments inevitably included dialogue with scripture, but by the nineteenth century colonial settlements were understood more generally as the achievements of civilisation and providence. Arguments from civilisation and Christian order informed the most influential version of the doctrine of discovery enshrined in American law by Justice John Marshall in *Johnson v. McIntosh* (1823). Even in earlier centuries of Protestant expansion, explicit warrants for colonisation drawn from the book of Joshua are surprisingly few, notwithstanding some early Puritan sermons.

Post-colonial critics have found it difficult to account for this pronounced silence in the North American records, when a metanarrative of scripture so clearly underwrites the colonial conceptions of providence. Bill Templer has argued that 'There seems to be an implicit understanding of the Joshua paradigm here ... perhaps a kind of discursive tactic to avoid explicitly invoking the most violent genocidal chapter in Biblical narrative'.[14] His study of the epic poem *The Conquest of Canaan* – published by Timothy Dwight in 1785 and dedicated to George Washington – shows how this poem is exceptional in its extended explicitness. More common in the colonial records are the abstract invocations of 'providence', civilisation, and manifest destiny, the abstract veneer of Indigenous dispossession. This is especially the case in Australia, where a self-centred New Israel typology was thoroughly implausible in the earlier years of settlement, not least because the penal colonies were configured more as experiences of exile than of exodus. The abstract language of providence grew with the years, veiling frontier violence much as it did in the American colonies. The foundation of the free settler colony in South Australia was something of an exception, although it was consistently framed by a rhetoric of peaceableness.[15]

---

[14]   B. Templer, 'The Political Sacralization of Imperial Genocide: Contextualizing Timothy Dwight's *The Conquest of Canaan*', *Postcolonial Studies* 9 (2006): 358–91, 383.

[15]   M. G. Brett, 'A Suitably English Abraham', in *Postcolonial Voices from Downunder: Indigenous Matters, Confronting Readings*, ed. J. Havea (Eugene: Pickwick, 2017), 110–21.

Remembering frontier violence 'through Canaanite eyes', Templer draws attention to a ritual of counter-memory, celebrated annually on Thanksgiving Day in Plymouth, Massachusetts, and organised by the United American Indians of New England. Since 1970, this post-colonial ritual has decried 'America's God', mindful that the first official Thanksgiving in 1637 was proclaimed by Governor John Winthrop during the Pequot War and marked the safe return of settlers who had slaughtered 700 Pequot women, children, and men. In their speech on the National Day of Mourning in 2004, Moonanum James and Munro Mahtowin put it this way: 'The myth of Thanksgiving, served up with dollops of European superiority and manifest destiny, just does not work for many people in this country. As Malcolm X once said about the African-American experience in America, "We did not land on Plymouth Rock. Plymouth Rock landed on us"'.[16]

Templer characterises these protests as 'post-colonial', but of course the legacies of coloniality are still with us. Among the enduring complexities illuminated by post-colonial studies have been the phenomena of religious and cultural hybridity, not just among migrant communities but also among Indigenous communities. Templer's account tends to elide the formation of Indigenous Christianities in North America, including among the Pequot. For example, writing in the 1820s and 1830s, the Pequot Methodist William Apess both absorbed and contested the colonial Christianity of his time. His writings have sometimes been criticised for being 'too Christianized', but this should not obscure his sustained critique of colonial nationalism.

Early in the nineteenth century, Apess was able to read the biblical literature through a Canaanite lens, and in this respect he was a 'post-colonial' critic before the rise of any academic theories under that name. Reflecting on the anniversaries of the Pilgrim's landing on Plymouth Rock, Apess wrote in 1836:

Let the children of the pilgrims blush, while the son of the forest drops a tear... as Job said about his birthday... let it be forgotten in your celebration, in your speeches, and by the burying of the Rock that your fathers first put their foot upon. For be it remembered, although the gospel is said to be glad tidings to all people, yet we poor Indians never have found those who brought it as messengers of mercy, but contrawise. We say, therefore, let every man of color

---

[16] B. Templer, 'The Political Sacralization of Imperial Genocide', 367.

wrap himself in mourning, for the 22nd of December and the 4th of July are days of mourning and not of joy.[17]

As foreshadowed here by Apess, a Day of Mourning that marks the arrival of first British fleet in New South Wales is also regularly held in Australia.[18] Like the Palestinian Nakba Day, which is generally celebrated on 15 May, these foci of memory reflect an originating trauma that can inform intractable social conflicts.[19]

8.4 JEWISH TRADITIONS

The rabbis concluded that Joshua routinely made offers of peace to the Canaanites (j. Sheb. 6:1), and he was more often construed as a Torah scholar than as a warrior.[20] After two disastrous wars in 66–73 CE and 132–135 CE, most Jews embraced a life of diaspora.[21] Especially after the Christianising of the Roman Empire, rabbinic Judaism adopted two main strategies for avoiding war. First, a re-examination of scripture produced a broad distinction between discretionary war (*milḥemet reshut*) and the 'commanded war' associated with Joshua's wars (*milḥemet mitswah*, notably in m. Sotah 8:7 and b. Sotah 44b). Without the leadership of a Jewish king, discretionary war was generally not considered possible. While a divinely commanded war might theoretically be sanctioned in defence of a diaspora community (y. Sotah 8:1, 22b), reasons provided in the 'Three Vows' made this scenario untenable (b. Ketub. 110b–111a). With peculiar halakhic (ethical) arguments built on the phrase 'do not wake or arouse love till it please' in the Song of Songs, it was resolved, first, that until the time of messianic redemption, Jews would not rebel against Gentile rulers; second, that there would be no mass emigration to the land of Israel; and third, that Gentile rulers were

---

[17]   W. Apess, *A Son of the Forest and Other Writings*, ed. B. O'Connell (Amherst: University of Massachusetts Press, 1997), 114; L. Donaldson, 'Son of the Forest, Child of God: William Apess and the Scene of Postcolonial Nativity', in *Postcolonial America*, ed. C. R. King (Urbana: University of Illinois Press, 2000), 201–22.

[18]   The Christian Aboriginal leader, William Cooper, first organized a Day of Mourning in Sydney on 26 January, 1938, marking the arrival of the first fleet in 1788. The celebration of Australia Day on 26 January is still a social wound.

[19]   See especially, D. Bar-Tal, *Intractable Conflicts: Socio-Psychological Foundations and Dynamics* (Cambridge: Cambridge University Press, 2013).

[20]   Farber, *Images of Joshua*, 366–454.

[21]   This brief discussion follows, in particular, R. Firestone, *Holy War in Judaism: The Fall and Rise of a Controversial Idea* (Oxford: Oxford University Press, 2012).

accountable to God and should not persecute the Jewish people beyond their capacity to endure.

Such views were widely held amongst religious groups up until modern times. By the beginning of the twentieth century, however, an overwhelmingly secular Zionism had begun to advocate for a return to the land of Israel. The Nazi horrors then turned the tide for many, who concluded that the Three Vows were invalidated after World War II. The first prime minister of the modern state of Israel, David Ben-Gurion, was styled as a new Joshua by some,[22] and then the Six Day War of June 1967 was seen as a miraculous watershed event by many Orthodox Jews. Stirred particularly by the teaching of R. Tzvi Yehuda Kook, religious Zionism began to assert national sovereignty over the entire land of Palestine, often encouraging Jewish settlements in the occupied territories. 'Commanded war' was thereby revived. A broad spectrum of Jewish groups have resisted this conclusion, including, amongst many others, an agency called the Rabbis for Human Rights.

8.5 HERMENEUTICAL CONCLUSIONS

There are a number of different theologies of landholding in the Hebrew Bible. For example, the book of Genesis provides a different and peaceable paradigm, along with the earlier priestly literature that does not extend to the theocratic warfare of Numbers and Joshua. It is important to acknowledge, however, that colonial discourses have arguably drawn more frequently from the books of Genesis and Isaiah than they have from the conquest traditions. Settler mandates are not exclusive to Deuteronomy and Joshua.

There is no responsible way for faith communities to draw ethical sanction from Joshua without attending to complex inner-biblical debates, as well as to the later religious traditions that hold these texts to be in some sense authoritative. Our discussion has shown, for example, that when St Augustine initiated the Christian reflections on 'just war', the divinely commanded wars of Joshua had little relevance. On this point, at least, rabbinic Judaism was largely in agreement, although the rabbis and their diaspora polities were not in a position to be tempted by the powers of Christian empire.

The violence of Joshua was not often endorsed within Christian ethics until the second millennium, when the conquest traditions began

---

[22]   R. Havrelock, 'The Joshua Generation: Conquest and the Promised Land', *Critical Research on Religion* 1 (2013): 308–26.

to be read in support of the crusades. Thomas Aquinas (1224–1274) did his best to limit the application of Joshua with his own conception of just war, outlined especially in his *Summa Theologiae* (II–II, Q 40). In the sixteenth century, Catholic ethicists re-formulated the theory particularly to deal with the abuses of Spanish settlement in the New World. Francisco de Vitoria developed a distinction between combatants and civilians, which invalidated the *ḥērem* legislation in Deuteronomy while at the same time defending the property rights of non-Christian peoples.[23] Nevertheless, the niceties of these early ventures in international legal theory, whether Catholic or Protestant, could not restrain the master narratives about providence, which underpinned settler colonial societies without needing to draw explicit sanction from the book of Joshua.

Post-colonial and de-colonial studies have criticised liberation theologians to the extent that the latter drew ethical inspiration from a metanarrative comprising both exodus and conquest. The focus of this critique has been on the history of the Bible's reception, rather than the history behind the text – but, for communities of faith, fresh and detailed consideration of the biblical texts themselves cannot be entirely irrelevant. Even the priestly tradition could arrive at the conclusion that citizens and immigrants (*'ezrāḥ* and *gēr*) should be subject to the same framework of justice (Exod 12:49; Lev 24:22). When Josh 8:30–35 reiterates this requirement on Mt Ebal, the outcome is paradoxical in the narrative context: in the midst of invasion, who hears the law as a citizen, and who hears it as an immigrant? Today, could it be that the very same readers might enter into each of these categories, for the purposes of study and self-critical reflection, but seek to resist being typecast?

In conversation with Native American theologians, Randall Bailey agrees that the reader's own experience of life will shape the capacity to identify with particular characters. He even puts a question mark against his own tradition in the black church of singing 'Joshua fit de battle of Jericho... I'm bound for the promised Land!'[24] But the Joshua tradition is deeply embedded in the stirring tradition of freedom songs, as is also revealed by the title of Ralph Abernethy's autobiography,

---

[23]   M. Mantovani, 'Francisco de Vitoria on the "Just War": Brief Notes and Remarks', in *At the Origins of Modernity: Francisco de Vitoria and the Discovery of International Law*, ed. J. M. Beneyto and J. C. Varela (Cham: Springer, 2017), 117–40. The status of non-combatants has been lost not just in terrorism, but also in nuclear strategies.

[24]   R. C. Bailey, 'But It's in the Text! Slavery, the Bible, and the African Diaspora', in *Black Theology, Slavery, and Contemporary Christianity*, ed. A. Reddie (Farnham: Ashgate, 2010), 36–7. See further, H.M. Kopelson, *Faithful Bodies: Performing Religion and Race in the Puritan Atlantic* (New York: New York University Press, 2014).

When the Walls Come Tumbling Down. There is a considerable difference, however, between identifying with Joshua as a coloniser and singing down the walls of Jericho in the civil rights movement. We find the same kind of hermeneutics 'from below' in the Maori prophet movement of the nineteenth century, when Te Kooti resolved to 'become Joshua' in his determination to drive the British from Aotearoa.[25] Empowering interpretations crafted from a position of weakness and marginality need not be confused hermeneutically with oppressive readings that legitimate the status quo. The social location of reading makes a difference.

Bailey suggests an alternative analogy between the black church and the historic exclusion of Samarian Yahwism, beginning with reflections on 2 Kings 17, which depicts non-Israelite converts to Yahwism who were never fully accepted by the southerners (Judeans). Bailey's new typology ironically fits very well with the history of the book of Joshua. What appears to be a simple narrative of colonial violence and imposition comprises many stories of resistance – to ancient imperialisms and to other forms of social exclusion. Reading with the grain of these historic complexities, it would be less surprising to discover William Apess reprising Rahab in the 1830s, lamenting the loss of his Pequot forebears, giving voice to all people of colour.

The more difficult challenge, arguably, is for the settler colonial churches to repent of their historic habits of 'reading as Israel'.[26] The New Israel typologies have done enough damage. If Christians wish to see themselves as honorary Jews, they cannot abandon the hermeneutical discipline of reading as Gentiles. Assuming the genealogy that begins Matthew's Gospel, we Gentiles hang from Rahab's thread. St Augustine's preface to the *City of God* might function as an apt warning to all readers of the book of Joshua: 'We must also speak of the earthly city, which, though it be mistress of the nations, is itself ruled by its lust of rule (*libido dominandi*)'.

FURTHER READING

Apess, W. *A Son of the Forest and Other Writings.* Edited by B. O'Connell. Amherst: University of Massachusetts Press, 1997.

---

[25] J. Binney, *Redemption Songs: A Life of the Nineteenth-Century Maori Leader Te Kooti Arikirangi Te Turuki* (Melbourne: Melbourne University Press, 1997), 115–16, 502–3.

[26] See further M. G. Brett, *Political Trauma and Healing: Biblical Ethics for a Postcolonial World* (Grand Rapids: Eerdmans, 2016).

Bailey, B. C. 'But It's in the Text! Slavery, the Bible, and the African Diaspora'. Pages 31–46 in *Black Theology, Slavery, and Contemporary Christianity*. Edited by A. Reddie. Farnham: Ashgate, 2010.

Davidson, S. "Gazing (at) Native Women: Rahab and Jael in Imperializing and Postcolonial Discourses." Pages 69–92 in *Postcolonialism and the Hebrew Bible: The Next Step*. Edited by R. Boer. Atlanta: Society of Biblical Literature, 2013.

Donaldson, L. 'Son of the Forest, Child of God: William Apess and the Scene of Postcolonial Nativity'. Pages 201–22 in *Postcolonial America*. Edited by C. R. King. Urbana: University of Illinois Press, 2000.

Farber, Z. *Images of Joshua in the Bible and their Reception*. BZAW 457. Berlin: de Gruyter, 2016.

Fleming, D. E. *The Legacy of Israel in Judah's Bible: History, Politics and the Reinscribing of Tradition*. Cambridge: Cambridge University Press, 2012.

Havrelock, R. *The Joshua Generation: Israeli Occupation and the Bible*. Princeton: Princeton University Press, 2020.

Hofreiter, C. *Making Sense of Old Testament Genocide: Christian Interpretations of Herem Passages*. Oxford: Oxford University Press, 2018.

Krause, J. J. 'Hexateuchal Redaction in Joshua'. *Hebrew Bible and Ancient Israel* 6 (2017): 181–202.

Mantovani, M. 'Francisco de Vitoria on the "Just War": Brief Notes and Remarks'. Pages 117–40 in *At the Origins of Modernity: Francisco de Vitoria and the Discovery of International Law*. Edited by J. M. Beneyto and J. C. Varela. Cham: Springer, 2017.

Miller, R.J., J. Ruru, L. Behrendt, and T. Lindberg. *Discovering Indigenous Lands: The Doctrine of Discovery in the English Colonies*. Oxford: Oxford University Press, 2010.

Noort, E. ed. *The Book of Joshua*. BETL 250, Leuven: Peeters, 2012.

Templer, B. 'The Political Sacralization of Imperial Genocide: Contextualizing Timothy Dwight's *The Conquest of Canaan*'. *Postcolonial Studies* 9 (2006): 358–91.

Williams, R. *The Bloudy Tenent of Persecution for Cause of Conscience*. London: J. Haddon [1644] 1848.

Wright, J.L. *War, Memory and National Identity in the Hebrew Bible*. Cambridge: Cambridge University Press, 2020.

9 David's Ethic of Togetherness and Its Victims

RICHARD G. SMITH

On any reading of 2 Samuel 9–20, Joab's ruse with the Tekoite woman in 14:2–21 is a pivotal scene. It portrays the moral reasoning which David adopted in order to allow Absalom to return to Jerusalem from exile in Geshur and a new development in the ethics of David's administration. The formal character of the king's decision as an official royal pronouncement sets it apart and makes it especially significant. Within the narrative, the account marks a turning point from which ethical thinking in David's court never seems to recover. The characters construct a theological ethic that places a premium on the communal "togetherness" of God's people, and the crown accepts it as justification for overlooking the bloodguilt of one of its most marginalized members. The half-life of this ethic in the ensuing narrative wreaks havoc on the kingdom, through two of its most maniacally vulnerable agents. Once blood*guilt* can be overlooked for the sake of togetherness, little remains to prevent members of the community from sanctioning the blood*shed* of any member perceived to threaten that togetherness. The troubles that follow after Absalom's return are not simply due to the mere fact that a maniacal member of God's estate was returned to run amok. Rather, they arise from the problematic ethic employed to justify his restoration. The king's response further exacerbates the situation. Contextualization within outworking of divine judgment on the king for his own acts of oppression adds another element to the narrative's portrayal of causality, part of 2 Sam 8:15–20:26's critical dramatization of David's efforts to establish "justice and righteousness for all of his people."

9.1 NARRATIVE CHALLENGES

Appreciation for the role of 14:2–21 in the broader narrative presupposes a certain literary and rhetorical demarcation of 2 Samuel 9–20 with respect to its themes and evaluative point of view. The narrative's literary sophistication and significance for the rest of the David

narratives has long been recognized. Indeed, 2 Samuel 9–20 may well be
the most ethically engaging and challenging of all the David narratives.
Here we find intimate portraits of the king, the members of his house,
the character of his reign, and the punishments for its crimes. The
narrative has proven most challenging with regard to its ethics, inasmuch as its evaluative point of view is bound up with its composition
and configuration. The perceived lack of a starting point for the narrative
is a particular problem. Nevertheless, most can appreciate Klaus-Peter
Adam's assertion that the books of Samuel "question the authority of
the Davidic king, and they bring out David's shortcomings as a lawful
ruler. In doing so, they in theory affirm the king's authority, yet they
confront this ideal with the way in which David exercises his actual
kingship."[1]

To ask after David's *lawfulness* is to ask about the basis for ethics in
the narrative. This is, in turn, linked to questions about where the
account of David's ethical history begins and to questions of causality. 2
Samuel 9–20 depicts a history determined by its characters as they feel,
reason, interpret, advise, act, and react with consequences. It also
depicts a history determined by the deity's involvement. That Yahweh
would cause "evil" (*rāʿāh*) to arise against David from within his own
house (12:11) implies a deity who works through natural human relationship systems. Subversion of human wisdom is part of this, as when
Absalom's court favors Hushai's counsel over Ahithophel's (17:14).
Yahweh also appears to use the natural ecological order, as when "the
forest became great, devouring more people than those whom the sword
devoured on that day" (18:8). 2 Samuel 9–20 has consequently figured
prominently in discussions of so-called "dual causality," namely,
explanations of events as natural or realistic or as directed by the hand
of God.[2] The challenges of 2 Samuel 9–20 may be appreciated by considering the following: How does Yahweh's decree concerning the rise of
evil relate to the evil that arises in the rape of Tamar, in Absalom's
revolt, and in Sheba's secession (13:16; 15:14; 16:8; 17:14; 18:32; 19:7;
20:6)? How is this related to the compromise of Amnon's character by
his father's undisciplined love (13:21); the compromise of Absalom's
character by his own narcissism, the people's admiration, his hatred of

---

[1]   K. -P. Adam, "What Made the Books of Samuel Authoritative in the Discourses of the
      Persian Period?: Reflections on the Legal Discourse in 2 Samuel 14," in *Deuteronomy-
      Kings as Emerging Authoritative Books: A Conversation*, ed. D. V. Edelman (Atlanta:
      Society of Biblical Literature, 2014), 182.

[2]   J. W. Gericke, "Rethinking the 'Dual Causality Principle' in Old Testament Research:
      A Philosophical Perspective," *OTE* 28 (2015): 86–112.

Amnon, and his father's refusal to recognize him (13:22; 14:24–27); the compromise of Joab's character by his involvement in Uriah's murder (11:14–25), his sense of validation by the king's endorsement of his wisdom (14:22), his sense of dishonor from David's mourning (19:1–8), and David's replacement of him in favor of Amasa (14:22; 19:1–8; 19:13); the compromise of Ahithophel's character by the esteem his wisdom brought him (16:20–23; 17:1–4, 23; cf. 23:34); the compromise of Sheba's character by his "man of *beliya'al*" disposition and the northern tribes' sense of having been spurned (19:41–20:2); and the compromise of the Abelites' character by their pride in their reputation for wisdom (20:18–19)? To what extent are these characters presented as independent agents, and to what extent are they presented as enmeshed in a relationship system in which David occupies a strategic place? To what extent do their already vulnerable dispositions and the relationship system in which they are embedded diminish their capacity for autonomous ethical functioning and "fate" them to certain behavior? Does the narrative presuppose naturally ordered forces, which the deity's decrees exploit? Why does David seem unable to rise above his own affections or the ethos of his court? Does the nature of David's responsiveness stand to impact not only the moral character of his court and kingdom but also the deity's punitive purposes?

The narrative depicts a complicated and mysterious moral world, in which the outworking of the divine will involves considerations of psychology, sociology, and ecology. Its conception of causation and ethical responsibility signals a certain perspective on individual humans and the relationship systems in which they function.

9.2 DAVID'S FAILURE TO ESTABLISH "JUSTICE AND RIGHTEOUSNESS"

The narrative of 2 Samuel 9–20 begins with 8:15–18, with the ingressive announcement, "and so David *began to do* justice and righteousness for all his people" (8:15). The following list of state officials, headed by Joab son of Zeruiah, forms an *inclusio* with 20:23–26, by which point Joab has become a ruthless murderer. 2 Sam 8:15 invokes "justice and righteousness" as the evaluative key to the ensuing narrative, with the lists of officials marking the narrative unit.[3]

---

[3]   For a more detailed presentation of this section's argument, see R. G. Smith, *The Fate of Justice and Righteousness during David's Reign: Narrative Ethics and Rereading the Court History According to 2 Samuel 8:15–20:26*, LHBOTS 508 (London: T&T

"Justice and righteousness" occurs only three times in the Enneateuch, though 2 Sam 15:4 in the Hebrew text comes provocatively close to a fourth.[4] Each instance assumes the reader knows what it means to "do justice and righteousness," but only in 2 Sam 8:15 (// 1 Chr 18:14) is the phrase found in the voice of a narrator. To grasp what is in view we depend on prophetic and poetic literature and cognates in ancient Near Eastern texts. On this basis, the expression represents a "thick" ethical concept for ancient readers, as "social justice" does today. "Justice and righteousness" represents a common moral tradition, shared throughout the ancient Near Eastern world. It was conceived as an expression of character and mental configuration, in synergy with the divine. As a practical exercise in wisdom, it functioned as a hermeneutical construct that guided the crafting of laws and historiography. What promoted "justice and righteousness" in a given situation was determined by ethical considerations drawing on a variety of standards. Ideally, "justice and righteousness" was inseparable from wisdom; kings in particular were responsible for both.

As a thick ethical concept, "justice and righteousness" drew other ancient ideals, institutions, and conventions into its semantic realm. The reference to David doing "justice and righteousness" in 2 Sam 8:15, coupled with the list of officials in 8:16–18, references this royal tradition; the narrative that follows capitalizes on it in many ways. The narrative's interest in royal functioning; synergy between deity and king; kindness toward orphans, widows, and aliens or foreigners; royal decrees; wisdom and folly; love and hate; good and evil; murder and adultery; rape and rapine; judicial decision; guilt and innocence; wars of defense and aggression; rebellion and secession; punishment of unjust kings; the importance of the people in the deity's land; and state-sponsored forced labor are all part of a notion of royal "justice and righteousness." The presentation of these things in relation to David's administration constitutes a socio-political and ethical-theological agenda based in an ethical tradition of "justice and righteousness."

9.3 FROM DOING KINDNESS TO DOING EVIL (2 SAM 8:15–14:1)

David's administration of "justice and righteousness" begins with his attempt to do "the kindness of God" toward Mephibosheth (2 Sam 9:3).

Clark, 2009); cf. M. Weinfeld, *Social Justice in Ancient Israel and in the Ancient Near East* (Jerusalem: Magnes, 1995).

[4]   Gen 18:19; 2 Sam 8:15; and 1 Kgs 10:9. Deut 33:21 could be a distributed hendiadys in which the second element in the pairing is pluralized.

This edict relegates Zibah and his house to virtual field hands (9:9–10) and will come back later to vex the king not once but twice during the story of his flight and return from Absalom's revolt (16:1–4; 19:24–30). The narrative also describes David's awkward attempt to do kindness to Hanun the Ammonite (10:1–5). The defensive war that erupts has David's military fighting "for the sake of our people and for the cities of our God" (10:12); but as the conflict develops into an aggressive campaign (11:1), David "does evil" from the deity's perspective (11:27) by committing adultery and murder. Yahweh enters the fray, via his prophet Nathan, to call this unjust king to account. Reflecting the notion that the gods punished oppressive kings through the proliferation of social ills, Yahweh declares that he will "cause evil to arise" (*mēqîm rā'āh*) against David from within his own house (12:11). The synergy ideally supposed to exist between deity and king for the sake of justice is now put into service by the deity to punish the king personally, demanding of him the very sorts of exercises required of royalty combating social injustice, inasmuch as the establishment of "justice and righteousness" presupposes the eradication of evil and evil doers. Unfortunately, a commitment to "justice and righteousness" will therefore require the destruction of members of David's house. David himself is forgiven (12:13), but punishment is not averted, nor is his own agency removed from the equation; it begins with transference of the death sentence to Bathsheba's illegitimate child (12:14–23). David will endure still further punishment – not unto death, but unto wishing he was dead (18:33). As this begins, with Amnon's incestuous rape of Tamar, David responds according to an ethic based in love-for-firstborn (13:21). Consequently, he does not punish Amnon or attend to Tamar. The same ethic drives his negative response to Absalom's killing of Amnon. David's animosity toward Absalom for killing his beloved Amnon overrides everything; Absalom's flight into exile seems motivated by fear of David's wrath while mourning for Amnon. According to 12:18, some feared that David was the sort of man for whom the death of a son could drive him to "do evil" – and not necessarily to himself.

9.4 THE WISE TEKOITE'S RUSE (2 SAM 14:2–21)

Once Yahweh's judgment against David is set in motion and the king's poor responses to it begin, everything eventually turns on 2 Sam 14:2–21. Regardless of whether 13:39 means David's feelings for Absalom were waxing or waning, the ruse is constructed on the basis of Absalom's assumed bloodguilt. Even the widow's appeal for the life of her fictitious fratricidal son is based not on her affections but on her son's importance for securing her own place and her husband's name in the divine estate. This fits the ethos of royal decision making, echoed in the use of "king" to refer to David and the absence of references to Absalom as "son." This scene highlights the crafting of principles and their significance, not the king's feelings. Even if there is an indirect attempt to play on David's paternal feelings, the arguments are for action on the basis of a principle rooted elsewhere. The situation heading into the meeting with the Tekoite is one in which the king has attributed bloodguilt to Absalom. The ethic employed to change the face of this affair, so that the king will allow Absalom to be returned to Jerusalem, is best described as "an ethic of togetherness."

The Widow's Case (2 Sam 14:4–11)

The widow's dramatic introduction suggests an attempt to manipulate the situation emotionally, describing her plight as a widow who has lost one of her two sons to fratricide. Unlike the narratives of the Amnon-Absalom conflict, there is no mention of any extenuating circumstances. This is because Joab and the woman know that David attributes bloodguilt to Absalom for killing Amnon. That Amnon might have deserved execution is not countenanced. The guilt of the fictitious fratricide is therefore a given, as the royal court continues to ignore the moral ramifications of Amnon's rape of Tamar and the king's refusal to address it. David's disposition has determined matters; no one can reason apart from the king's premise.

The woman claims that "the whole family" has arisen against her, demanding that she hand over the fratricide so that they might put him to death. The clan is not deterred by the fact that the murderous son is the sole heir. The significance that the woman attributes to this is specified in the last half of the verse: "Thus they would quench my one remaining ember, and leave to my husband neither name nor remnant on the face of the earth" (14:7). This signals Joab's intention to confront the king with a case involving a clash of generational interests, pitting the interests of the clan for blood vengeance against the interests of the widow for a name and remnant for her husband. Joab thereby ensures that if the king sides with the clan he oppresses the widow; if he sides with the widow, he allows a murderer to go unpunished and denies justice to the clan. David's alternatives involve classic "justice and righteousness" motifs, which no ancient Near Eastern king could afford to ignore, and highlight the ethical tension between the interests of the individual and those of the community. The king's response, though slightly reassuring, is accordingly guarded. He ducks the dilemma by focusing only on the welfare of the widow herself: "Go to your house and I will give orders concerning you" (14:8). This seems to guarantee the woman's welfare and allows the king to separate the issue of her welfare from the issue of her murderous son's life. The widow will be cared for irrespective of the clan's pursuit of blood vengeance.

This shrewd ruling nearly thwarts Joab and the Tekoite, who seek to persuade the king to subordinate the justice of punishing a fratricide to the righteousness of maintaining the unity of God's estate. The widow accordingly attempts to maintain her audience with the king, pressing him again to rule against the interests of the clan. She calls for any "guilt" to be on her and her father's house, not on the "guiltless" king or his throne, implying that he is concerned about his own liability (14:9). The king, however, does not take the bait. Instead, he maintains his original strategy of guaranteeing her welfare, saying, "If anyone says anything to you, bring him to me, and he shall never touch you again" (14:10). The king's words appear to refer to the "avenger of blood," but he makes no promise to protect the fratricidal son from the avenger's approach. He merely repeats his assurance of protection for the widow.

The woman responds by pressing David even harder, going all-in to engage the king in explicit theological reflection. This time she hits a nerve. She urges, "May the king keep the LORD your God in mind, so that the avenger of blood may kill no more, and my son not be destroyed" (14:11a). The woman counters the king's strategy by linking her surviving son's welfare to the king's responsibility to prevent the escalation of violence, implying that the king is neglecting his duty before God. David now reacts strongly, swearing an oath that finally rules against the interest of the clan regarding blood vengeance: "As the LORD lives, not one hair of your son shall fall to the ground" (14:11b).

The Widow's Indictments of David (2 Sam 14:12–14)

With the king's ruling now finally in hand, the widow moves to use it against David. Her carefully worded indictment accuses the king of ignoring the precedent just set in her own case and of resisting the plans of Yahweh to return an exile. These charges are premised on the supposed justice of keeping all the people of God together in God's estate. They are not made for the sake of justice for Absalom and there is no appeal to any affection that David might still harbor for him as his son.

After receiving permission to speak further, the woman asks, "Why then have you planned such a thing against the people of God?" (14:13a). The verb refers to David's judicial reasoning regarding the widow's case;

the question links the preceding discussion and the Tekoite's exposition that follows. First, she explains why the king's ruling in her case is detrimental to the people of God: "For in giving this decision the king convicts himself" – or, more literally, "is like a guilty person." The Tekoite chooses her words; she does not say that the king *is* guilty. Rather, he is *like* a guilty person. This conviction is not quite so brutal as Nathan's "You are the man!" in 12:7. While Nathan represented the voice of Yahweh, accusing David of crimes that cannot be reversed, the Tekoite represents the voice of "wisdom," carefully exposing a more subtle sort of hypocrisy that the king still has an opportunity to rectify. In the most careful way possible, she suggests that the king is a hypocrite, but not yet guilty of a crime. He is in danger of becoming a veritably guilty person, "inasmuch as the king does not bring his exiled one home again" (14:13b).[5] Throughout, the woman avoids mentioning Absalom by name, reflecting her awareness that he is persona non grata with David.

The woman's expansion of her indictment in 14:14 is much more difficult to interpret. The following is based on MT, which we translate as follows:

> Indeed, we humans will certainly die, even like water poured out on the ground which cannot be gathered up. And God does not lift up [i.e., "restore"] life, but he does devise plans to restore an exile who has been exiled from us.

The first clause of the second sentence is the crux. Having addressed it at length elsewhere, the main point is that *nś᾽ npš* is best translated as "lift up life," in the sense of restoring life.[6] This fits the immediate sense, as a person's death is as irreversible for humans as water spilled on the ground. The final prepositional phrase may mean either "from him (= God)" or "from us (= the people of God)"; the latter is preferable in this context, explaining why David's reasoning has been against the people of God. The dead are gone; humans cannot bring them back and God does not raise them up. This is a basic wisdom sentiment; similar statements about the irreversibility of human mortality occur in 11:25 and 12:22. Indeed, this was the supposed basis of the widow's plight all along. However, when it comes to exiles and banishment, God is actively engaged in devising plans to restore exiles back to "us," the

---

[5]   NRSV's "banished" implies that David sent Absalom into exile, but 13:37–38 makes clear that Absalom fled of his own accord.

[6]   See Smith, *Fate of Justice and Righteousness*, 168–72.

people of God. According to the widow, none of the people of God should be excluded from the rest of the community.

The woman's words highlight the lack of synergy between the king's reasoning (14:13) and God's reasoning (14:14). God's plans to restore the exile are in opposition to the king's refusal to have the exile returned. The implication is clear: The present meeting is a divine device to restore the exile to the community. This argument is a bold one. It highlights the king's inner life and implies that the divine will is being made manifest to him in the wisdom of the moment; the king is on the threshold of a divine work of restoration for the sake of the community. Indeed, the wisdom being put forth is implied to be a revelatory moment of the deity's reasoning. Ironically, readers of Samuel have heard similar efforts of persuasion in 1 Sam 24:4 and 25:8, where David's men seek to justify taking advantage of and killing Saul! Then David resisted, because the liabilities of committing bloodshed were clear to him. Now, however, he will be unable to resist the argument; the blood has already been spilled and the moral goods of life and togetherness seem to justify overlooking it.

Concern for the King's Reputation (2 Sam 14:15–17)

The Tekoite returns to her own case to show how the king's consistency stands to affect her own situation. Although some suggest that these verses have been transposed from their original place between 14:7 and 14:8, our interpretation follows MT. The Tekoite's words make sense if they are understood to be recounting what she originally said to the people terrorizing her. She recounts in 14:16 how she pleaded with the people to let her speak to the king, telling how she declared her confidence that the king would act to "deliver his maidservant from the grasp of the man who is seeking to eradicate me and my only son from the estate of God (naḥălat 'ělōhîm)." This expression occurs only here. If 'ělōhîm is God, it has in view the idea of Yahweh's estate, encompassing both land and people; it thereby relates to the issue of God's people in God's land and the king as steward of it. If 'ělōhîm refers to the dead, the expression has in view the estate of the widow's dead husband.[7]

The woman then goes on to inform David how she persuaded the people to defer to the king's decision, boasting about the king's sapiential moral discernment, implying that there was popular respect for the king and his sense of justice and hinting that the king will jeopardize his

---

[7]   Smith, *Fate of Justice and Righteousness*, 165; T. J. Lewis, "The Ancestral Estate (*nachalath'elohim*) in 2 Samuel 14:16," *JBL* 110 (1991): 597–612.

reputation for wisdom – and ultimately the people's respect – if he shows duplicity in his dealings with Absalom. Perhaps this is why the woman ends her speech with, "The LORD your God be with you" (14:17). It is a wry sort of wish similar to 14:11; both invoke the ideal of synergy between God and king for justice and show that something remains to be done to avert an undesirable outcome. In 14:11 it was the need for a ruling concerning the preservation of her son. In 14:17 Absalom needs to be returned. The woman's flattery is designed to put the king under the pressure of public opinion. It may also suggest that Joab was concerned about the king's reputation as a just ruler.

The Tekoite's argument may be paraphrased as follows: "If you, O king, would deny a clan's right to blood vengeance in order to protect a widow's place in Yahweh's estate by assuring that her remaining son may live, then you should set aside your own ambivalence toward Absalom and return him from exile in order to protect the heritage of the people of God in God's land. God does not bring back the dead, but he works to bring back exiles. Do not oppose the will of Yahweh by refusing to have Absalom returned. It would violate the synergy between the king and God for justice and runs the risk of undermining popular respect for the king's wisdom."

The King's Discernment and Directive (2 Sam 14:18–21)

Once confronted about Joab's involvement, the Tekoite contends that Joab's intention was to put a crucial new "spin" on the Absalom problem, to get the king to see it from another theological and social angle. Despite the ruse, David accepts the arguments and orders Joab to have Absalom returned. It appears Joab has not been trying to trap the king into a binding legal judgment so much as change his moral perspective. Nevertheless, the fact remains that David, Joab, and the Tekoite have all failed to address the justice of Absalom's killing of Amnon, instead creating an ethic to justify overlooking, for the sake of community, fratricidal bloodguilt – a primeval ethical category of antisocial behavior if there ever was one. The basis for this is a folk theology of Yahweh's estate that relies for its persuasive force on the king's desire to be in synergy with the supposed will of the deity and with public opinion.

Though the king makes the final decision, this has been a group process. The king represents the deity, Joab the royal court, and the Tekoite woman a wisdom tradition subservient to both. Their collective focus on togetherness results in a court more favorable to some than others. The Tekoite woman completely bows out in the end, having been little more than Joab's mouthpiece, while Absalom will eventually force consideration of the implications of his *full* return in this ethic of "togetherness" (14:28–32). The group process should not be minimized when the narrative subsequently portrays its members as becoming (more) dysfunctional individuals. The narrative requires the reader to think of the development of these characters as the product of the interface among their dispositions, the new moral ethos, and an evolving relationship system.

9.5 THE CONSEQUENCES OF THE "ETHIC OF TOGETHERNESS" (2 SAM 14:22–20:26)

The moral fallout from David's decision to prioritize unqualified togetherness over fratricidal bloodguilt is immediate. The victims of this ethic of togetherness are those whose moral characters it poorly serves and those whose lives are snuffed out on its account. Joab and Absalom are individually compromised; Israel and Judah are corporately deconstructed. Amasa and Sheba lose their lives. The personal woe that Absalom and Joab effect for the king becomes the basis for David's decisions, as he mismanages his return to the throne after Absalom's defeat.

Of the six verses that follow David's decision to return Absalom, four reveal something of the inner lives of Joab and Absalom (2 Sam 14:22, 25–27). Absalom's prominence makes it easy to overlook how Joab is introduced in 14:22–24 as the first victim of an unqualified ethic of togetherness. His uncharacteristically ostentatious display of obeisance reveals a deep sense of personal validation. Whether this suggests that Joab has been out of David's favor since the death of Abner is hard to say. More significantly, it indicates that this ethic found an empathetic host in Joab precisely because it was from his sapiential incubation chamber that it sprang (14:2–3, 19b–20a). For Joab, the king's decision is royal validation. This goes a long way toward explaining why Joab will show such chutzpah when defying David's order to spare Absalom (18:5, 10–15) and when disemboweling Amasa (20:8–10), using him to send a message to potential supporters of David (20:11–12), which proved counterproductive (20:13). At the end of the story of the Absalom affair we see Joab pushed to the limits of frustration with a king who neglects his responsibility to acknowledge the faithfulness of his vassals (19:5–8). David refuses to acknowledge the justice of Joab's execution of Absalom, just as he refused to acknowledge the justice of Absalom's execution of Amnon for the incestuous rape of Tamar.

As for Absalom, only in 14:25–27 does the narrator reveal aspects of his character that dispose him to be a casualty of the togetherness ethic. Superficially, there was no man worthier of the king's court than Absalom, possessed of the power and virility associated with divine blessing. Absalom appears to have reveled in this, as his narcissistic weighing of his own hair seems to suggest. That he fathered three sons served to support his popular estimation. Yet the reference to Absalom's daughter, Tamar, bespeaks something deeper, suggesting that the injustice done to his sister was never far from his mind. Moral preening, righteous indignation, long-term resentment, and natural vanity are an explosive combination.

Yet it is Absalom's delayed reintegration into the court that unleashes his sociopathic potential (14:28–32). The results are catastrophic for justice. By the time David is compelled to recognize Absalom, the damage is done, his already vulnerable character thoroughly deconstructed. The king's wordless kiss of acceptance is ambiguous as to whether Absalom is exonerated or forgiven of bloodguilt (14:33b). The king's failure to take a clear stand leads Absalom, apparently convinced that his justice has been vindicated, to dupe the people with his claims about his character (15:4). Eventually, Absalom justifies plotting to kill his own father for the sake of community justice (15:12–14). The "togetherness" ideal appears again in the coup d'etat; Ahithophel claims that David's death alone will restore Israel, "as a bride comes home to her husband," so "all the people will be at peace" (17:3). Despite the emphasis on the ethic of togetherness, Absalom's behavior defies the social relations that should characterize the establishment of "justice and righteousness." The men of Israel are victims of David's royal ethic of togetherness, misled as to where "justice and righteousness" resided and who was able to establish it – to say nothing of its use to justify patricidal regicide. Absalom, criminal that he is, is a tragedy for the nation as a community and David as an individual. The narrative thus undermines any efforts to read Absalom's death in pro-Davidic terms. This is driven home in the account of the two messengers who could not, despite their best efforts, put a pro-Davidic interpretation on the battle that defeated Absalom's forces, precisely because of the death of the king's son. Joab is presented as having recognized the futility of this from the start (18:19–33).

The final section of 19:9–20:26 is characterized by relationship breakdown at virtually all levels of the kingdom, from the king's house in Jerusalem, through the tribes of Judah and Israel, to a prominent city on the northern border, as a result of David's spiteful and self-centered decision making.[8] In this more anthropocentric narrative David has not gained greater moral awareness after Absalom's death, nor is he presented as weak or broken. Rather, he is less pious, more secular, and more spiteful. At key points he responds poorly to events; most prominently, his favoring of Judah over Israel and Amasa over Joab (19:9–15) fostered the dissolution of Israel and Judah as well as Joab and Amasa (19:41–20:22). Israel's willingness to have David returned as king was an opportunity to leave the bitter days behind. This opportunity is squandered when David spurns Israel, honors Judah, and replaces Joab with Amasa. This prompts Israel to follow an even less virtuous rebel, Sheba, and pushes Joab into murdering Amasa. David's favoritism even corrupts Judah, which resorts to rank stubbornness to deny the claims of the northern tribes (19:43). By the time we come to the siege of Abel (20:14–22), David's original declaration regarding Mephibosheth has been completely undone (19:24–30) and Joab is transformed into an oppressor who returns to serve the king (20:14–23). Throughout 19:9–20:26, it is David's character, not the outworking of Yahweh's judgment against him, that is responsible for the course of affairs. The closing picture is one of institutionalized oppression (20:23–26).

Faced with an obligation to stem the tide of violence and a need to secure popular respect, in 2 Samuel 14 David unleashed an ethic born of the very emotional matrix he was trying to transcend. This ethic subordinated bloodguilt to the unity of the people. Little wonder that it increased the tide of violence, undermined the king's moral authority, and promoted intolerance for anything that threatened community unity. The ethic of unqualified togetherness is thus presented as having increased social injustice and institutionalized oppression.

9.6 IMPLICATION FOR MODERN DISCUSSIONS OF ETHICS

Second Samuel 8:15–20:26 reflects the interests of its ancient author(s) in the systemic emotional forces at work in the ethical life of David's kingdom. The narrative presents individual characters and dispositions intersecting with others, including the deity, in a hierarchically ordered system. Those at the top are portrayed as in pursuit of an ethical vision with ethical significance beyond individual characters. David's sins violate an entire network of relationship ties and commitments; his

[8]   See Smith, *Fate of Justice and Righteousness*, 205–28.

divinely orchestrated punishment involves violation of the same, within his own house and ultimately the nation. The narrative especially highlights the critical role of the deity and the king for the ethical functioning of others in the system. In the process, the ancient crafters of this narrative have anticipated some modern developments in family systems theory and character/virtue ethics.

The Bowen Theory of family systems is a conceptual framework able to account for the complexity of evolving relationship systems and is helpful in clarifying the morally significant realities with which ethical deliberation and functioning must contend.[9] In particular, its explanation of human functioning as a natural and thinking system relates directly to biblical creation and wisdom theologies. It is concerned with how complex emotional relationships – across generations, throughout societies, and within families – affect the functioning of individuals and how the tension between the community and the individual relate to biology and learning. At the level of leadership, Bowen Theory is interested in how individuals manage themselves as a therapeutic modality for good amidst systemic relationship forces.[10]

Bowen Theory sees togetherness as that which propels us to follow the directives of others, becoming a dependent, connected, and indistinct entity. Togetherness manifests in pressure for oneness, sameness, and agreement; seeking love, approval, and closeness, and assigning positive value to thinking about the other before the self; and holding others responsible for one's own happiness or holding the self responsible for the happiness of others, or both. The intensity of the togetherness impulse is influenced by learning, including the conditioning of emotional and feeling responses and the acquisition of values and beliefs. ("Emotion," note, is not equated with "feelings" in Bowen Theory. Emotion may involve feelings, but the term is used to designate human instinct.)

Individuality is what propels a person to follow his or her own directives, becoming an independent and distinct entity. This is reflected in the motivation to feel, think, and act for oneself and a lack of concern about whether others feel, think, and act the same. Bowen Theory understands individuality to manifest in autonomy for self, goal-

---

[9]   M. E. Kerr, *Bowen Theory's Secrets: Revealing the Hidden Life of Families* (New York: W. W. Norton, 2019); M. E. Kerr and M. Bowen, *Family Evaluation: An Approach Based on Bowen Theory* (New York: W. W. Norton, 1988) with further references.

[10] On the application of Bowen Theory to faith communities see E. H. Friedman, *Generation to Generation: Family Process in Church and Synagogue* (New York: Guilford, 1985).

directed behaviors, productivity, and being governed by principle versus feelings of the moment. The development of individuality is also based on learning, including the conditioning of emotional responses to the intellectual acquisition of knowledge. This intellectual and knowledge component distinguishes learning under force of individuality from learning under force of togetherness.[11]

Bowen Theory attempts to account for the interplay and tension between individuality and togetherness forces through eight interlocking concepts, of which the most important are differentiation of self and the emotional triangle. Differentiation refers to one's capacity to be an emotionally separate person. The more differentiated a self, the more a person is able to be an individual while still in emotional contact with the group. That is, the capacity for a person to function as part of a group is not contingent on giving up individuality. An ability to think and reflect, rather than respond automatically, is what enables an ability to restrain selfish and spiteful urges, even during periods of high anxiety. The higher the differentiation of individual members of a family or social group, the more they are able to cooperate, look out for each other's welfare, and stay in contact with one another during stressful periods. The lower their differentiation, the more likely it is that the group will regress into selfish, aggressive, and avoidance behaviors, breaking down cohesiveness, altruism, and cooperativeness. As differentiation decreases, "individuality is less well-developed, togetherness needs are stronger, emotional reactivity is more intense and more easily triggered, and subjectively based attitudes are more influential."[12] Emotional boundaries become blurred and, as these boundaries dissolve, anxiety becomes increasingly infectious. People then become "more reactive to each other's distress and consume more energy trying to avoid saying and doing things that might cause upset"; as a result, "there is increased pressure on people to think, feel, and act in ways that will enhance one another's emotional well-being."[13] As differentiation increases, however, individuality is better developed, togetherness needs are less intense, and emotional reactiveness is better modulated. Togetherness is felt "not as deep yearnings and needs, but as a basic attraction and interest in one's fellow man."[14] This is conducive of more responsible ethical reflection and behavior.

---

[11] Kerr and Bowen, *Family Evaluation*, 64–5; Kerr, *Bowen Theory's Secrets*, 68.
[12] Kerr and Bowen, *Family Evaluation*, 75.
[13] Kerr and Bowen, *Family Evaluation*, 77.
[14] Kerr and Bowen, *Family Evaluation*, 69.

How one conceives of the processes governing human relationships impacts one's capacity for and conception of ethical functioning. An ethical endgame – such as "justice and righteousness" – that does not attend to the capacity of individuals to self-regulate their emotions practically assures that it will be undermined by leaders who violate boundaries, deconstruct virtues, and foster the moral corruption of other members in the system. As the David narratives suggest, the capacity for remaining connected without sacrificing the integrity of self is crucial to ethical functioning, precisely because self-differentiation is what puts ethical expertise at one's disposal in the pursuit of "justice and righteousness." David, Joab, the Tekoite, Absalom, and Ahithophel are powerful illustrations of the consequences of failure.

FURTHER READING

Adam, K.-P. "What Made the Books of Samuel Authoritative in the Discourses of the Persian Period?: Reflections on the Legal Discourse in 2 Samuel 14." Pages 159–86 in *Deuteronomy-Kings as Emerging Authoritative Books: A Conversation*. Edited by D. V. Edelman. Atlanta: Society of Biblical Literature, 2014.

Friedman, E. H. *Generation to Generation: Family Process in Church and Synagogue*. New York: Guilford, 1985.

Friedman, Edwin H. *A Failure of Nerve: Leadership in the Age of the Quick Fix*. Edited by Margaret M. Treadwell and Edward W. Beal. Revised edition. New York: Church Publishing, 2017.

Gericke, J. W. "Rethinking the 'Dual Causality Principle' in Old Testament Research: A Philosophical Perspective." *OTE* 28 (2015): 86–112.

Kerr, M. E. *Bowen Theory's Secrets: Revealing the Hidden Life of Families*. New York: W. W. Norton, 2019.

Kerr, M. E., and M. Bowen. *Family Evaluation: An Approach Based on Bowen Theory*. New York: W. W. Norton, 1988.

Lewis, T. J. "The Ancestral Estate (*nachalath'elohim*) in 2 Samuel 14:16." *JBL* 110 (1991): 597.

Rosenberg, Joel. *King and Kin: Political Allegory in the Hebrew Bible*. Indiana Studies in Biblical Literature. Bloomington: Indiana University Press, 1986.

Smith, R. G. *The Fate of Justice and Righteousness during David's Reign: Narrative Ethics and Rereading the Court History According to 2 Samuel 8:15b–20:26*. LHBOTS 508. London: T&T Clark, 2009.

Weinfeld, Moshe. *Social Justice in Ancient Israel and in the Ancient Near East*. Jerusalem: Magnes, 1995.

10 Ethics and Ethnicity in the Deuteronomistic History

BRIAN RAINEY

Debates about immigration, national identity, and the inclusion of ethnic minorities have been a prominent part of the twenty-first century thus far. Yet, ethical questions such as how to define one's community and whether and to what extent to include those deemed foreign are ancient. The Hebrew Bible offers a variety of viewpoints – many of them conflicting – on how to define "Israelite" and non-Israelite, native and foreign, insider and outsider. Among these is the perspective of the Deuteronomistic History (Joshua to 2 Kings), a group of texts united by a somewhat coherent ideological perspective and the focus of this essay. Even within this collection, however, are expressed a variety of positions on the treatment of different peoples in the world of ancient Israel.

According to Genesis 10, all of humanity descended from the sons of Noah; these descendants spread out around the world by "national" groups (gôy, 10:5, 20, 31–32). Deuteronomy 32:8–9 says that Yahweh divided humanity into nations (gôy) and "peoples" ('am), who lived within divinely ordained boundaries. These texts, like others in the Hebrew Bible, envision a world in which human beings are classified according to "nations" and "peoples," of which the nation and people of Israel is one (Exod 33:13; Deut 4:6; 32:9; 2 Sam 7:23). These national and people groups are usually delineated by a demonym, such as Israelite, Canaanite, Philistine, Ammonite, or Amalekite. It is not immediately clear that these groups should be understood as ethnic or racial categories. Since there are no biblical Hebrew words for "race" or "ethnicity," the interpreter must infer such concepts in the biblical texts. There are also many conflicting, contested modern theories about how to define "ethnicity" and "race." Whether there is a difference between the two terms and (if so) the relationship between them is contentious. It is not uncommon for aspects of one person's definition of race to overlap with another person's definition of ethnicity, and vice versa. "Ethnicity" is perceived by some as a more neutral and less hierarchical term than "race," a concept many believe developed as a result of the slave trade

and European imperialism. It is also common to argue that race differs
from ethnicity insofar as race emphasizes physical characteristics as an
important basis by which to categorize peoples. This is certainly an
important aspect of race in the modern era, though some have argued
that rudimentary concepts of race can already be found in the
ancient world.

If we assume that race emphasizes physical characteristics, what are
the important features of ethnic categorization? Some argue that ethnicity should be understood as a manifestation of the social importance
ascribed to cultural features. Others argue that common ancestry is the
primary criterion by which people divide into ethnic groups. Ethnic
group members are believed to share some kind of hereditary link,
perhaps a belief that members of the group descended from a common
ancestor or a belief that the ethnic appellation is hereditary and fixed
from birth. Others contend that ethnicity is a phenomenon in which
people are imbued with an indelible essence that defines them as permanent, unchangeable members of a social group.[1]

It is impossible to explore all of the various theories about ethnicity
here, nor will it be possible to mount an adequate defense of a particular
theory of ethnicity. Instead, I will assume that the people and nation
categories in the Hebrew Bible, usually identified by demonyms (e.g.,
Israelite, Philistine, the various peoples designated Canaanite or
Amorite, Amalekite, Egyptian, etc.), constitute ethnic groups (Num
24:20; Deut 4:6, 27; 7:1; 32:8–9; 2 Sam 7:23; 2 Kgs 6:18; 19:12). Those
who are not Israelites (bĕnê yiśrā'ēl) will be referred to as foreigners, with
the understanding that these foreigners are also ethnically distinguished
from Israelites. Whatever one calls the separation of humanity by nation
and people, biblical texts usually portray these demonymic categories as
stable, enduring, and permanent. "Ethnicity," then, seems to be a term
that appropriately communicates the sense of immutability that
characterizes these nation and people categories. Additionally, because
physical descriptions of peoples are rare (though certainly attested),[2] and
humanity as a whole is not organized into a taxonomy based on physical
descriptions, "ethnicity" seems to be a more appropriate term
than "race."

---

[1] For a review of many, but certainly not all, theories of ethnicity, see B. Rainey,
    *Religion, Ethnicity and Xenophobia in the Bible: A Theoretical, Exegetical and
    Theological Survey* (London: Routledge, 2019), 19–53.
[2] Giants as part of the population of Canaan: Deut 1:28; 2:10, 21; 9:2; 2 Sam 21:20.
    Cushites: Isa 18:1–2, 7; Jer 13:23.

The ethical framework I use to assess ethnicity in biblical texts assumes that empathy is fundamental for ethics. I define empathy as "perceiving that another being is experiencing some particular emotion (or feeling) and, as a result of this perception, experiencing an emotion similar to what the other being is experiencing."[3] Empathy is to "'feel with' another as if from a first-person perspective"; this is distinct from sympathy, which is to "'feel for' another – to feel concern for another's welfare... more from a third-person perspective."[4] Empathy seems to be part of a universal human experience and can also be found in other animals, particularly other primates. Consequently, empathy can be a helpful concept by which to assess an alien cultural context ethically, including the sociocultural world of ancient Israel as depicted in their literary texts. Debates over the use of empathy as a foundation for ethics – even virtue ethics – will not be reviewed here, but it has been cogently and competently defended.[5] Pertinent to the current discussion is that in-group bias demonstrably affects empathy: People are likely to show more empathy toward the familiar, including those perceived to be within their own group, than toward outsiders and the unfamiliar.[6]

I have chosen empathy as a framework with respect to ethnicity because biblical texts seem to appeal to empathy when arguing that Israelites should not mistreat the resident alien (gēr), who is understood in most cases to be a foreigner: "You shall not oppress a resident alien. You yourselves know the spirit (nepeš) of a resident alien because you were resident aliens in the land of Egypt" (Exod 23:9; similarly, Exod 22:20 [ET 22:21]; Lev 19:33–34; Deut 10:18–19).[7] The reference to the nepeš of the resident alien, in particular, suggests that the passage enjoins hearers to take an empathetic stance toward them.[8] While the

---

3   A. Simmons, "In Defense of the Moral Significance of Empathy," *Ethical Theory and Moral Practice* 17 (2014): 99.

4   Simmons, "Moral Significance," 100. Simmons argues that empathy in the fullest sense has both a cognitive and an affective aspect. One must both grasp the other's concerns and purposes and also affectively share in those concerns and purposes (102).

5   Simmons, "Moral Significance," 97–110 (for an overview of these debates, see 100–1).

6   See discussion in M. L. Hoffman, *Empathy and Moral Development: Implications for Caring and Justice* (Cambridge: Cambridge University Press, 2000), 206–9.

7   The relationship between foreignness and the resident alien is complicated and debated. See S. M. Olyan, *Rites and Rank: Hierarchy in Biblical Representations of Cult* (Princeton: Princeton University Press, 2000), 68–71.

8   Translating *nepeš* as "spirit" in the sense of the core characteristics, emotions, and moods of a person. It does seem that the *nepeš* encompasses the part of a person that includes desire and longing (HALOT 2, 713). Consequently one could reasonably argue that Exod 23:9 communicates something like an affective component of empathy (*nepeš*) as well as a cognitive component (*yd'*).

passage refers to an event in Israel's historical memory, instead of a contemporaneous experience, it commands Israelites to think about the experience of others as a foundation for the treatment of these foreigners. This coincides with the definition of empathy outlined above. These passages invite the hearer to "feel with" the concerns and purposes of resident aliens, from a first-person perspective.[9]

10.1 CONSTRUCTING ETHNICITY IN ISRAEL

Biblical texts that take pains to differentiate between Israelites and non-Israelites may be difficult to reconcile with modern theologies and ethical outlooks that emphasize universality and the equality of all people. It is especially difficult to reconcile texts that promote discrimination, even violence, based on ethnic background. A number of theorists of ethnicity argue that the construction of the self necessarily requires the creation of "others" or "outsiders" and a division between "us and them."[10] Whether categorizing people into types, groups, or making "us/them" distinctions is a morally positive, neutral, or negative human behavior is an open question. If people naturally, unreflexively, or unconsciously divide human beings into categories and types, can people – ancient or modern – be held morally responsible for categorizing? Perhaps the division of people into categories is morally neutral – even good in some contexts – but the introduction of hierarchies, especially those that divide people into superior and inferior groups, is wrong. Another possible argument is that human beings should critically assess all human categorization (i.e., "putting people in boxes"), with the goal of eliminating categorical distinctions altogether and viewing people as individuals. These arguments are based on the notion that dividing people into "us and them" inevitably leads to hierarchical distinctions. Because in-group bias affects levels of empathy, categorization could unjustly deprive out-group members of appropriate levels of empathy.

Biblical texts are certainly interested in dividing people into "Israelite" and (various types of) "non-Israelite." Deuteronomistic texts, in particular, frequently describe the nation and people of Israel using

---

9   Simmons notes that empathy must have an imaginative aspect that requires a person to take the perspective of another person or animal in order to be expressed fully ("Moral Significance," 102–5).

10   Summary in Rainey, *Religion, Ethnicity and Xenophobia*, 11–13, especially sources in nn. 36 and 42; L. M. Wills, *Not God's People: Insiders and Outsiders in the Biblical World* (Lantham: Rowman and Littlefield, 2008), 1–19.

familial language. Deuteronomy repeatedly describes the Israelites as a community of "brothers" (*'aḥîm*) and contrasts the "brotherhood" of Israel with the resident alien or foreigner (Deut 1:16; 14:21; 15:2; 17:15; 23:21; 24:14). Similarly, the books of Joshua, Judges, Samuel, and Kings regularly use the language of brotherhood to describe smaller kinship groups such as families and clans (Josh 6:23; Judg 9:1, 3, 26, 31, 41; 14:3; 16:31; 18:8; 2 Sam 15:20; 2 Kgs 10:13; 23:9), as well as the larger "kinship" group of the people, Israel (Josh 1:14; Judg 19:23; 20:13, 23, 28; 21:6; 2 Sam 2:26; 19:12, 41; 1 Kgs 12:24). Membership in the brotherhood of Israel comes with privileges and obligations. Some passages mandate heartfelt acts of generosity toward fellow Israelites that are not available to outsiders. In Deuteronomy 15, a fellow Israelite (*'aḥ, rēᵃ*) and not a foreigner (*nokrî*, 15:3) is entitled to a remission of debts (*šĕmiṭṭâ*) every seven years, as well as a generous release from debt slavery. Passages outside the Deuteronomistic corpus command addressees to create a special regime of economic justice for their fellow Israelites that prevents exploitation (Leviticus 25). The same level of protection from economic exploitation is not offered to foreigners and resident aliens (Lev 25:44–46).

The use of brotherhood terminology to describe Israel supports theoretical views holding that ethnicity is, at least partially, related to notions of common ancestry. Familial language also serves to imbue the category "Israelite" with a sense of permanence and endurance, rooting it in heredity and birth. It is noteworthy that the Edomites, a neighboring people also known as the descendants of Esau (*bĕnê 'ēśāw*), are sometimes called the "brethren" of Israelites (Deut 2:4, 8; 23:8 [ET 23:7]). The close relationship between Edomites and Israelites probably stems from traditions about Esau and Jacob, the ancestors of Edom and Israel, as brothers (Genesis 25–27; 32–33). The fact that ancestors are significant for explaining the relationship between different peoples and nations reinforces the familial and hereditary links that give ethnic groups in the Bible their sense of fixedness and immutability (see also Genesis 10).

10.2 RESIDENT ALIENS

Biblical passages encourage an empathetic stance toward the resident alien, but the resident alien is not just any non-Israelite. Deuteronomy's dietary law separates the resident alien both from the Israelite and from the general "foreigner" (*nokrî*): "You [Israelites] shall not eat anything of itself; you may give it to a resident alien (*gēr*) or you may sell it to a foreigner (*nokrî*)" (Deut 14:21). Deuteronomy's distinction between the resident alien and the foreigner seems similar to the differentiation between the resident alien and foreigner (*ben-nēkār*) in Exod 12:43, 48, a Holiness passage. Resident aliens are usually foreigners, but not all foreigners are resident aliens. Yet, while resident aliens are protected members of Israelite society, they are not socially equal to Israelite male heads of household. When addressed in Deuteronomistic material, they are grouped with women, children, and slaves and referred to in the third person (Deut 5:14; 16:14; 29:11; 31:12; Josh 8:35), whereas the Israelite head of household is addressed in the second person.[11]

It is unclear what protection from oppression means for the resident alien. Verses that mention the Israelites' sojourn in Egypt imply that Egypt abused the Israelites who lived there as resident aliens by forcing them into servitude (Deut 26:5).[12] Israelites are not to treat resident aliens the way Egypt treated Israel, suggesting that resident aliens should be exempt from forced labor. Yet, Deut 29:9–11 says that resident aliens hew wood and draw water like the enslaved Gibeonites, possibly suggesting that resident aliens constitute a servant class somehow (compare Josh 9:21–27). Similarly, Lev 25:44–46 authorizes the use of resident aliens as chattel slaves. Although some passages suggest that there are circumstances in which a resident alien might achieve power over an Israelite (Deut 28:43–44; see also Lev 25:47–54), such a situation is considered extraordinary; it comes about as a result of Yahweh's judgment or is an aberration that must be urgently remedied.

The protection of resident aliens in the Hebrew Bible corresponds with ancient Near Eastern ideologies of justice, which require the protection of vulnerable populations. In Deuteronomy, the resident alien is grouped with other vulnerable populations commonly mentioned in ancient Near Eastern legal texts, such as the widow and the orphan (Deut 10:18; 14:29; 16:11, 14; 24:17, 19, 21; 26:12; 27:19) and the poor (24:14). Notably, however, these extrabiblical texts do not include resident aliens or foreigners. For example, in the prologue to the Laws of Ur-Nammu – the earliest extant written law code in the world – the king boasts that "I did not deliver the orphan to the rich; I did not deliver the widow to the mighty; I did not deliver the man with but one shekel

---

[11]   Olyan, *Rites and Rank*, 76–8.
[12]   That is, corvée labor (*mas*, Exod 1:8–14), a function that the Canaanites who were not annihilated in the conquest serve (Josh 9:3–27; 16:10; Judg 1:27–36; 1 Kgs 9:21).

to the man with one mina."[13] He makes no mention of foreigners. In some nonlegal Akkadian texts, there are implicit references to the protection of certain foreign guests, such as the *ubāru*. In the Amarna letters, for example, this word appears to refer to foreign guests of an official or diplomats from a foreign land, and one Amarna letter even appears to condemn an official for mistreating the *ubāru*.[14]

10.3 ETHNIC VIOLENCE AND HOSTILITY

In contrast to the empathetic stance these passages take toward the resident alien, numerous other texts promote violence, marginalization, and discrimination toward foreigners. Deuteronomistic writers also frequently describe the religious practices of which they disapprove as "foreign" and not native to Israel.[15] Such practices are associated with the indigenous, non-Israelite population of the land of Canaan and serve as justifications for their brutal suppression (Deut 7:1–6, 25–26; 20:17–18). Deuteronomistic texts fear that, if allowed to remain in the land, the native population of Canaan will entice Israelites to follow these forbidden practices. It has been noted by numerous modern interpreters that archaeological evidence does not support the Deuteronomistic portrayal of these practices as non-Israelite. Rather, Deuteronomistic texts employ the label "foreign" rhetorically, in order to slander *Israelite* religious practices they seek to suppress.

Certain passages promote the complete destruction of the Canaanites, while others seem more circumspect, resigning themselves to a continuous but marginalized Canaanite presence in the land (e.g., Josh 13:1–6, 13; Judg 1; 2:2–4). Deuteronomistic passages that depict life in the early monarchy claim that Canaanites lived in Israel, sometimes in urban enclaves, but typically as servants or as a source of forced labor (*mas*, Josh 16:10; 17:13; Judg 1:28–35; 1 Kgs 9:21). Compared to the

---

[13]   An accessible version can be found in M. T. Roth, *Law Collections from Mesopotamia and Asia Minor* (Atlanta: Scholars, 1995), 16.

[14]   All but three of the Amarna Letters, which record Egypt's diplomatic correspondence in the latter part of the fourteenth century BCE, were composed in Akkadian, not Egyptian. For Amarna examples, see W. L. Moran, *The Amarna Letters* (Baltimore: Johns Hopkins University Press, 1992), 48–9 incl. n. 16, 93, 250 (letters 20:72; 29:32; 162:75). For more discussion on the term *ubāru*, often translated "foreign resident," see J. Lewy, "Some Institutions of the Old Assyrian Empire," *HUCA* 27 (1957): 58–61, esp. n. 250; H. Lewy, "The Nuzian Feudal System (Concluded)," *Or* 11 (1942): 320–2; CAD, U/W, 10–11.

[15]   Deut 4:19; 6:14; 7:2–4, 16; 13:2, 6; 12:2, 30; Deut 31:16; 32:12; Josh 24:20, 23; Judg 10:16; 1 Sam 7:3.

resident alien, Deuteronomistic texts show considerably less empathy for the indigenous Canaanites. One text even explicitly prohibits empathy toward Canaanites, saying, "You shall have no pity for them" (Deut 7:16). This unpitying sentiment is usually expressed through the practice of "the ban" or ḥērem/ḥrm (Deut 2:34; 3:6; 7:2; 20:17; Josh 2:10; 6:17–18, 21; 8:26; 11:20, et passim). This ostensibly involves killing all men, women, and children in a particular locale, though descriptions of the practice vary. Descriptions of Israelite cruelty toward Canaanites include gibbeting, torture, and mutilation (Josh 10:24–27; Judg 1:6–7).

A notable example of ḥērem involves the Amalekites (1 Samuel 15), who are not Canaanites. In this ban, all of the people as well as the livestock are to be destroyed. Because Saul disobeys, sparing the king of Amalek and the livestock, he is punished severely (1 Sam 15:22–29; cf. Achan in Josh 7:22–26). Unlike the case of the Canaanites, the rationale for this ban does not stem from fear that Amalekites will entice Israel to participate in forbidden religious customs, nor because they pose an immediate threat to Israel. Rather, the Amalekites are to be destroyed because of an act that was committed in the past (1 Sam 15:2; Deut 25:17–19). This is not the only passage that imposes punishments on ethnic groups because of a past event. A notable example includes Deut 23:4–5 [ET 23:3–4], which excludes Ammonites and Moabites from the community because they were inhospitable to the Israelites during their time in the wilderness and hired a prophet to curse Israel.

Interestingly, Deuteronomistic texts use similar rhetoric against Israelites who violate social or religious norms. Deuteronomy 13 mandates that Israelites execute ḥērem against Israelite towns whose inhabitants worship forbidden deities (Deut 13:13–19 [ET 13:12–18]). As with the Canaanites, the people are to have no pity for Israelites who contravene religious norms (Deut 13:5–9 [ET 13:6–8]). Israelites should also have no pity for compatriots who break certain social rules (Deut 19:13, 21; 25:11–12). In one significant example, Israelites execute a limited ban against the tribe of Benjamin (Judg 21:11), who are also Israelites, because they protected the men responsible for the rape and murder of a Levite guest's concubine (Judges 19–20). This act of savagery, similar to the behavior of the people of Sodom (Genesis 19), is described as something beyond the pale (nĕbālâ, Judg 20:6). It is so far outside the bounds of socially acceptable behavior that the Levite declares to his fellow Israelites, "Has such a thing ever happened since the day the Israelites came out from Egypt until this day?" (Judg 19:30). Ultimately, however, the other tribes of Israel take pity on the Benjaminites (Judg 21:6, 15). The compassion that the Israelites show toward their fellow Benjaminites, even when executing the ban, attests to the problematic relationship between empathy and in-group bias. While some texts say that Israelites should not pity Canaanites under any circumstances (Deut 7:16), Israelites spare the tribe of Benjamin despite their outrageous actions.

Before assessing these violent passages from an ethical perspective, it might be useful to situate the violence in the context of the ancient Near East. Ancient Israel was not the only ancient society that had a concept of the ban (ḥrm) and was certainly not the only society to discuss inflicting mass violence on foreigners and subjugated peoples. In the Mesha Stele, which dates to the mid-ninth century BCE, the king of Moab boasts that he executed the ban against Atarot and Nebo, in Israel.[16] Echoing the Israelite conquest of Jericho, Mesha brags that he slaughtered not only Israelite men and women but also slaves and even aliens (gr), as ḥrm for Moab's national god, Chemosh. He also took cult objects of Yahweh and presented them to his own god (compare Josh 6:19, 24). According to 2 Kgs 19:11, Assyrians routinely executed the ban (haḥărîm) against the peoples they conquered. While Assyrian texts do not describe a practice exactly like the Israelite and Moabite ḥrm, Assyrian kings certainly boasted about the mass killing, torture, and mutilation of enemies in the name of their national god, Assur. For example, Shalmaneser III says of one of his early campaigns:

> I besieged the city [of Aridu], captured (it), massacred many of his (people), (and) carried off booty from him. I erected a tower of heads in front of the city (and) burned their adolescent boys (and) girls.[17]

It is interesting that a biblical author would use an indigenous term, ḥrm, to understand Assyrian violence; it suggests that the conquest of Canaan is modeled on Assyrian conquest rhetoric.

In responding to these portrayals of violence, modern scholars sometimes note that the Canaanite conquest was not a historical event, and they often contend that passages advocating mass killing of Canaanites were created to promote the radical changes to the cult of Yahweh that Deuteronomistic writers supported.[18] Those who view the Canaanite conquest as fictional may also point to the similar language used to describe Israelites who violate Israelite religious or social mores,

[16] ANET, 320–321.

[17] A. K. Grayson, *Assyrian Rulers of the Early First Millennium BCE 858–745 BCE*, vol. 2, RIMA 3 (Toronto: University of Toronto Press, 1996), 14.

[18] See discussion in J. S. Kaminsky, "Did Election Imply Mistreatment of the Canaanites?" *HTR* 96 (2003): 403; Wills, *Not God's People*, 29–31.

suggesting that the Canaanite conquest is largely rhetorical and targeted at dissenters within Israel.

Yet the brutality in these texts requires explanation, especially since these texts have been used to justify atrocities committed by people who believe that they do, in fact, represent historical events. That some passages claim that the extermination of the Canaanites is unsuccessful does not change the fact that passages advocate the complete destruction of entire peoples – what a modern reader might label "genocide." "Genocide" is a modern term developed in the early twentieth century, which has the force of international law; Israelite texts, conversely, participate in a discourse of violence common to the ancient Near East. As modern cases attest, genocides are rarely successful in eliminating the targeted population entirely. They may, however, be successful in suppressing a people to the point that only small remnants remain (e.g., Native Americans, Armenians, European Jews) – precisely the image of the Canaanites that appears in Judges, for example. Contemporary human rights law does not limit the definition of genocide to acts of mass slaughter, but includes the intent to eradicate, even in part, an ethnic or national group by any means. Some biblical texts explicitly say that Israelites seek to destroy the religious and cultural practices of the Canaanites and to drive them from the land (Num 33:52–55; Deut 7:1–17). Additionally, genocide is not the only way to express profound ethnic violence. Supporters of African slavery – especially in the United States – relied on portrayals of the Canaanites, and their descent from Noah's son Ham, to justify the enslavement of blacks (Gen 9:20–27; 10:6–20).[19] Passages that depict Canaanites as a servant class, or passages that allow foreigners to be enslaved, were also useful for prominent proslavery interpreters, such as Josiah Priest.[20] These racist theologians typically identify their own conquering or enslaving society with ancient Israel.

But the Israelites' continued occupation of the land they conquered brutally was contingent on strict adherence to Yahweh's covenant. According to the Deuteronomistic History, they failed. The punishment for breaking the covenant is defeat and exile. The Deuteronomistic History promotes conquest, stereotyping, genocidal violence, enslavement of native peoples, and zealous loyalty to a national God. On the other hand, the Deuteronomistic History portrays Israel as a people who

[19]   J. Priest, *Bible Defence of Slavery; and Origin, Fortunes and History of the Negro Race*, (Glasgow: W. S. Brown, 1852), 174–202.

[20]   Priest, *Bible Defence*, 119, 149–50.

could not adhere to the very standards used to justify the extermination of the Canaanites. This profound contradiction, and the failure of Israel to sustain its occupation of the land, might suggest that the idea of a God who authorizes one nation's conquest and violence against other nations is ultimately incoherent and untenable.

10.4 INCLUSION OF NON-ISRAELITES

There are numerous depictions of foreigners in the Deuteronomistic History that portray them as members of ancient Israel's society, even if not fully enfranchised members. The resident alien is one example; another is the incorporation of the Canaanite Rahab and her kinfolk in the aftermath of the destruction of Jericho. According to this story, the Israelites spare Rahab and her family from the fiery demise of Jericho because she decided to hide Joshua and Caleb as they were spying on the city. Joshua 6:25 says that Rahab and her kin end up living "in the midst of Israel (*běqereb yiśrā'ēl*) until this day," indicating that the people of Rahab were thought to be an enduring presence among Israel. Nevertheless, Rahab and her family are placed outside of the Israelite war camp (Josh 6:23), suggesting that Rahab's relatives are not considered a part of the people of Israel even if they are "in the midst" of Israel. It is also possible that there is a stigma associated with Rahab's location, because war camp rules take great pains to exclude impurity from the camp (Deut 23:10–15 [ET 23:9–14]).[21]

Those who live among Israel but are not a part of Israel also include servant classes made up of the remnants of Canaanites not annihilated in the conquest (Josh 9:3–27; 16:10; Judg 1:27–36; 1 Kgs 9:21). Of particular note are the Gibeonites, a Canaanite group that makes a treaty with Joshua and the Israelites by pretending to be from a faraway land (and thus probably outside of the parameters of the ban, Deut 20:10–18). According to Josh 9:3–15, the treaty entails sparing the lives of the Gibeonites in exchange for their general servitude ('*ăbādêkā 'ănāḥnû*, 9:9, 11). When Joshua and the rest of the congregation of Israel discover the deceit of the Gibeonites, Joshua curses them to perpetual servitude as "hewers of wood and drawers of water" (Josh 9:21, 23, 27). While the Gibeonites are relegated to servitude, they are protected from extreme violence because of their treaty with Israel. When Saul violates this

---

[21] See also purity in the wilderness camp in Num 5:1–4 (H).

treaty, Yahweh imposes a three-year famine that can only be remedied by the execution of Saul's sons (2 Sam 21:1–9).

Other Canaanites said to live in the land of Israel after the conquest "until this day" include the Geshurites and Maacthites (Josh 13:13), the Jebusites (Josh 15:63; Judg 1:21), and various urban enclaves of "Hivvites and Canaanites" (2 Sam 24:6). The status of these various Canaanites is not always clear, but if the references to forced labor are any indication they seem to constitute a marginalized class. It is not clear whether they are considered "foreigners" (nokrî) or, as Canaanites, constitute a class unto themselves.

Notably, Philistines (Cherethites, Pelethites, Gittites), Hittites (one of the Canaanite nations), and other foreigners such as Cushites (Ethiopians) serve in the royal administration and the military (2 Sam 8:18; 11:2–26; 15:18–22; 18:2, 12, 21–32; 20:23; 1 Kgs 1:38, 44; compare Jer 38:7–13; 39:15–18). Foreign members of Israel's professional military can be depicted as extraordinarily loyal and righteous, as the examples of Uriah the Hittite and Ittai the Gittite demonstrate. Uriah (whose name suggests that he worships Yahweh) is so dedicated to David that he refuses to abandon the king even when David gives him leave. David wants Uriah to go home and sleep with his wife, Bathsheba, because David is trying to cover up an adulterous affair. Uriah's loyalty contrasts starkly with David's treachery and shows that foreigners – a Canaanite, no less – can display greater righteousness than even the king of Israel. Similarly, Ittai the Gittite, a military official in David's army, refuses to leave David's side even though David gives him permission to do so, in radical contrast to the rebellious behavior of David's own son, Absalom (2 Sam 15:19–22). Ironic passages in which the misbehavior of Israelites is brought into relief by foreigners – especially Canaanites – occur more than once. In the story about the Levite's concubine, the Levite avoids Jebus (Jerusalem), a city inhabited by the Jebusites, preferring to lodge among fellow Israelites in Benjamin (Judg 19:10–11). The disasters that follow on from this decision imply that the Levite might have been safer with the Canaanites. These positive portrayals of highly stigmatized foreigners, especially when juxtaposed with the scurrilous behavior of Israelites, clash with the extremely negative portrayals of them elsewhere, especially texts that call for their extermination because of their allegedly corrupting influence.

Some foreigners are able to access Israelite religion without becoming a member of Israelite society. First Kings 8:41–43, for example, asks Yahweh to listen to a foreigner (nokrî) who comes to the Temple in Jerusalem to supplicate him (compare Isa 56:3, 6–8). The Aramean general Naaman is another interesting example of a foreigner who participates in Israelite religion without joining Israelite society. Naaman sought Yahweh in order to heal his skin disease (2 Kings 5); after some minor disagreement this takes place, thanks to the intervention of the prophet Elisha. As a result, Naaman recognizes Yahweh as the only God on the entire earth and wishes to sacrifice only to Israel's God in the future. The pericope introduces a series of stories about Israel's and Judah's wars with the Arameans, beginning in 2 Kgs 6:8. Despite these ongoing conflicts, Naaman is not the only Aramean who seeks help from Israel's God: Ben-Hadad, another ailing Aramean king, also inquires of Yahweh through Elisha (2 Kgs 8:7–15).

These examples show the complications involved in forging and policing ethnic boundaries. Some texts set up a clear demarcation between Israelites and Canaanites, promoting hostility toward Canaanites for their allegedly foreign religious customs to the point of advocating their extermination. Other texts allow for the continued presence of Canaanites in the land; some even recognize that individual Canaanites can display more righteous behavior than Israelites. Additionally, foreigners whose nations are portrayed as hostile in certain texts, such as Philistines and Arameans, are nevertheless able to interact positively with Israelite society, by becoming part of the military or seeking the help of Israel's God.

10.5 CONCLUSION

The Hebrew Bible mandates an empathetic stance toward certain foreigners. Of particular note is that biblical texts group resident aliens with people recognized throughout the ancient Near East as vulnerable populations, such as widows, orphans, and the poor, who are entitled to special protection. If empathy constitutes a basis for ethics, these passages resonate with modern notions of justice for ethnic minorities, immigrants, and other marginalized groups. Yet, the depiction of the resident alien is not without complications. Resident aliens are portrayed as a dependent, subordinate class within Israel. Such depictions conflict with modern concepts of egalitarianism and opposition to social discrimination based on ethnicity.

Moreover, some passages advocate the complete extermination of foreigners such as the Canaanites and the Amalekites. Such passages fly in the face of contemporary models of human rights, especially the widely held opposition to ethnically based violence and the international abhorrence of genocide. They may also be offensive insofar as they expressly forbid any empathy toward such foreigners. Passages that advocate the extermination of the Canaanites because they might entice Israelites to engage in forbidden religious customs could also be seen as extreme stereotyping and as an unfair monolithic caricature of the people in question. Biblical texts also turn this extraordinarily violent rhetoric inward, but using rhetoric normally reserved for despised foreigners on (perceived) deviants in one's own community seems to buttress the hatred of foreigners and their customs rather than mitigate it.

In many cases, however, this rhetoric does not match the reality. The variety of ways in which foreigners are portrayed in the Hebrew Bible suggest that ancient Israelite writers struggled with how best to articulate ethnic boundaries, even as many passages make broad, seemingly inflexible pronouncements about ethnic groups. This apparent inconsistency reflects a truth about ethnic boundaries: Ethnicity can be fixed, immutable, and enduring in people's minds and in their rhetoric, but in practice it is fluid, unstable, and dependent on context. Conflicting passages about foreigners in the Hebrew Bible remind us that the task of organizing people into stable ethnic categories is fraught with difficulties and that on-the-ground realities will constantly disrupt attempts to place people in ethnic "boxes."

FURTHER READING

Grayson, A. K. *Assyrian Rulers of the Early First Millennium BCE 858–745 BCE.* Vol 2. RIMA 3. Toronto: University of Toronto Press, 1996.

Hoffman, M. L. *Empathy and Moral Development: Implications for Caring and Justice.* Cambridge: Cambridge University Press, 2000.

Kaminsky, J. S. "Did Election Imply Mistreatment of the Canaanites?" *HTR* 96 (2003): 397–425.

Lewy, H. "The Nuzian Feudal System (Concluded)." *Or* 11 (1942): 297–349.

Lewy, J. "Some Institutions of the Old Assyrian Empire." *HUCA* 27 (1957): 1–79.

Olyan, S. M. *Rites and Rank: Hierarchy in Biblical Representations of Cult.* Princeton: Princeton University Press, 2000.

Rainey, B. *Religion, Ethnicity and Xenophobia in the Bible: A Theoretical, Exegetical and Theological Survey.* London: Routledge, 2019.

Roth, M. T. *Law Collections from Mesopotamia and Asia Minor.* Atlanta: Scholars, 1995.

Simmons, A. "In Defense of the Moral Significance of Empathy." *Ethical Theory and Moral Practice* 17 (2014): 97–111.

Wills, L. M. *Not God's People: Insiders and Outsiders in the Biblical World.* Lantham: Rowman and Littlefield, 2008.

Part III

Prophetic Ethics

11   Religion and Ethics in Isaiah

BOHDAN HROBON

'It should never be forgotten that the prophetic demand was religious, and that it sprang from the conception of God'.[1] This essay aims to explore the relationship between religion and ethics, arguing that the ethical appeals in Isaiah were based on and prompted by largely the same conception of God and of religion as appear in the priestly literature of the Pentateuch. First, we sketch from the priestly sources the essence and the interrelatedness of certain key concepts, namely, rituals, holiness, and (im)purity. Second, we investigate the relationship of these concepts to ideas expressed in Isaiah.

11.1   PRIESTLY RELIGION AND ETHICS

Where there is religion, there is ritual: 'it is a mistake to suppose that there can be religion which is all interior, with no rules, no liturgy, no external signs of inward states. As with society, so with religion, external form is the condition of its existence'.[2] In the religion of ancient Israel, primary responsibility for performing and maintaining rituals was assigned to priests, whose priestly traditions are therefore naturally dominated by the description and prescription of cultic rituals such as purification and sacrifices.

De Vaux aptly described the purpose of such rituals as 'all those acts by which communities or individuals give outward expression to their

This essay is the result of research funded by the Czech Science Foundation as project GA ČR 18-01995S/P401, 'Cult and Politics in "Proto-Isaianic" Tradition. Divergence and Convergence of Hebrew and Greek Versions'.

[1]   H. H. Rowley, *The Faith of Israel: Aspects of Old Testament Thought* (London: SCM, 1956), 128.

[2]   M. Douglas, *Purity and Danger: An Analysis of Concept of Pollution and Taboo*, Routledge Classics (London: Routledge, [1966] 2002), 77.

religious life, by which they seek and achieve contact with God'.[3] Sacrifices are the most notable of such acts in the Old Testament. The main function of these is too often and too quickly identified, at least in Christian contexts, with atonement. Yet, 'just like a magic ceremony or prayer, which can serve at the same time as an act of thanksgiving, a vow, and a propitiation, sacrifice can fulfil a great variety of concurrent functions'.[4] Marx has persuasively argued that, according to priestly literature, the primary purpose of the sacrificial cult 'is to establish a relationship with YHWH by means of an offering', with different types of sacrifices serving this purpose differently.[5] Those that are 'of pleasing odor to the LORD',[6] such as the whole-offering (ʿolāh), cereal offering (minḥāh), and well-being offering (šelem), serve to establish communication with God. The function of those that atone, such as the purification offering (ḥaṭṭāʾt)[7] and the reparation offering (ʾāšām), is subsidiary, ritually purifying the worshipper before approaching God.

Such purification is necessary because God is holy; any impurity is offensive and repulsive to his holiness. Indeed, 'impurity and holiness are antonyms'.[8] A closer look at holiness illuminates this. Whereas modern understandings of holiness carry predominantly ethical connotations, holiness was originally a cultic notion. Only subsequently did an ethical meaning shape and infiltrate terms like Hebrew qōdeš, Greek agios, or Latin sanctus; their original substance was non-ethical (or ethically neutral) and non-rational, namely, a feeling-based response to the presence of divinity – the 'extra Something' in the meaning of 'holy', which Otto calls 'numinous'.[9] Holiness is the essential attribute of God, intrinsically connected with his presence and visibly manifested by his glory. With regard to people and the land one can only speak of derivative holiness: 'it was only in virtue of its relation to God as his property

[3] R. De Vaux, *Ancient Israel: Its Life and Institutions*, trans. John McHug (London: Darton Longman and Todd, 1961), 271.
[4] H. Hubert and M. Mauss, *Sacrifice: Its Nature and Function* (Chicago: University of Chicago Press, 1964), 97.
[5] A. Marx, 'The Theology of the Sacrifice According to Leviticus 1–7', in *The Book of Leviticus: Composition and Reception*, ed. R. Rendtorff, R. A. Kugler, and S. S. Bartel, VTSup 93 (Leiden: Brill, 2003), 111.
[6] Biblical quotations are from NRSV unless stated otherwise.
[7] ḥaṭṭāʾt is often rendered as 'sin offering', but compare Milgrom, 'Sin-Offering or Purification-Offering?', 237–9.
[8] J. Milgrom, *Leviticus 1–16*, AB 3 (New York: Doubleday, 1991), 46.
[9] See R. Otto, *The Idea of the Holy: An Inquiry into the Non-rational Factor in the Idea of the Divine and Its Relation to the Rational*, trans. J. W. Harvey, 2nd ed. (London: Oxford University Press, 1950), 5–7.

that anything became holy'.[10] Ethics enters the picture as one of the effects of this derivative holiness. As aptly put by Raphael:

> the sense of the numinous is 'translated' into the sense of the holy and one's proper duties towards it. Some of these duties will be ritual, others ethical, so that holiness and morality may come to overlap in the finite world. But this does not entail that the beginning and end of morality cannot, ultimately, be absorbed into the holy as its source and judge.[11]

From the perspective of divine holiness, it makes no difference whether an impurity is caused by a childbirth or a murder; both 'invade and contaminate the divine abode and ... unchecked they drive the divine Presence away'.[12] However, for cultic and ethical purposes it is important to distinguish between ritual impurity and moral impurity.[13] Sources of ritual impurity are generally natural and more or less unavoidable, such as childbirth (Lev 12:1–8), scale disease (Lev 13:1–14:32), genital discharges (Lev 15:1–33), the carcasses of certain impure animals (Lev 11:1–47), or human corpses (Num 19:10–22). Therefore, ritual impurity is not sinful and can be reversed straightforwardly by performing various purificatory procedures.[14]

The second kind of defilement, moral impurity, results 'from committing certain acts so heinous that they are explicitly referred to as defiling', such as certain sexual sins (e.g., Lev 18:24–30), idolatry (e.g., Lev 19:31; 20:1–3), or bloodshed (e.g., Num 35:33–34). These acts defile not only the sinner, but also the land and the temple. No ritual can purify moral impurity, and thus 'the defilement of sinners and the land by grave sins is, for all practical purposes, permanent'.[15] The reversal of this status is only possible for – and is solely up to – God. Without God's forgiveness, moral impurity brings permanent separation from God:

---

[10]   O. R. Jones, *The Concept of Holiness* (London: Allen and Unwin, 1961), 107.

[11]   M. Raphael, *Rudolf Otto and the Concept of Holiness* (Oxford: Clarendon, 1997), 130.

[12]   B. J. Schwartz, 'The Bearing of Sin in the Priestly Literature', in *Pomegranates and Golden Bells: Studies in Biblical, Jewish and Near Eastern Ritual, Law, and Literature in Honor of Jacob Milgrom*, ed. D. P. Wright, D. N. Freedman, and A. Hurvitz (Winona Lake: Eisenbrauns, 1995), 4–5.

[13]   These cathegories were suggested by J. Klawans. For a survey of studies that categorize impurity in the priestly tradition on the same basis but use different labels, see J. Klawans, *Impurity and Sin in Ancient Judaism* (New York: Oxford University Press, 2000), 3–20.

[14]   Klawans, *Impurity and Sin*, 23.

[15]   Klawans, *Impurity and Sin*, 26 and 31.

death and exile.[16] This perspective rearranges our understanding of the relationships between these concepts: 'It might seem to us that impurity was treated as a "sin", but the reverse is probably the case: to break ethical norms is a form of impurity and impairs the holiness of Israel before the holy God'.[17]

We may sum up as follows. First, the main purpose of rituals – and of the sacrificial cult in particular – was to attract and maintain God's presence among the people. Second, because God is holy, his presence requires purity of the people, the land, and the temple. Third, some impurity can be removed by purificatory rituals, but no ritual can cleanse the impurity caused by such grave sins as idolatry, murder, or adultery (i.e., moral impurity). Moral impurity defiles not only the sinner, but also the land and the temple and, unless blotted away by God (forgiveness), results in separation from God through punishments including death and exile; it thereby reverses the communion with God that rituals produce.

II.2 RELIGION AND ETHICS IN ISAIAH

Comparing this sketch of priestly ethics and religion with the picture of religion and ethics presented by Isaiah must take into consideration that the book as we have it covers over two hundred years of Israel's and Judah's history. These centuries were full of dramatic events and radical changes. One helpful navigation device throughout this complex material is the division of the book into the three parts: Proto-Isaiah (PI, chapters 1–39), containing words associated with the eighth-century BCE prophet Isaiah; Deutero-Isaiah (DI, chapters 40–55), the work of an anonymous sixth-century prophet written during the Babylonian exile; and Trito-Isaiah (TI, chapters 56–66), composed shortly after the return from the exile. As these historicised descriptions indicate, the prophets spoke by and large to their contemporaries, addressing their immediate state of affairs. Therefore, the following enquiry is undertaken in stages, mindful of these backgrounds. Within the present confines, we will examine one exemplary text from each part of the book: Isaiah 1; Isa 43:22–28; and Isaiah 58. These texts represent a serious

---

[16] Apparently, moral impurity as defined above blurs the modern distinction between cult and ethics, for, even if the cause can be ethical, its effect is cultic.

[17] Cyril Rodd, *Glimpses of a Strange Land: Studies in Old Testament Ethics*, Old Testament Studies (Edinburg, T & T Clark, 2001) 8. As he concludes there, 'securing holiness in Israel requires both obedience to the ethical norms and upholding ritual purity'.

challenge to the thesis that the prophets understood religion in a manner essentially identical to that of the priests.

Religion and Ethics in Proto-Isaiah

Chapters 1–39 reflect the ministry of 'Isaiah son of Amoz' (1:1) who lived and prophesied in Jerusalem in the second half of the eighth century. He was an adamant advocate of applying God's law and justice to interpersonal relationships. He fiercely criticised the rich and powerful, including the judges, priests, and kings. He respected a hierarchical ordering of society (king first; then nobility, priests and prophets; then everybody else), but put God above all. God alone could be 'high and lofty' (6:1). Isaiah therefore proclaimed judgement against any form of human pride or arrogance, including reliance on something or someone other than God. He rebuked King Ahaz for turning to Assyria when threatened by the Syro-Ephraimite coalition (7:1–25) and commended King Hezekiah for trusting only in God when surrounded by the Assyrians (37:21–38). The later episode is a rare exception among an otherwise gloomy picture of Israel, Judah, and surrounding nations. The disasters of which Isaiah warned constituted not only punishment for religious and ethical misconduct but also means of restoration, via lessons of God's superiority and sublimity.

Although Proto-Isaiah is full of texts concerning ethical conduct, its first chapter epitomises the relationship between religion and ethics: it concerns loving God (the core of religion) and loving neighbour (the core of ethics). In a form resembling ancient Near Eastern lawsuits, Isaiah describes the people's failures in these two fundamental relationships, vitally interrelated and deeply misunderstood and ignored by his audience.

To make his point, Isaiah uses two images. The first (1:2b) is of a parent and his rebellious children. Such behaviour by the children is totally unacceptable. According to Torah, it even deserves capital punishment (Deut 21:18–21), because it threatens the very fundaments of society. It is not only immoral, but very stupid – as becomes even more apparent in the second image (1:3), borrowed from agriculture: even an ox or a donkey seems to have more common sense than the people of God!

Isaiah 1:4–9 yields what may be the most disturbing diagnosis of the nation in the whole Bible: full of sin and guilt, corrupt in every part and in every way. This is even more shocking in light of the title 'the Holy One of Israel'. Holiness requires purity; because God is holy, Israel is summoned to cleanliness. Instead, this 'sinful nation is laden with iniquity', impure through and through – 'from the sole of the foot even to the head' (1:6). In this context, 'the Holy One of Israel' not only sounds like an oxymoron but presents a grave danger to Israel, because impurity and holiness do not mix. As God's other title – 'the LORD of hosts' (1:9) – implies, God takes drastic measures to deal with impurity. It would be both reasonable and self-preserving for his people to strive for purification – but Israel is anything but reasonable. Bent on self-destruction, despite their 'bruises and sores and bleeding wounds' (1:6), the people 'do evil, deal corruptly, have forsaken the LORD, have despised the Holy One of Israel, are utterly estranged, ... seek further beatings', and 'continue to rebel' (1:4–5).

Further indictment is spelled out in Isa 1:10–17. There is no better place to illustrate the problem of impurity than the temple, where God and the people meet face to face. Yet the first part of this passage (1:11–15) has been frequently misunderstood, because it appears to be critical of – even hostile to – rituals. This is juxtaposed with a commendation of virtuous ethical behaviour in Isa 1:16–17, creating an impression that ethical behaviour is preferred over cult. Paradoxically, the message of this passage is probably the very opposite. A closer look yields the following picture: the people of Israel are gathering for 'solemn assemblies' (1:13), seeking communion with the LORD via cultic means designed for this very purpose – 'sacrifices', 'offerings', 'prayers', and other rituals (1:11–15). They come 'to appear before' him (1:12, lit. 'to see his face'), the ultimate exposure of humans to God's holiness. In this moment, the people's impurity – caused by 'iniquity' (1:13) and murder (1:15, lit. 'hands full of blood') – turns their sacrifices, offerings, and even their prayers into 'an abomination' (1:13). They thus accomplish the exact opposite of the ritual's purpose, as the LORD 'hides' his 'eyes' from the people (1:15). Isaiah, aware of the disastrous effect of such cultic practice, calls for the people's purity (1:16, 'wash yourselves; make yourselves clean'). He must also have been aware that impurity already incurred through murder, idolatry, and other grave sins could not be removed by ritual. Nevertheless, he calls for the termination of its causes, namely, the unethical conduct of the people (1:16–17), and aches for their purification. Isaiah's ultimate concern is the people's fellowship with the Holy One (as materialised in rituals) and his presence in the people's midst. The major impediment to this is cultic practice that mixes impurity with holiness, as expressed in the key phrase of the passage: 'I cannot endure solemn assemblies with iniquity' (1:13).

The words in Isa 1:18 about 'sins' that are 'red like crimson' or 'like scarlet' recall the 'hands full of blood' (1:15) and represent the impurity of which the people are guilty. As noted, this moral impurity cannot be removed by human effort; only God can turn the redness of such sins into the whiteness of purity and holiness. What people can do, however, is to stop 'rebelling' (1:2) and begin to be 'willing and obedient' (1:19–20) 'to the Lord' (LXX). This is not just a matter of proper religious practice, but a choice between good life ('you shall eat the good of the land', 1:19) and violent death ('you shall be devoured by the sword', 1:20).

The rest of Isaiah 1 develops the themes of the first part: Israel's impurity, its sources, and how the LORD will deal with it. In one last indictment (1:21–23), the prophet expresses amazement and grief over the gross difference between the former and the present state of Jerusalem. The ideal of the past is described as 'the faithful city', characterised by 'justice' and 'righteousness'. These two terms appear throughout the book as insignia of perfect rulership. Since God is just and righteous, his people and their rulers should 'maintain justice and do what is right' (56:1). But now, they are 'murderers' (1:21), 'rebels and companions of thieves' (1:23), doing the very opposite of what their God is about. This is, in metaphor, mixing 'wine with water', or 'silver' becoming 'dross' (1:22). Mixing holiness with impurity is what turns the once 'faithful city' into a 'whore' (1:21) and the people of God into his 'enemies' and 'foes' (1:24) – just as their sacrifices and offerings were turned into abominations (1:11–15). 'Therefore', the verdict is drastic, definite, and sure to be executed, as the invocation of the titles 'Sovereign', 'LORD of hosts', and 'Mighty One of Israel' confirm (1:24–25). Yet, the goal is not extermination but radical purification for the future pronounced in Isa 1:26. God's holy presence will abide in 'the city of righteousness, the faithful city' that will be run by God-like 'judges' and 'counsellors'.

The final verses compound the impurity with idolatry. Though idols or foreign gods are not explicitly mentioned, idolatrous cult practices are implied by references to 'the oaks' and 'the gardens' where it took place (1:29, cf. 57:5; 65:3; 66:17). In addition, the Hebrew verb ḥmd, translated here as 'delighted', also means 'to covet' – as in the last commandments of the Decalogue (Exod 20:17; Deut 5:21). The problem is not one of liking things, but of putting one's hopes and faith in it. Idolatry is clinging to someone or something other than God.

Religion and ethics in this material may be summed up as follows. The people live in their land and worship in the temple, but their sins are polluting them, the land, and the temple with moral impurity – and this is reaching the point of intolerability for God. This impurity also means that rituals designed to attract and maintain God's presence are counter-productive. The only way the people can prevent – or at least delay – judgement is to adopt ethical behaviour, so as not to increase impurity further.

Religion and Ethics in Deutero-Isaiah

The tenor of chapters 40–55 is substantially different, as established by the first verse: 'Comfort, O comfort my people, says your God' (40:1). This portion of the book speaks to the people in Babylonian captivity, around 150 years after events described in the previous chapters. Deutero-Isaiah comforts his weary people by announcing the impending end of exile. Moreover, he builds up their courage by explicating God's plan of deliverance and portraying the Holy One of Israel as the almighty one and only Lord of the whole universe, capable of carrying out his plans for salvation. The prophet praises the LORD over all other gods, whom he considers merely the impotent products of human hands. One of the signs of God's universal sovereignty is his use of Cyrus, the king of Persia, as 'his anointed' (45:1). An even greater role is assigned to the 'servant', called to 'bring forth justice' and to be 'a light to the nations' (42:1; 49:6), as a wise and gracious ruler. This mission, however, involves misapprehension and contempt, even condemnation, and pain and grief inflicted by his own people. Even more shocking is that his suffering is vicarious (53:5) and his vindication is divine – 'he shall be high and lofty' (52:13; cf. 6:1).

The concept of the servant, especially in 52:13–53:12, takes religion and ethics to a new level. It is clearly out of the box – 'Who has believed what we have heard?' (53:1) – and runs against the theology that God blesses the righteous and curses the wicked. Moreover, it seems grossly unjust for the righteous to suffer for the wicked and for the wicked to be declared innocent because of this suffering. Yet, even this supra-ethics (whose closer definition would require a separate study) is deeply related to cult. As Blenkinsopp has recently argued, the Hebrew term 'šm in 53:10 'refers to the sacrificial ritual of the guilt offering'; he therefore concludes that 'the suffering and death of this Servant of the LORD is to be understood as sacrificial by analogy with the ritual of the guilt or reparation offering in the book of Leviticus'.[18]

There is otherwise very little concerning the people's religious or ethical practices in Deutero-Isaiah. While conditions for religious practices must have been very limited without the temple, one would expect an appeal akin to that of Trito-Isaiah: for the people to do the best they

---

[18]   J. Blenkinsopp, 'The Sacrificial Life and Death of the Servant (Isaiah 52:13–53:12)', *VT* 66 (2016): 1.

can under the circumstances, religiously and ethically, to enhance the chances of God's deliverance. Deutero-Isaiah, however, seems to accept that 'all we like sheep have gone astray; we have all turned to our own way' (53:6); thus God has decided to use the servant for his salvific plan instead. The role of the people and their lack of religious and ethical activities are addressed in Isa 43:22–28.

This passage has often been mistreated as a judgement oracle,[19] by which 'Yahweh rebukes Israel for not bringing offering and sacrifices'.[20] Such an accusation is unlikely if this passage is addressed to the people in exile, where practising Yahwism was constrained by the circumstances. Even the text itself speaks against such interpretation, as God asserts, 'I have not burdened you with offerings, or wearied you with frankincense' (43:23b). Furthermore, it goes against the grain for God to accuse his people of not practising rituals to the point that they weary themselves (43:22), of not buying expensive 'sweet cane' (43:24), and not soaking him in the fat of their sacrifices (43:24).[21] Finally, charging people with miserliness in the cultic sphere – or even reluctance – when they had 'burdened' God with their 'sins' and 'wearied' him with their 'iniquities' (43:24b) misses the mark, regardless of geographical or political context. Such behaviour would make any sacrificial cult invalid; the more lavish one would appear even more preposterous. Booij is right to conclude that 'the opinion that in Isaiah 43 Israel is reproved on account of its sacrifices, to the effect that it is blamed of cultic neglect, is probably the most serious misunderstanding of this text'.[22]

It makes better sense to read Isa 43:22–28 as a 'theological dispute concerning the basis for Israel's future deliverance'.[23] Isaiah 43:22–24 is not an accusation, but a description. Israel did not outdo itself in worshipping God; the only activity in which Jacob/Israel outdid itself was burdening God with its people's sins and wearing him with their iniquities. Isaiah 43:27–28 provides a list of reasons why Israel is bound to fail the challenge 'to set forth your case, so that you may be proved right' (43:26). Israel's 'first ancestor sinned' and its subsequent leaders

[19] Watts declares that Isa 43:22–28 'is cast in the form of a judgment as virtually everyone ... has recognized', J. D. W. Watts, *Isaiah 34–66*, WBC 25 (Waco: Word, 1987), 143.

[20] W. Brueggemann, *Isaiah 40–66* (Louisville: Westminster John Knox, 1998), 61.

[21] For this rendering, see B. Hrobon, *Ethical Dimension of Cult in the Book of Isaiah*, BZAW 418 (Berlin: de Gruyter, 2010), 125–30, 141–6.

[22] T. Booij, 'Negation in Isaiah 43:22–24', *ZAW* 92 (1982): 390–400.

[23] R. F. Melugin, *The Formation of Isaiah 40–55*, BZAW 141 (Berlin: de Gruyter, 1976), 49.

('your interpreters') 'transgressed against' God (43:27).[24] Moreover, the present leadership has been 'profaned', with Jacob turned into an impurity and Israel into a blasphemy (43:28).[25] The oracle makes clear to the people that they have no justification: neither their present or past moral actions (43:24b, 27), nor their present cultic activities or cultic status (43:22–24a, 28). Isaiah 43:25 should then be read in contrast: as already argued by Calvin, God

> contrasts his mercy with all other causes, as if he declared that he is not induced by anything else to pardon sins, but is satisfied with his mere goodness, and, consequently, that it is wrong to ascribe either to merits or to any sacrifices the redemption of which he is the Author by free grace.[26]

Isaiah 43:22–28 thus depicts Israel's cultic activities as inadequate, with their cultic status the opposite of holiness. Moreover, no claim to righteousness can be derived from past or present; it is annulled by sin from the beginning, throughout history, and into the present. It suggests that neither the religious practice nor the ethical behaviour of Israel could reverse the situation that resulted from its sin. It is exclusively God's forgiveness and his holy status that abolish sin and make salvation possible.[27] In this soteriological disputation, the omnipotence of God is contrasted with the impotence of Israel, and the holiness of God with the impurity of Jacob.

This lesson is consistent with priestly teaching: sin and transgression lead to desecration and cause impurity that can be removed by neither rituals nor ethics. Moral impurity can be put aright only by God's grace and only for his own sake. The good news of Deutero-Isaiah for Israel is that God is about to forgive their sins and deliver them from the oppression.

Religion and Ethics in Trito-Isaiah

Visions of Zion's future occur also in the third part of the book (especially Isa 60–62). However, most of Trito-Isaiah reflects the

---

[24] The Hebrew term *mĕlîṣêkā*, translated as 'your interpreters', may refer to the nation's prophets, priests, and/or kings.

[25] For this rendering, see Hrobon, *Ethical Dimension of Cult*, 135–40.

[26] Calvin, *Isaiah*, Crossway Classic Commentaries (Wheaton: Crossway, 2000), 348–9.

[27] As Goldingay points out with reference to Isa 43:25, '"for YHWH's [name's] sake" ... is the consideration that comes into play when there is no other to appeal to' (J. Goldingay and D. F. Payne, *A Critical and Exegetical Commentary on Isaiah 40–55*, ICC [London: T&T Clark, 2006], 313).

disillusionment of the returnees from Babylon over the difference between expectations and reality. According to Trito-Isaiah, the main reason for their hopes' lack of fulfilment is spiritual and moral decline: the people's idolatry, syncretism, and religious formalism, along with social injustice, violence, and lack of concern for one's neighbour, have upset the realisation of Deutero-Isaiah's vision of life with God in the land. Yet, there seems to be a handful of the faithful, who cling to the eschatological message of the prophet despite oppression by their own people (66:5). Because they 'are contrite and humble in spirit', 'the high and lofty one who inhabits eternity' promises to 'dwell also with' them (57:15).

There is no better passage in Trito-Isaiah to demonstrate the relationship of religion and ethics than Isaiah 58. Before turning to this text, a closer look at two religious practices that come to prominence during and after the exile is useful: fasting and the Sabbath.

Herr rightly observes that many biblical passages indicate that 'fasting is basically an act of penance, a ritual expression of remorse, submission, and supplication'.[28] However, fasting itself never has an expiatory function.[29] Rather, its main purpose was to evoke God's (favourable) attention (Jer 14:12a; cf. Isa 58:2–3). Because 'one's demeanor toward God should be commensurate with one's demeanor toward one's fellow human beings', 'social action constitutes an expression of true fasting'.[30]

The social character of Sabbath observance is explicit (Deut 5:14; Exod 23:12). The rationale in Deut 5:15 – 'Remember that you were a slave in the land of Egypt . . . therefore the LORD your God commanded you to keep the sabbath day' – and the fact that references to exodus are often used as motivators of social justice (Deut 24:18–22; 10:19; Exod 23:9; Lev 19:34) underline the ethical dimension of Sabbath. This becomes even more apparent when one understands Sabbath as a *quality* of time or activity. This brings into discussion other religious festivals that involve the Sabbath: the Day of Atonement (Lev 16:31; 23:32), New Year's day (Lev 23:24), the first and the eighth days of the Feast of Booths (Lev 23:39), and the Sabbath year (Lev 25:4–5). The ethical dimension of these festivals is manifest. Thus, for example, Deuteronomy gives deliverance from slavery in Egypt as the rationale

---

[28] M. D. Herr, 'Fasting', *EncJud* 6:1190.

[29] As Preuss correctly points out, 'fasting is not attested in the OT as an atonement ritual', H. D. Preuss, 'צום', *TDOT* 12:298.

[30] Preuss, 'צום,' 12:300.

for the Sabbath year (15:15) as well as for keeping the Sabbath (5:15). The Sabbath year – with its extension in the year of jubilee – puts a special emphasis on this social aspect, demanding concern for the hungry (Exod 23:11), remission of debts (Deut 15:1), setting the slaves free (Deut 15:12), and so on. The Sabbath day functions as a weekly celebration of the same principles, representing the intersection of religious practice and ethical behaviour.

Isaiah 58 uses fasting and Sabbath observance to illuminate this relationship, as it responds to the people's question about God's apparent lack of response to their fasting (58:3a). The problem is not with God's ability nor with his willingness or readiness to act; nor is it an issue with the object of people's desires (58:2) or the people's cultic expressions (58:5).[31] The problem is the people's 'rebellion' and 'their sins' (58:1b), which most likely consist of their disregard for righteousness and justice (58:2). This is the result of selfish desires (58:3b, 13), documented most visibly in the ill-treatment of the weaker members of society (58:3b–4, 6–7, 9b–10a). Yet, since 'the LORD of hosts is exalted by justice, and the Holy God shows himself holy by righteousness' (5:16), the positive manifestation of his presence in the midst of people who pervert justice and righteousness is impossible. Pursuing one's 'own interests' on God's 'holy day' (58:13) is a serious distortion of Yahwism, missing its ethical dimension. Fasting thus 'will not make your voice heard on high' (58:4b), for this would suggest that God consecrates this distorted image.[32]

The prophet emphasises the social dimension of fasting and Sabbath not at the expense of but alongside their cultic dimension. Williamson aptly summarises the need for such a message:

> Just as ceremony can easily degenerate into a purely personal and self-satisfying activity of the ghetto, so the practice of ethics can become an independent goal in itself, divorced from its biblical roots in a proper relationship with God. Neither is correct, according to this chapter. Rather, the point is to establish both on a proper footing.[33]

---

[31] The possibility of fulfilment of these desires is indicated in Isa 58:8–9a, 10b–12, 14.

[32] For more arguments along these lines, see H. Schüngel-Straumann, *Gottesbild und Kultkritik vorexilischer Propheten*, Stuttgarter Bibelstudien 60 (Stuttgart: KBW Verlag, 1972).

[33] H. G. M. Williamson, 'Promises, Promises! Some Exegetical Reflections on Isaiah 58'. *WW* 19 (1999), 158.

Trito-Isaiah, like Proto-Isaiah, believes that ethical behaviour and cultic practice are two sides of the same coin. He likely agrees with Deutero-Isaiah that this coin cannot buy salvation; God saves for his own sake, out of grace alone. Yet the people can obtain a very precious commodity for it – communion with the LORD. When a purified people are back in a purified land, rebuilding their religious and social life, the conditions of time and space are right for God to live in the midst of his people. God's presence remains an act of grace, for it was he who granted these conditions and chose to abide among the people in this land. Nevertheless, his presence creates conditions for the people and the land: the only way to live with the Holy One is to remain pure, because holiness and impurity do not mix. This God-with-us element accounts for the positive role of ethics as well as of religion in Trito-Isaiah.

11.3 CONCLUSIONS AND IMPLICATIONS

The exact function of religious practice and ethical behaviour varies in the book of Isaiah depending on the state of affairs and the issue at stake, clearly demonstrating 'that the mission of the prophet is dependent on the conditions of time and space'.[34] Yet, the underlying assumptions about the essence and the interrelatedness of concepts like rituals, holiness, and (im)purity appear largely unchanged, and compatible with their definitions in the priestly traditions. Indeed, reading this material in light of the priestly literature renders them more intelligible, as the priestly perspective makes clear that simply to label them critical of the cult is wrong, and even that the idea that they favour ethics over ritual is misleading. The book's understanding of the value of ritual and the significance of purity and holiness is essentially the same as in Torah. Mixing ritual behaviour with the impurity caused by the sinful behaviour of the people poses a grave danger. These texts' passionate cry for ethical behaviour and the purity for which such behaviour constitutes a prerequisite resulted from an understanding of this fact and from a desire to maintain the presence of the Holy One of Israel in the people's midst. We should speak not of ethics as a separate category, but rather of the ethical dimension of religion.

This understanding of Isaiah's ethics presents serious challenges as well as opportunities for practitioners of modern Judaism and Christianity. The main challenge is to connect ethics to religion in such a way

---

[34] J. Jensen, *Ethical Dimensions* (Collegeville: Liturgical, 2006), 159.

that loving one's neighbour would result from loving God – from the desire to be with him here and now. This necessitates making a 'distinction between the holy and the common' and teaching 'the difference between the unclean and the clean' (Ezek 22:26). The challenge is not to reinstitute ancient dietary laws or dress codes, but to consider all that people do, as a community and as individuals, from the perspective of divine holiness, and to eliminate everything that upsets God's presence in their midst.

The distinct emphases of the three parts of the book of Isaiah with regard to religion and ethics also have potential implications. Proto-Isaiah reminds us to take religion seriously, including its external forms – liturgy, songs, prayers, festivals, and so on. The quest for less formal alternatives to traditional forms of worship is understandable but often misguided. Forms of worship as such are not the problem; they are merely external signs of the inward states of worshippers – their sign-language to God, if you will. If the worshipper is impure, even the purest forms of that language is profane to the holy God.

Trito-Isaiah warns especially of the dangers of separating religion and ethics. Religious communities that confine expressions of faith to rituals conducted on their premises cut themselves from the outside world and thereby from its Creator. If we want to fully enjoy communion with the Creator, we must learn how to serve creation in its midst.

Last but not least, Deutero-Isaiah reminds us that what ultimately matters is God's grace; proper religion and ethics are only our grateful responses to it. The good news is that God will not deal with us according to our religio-ethical practices, but 'according to his mercy, according to the abundance of his steadfast love' (Isa 63:7).

FURTHER READING

Blenkinsopp, J. 'The Sacrificial Life and Death of the Servant (Isaiah 52:13–53:12)'. *VT* 66 (2016): 1–14.

Booij, T. 'Negation in Isaiah 43:22–24'. *ZAW* 94 (1982): 390–400.

Douglas, M. *Purity and Danger: An Analysis of Concept of Pollution and Taboo.* Routledge Classics. London: Routledge, [1966] 2002.

Hrobon, B. *Ethical Dimension of Cult in the Book of Isaiah.* BZAW 418. Berlin: de Gruyter, 2010.

Hubert, H. and M. Mauss. *Sacrifice: Its Nature and Function.* Chicago: University of Chicago Press, 1964.

Jensen, J. *Ethical Dimensions of the Prophets.* Collegeville: Liturgical, 2006.

Jones, O. R. *The Concept of Holiness.* London: Allen and Unwin, 1961.

Klawans, J. *Impurity and Sin in Ancient Judaism.* New York: Oxford University Press, 2000.

Rodd, C. S. *Glimpses of a Strange Land: Studies in Old Testament Ethics*. OTS. Edinburgh: T & T Clark, 2001.

Schwartz, B. J. 'The Bearing of Sin in the Priestly Literature'. Pages 3–21 in *Pomegranates and Golden Bells: Studies in Biblical, Jewish and Near Eastern Ritual, Law, and Literature in Honor of Jacob Milgrom*. Edited by D. P. Wright, D. N. Freedman, and A. Hurvitz. Winona Lake: Eisenbrauns, 1995.

Williamson, H. G. M. 'Promises, Promises! Some Exegetical Reflections on Isaiah 58'. *WW* 19 (1999): 153–60.

12 Covenant in the Book of Jeremiah

ELSE K. HOLT

Ethics is not the main problem in the book of Jeremiah. The professor who wants to prepare for teaching a course on ethics in the prophetic books would rather begin in the book of Amos, where social matters are of the utmost importance for the religious message, a book that from the outset has very little in common with the book of Jeremiah. Or she would go to the book of Hosea, where religious and social issues are ingeniously combined. In Jeremiah, apostasy and the pursuant divine punishment are far more important matters. This does not mean that ethics is of no importance in Jeremiah, but ethics in general is a derivative from the central issue, namely, the question of theodicy in the wake of the catastrophes in 597 and 587 BCE and the Babylonian exile.

12.1 EXILE AND TRAUMA

It is commonplace in today's scholarly community to date the composition of the book of Jeremiah in the exilic and postexilic periods, and there is no need to repeat the discussion here. There is no reason, either, to argue for the problems of identifying the *ipsissima verba*, the indisputably original words of the prophet, in the book of Jeremiah. These questions have been meticulously discussed in the commentaries and in scholarly articles since Robert P. Carroll's epoch-making commentary from 1986.[1] In what follows, the exilic and postexilic dating will be taken for granted. Carroll's aim was to warn against a naive belief in the book's own claims of a Jeremian authorship; the only connection between the book and its alleged author, according to Carroll, derived from secondary editorial interpolations and was thus not to be considered historical information. On this reading, the prophet disappears as a historical person, and his historical framework, as described in the

---

[1] R. P. Carroll, *Jeremiah: A Commentary* (London: SCM, 1986).

book, turns more or less into a scholarly fata morgana. Instead, the book of Jeremiah (MT) should be considered the result of a long compositional growth; though this might have begun with the memory of the message of a historical prophet, this is now almost impossible to identify. Over time and translations, the book of Jeremiah has developed into its present, final form, reflecting issues and discussions from at least four centuries.

Its ethical discourse thus reflects issues from the early exilic to the Persian period. Common to these periods is the imprint of trauma.[2] Biblical scholars borrow the term "trauma" from psychology and sociology; some scholars understand it as a development of the psychological diagnosis post-traumatic stress disorder (PTSD) and propose a reading of the texts based on the impact on the text of the author's individual psychological profile. With the aforementioned caution against the identification of the voice of the historical Jeremiah taken into consideration, this approach is fraught with insecurities in the case of the book of Jeremiah. At best, such an approach leads to a psychological profile of the implied author or of the literary persona, or both: the "prophet Jeremiah." The traces of trauma in the book of Jeremiah are better understood as expressions of communal or collective trauma.

Applying the American sociologist Jeffrey C. Alexander's concept of "cultural trauma," the book of Jeremiah can be understood as an example of a society's attempt to cope with a traumatizing event.[3] In seeking to understand the collapse of their worldview, a society's members look for healing. This especially is the case among so-called "carrier groups," who have the responsibility and intellectual resources to contemplate the past and future of the traumatized community.

---

[2] On trauma as hermeneutical lens in Hebrew Bible research see E. Boase and C. G. Frechette, "Defining 'Trauma' as a Useful Lens for Biblical Interpretation," in *Bible Through the Lens of Trauma*, ed. E. Boase and C. G. Frechette (Atlanta: Society of Biblical Literature, 2016), 1–23; D. Carr, *Holy Resilience: The Bible's Traumatic Origins* (New Haven: Yale University Press, 2014); K. M. O'Connor, *Jeremiah: Pain and Promise* (Minneapolis: Fortress, 2011); L. Stulman, "Reflections on the Prose Sermons in the Book of Jeremiah: Duhm's and Mowinckel's Contributions to Contemporary Trauma Readings," in *Bible Through the Lens of Trauma*, ed. E. Boase and C. G. Frechette (Atlanta: Society of Biblical Literature, 2016), 125–39.

[3] J. C. Alexander, "Toward a Theory of Cultural Trauma," in *Cultural Trauma and Collective Identity*, ed. J. C. Alexander (Berkeley: University of California Press 2004), 1–30; J. C. Alexander, *Trauma: A Social Theory* (Cambridge: Polity, 2012). For an application of Alexander's theories to the book of Jeremiah, see E. K., Holt, "Daughter Zion: Trauma, Cultural Memory and Gender in OT Poetics," in *Trauma and Traumatization in Individual and Collective Dimensions: Insights from Biblical Studies and Beyond*, SANt 2 (Göttingen: Vandenhoeck & Ruprecht, 2014), 162–76.

Alexander defines carrier groups as groups of influential persons who "broadcast symbolic representations – characterizations – of ongoing social events, past, present, and future," and present a "claim to some fundamental injury, and exclamation of some sacred value, a narrative about a horrible destructive social process, and a demand for emotional, institutional, and symbolic reparation and reconstruction."[4]

In the book of Jeremiah, the collective trauma identified by the carrier group – scribes and scholars of the exilic and postexilic ages – is basically understood in terms of the people's forsaking of their obligation to the one, national God, YHWH. Though collected, composed, and recomposed over two to four centuries, the basic problem in Jeremiah remains the relationship between the people's responsibility for the collapse of Jerusalem and God's responsibility. The book of Jeremiah, in all its multilayered appearance, is a theodicy *and* a soul-searching by the people. The answers to the questions are diverse and run in all directions; the heavily redacted book of Jeremiah can be compared to a *Reader's Digest* of the theologies of the entire Hebrew Bible. One of these is the Deuteronomistic theology, which – put very simplistically – works as a redactional backbone of the book. With this Deuteronomism comes the concept of covenant, to which we now turn.[5]

12.2 RELIGIOUS AND ETHICAL TRANSGRESSIONS

In a modern – at least Christian – context, religious transgressions may be easily confused with ethical misdemeanors. To be a person of religion is thought to mean being a person of a certain moral standard (though reality often proves differently). This is only partly the case in the Hebrew Bible, where religious orthodoxy is often closely connected to adherence to cultic rules that should not be confused with ethical or moral instructions. Many of these instructions are written in the Torah and thus belong to divine teaching. Alongside such cultic matters, however, are ethical instructions conceived as a consequence of the covenant – symbolized by the placing of the Decalogue right after the epiphany at Sinai (Exodus 19–20), followed by the record of the making of the covenant in Exodus 24. The message of the parallel text in Deuteronomy is the same: "I am the LORD your God, who brought you out of the land of Egypt, out of the house of slavery" (Deut 5:6).

---

[4] Alexander, "Cultural Trauma," 11.
[5] See L. Stulman, *Order amid Chaos: Jeremiah as Symbolic Tapestry* (Sheffield: Sheffield Academic, 1998).

The commandments and rules of conduct that follow are thus set within the history between God and his people. Ethics in the Hebrew Bible is grounded in the will of God as a matter of revelation. This is symbolized most prominently by the concept of covenant, the most forceful metaphor for the divine demand for exclusivity.

This image of ethics as simply a matter of direct divine revelation, however, is too simplistic. As John Barton states, "The biblical writers often argue from what is apparent on the basis of the nature of human life in society."[6] From a historical perspective, much of the ethical material in the Hebrew Bible is based on common rules of conduct and on knowledge of what will breach the natural order of things. Indeed, this includes the commands in the Decalogue, read without the introductory verses (Exod 20:1–11; Deut 5:6–15). Nevertheless, in the context of torah and in the book of Jeremiah, all such regulations are set within a covenantal framework.

12.3 YHWH'S DEMAND FOR EXCLUSIVITY

YHWH's demand for exclusivity is a constitutive element in the book of Jeremiah; the people must worship YHWH and YHWH alone, if they want to stay in the land that he has given them and where he brought them in the days of their ancestors.[7] One of the basic accusations against Judah is that it has forsaken (ʿāzab, Jer 1:16; 2:13, 17, 19; 5:7, 19; 16:11 [twice]; 17:13 [twice]; 18:14; 19:4; 22:9) or forgotten (šākaḥ, Jer 2:32; 3:21; 13:25; 18:15; 23:27; 50:6) YHWH. This is often followed by the accusation that its people follow other gods (ʾĕlohîm ʾăhărîm) and thus have transgressed the divine demand for exclusivity. These accusations are found in the poetic as well as the prose parts of the book of Jeremiah, but never in a context of the covenant (bĕrît, Jer 3:16; 22:9; 31:31; 32:40; 34:8, 13, 15; 50:5). Remembrance and covenant seem to be two different, though supplementary, metaphors for the (same) demand for exclusivity and form the backdrop of the judgment and punishment discussed by the traumatized Judeans. They are thus essential to the exoneration of God from accusations of injustice. Other images, including accusations of

---

[6] J. Barton, *Ethics and the Old Testament* (Harrisburg: Trinity Press International, 1998), 61; also J. Barton, *Ethics in Ancient Israel* (Oxford: Oxford University Press, 2014).

[7] M. Rose, *Der Ausschließlichkeitsanspruch Jahwes: Deuteronomistische Schultheologie und die Volksfrömmigkeit in der späten Königszeit*, BWANT 106 (Stuttgart: Kohlhammer, 1975), 8.

infidelity (2:1–4:4) and foolishness, also appear.[8] The diversity of the imagery points partly to the historical development of the text over the centuries and partly to the fragmented memories and expositions of the blow that traumatized both the voices behind and the audience before the traditions that now constitute the book of Jeremiah.

Covenant and Exclusivity

Jeremiah 11:1–14 is the best and most explicit example of covenant theology in Jeremiah. It emphasizes the words of the covenant, transmitted from God through his spokesperson, Jeremiah, to the Judeans and the inhabitants of Jerusalem. God commands Jeremiah to speak to the people, saying, "Hear the words of this covenant" (11:2). At first, however, the content of the covenant is not specified – only its circumstances. In formulaic Deuteronomistic language, God curses anyone who does not heed (šāmaʿ) "the words of this covenant" (11:3), which they have known since God brought them out of Egypt. The content of the covenant is not a matter of cognitive knowledge or rules of conduct, but the people's obedience to the – unspecified – words of God. If they listen to God's voice and do all that he commands them, "So shall you be my people, and I will be your God" (11:4). This conditional promise, in the form of the so-called "bilateral covenant formula," has all the authority of formulaic language and stresses the importance of obedience. The promise of the land was – and is for the audience – dependent on obeisance. Jeremiah's answer to the command is the model reaction for the people: "So be it, LORD" (11:5).

The following pericope, 11:6–8, repeats the command to tell the people to listen and remember the exodus as the point of departure for God's teaching of obedience and the peoples' disobedience:

> For I solemnly warned your ancestors when I brought them up out of the land of Egypt, warning them persistently, even to this day, saying, Obey my voice. Yet they did not obey or incline their ear, but everyone walked in the stubbornness of an evil will. So I brought upon them all the words of this covenant, which I commanded them to do, but they did not. (11:7–8)

---

[8]   See A. R. P. Diamond and K. M. O'Connor, "Unfaithful Passions: Coding Women Coding Men in Jeremiah 2–3 (4.2), in *Troubling Jeremiah* ed. A. R. P. Diamond, K. M. O'Connor, and L. Stulman, JSOTSup 260 (Sheffield: Sheffield Academic, 1999): 123–45; O'Connor, *Jeremiah: Pain and Promise*: 35–45; H. S. Pedersen, "The Retributive and Suffering God of the Book of Jeremiah: A Study of YHWH's ʿazab-Complaints" (PhD DISS., MF Norwegian School of Theology, 2018).

The basic message is that God, from the earliest times, has repeatedly warned his people against disobedience. The blame for the disaster thus lies entirely on the people. Jeremiah 11:9–13 unpacks this general accusation. The Judeans and the inhabitants of Jerusalem have "gone after other gods" and "broken the covenant" by building altars to gods who, when the disaster hits, will not be able to help. But YHWH will not help, either; his is the hand behind the disaster.

This demonstrates that "covenant" does not mean "commands," but rather "exclusive worship of YHWH." But, as already intimated, this is part of the background for ethics in the book of Jeremiah. Jeremiah 11 is a typically Deuteronomistic pericope: a prose sermon that, together with the prose sermon in 17:19–27, brackets chapters "laden with anomie and dissymmetry."[9] Jeremiah 11 also serves as an interpretive reminder of the preceding chapters, forming part of a *Spannungsbogen* – a narrative connection arcing back to the ethical discourse in Jeremiah 7.[10]

The Book of Jeremiah and the Deuteronomists

Covenant, torah, and the fact that God "brought them up out of the land of Egypt" are the key Deuteronomistic arguments for YHWH's demand for exclusivity and attendant ethical commands.[11] The introduction to the oracles concerning the kings in Jeremiah 22 is a fine example of Deuteronomistic ethical demands in the book of Jeremiah. It follows an oracle to the house of David in Jer 21:12–14, warning that the king must

> Execute justice in the morning,
> and deliver from the hand of the oppressor anyone who has been
>   robbed,

---

[9]   Stulman, *Order amid Chaos*, 44–5.
[10]   Cf. Stulman, *Order amid Chaos*, 18.
[11]   The present essay is unable to address redaction critical matters in detail due to space, although we point the reader especially to the enduring legacy of S. Mowinckel, *Zur Komposition des Buches Jeremia* (Kristiania: Jacob Dybwad, 1914) as well as the work of W. Thiel, *Die deuteronomistische Redaktion von Jeremia 1–25*, WMANT 41 (Neukirchen: Neukirchener Verlag 1973); W. Thiel, *Die deuteronomistische Redaktion von Jeremia 26–45*, WMANT 52 (Neukirchen: Neukirchener Verlag 1981); L. Stulman, *The Prose Sermons of the Book of Jeremiah: A Redescription of the Correspondences with the Deuteronomistic Literature in Light of Recent Text-Critical Research*, SBLDS 83 (Atlanta: Scholars, 1986); and T. Römer, "Is There a Deuteronomistic Redaction in the Book of Jeremiah?" in *Israel Constructs Its History: Deuteronomistic Historiography in Recent Research*, ed. A. de Pury, T. Römer, and J. -D. Macchi (Sheffield: Sheffield Academic, 2000), 399–421.

or else my wrath will go forth like fire,
and burn, with no one to quench it, because of your evil doings.

(21:12)

This introductory poem is connected to a Deuteronomistic cycle in which the prophet is commanded to speak to the king of Judah and tell him to adhere to the words of YHWH (22:1–5). The king is to take care of the vulnerable groups in society and to "act with justice and righteousness." If he obeys these words, God will support him, his servants, and his people. If not, the royal house shall become "a desolation."

The discourse concerning the freeing of Hebrew slaves in Jer 34:8–22 may be another example of covenant-based ethical teaching. This is not the place to go into details with this peculiar narrative, which seems to be a very late addition to the book; here it suffices to say that ethics does not seem to be the main interest of the discourse. Rather, the transgression of the covenant by the elites is the core message of the pericope.

12.4 THE DECALOGUE

Jeremiah 7 has been the focus of much research; in Stulman's representation, it forms one of the key structuring chapters in the book. In it, the so-called Temple Sermon discusses the connection between cult, ethics, and deportation. As always, the discourse is *ex eventu*, superficially discussing the possibility that the Judeans and Jerusalemites might stay in "this place" but really asking, "Why did we lose Jerusalem?" There is a special focus on the role of the temple, as opposed to the Decalogue (and thus, tacitly, the covenant).

The sermon begins with an adamant summons to the prophet: "Stand in the gates of the LORD's house, and proclaim there this word, and say, Hear the word of the LORD ... 'Amend your ways and your doings.'" (7:1–4). Unlike the sermon in Jeremiah 11, which is initiated by the same call to the people to hear, this sermon highlights the divine word and how the people are supposed to amend their ways in response to it. If the people will refrain from oppressing the alien, the orphan, and the widow or shedding innocent blood in this place, and if they do not go after other gods (7:6), then God will let them "remain/live in this place, in the land that I gave of old to your ancestors forever and ever" (*wĕšikkantî'etkem bammāqôm hazzeh*, 7:7; note that the NRSV translates differently). In other words: If the people will adhere to two fundamental pillars of Deuteronomistic law – care for the vulnerable and exclusive worship of YHWH – God will let them stay in the Jerusalem temple and in the land. So far, so good.

The people, however, seem unwilling to adhere to the content of the covenant. They listen not to the divine command but to deceptive words (dibrê-haššeker) that – it is implied – turn them away from the commands of the Decalogue. These are recounted in the form of an accusation:

> Will you steal, murder, commit adultery, swear falsely, make offerings to Baal, and go after other gods that you have not known, and then come and stand before me in this house, which is called by my name, and say, "We are safe!" – only to go on doing all these abominations? (7:9–10)

The word "covenant" is not used here in connection with these commands from the Decalogue. But the content is an informative supplement to the general demand for obedience to the words of God, mentioned in the preceding paragraph. Ethics, in the form of responsibility for the unguarded and with reference to basic societal and religious regulations of the Decalogue, fulfills the divine demand for exclusivity. Performing cultic activity is not enough; this Deuteronomistically influenced theology emphasizes that adherence to the divine words, whatever their content, is the *conditio sine qua non*, the ultimate requirement. There is nothing wrong with participation in the cult – the Temple Sermon does not condemn the Jerusalem cult in principle – but the words of God's unnamed opponents – the deceptive words, opposed to God's words – have led the people to believe that participation in the cult is enough. It isn't![12] Adherence to God's teaching – signaled here in the form of an allusion to some of the Ten Commandments – is the only way to remain in the land.

It might be important to note which commandments are mentioned in Jeremiah 7. The prohibition of stealing (Deut 5:19 // Exod 20:15), murdering (Deut 5:17 // Exod 20:13), committing adultery (Deut 5:21 // Exod 20:14), and swearing falsely (Deut 5:11 // Exod 20:16) all deal with a person's relationship with socially vulnerable groups. Going after other gods (Deut 5:7–10 // Exod 20:3–6) is the ultimate Deuteronomistic offense (Deut 4:28 et passim). Amos 2:6–8; 5:10–13 offer examples of these offenses and show that those who are in the greatest danger of becoming victims of theft, murder, and lies in court are the vulnerable who lack protection from an extended or influential family. Likewise, the man whose wife is stolen from him – in this context adultery is

---

[12] See Römer, "Deuteronomistic Redaction," 414–15.

considered a violation of property rights – is the man who is too weak to present a threat to the offender. The final accusation – offering sacrifices to Ba'al and going after other gods in general – restates the overall concern. Thus, the ethical discourse in Jeremiah 7 should be seen as exemplifying the Deuteronomistic concern for the weakest groups in society, as stated in, for example, Deut 24:12–22.

In a later elaboration of the Temple Sermon in 7:21–28, the conditional bilateral covenant formula forms a literary link to the Deuteronomistic sermon in Jeremiah 11: "Obey my voice, and I will be your God, and you shall be my people; and walk only in the way that I command you, so that it may be well with you." (7:23; cf. 11:5). In this part of the extended Temple Sermon, YHWH – after a long denunciation of the people's (especially the women's) service of "other gods" (7:14–19) – denies that he has ever demanded sacrifice and makes clear that sacrifice is not a viable means of access to him. Here, the message of the first part of the sermon – that sacrifice will not do without obedience to the divine teaching – is radicalized; there will no longer be a way for the people to approach God through sacrifices, or indeed any other means. His spurning of them is complete and final; ethical discourse and admonition are of no use. They have forfeited their chance of being God's chosen people.

12.5 CONCERN FOR THE WEAK

Two passages in Jeremiah 5 substantiate the argument that ethics in the book of Jeremiah is primarily a matter of care and concern for the weaker groups in society.[13] These texts, however, are not as influenced by Deuteronomistic formulaic language as are Jeremiah 7 and 11, and ethics is not explicitly understood within a covenantal framework. Rather, the background is a more general ancient Near Eastern ethos, albeit one that also comes to the fore in the Deuteronomistic writings. The context connects this ethical discourse in Jeremiah 5 with the issue of divine punishment for Israel's disobedience and unfaithfulness: Jeremiah 5 is encircled by two chapters, Jeremiah 4 and 6, in which God threatens the Judeans with the coming of an almost mythical enemy from the North, who will defeat Jerusalem.

---

[13] For a thorough reading with focus on ethics in Jeremiah 5, see W. J. Wessels, "Prophet and Ethics: A Study of Jer 5:26–29," in *Psalmody and Poetry in Old Testament Ethics*, ed. D. J. Human (London: T&T Clark, 2012), 181–96.

Jeremiah 5:1–6 begins with a summons from God to an unidentified audience to walk the streets of Jerusalem, in search of "one person who acts justly and seeks truth (*'ośeh mišpat mĕbaqqeš 'ĕmûnâ*) – so that I may pardon Jerusalem." As becomes clear from the following verses, the search is in vain; the prophet ascertains that both the poor (*dallîm*) and the educated elite (*haggədolîm*) have forgotten "the way of the LORD, the law (*mišpat*) of their God" (5:4–5). This is the twofold way of social justice (*mišpat*) and divine truth (*'ĕmûnāh*), demanded by God in one breath (5:1). As a consequence of the people's forgetfulness, they will be devoured by wild animals – an image of the enemy from the North – that lie in wait outside the city, "because their transgressions are many, their apostasies are great" (5:6). In this conclusion as in 5:1c, we find again a parallel between transgression of the law (*piš'êhem*) and apostasy (*mĕšûbotêhem*). The two offenses are two peas in a pod. (The pericope bears similarities to the narrative of Abraham's discussion with YHWH of justice of the fate of Sodom and Gomorrah in Gen 18:16–33, although the iniquities in Jer 5:1–6 are different from the transgressions of Sodom, as unfolded in Genesis 19.)

Jeremiah 5:1–6 is followed by an announcement of judgment against Judah, which is personified as the enemy from the North (5:7–13, 14–17) and a subsequent modification thereof (5:18–20). In the following unit (5:20–31), YHWH refers to himself as the creator and sustainer of the world and its fertility. The "foolish and senseless people," however, do not see and hear (5:21) and their inequities and sins (*'ăwonôtêkem ... wĕḥaṭṭo'têkem*) have thereby disturbed the balance of nature (5:25). The nature of these inequities is defined in the following verses (5:26–28). In the imagery of the fowler who sets traps, the "scoundrels" (*rĕšā'îm*) among the people are accused of setting traps for human beings. Therefore, they have become great and rich, grown fat and sleek, knowing no limits in deeds of wickedness (*dibrê-ra'*): "They do not judge with justice the cause of the orphan, to make it prosper, and they do not defend the rights of the needy" (5:27–28). Again, the transgression of ethical limits is set within the framework of the proper social balance, characteristic of ancient Near Eastern codes of conduct; here, however, the legitimizing authority behind the demands is emphasized as God, the creator and sustainer, rather than the God of the covenant. Read at the surface level, the theological framework and likewise the punishment are different from that of Jeremiah 7. The balance of the natural world, which when cultivated should feed the people, has been disturbed as a direct consequence of their transgressions; the creator God either will not or cannot any longer uphold the order of creation (5:24–25). There is no mention here of covenant or commandments. This line of thought is in no way unique to Jeremiah 5; the thematic parallel to Amos 4 and maybe even Joel 1 is blatant. Another close intertext is Deut 11:13–17, especially 11:14. The larger section of which this is a part (Deut 10:11–11:20) uses blessings and curses to close the first half of the frame around the legal core (Deuteronomy 12–26), interweaving and uniting the images of YHWH as the God of history and salvation, as the God of justice and care for the needy, and as the God of creation, fertility, and sustenance. Deuteronomy 11:13–17 thus explicitly connects fertility and sustenance with the exclusive adoration of YHWH, that is, with the covenant, paralleling drought and hunger with turning away from YHWH and following other gods. What unites Jer 5:26–28 and Deut 11:13–17 is thus the connection between transgression of the divine will – be it idolatry or lack of ethics – and ecological disaster. Moreover, the ecological disaster in Jeremiah 5 goes hand in hand with, or is even caused by, the threat of warfare by the enemy from the North. This enemy embodies the latent threats of the divine wrath in Deuteronomy.

The issue of unethical societal dissymmetry as a transgression of the divine will and cause for destruction continues in Jer 6:6–8. As punishment for oppression and wickedness, God summons the enemy to make a siege ramp around Jerusalem (the normal means in the period of attacking and defeating a city). Maybe the city is already under siege: Violence and destruction, sickness and wounds are already in it and recognized by God (6:7b). The threat in 6:8 – or rather, the invitation to Jerusalem to learn and change its ways – is consistent with the war imagery. The defeated land will be an uninhabited desolation, as the ecological and military disasters go hand in hand.

What becomes clear in these examples in Jeremiah 5–6 is that the ethical discourse of the book of Jeremiah is not a discourse of ethics per se, but deeply enmeshed in discussions about the cause of Jerusalem's demise among the exiles and their descendants in the Persian period – the elitist carrier group that shaped the communal memory of these events and thereby reshaped the collective identity of a shattered and traumatized people. These discussions about failing ethics in predisaster Jerusalem and their consequences is a means of formulating a way out of the loss among the traumatized of their existential foundations, namely, their trust in God. Two small details point in this direction: first, the rhetorical question in 5:31c ("but what will you do when the end comes?") and, second, the warning in 6:8 that leaves open the possibility of change among the audience – both the imagined predisaster Jerusalemites, as well as the implied postdisaster groups.

12.6 THE NEW COVENANT

The pericope of the new covenant in Jeremiah has been of enormous theological import for the understanding of the book and for its reception in the New Testament and Christianity. One might expect that ethics would play an important role in such a radically new relationship between God and his people. Yet, it does not. The content of the new covenant is not its ethical character, as such; rather, it is a matter of divine teaching. The demand of the new covenant is to *know* the LORD. This demand will be made easy by God, who in the days to come will put torah – the knowledge of God – into the hearts and minds of his chosen people. There will no longer be any use for covenant teaching, for they will remember and know him, from the least to the greatest. The danger of forgetting and forsaking the covenant and thus the insistence on the demand for exclusivity will be bygone; God's acts prevent any human transgressions. This image of the new covenant thus substantiates the impression that ethics in the book of Jeremiah is always secondary, derived from a primary concern with the divine demand for exclusivity.

12.7 THE TEACHING OF JEREMIAH IN A CONTEMPORARY CONTEXT

It appears from the preceding discussion that there is little to learn about ethics from the book of Jeremiah, insofar as it makes no new or original ethical considerations – no appeal to the better self not posed elsewhere in the Old Testament. Instead, we suggest, the ethical teaching lies within another framework, namely, how to undertake ethical reads of authoritative texts.

The book of Jeremiah is a perplexing and disturbing book. It presents God as a vengeful and violent God and the people as hopelessly unchangeable sinners. Only in a few instances is God presented as a merciful and forgiving God, most particularly in the so-called Book of Consolation (Jer 30–31; 32–33). After these more hopeful chapters, however, follow chapter after chapter of diatribe, divine wrath, onslaught of the enemy, destruction, and hopelessness (Jeremiah 34–44). Only in the Oracles against the Nations, which in the Masoretic version of the book are placed after Jeremiah 45, does the book allow a slight vestige of hope for Israel/Judah. Yet this hope is at the expense of Judah's neighbors and conquerors, whom YHWH promises to strike even harder than his own people (Jeremiah 46–51). Its imagery is full of misogynic outbursts, disciplinary methods that evoke child molestation, and sexually laden parables. What then to do with the book of Jeremiah from an ethical point of view?

First of all, we must acknowledge the disturbing features of the text, not exonerate them out of reverence for the authority of the text or, conversely, totally dismiss them as antiquated and outlandish. We must acknowledge the importance of the time gap between us and the biblical text, asking after the circumstances in which it was written and handed down through the centuries. Only against the backdrop of the text's immediate otherness – the recognition that the text is not a textbook or a manual – can we return to the text and try to understand it as a testimony of circumstances, known to us. The book of Jeremiah is a book of disaster and trauma. It reflects the thoughts of a people (or rather, the intelligentsia of a people) who struggled to reconcile with their own past and their perception of the world – their God and their relationship to him. As beautifully stated by Kathleen M. O'Connor,

> Beliefs and traditions... the society's "symbolic tapestry," those interlocking ideas and institutions that once secured them firmly on the earth and kept them grounded in daily life and communal identity – those no longer seem reliable. After all, God did not protect them, nor did prayer comfort them, nor is worship any longer possible because the gods of chaos rule the cosmos. No longer is there a stable, secure foundation upon which to stand.[14]

Reading the book of Jeremiah ethically first and foremost means to understand what loss of worldview and moral orientation or dissonance of belief does to the traumatized. The individual as well as society seeks coherence, trying to establish coherence where there is none or where the old coherence has shown itself to be lost or wrong. The answers they found might not accord with the current reader's experience or belief system, and may thus from the outset seem to be unusable. But acknowledging the traumatic background of the texts in Jeremiah opens up at least two uses of the text. First, it offers words to those numbed by trauma and shows to the safe that perplexity and lament have their place in religious life. It thus poses an ethical demand for lament to be allowed and heard. Second, reading these texts by the more recently traumatized might lead them to a deeper understanding of their own circumstances and, by recognizing the patterns of loss of meaning in the biblical text as parallel to his or her own, offer a way to recuperation and resilience.

---

[14]   O'Connor, *Jeremiah: Pain and Promise*, 4.

FURTHER READING

Alexander, J. C. "Toward a Theory of Cultural Trauma." Pages 1–30 in *Cultural Trauma and Collective Identity*. Edited by J. C. Alexander. Berkeley: University of California Press, 2004.

Alexander, J. C. *Trauma: A Social Theory*. Cambridge: Polity, 2012.

Barton, J. *Ethics and the Old Testament*. Harrisburg: Trinity Press International, 1998.

Boase, E. and C. G. Frechette, eds. *Bible through the Lens of Trauma*. Atlanta: Society of Biblical Literature, 2016.

Carr, D. *Holy Resilience: The Bible's Traumatic Origins*. New Haven: Yale University Press, 2014.

Carroll, R. P. *Jeremiah: A Commentary*. London: SCM, 1986.

Holt, E. K. "Daughter Zion: Trauma, Cultural Memory and Gender in OT Poetics." Pages 162–76 in *Trauma and Traumatization in Individual and Collective Dimensions: Insights from Biblical Studies and Beyond*. SANt 2. Göttingen: Vandenhoeck & Ruprecht, 2014.

Römer, T. "Is There a Deuteronomistic Redaction in the Book of Jeremiah?" Pages 399–421 in *Israel Constructs Its History: Deuteronomistic Historiography in Recent Research*. Edited by A. de Pury, T. Römer, and J. -D. Macchi. Sheffield: Sheffield Academic, 2000.

Rose, M. Der *Ausschließlichkeitsanspruch Jahwes: Deuteronomistische Schultheologie und die Volksfrömmigkeit in der späten Königszeit*. BWANT 106. Stuttgart: Kohlhammer, 1975.

Stulman, L. *Order amid Chaos: Jeremiah as Symbolic Tapestry*. Sheffield: Sheffield Academic, 1998.

Wessels, W. J. "Prophet and Ethics: A Study of Jer 5:26–29." Pages 181–96 in *Psalmody and Poetry in Old Testament Ethics*. Edited by D. J. Human. London: T&T Clark, 2012.

13 Ezekiel and Criminal Justice Reform

C.L. CROUCH

But if the wicked turn away from all their sins that they have committed and keep all my statutes and do what is lawful and right, they shall surely live; they shall not die. None of the transgressions that they have committed shall be remembered against them; for the righteousness that they have done they shall live. (Ezek 18:21–22)

Few Americans are aware that someone convicted of a crime in the United States emerges from the courtroom condemned to a lifetime of discrimination. Individuals with a criminal record are required to declare their conviction to prospective employers, who are overwhelmingly averse to hiring them, and to prospective landlords, who are averse to housing them.[1] They are prohibited from practicing a wide range of professions, many of which bear no relation whatsoever to the crime they may have committed. They are barred from public housing and limited in their recourse to food stamps and other forms of government assistance, if not outright prohibited from it. These and other forms of systemic, legalized discrimination against individuals with criminal records means that the end of a prison sentence marks not the end of punishment, but only a transition to its next stage.

With thanks to my Spring 2019 Ezekiel students at Fuller Theological Seminary, especially Teesha Hadra, September Penn, and Samuel Ansong, whose attention to the ancient and the modern contexts of the book inspired many fruitful conversations and, in turn, this essay.

[1] For documentation and analysis, see M. Alexander, *The New Jim Crow: Mass Incarceration in the Age of Colorblindness*, rev. ed (New York: New Press, 2012); E. Hinton, *From the War on Poverty to the War on Crime: The Making of Mass Incarceration in America* (Cambridge: Harvard University Press, 2016); D. Pager, *Marked: Race, Crime, and Finding Work in an Era of Mass Incarceration* (Chicago: University of Chicago Press, 2007); R. Perkinson, *Texas Tough: The Rise of America's Prison Empire* (New York: Picador, 2010). T. Coates, "The Black Family in the Age of Incarceration," in *We Were Eight Years in Power: An American Tragedy* (New York: One World, 2017), 223–81 provides an accessible overview.

This system of perpetual punishment is not limited to violent criminals or drug kingpins. Even petty drug offenders may be sentenced to a term of probation, community service, and court costs.

Unbeknownst to such offenders, and to most other actors in the sentencing process, their conviction may mean that they are ineligible for federally funded health and welfare benefits, food stamps, public housing, and federal educational assistance. Their driver's license may be automatically suspended, and they may no longer qualify for certain employment and professional licenses. If they are convicted of another crime they may be subject to imprisonment as repeat offenders. They will not be permitted to enlist in the military, or possess a firearm, or obtain a federal security clearance. If citizens, they may lose the right to vote; if not, they become immediately deportable.[2]

An extensive study of the employment prospects of ex-offenders rightly concluded that "the punishing effects of prison do not end upon an inmate's release"; rather, the civil penalties levied upon the formerly incarcerated result "in the exclusion of ex-offenders from valuable social and economic opportunities."[3] The nature and the extent of such penalties, "although not considered punishment by our courts, often make it virtually impossible for ex-offenders to integrate into the mainstream society and economy upon release."[4] In some cases the obstacles reach the level of the absurd: Prisoners trained and deployed as firefighters against wildfires in California, for example, are disqualified by their criminal conviction from employment in any civilian fire department.[5] As a result of such limitations,

> people who have been convicted of felonies almost never truly reenter the society they inhabited prior to their conviction. Instead, they enter a separate society, a world hidden from public view, governed by a set of oppressive and discriminatory rules and laws that do not apply to everyone else.[6]

---

[2]   Alexander, *New Jim Crow*, 143, citing American Bar Association, Task Force on Collateral Sanctions, *Introduction, Proposed Standards on Collateral Sanctions and Administrative Disqualification of Convicted Persons*, Jan. 18, 2002.

[3]   Pager, *Marked*, 58.

[4]   Alexander, *New Jim Crow*, 143.

[5]   J. Raphling, "California's Prisoner Firefighters Deserve a Chance at a New Life," *The San Francisco Chronicle*, November 5, 2019. www.sfchronicle.com/opinion/openforum/article/Inmate-firefighters-deserve-a-chance-at-a-new-life-14806236.php.

[6]   Alexander, *New Jim Crow*, 186–7.

Even for an ex-offender desperately desirous of a full – and fully legal – reintegration, the legal and social environment into which he or she is released make this all but unattainable.

It is no surprise that those who face such substantial obstacles to gainful employment often land back in prison – and that those who do not are ten times more likely to be homeless than the general public.[7] In Ta-nehisi Coates's powerful prose: "Incarceration pushes you out of the job market. Incarceration disqualifies you from feeding your family with food stamps. Incarceration allows for housing discrimination based on a criminal background check. Incarceration increases your risk of homelessness" – and "incarceration increases your chances of being incarcerated again."[8]

The racialized character of this system is impossible to ignore. Though explicit forms of discrimination are illegal, militarized policing tactics focused on poor and minority neighborhoods, combined with sentencing laws dictating harsher penalties for certain crimes, have overwhelmingly and disproportionately increased the rates of incarceration among persons of color. Combined with the number and extent of policies permitting employers, landlords, and government agencies to discriminate against the formerly incarcerated, the consequences have been disastrous. A series of government "wars" on crime and on drugs have effectively relegated persons of color – especially though not exclusively African American men – to a new second-class status, akin to that formally encoded in the pre-civil rights era Jim Crow laws.[9]

Moreover, as Coates observes,

> the chasm in incarceration rates is deeply tied to the socioeconomic chasm between black and white America. The two are self-reinforcing – impoverished black people are more likely to end up in prison, and that experience breeds impoverishment. An array of laws, differing across the country but all emanating from our tendency toward punitive criminal justice – limiting or banning food stamps for drug felons; prohibiting ex-offenders from obtaining public housing – ensure this. So does the rampant discrimination against ex-offenders and black men in general. This, too, is self-reinforcing. The American population most discriminated against is also its most incarcerated – and the

---

[7] L. Couloute, "Nowhere to Go: Homeless among Formerly Incarcerated People," *Prison Policy Initiative*, August 2018. www.prisonpolicy.org/reports.housing.html.

[8] Coates, "Age of Incarceration," 271.

[9] Hinton, *War on Poverty*; Alexander, *New Jim Crow*.

incarceration of so many African Americans, the mark of criminality, justifies everything they endure after.[10]

Discrimination on the basis of race may be illegal, but discrimination on the basis of criminal record is not only legal but widespread. Though few of its practitioners would acknowledge it, the latter masks an ongoing epidemic of the former. Those with a criminal record immediately "become members of an undercaste – an enormous population of predominately black and brown people who, because of the drug war, are denied basic rights and privileges of American citizenship and are permanently relegated to an inferior status."[11]

*

What has the book of Ezekiel to do with this systemic miscarriage of justice? The book seems hardly the most likely source of relief – it is the epitome of prophetic moral severity. Indeed, it is off-putting to many readers precisely because of its insistence on the sinfulness of the people and the justice of YHWH's punishment. Unlike the more hopeful message of Second Isaiah, with its emphasis on YHWH's ongoing care for the people (43:4; 48:14; 54:8, 10; 55:3), or even the doom-laden judgment oracles of Hosea, which nevertheless affirm YHWH's perpetual love for the people (2:19; 3:1; 11:1, 4; 14:4), the book of Ezekiel never draws attention to YHWH's positive emotional attachment to the Israelites. The deity's relationship with the people is driven not by affection but by concern for YHWH's own reputation: When YHWH acts on the people's behalf, he does it "for the sake of my (holy) name" (20:9, 14, 22; 36:22; cf. 20:44; 36:20–23; 39:7; 43:7–8).

Even the book's promises of restoration are dwarfed by the focus on sin and judgment. Unlike other prophetic figures, Ezekiel is given no intercessory function; his role is not to plead with YHWH on the Israelites' behalf – to "forgive, I beg you!" (Amos 7:2, cf. 7:5). Rather, he is to proclaim to the Israelites their punishment and to ensure that they understand that this punishment arises directly from their own sinfulness. Indeed, the need for the people to acknowledge the relationship between their sins and their punishment is so central to the book's agenda that Ezekiel is repeatedly warned that any failure to convey this

<hr />

[10] Coates, "Age of Incarceration," 279.
[11] Alexander, *New Jim Crow*, 186–7.

point clearly will bring down punishment on his own head, rather than on the people (3:19–21; 33:2–9).

The judgment Ezekiel is compelled to communicate calls for the destruction of Jerusalem and the death or deportation of the city's inhabitants (chs 4–5; 9; 11; 14; 15; 17; 20; 23; 24; 33). Immediately following the prophet's commission in chapter 3, he is instructed to illustrate this point using his own body, in a series of symbolic prophetic actions (chs 4–5). First, he is to enact a siege against the city, so that he may lay before it and "bear [the house of Israel's] iniquities" (4:4). Famine, exile, and death follow, all under the banner of punishment for Israel's various crimes.

These crimes themselves are enumerated in the following chapters. In one form or another, they all constitute a variation on failure to follow YHWH's "ordinances and statutes" (5:6–7; cf. 11:12). The worship of other gods is prominent (chs 6; 8; 14; 16; 20; 23), as one might expect, but so are less overtly theological offenses: love of violence and its execution (chs 7; 11; 19; 20; 22), perversion of justice (chs 11; 18; 22; 33), and failures of leadership (chs 11; 12; 13; 17; 19; 21; 23; 34). The commissioning of the unnamed figure to kill the inhabitants of Jerusalem follows on from a description of religious apostasy (ch. 8) and is explained as a consequence of the bloody injustices of town and country (9:9). Violent slaughter awaits those who committed it against others (11:6–8, cf. 12:19).

The moral and theological outlook engendered by this material is unremittingly "tough on crime." Indeed, it exhibits what we might describe as a "law and order" mentality: Israel's punishment is expressly articulated as a consequence of its failure to follow the "statutes and ordinances" laid down by YHWH for Israel's well-being. Already in the opening series of prophetic sign-acts, YHWH explains that the siege, famine, exile, and death that Ezekiel's actions anticipate are the consequences for this failure to obey the law:

> But [Jerusalem] has rebelled against my ordinances and my statutes, becoming more wicked than the nations and the countries all around her, rejecting my ordinances and not following my statutes. Therefore thus says the LORD God: Because you are more turbulent than the nations that are all around you, and have not followed my statutes or kept my ordinances, but have acted according to the ordinances of the nations that are all around you; therefore thus says the LORD God: I, I myself, am coming against you; I will execute judgements among you in the sight of the nations. (5:6–8)

This point is repeated multiple times. The climactic accusation against the elders at the temple, for example, culminates with a declaration of their failure to obey the law: "Then you shall know that I am YHWH, whose statutes you have not followed and whose ordinances you have not kept" (11:12). The subsequent promise of restoration identifies obedience to the law as a critical component of any future relationship between the people and YHWH (11:20). Indeed, though the book imagines a variety of possible futures, these visions consistently prioritize law and order (37:24; 43:11; 44:24). In the exploration of individual and generational punishment in chapter 18, (non-)obedience to YHWH's "statutes and ordinances" is likewise determinative of a person's wickedness or righteousness (18:9, 17, 19, 21). The litany of chapter 20 recalls how YHWH provided these statutes and ordinances to the people as the key to life (20:11) and makes explicit the connection between the people's failure to obey these laws and their current punishment (20:13, 16, 18–20, 24).[12] That punishment has been repeatedly delayed only underscores the strength of the expectation that disobedience normally results in punishment.

At this point in Israel's history, punishment is guaranteed. This is, in part, because YHWH's earlier attempts at leniency have been a complete and utter failure. Chapter 20 elaborates how generation after generation were given an opportunity to repent, as YHWH repeatedly forestalled the punishment appropriate to their extensive sins. But these attempts at leniency proved futile; instead of making better choices and obeying the law, the Israelites compounded their disobedience: sin upon sin, generation upon generation. YHWH's patience has now worn out: The divine judge gave the Israelites multiple chances, but the Israelites refused to change. YHWH has therefore concluded that only an unmistakable act of punishment will bring home the severity of condemnation of the Israelites' behavior and perhaps effect the hoped-for change. The Israelites must bear their punishment, recognize the consequences of their choices, and make better ones in future. Responsibility for the catastrophe is laid at the feet of a morally impenetrable people.

YHWH's change in tactics is motivated by the threat to the divine reputation posed by Israel's failures. International onlookers have begun to view YHWH's willingness to forestall punishment as a reflection of a

---

[12]   Ezekiel 20:25 (in)famously inverts the connection between law and life; for attempts to understand this verse, see, e.g., D. E. Callender, Jr., "'I Gave Them Laws That Were Not Good' (Ezek 20:25): A Biblical Model of Complex Subjectivity and the Prospects of Multi-Ethic Contextual Reading," *In Die Skriflig* 48 (2014): 3–10, and below.

flaw in YHWH's character – either he is impotent and incapable of acting, or he lacks a true commitment to justice and cannot be bothered. With its long-lensed perspective, chapter 20 emphasizes that divine justice concerning Israel's sin is the engine behind the book's message of judgment: YHWH must bring down the gavel, lest the justice system he has sworn upon his own life to uphold be called into question ("as I live"; 5:11; 14:16, 18, 20; 18:3; 20:3, 31, 33).

Though severe, the book's litany of Israel's sins against the divine moral order serves a juridico-theological purpose: It depicts the people's fate as justified punishment for offenses against the divine law – not random chance, neglect (or malevolence) on the part of the deity, or the greater power of enemy gods. The prophet's job is to ensure that the people recognize the justice of the punishment inflicted upon them. YHWH is neither capricious nor cruel, but a God whose punitive actions against Israel are proportionate to the crimes they have committed. The people must acknowledge their responsibility for the suffering that they now experience.

*

Comparative social-scientific research suggests that the book's focus on the people's failures represents a typical response to the traumatic experience of involuntary migration.[13] Ezekiel's community at the River Chebar is such a community: involuntary migrants for whom the world has descended into unremitting chaos. The state of existential disorientation in which the community now finds itself demands an explanation: Why did this happen?

One route through this wilderness of dispossession is to identify specific past behaviors as the source of a community's current suffering. This enables the community to re-assert the existence of a causally ordered universe, reconstructing a coherent narrative of the community and its fate in a way that reestablishes meaning and order.[14] Though terrible, the situation is explicable. Such moral reckonings serve to assert migrants' agency: Their present distress is not random, but the

---

[13]   L. Malkki, *Purity and Exile: Violence, Memory, and National Cosmology among Hutu Refugees in Tanzania* (London: University of Chicago, 1995).

[14]   C. Caruth, *Unclaimed Experience: Trauma, Narrative, and History* (Baltimore: Johns Hopkins University Press, 1996); J. Fentress and C. Wickham, *Social Memory* (Oxford: Blackwell, 1992); N. King, *Memory, Narrative, Identity: Remembering the Self* (Edinburgh: Edinburgh University Press, 2000). For the use of such work to interpret Jeremiah see K. M. O'Connor, *Jeremiah: Pain and Promise* (Minneapolis: Fortress, 2011).

result of previous offenses. The people are complicit in the circum-stances in which they find themselves.

Significantly, these assertions also constitute a claim to the people's moral autonomy over the future: If their current circumstances are the result of bad choices in the past, changing their behavior in the present may stave off similar disasters in the future. Though the Israelites' lives may appear to be wildly beyond their control, in fact their choices and behaviors have value. Changed behavior – careful avoidance of the problematic activities that brought about the disaster – will prevent the recurrence of punishment and thereby ensure their future well-being.

Echoing the psychological literature on coping mechanisms in response to trauma, Smith-Christopher describes this as a kind of "our fault" theology. Although strange to the modern ear – and especially disconcerting to audiences sensitive to the psychological pitfalls of victim-blaming – Smith-Christopher argues that such an approach "ironically empowers... by offering the hope of cultural recovery. *Our own* mistakes offer hopeful possibilities in ways that outside imperial conquest does not."[15] Emphasizing the community's guilt is a way of emphasizing its capacity to affect the future; if the people acknowledge responsibility, they will be able to change their behavior and avoid future punishment. Ezekiel's recitation of Israel's past misdeeds thus represents an assertion of Israel's ability to achieve a better future for itself. Although discomfiting to readers accustomed to the late twenti-eth century's attention to the deity's more gracious aspects, in a com-munity of traumatized migrants this makes perfect sense.

*

In the midst of such unremitting emphasis on Israel's sinfulness, it is especially startling to read the declaration that forms the epigraph to this essay:

> But if the wicked turn away from all their sins that they have committed and keep all my statutes and do what is lawful and right, they shall surely live; they shall not die. None of the transgressions that they have committed shall be remembered

---

[15] D. L. Smith-Christopher, "Reading Jeremiah as Frantz Fanon," in *Jeremiah (Dis) Placed: New Directions in Writing/ Reading Jeremiah*, ed. A. R. P. Diamond and L. Stulman (London: T&T Clark, 2011), 116–17 (italics original).

against them; for the righteousness that they have done they shall live. (18:21–22)

How can this be? That the wicked will suffer the consequences of their wickedness is one of the most fundamental tenets of the book's moral logic: Chapter after chapter is dedicated to drawing an explicit and irrefutable connection between the crimes that the people have committed and the punishment that they now experience.

Even the chapter in which this remarkable statement is found is designed to emphasize that none of Ezekiel's audience who are now suffering do so in innocence. They may wish to blame the misdeeds of their parents, claiming that the consequences of their sin have fallen upon them: "The parents have eaten sour grapes, and the children's teeth are set on edge" (18:2). But the chapter denies this disavowal of responsibility. If the people are suffering YHWH's judgment, it is because they have sinned.

Such a strict system of retribution and reward has its problems; in the contemporary context, this type of logic underpins the prosperity gospel's simplistic claims that rewards will come to the righteous and that material suffering signifies moral depravity. An idealized schema in which a good life follows upon good deeds and evil follows upon evil deeds surfaces in parts of Proverbs, as it encourages young men in their pursuit of wisdom – but reality gives rise to the other biblical voices that contest this schema. Job is declared unfailingly righteous, yet suffers great loss and prolonged physical and mental pain. Ecclesiastes wonders at the irregularity with which the pursuit of wisdom produces predictable results. Psalms lament. In the context of the sixth century BCE, Ezekiel's extreme emphasis on the correlation between sin and punishment represents a reaction to the refusal of the people to acknowledge the depravity of their actions and accept responsibility for their consequences.

Yet, despite the urgency with which the book presses this point, Ezekiel allows room for the possibility that even the most inveterate sinner might turn aside from his wickedness and sin no more. In such a case, the chapter avows, "none of the transgressions that they have committed shall be remembered against them."

*

This injunction to reckon the sins of the past as though they were nothing constitutes a powerful condemnation of the widespread and entirely legal forms of discrimination currently practiced against the formerly incarcerated. Rather than offering ex-offenders a genuine chance to turn their lives around – to "turn away from all their sins that they have committed and keep all my statutes and do what is lawful and right" – ex-offenders are turned out into a system that could hardly be more effectively designed to ensure recidivism.[16] Limited access to gainful employment is a critical link in this chain; because they are denied the ability to support themselves legally, it is not surprising to find ex-offenders resorting to illegal forms of employment or theft.

The specific limitations arising from the criminal record are compounded by the fact that many ex-offenders had few employable skills to begin with. Robert Perkinson estimates that "roughly half of today's prison inmates are functionally illiterate."[17] The prison system as it stands does little to rectify this; over the last fifty years, prisons and jails have all but abandoned efforts to reform those condemned to them.[18] The criminal justice system has become little more than a vast warehousing system for America's most marginalized citizens. The exponential increase in the prison population over the last several decades is the result of a schools-to-prison pipeline fed by economic impoverishment, failing schools, and poor health care – abetted by private companies' profit margins and characterized by a callous disregard for the vulnerable individuals caught in its net.

Ezekiel condemns this. Israel's punishment is depicted as a consequence of its past failure to obey the law, but it is not conceived as punishment for its own sake or as an end in itself. Rather, Israel's punishment is meant, first, to draw the people's attention to the detrimental consequences of their current behavior – for the well-being of a community devastated by violence, as well as for themselves personally. Second, it is meant to provide a route to future obedience. After Israel's punishment has come to an end, the people will be able to "follow my statues and keep my ordinances and obey them" (11:20). Punishment is exacted in order to bring about a change in the people's behavior – specifically, change that leads to law-abiding membership in the community. Warehousing human beings without seeking to transform them is antithetical to Ezekiel's theology. If criminal justice proceeds through incarceration, prison must include routes to rehabilitation that enable ex-offenders to enter fully into society upon their release.

[16]   Alexander, *New Jim Crow*, 176.
[17]   Quoted in Coates, "Age of Incarceration," 241.
[18]   Pager, *Marked*, 15–22.

With this in mind, Ezekiel's depiction of the change Israel undergoes during the term of its punishment merits close attention. Perhaps surprisingly, the book envisions Israel's reformed future arising not out of some spontaneous transformation on the part of the people, but from changes in their circumstances, brought about by YHWH specifically in order to facilitate obedience to the divine law: YHWH promises to give the people "one heart" and a "new spirit" (11:19; 36:26; cf. 18:31). The goal of YHWH's dramatic intervention in Israel's history, these passages emphasize, is not merely a temporary disruption, undertaken in resigned expectation of the Israelites' eventual return to their previous circumstances. Rather, YHWH recognizes the magnitude of the obstacles that obstruct the Israelites' path to obedience and grants the people the resources they need to overcome them. Punishment is envisioned as a radical break from the past, effected by YHWH through the gift of "one heart" and a "new spirit." On the other side of punishment, the Israelites will be able to live lives in accord with the divine will, fully resourced by the divine judge who sentenced them. This one heart and this new spirit will enable the Israelites to live the kind of law-abiding lives they previously found impossible. These passages recognize that, without a change in circumstances, the Israelites will remain trapped in an endless cycle of crime and punishment. Indeed, chapter 20 makes clear that YHWH's repeated injunctions to obedience were not, on their own, enough to bring about the change YHWH desired; the Israelites kept falling into sin. After reporting Israel's multiple failures, the chapter finally acknowledges that the law, on its own, could bring only death (20:25). Something more was required for life.

To twenty-first-century America, Ezekiel issues a summons: Transform the death-dealing circumstances that feed and facilitate the prison-industrial complex. It is well established and widely acknowledged that a number of material risk factors dramatically increase one's chances of incarceration, including poverty, illiteracy, mental illness, and addiction.[19] The long shadow of racial discrimination – housing restrictions, bars to employment, inadequate medical care, underfunded schools, and so on – link these risk factors disproportionately to individuals and communities of color. Once swept into the system, the exclusion of ex-offenders from housing, employment, and other basic benefits establishes significant obstacles to successful reentry into mainstream society. These legal forms of discrimination add their compounding effect to

---

[19]   Coates, "Age of Incarceration," 241.

the risk factors associated with initial incarceration – and so incarceration breeds more incarceration. Nearly two-thirds of those recently released from prison are charged with new crimes; more than 40 percent return to prison within three years.[20] Unless we address the circumstances at the root of mass incarceration, this cycle – what Loïc Wacquant describes as a "closed circuit of perpetual marginality" – will continue.[21] Moreover, we must recognize that these circumstances are fundamentally material, rather than moral: "Mass incarceration," Coates writes, "is, ultimately, a problem of troublesome entanglements. To war seriously against the disparity in unfreedom requires a war against a disparity in resources."[22] In one of the wealthiest countries in the world, there is no question that these resources exist; what we require is the will to use them.

Ezekiel's promises of divine intervention, we should note, do not constitute a simple carte blanche; the people must do more than sit back and wait passively for divine transformation. In chapter 18, the "new heart and a new spirit" are promised in the imperative: "Cast away from you all the transgressions that you have committed against me, and get yourselves a new heart and a new spirit!" (18:31). As in the book's depiction of the people's earlier offences, the passage emphasizes the Israelites' own moral agency: Change requires them to act, as well. Although YHWH's gifts are meant to facilitate obedience, they do not guarantee it; further recidivism will still bring consequences (11:21). Nevertheless, both the first and the last iterations of YHWH's promise to change the Israelites' circumstances recognize that this individual will to change is not, on its own, enough (11:19; 36:26) – the turn away from wickedness and toward righteousness is not a simple matter of resolve. Not only the resolve of the individual to pursue a life of righteousness and obedience to the divine law must change; the circumstances in which the individual finds him- or herself must also be transformed.

This attention to both the divine and the human responsibility for change is significant. A similar balancing act is appropriate also to our conversation about criminal justice reform. Of the system in its present state, Alexander concludes that "it is difficult to imagine a system better

---

[20]   Pager, *Marked*, 2. Alexander cites a Bureau of Justice Statistics study that reports a 30 percent re-arrest rate in the first six months and a 68 percent rate within three years (*New Jim Crow*, 94).

[21]   Alexander, *New Jim Crow*, 95.

[22]   Coates, "Age of Incarceration," 279. On ethics of the marginalized, see the essay by Strine in this volume.

designed to create – rather than prevent – crime."[23] Ezekiel (like Augustine) might conceive of this in terms of the all-but-universal propensity
toward sin – the Israelites seem hardly able *not* to sin, immersed as they
are in a pervasively sinful society. Alexander, in the contemporary
context, points to widespread discrimination against those with a criminal record as propelling many ex-offenders (back) into criminal activity.[24] Yet, while Alexander weighs very highly the significance of these
circumstantial obstacles to righteousness – full participation in the
mainstream society and economy, in her terms – she denies that it is
the *sole* determining factor of recidivism:

> None of this is to suggest that those who break the law bear no
> responsibility for their conduct or exist merely as "products of their
> environment." To deny the individual agency of those caught up in
> the system – their capacity to overcome seemingly impossible
> odds – would be to deny an essential element of their humanity.
> We, as human beings, are not simply organisms or animals
> responding to stimuli. We have a higher self, a capacity for
> transcendence.[25]

Although the responsibility of the individual ex-offender to successfully
pursue a form of life that does not lead back to prison is not Alexander's
primary interest, like Ezekiel she recognizes that individual will is
relevant to the equation. Ezekiel's imperative to the Israelites to "get
yourself a new heart and a new spirit" reminds us that a change in
circumstances alone – even a radical one – is not of itself enough to
guarantee a future free of recidivism. The individual must also choose.
At the same time, as Alexander argues,

> our ability to exercise free will and transcend the most extraordinary
> obstacles does not make the conditions of our life irrelevant. Most of
> us struggle and often fail to meet the biggest challenges of our
> lives... As a society, our decision to heap shame and contempt

---

[23] Alexander, *New Jim Crow*, 176.

[24] Alexander observes significant data regarding the number of wrongly convicted or
      unconvicted individuals (that is, those who pled guilty rather than face trial) currently
      incarcerated; not all those who bear the stigma of a criminal record have previously
      engaged in criminal activity (*New Jim Crow*, 84–9). There is likewise extensive
      evidence concerning the cultural construction of the "criminal" as black (or brown)
      and male, with systemic and detrimental effects on black (and brown) men who have
      no criminal record at all (Pager, *Marked*, 5; Coates, "Age of Incarceration,"
      239–40, 279).

[25] Alexander, *New Jim Crow*, 176.

upon those who struggle and fail in a system designed to keep them locked up and locked out says far more about ourselves than it does about them.[26]

*

As noted already, Ezekiel depicts YHWH's actions on behalf of the Israelites as actions "for the sake of my name." YHWH provides for the Israelites one heart and a new spirit and restores the people to a life-giving land where they will dwell in safety forever – lest the nations look upon the Israelites' suffering and conclude that YHWH is powerless to protect his people. Rather than focusing on YHWH's concern for the people's well-being, these passages emphasize that YHWH acts out of concern for YHWH's reputation, especially as it concerns the nations.

In secularized society, claim to the deity's position of sovereign power is made by the nation-state. In this modeling of the locus of ultimate power, the source of the legislation that authorizes discriminatory practices and the gatekeepers of the resources needed to support the formerly incarcerated in their efforts to (re)enter mainstream society is the state. In its combined federal and state forms, the American criminal justice system incarcerates more people, and at higher rates, than any nation on earth. The nations rightly look upon us in horror. As YHWH acted on Israel's behalf for the sake of his reputation, the United States must likewise act – dismantling systems of criminal injustice for the sake of its reputation. If the state arrogates the sovereignty of God, it inherits its obligations as well.

Although the moral logic of *imitatio Dei* is dangerous when it leads to abuses of power by the powerful, its invocation in this instance recognizes that action on behalf of the formerly incarcerated, together with the radical reformation of a system that puts so many of society's most marginalized members behind bars, may legitimately be motivated by a concern for national reputation. Many of the Hebrew Bible's most powerful invocations to care for the marginalized are similarly predicated on right behavior as a form of *imitatio Dei*. Deuteronomy declares that

> YHWH your God is God of gods and Lord of lords, the great God, mighty and awesome, who is not partial and takes no bribe, who executes justice for the orphan and the widow, and *who loves the*

[26]   Alexander, *New Jim Crow*, 176.

strangers, providing them with food and clothing. *You shall also love the stranger*, for you were strangers in the land of Egypt. (Deut 10:18–19)

Imperatives and adjurations reflecting this principle appear frequently, including within Ezekiel. YHWH's holiness requires holiness on the part of the people; it is because the Israelites failed so comprehensively to live lives of holiness that the Holy One of Israel was obliged to abandon Jerusalem (Ezek 8–11; cf. Leviticus and Isaiah). Elsewhere, prophetic exhortations to justice and righteousness are implicitly or explicitly based on the attribution of these characteristics to YHWH (Amos 5, Isaiah 56, and so on). Because human beings are made in the image of God (Gen 1:26–27), ideas about what God is like may serve as a guide to what human beings should be like.

Ezekiel unabashedly acknowledges that it is part of the divine character to care whether human beings comprehend YHWH's character. It is not, to be clear, that Ezekiel's YHWH is an arrogant God concerned only with being the object of international praise. Rather, it is YHWH's commitment to *justice* that is at stake – this is what prompts YHWH's punishment of the people for their wrongdoings, as well as YHWH's recognition that punishment, once wrought, must ultimately come to an end.[27]

The United States of America is a nation that promises "liberty and justice for all." This promise is countermanded by a system that abuses its sovereignty to deny astonishing numbers of persons – overwhelmingly black and brown persons – their freedom, first by locking them up in jails and prisons, then by condemning them to a shadow existence, barred from the means by which they might become functioning members of the community. The nations round about look upon these actions and doubt the American character. Ezekiel summons us, like YHWH, to bring about a society that reflects a genuine commitment to liberty and justice for all.

FURTHER READING

Alexander, M. *The New Jim Crow: Mass Incarceration in the Age of Colorblindness.* Rev. ed. New York: New Press, 2012.
Coates, T. "The Black Family in the Age of Incarceration," in *We Were Eight Years in Power: An American Tragedy*, 223–81. New York: One World, 2017.

[27] See C. L. Crouch, "Ezekiel and the Foreign Nations," in *Oxford Handbook to Ezekiel*, ed. C. L. Carvalho (Oxford: Oxford University Press, forthcoming.)

Joyce, P. M. *Divine Initiative and Human Response in Ezekiel*. Sheffield: JSOT, 1989.

Lapsley, J. E. *Can These Bones Live? The Problem of the Moral Self in the Book of Ezekiel*. Berlin: de Gruyter, 2000.

Mol, J. *Collective and Individual Responsibility: A Description of Corporate Personality in Ezekiel 18 and 20*. Boston: Brill, 2009.

Pager, D. *Marked: Race, Crime, and Finding Work in an Era of Mass Incarceration*. Chicago: University of Chicago Press, 2007.

Perkinson, R. *Texas Tough: The Rise of America's Prison Empire*. New York: Picador, 2010.

14 Poverty and Social Justice in Micah

MATTHEW J. M. COOMBER

The book of Micah is both a complicated work and literarily cluttered. While the book is set in Judah during the mid-to-late eighth century BCE, much of it was composed in the exilic and postexilic periods. Any eighth-century components have been heavily redacted. For present purposes, however, the turbulent period in which Micah's authors set their work is more important than time(s) of actual authorship. The book's eighth-century Judean setting gives clues as to its authors' intents as well as signaling the book's relevance to a variety of audiences. Eighth-century Judah's contexts of suffering conquest and subjugation – with the political, economic, and religious changes that follow – resonate with marginalized peoples across time. Furthermore, Micah's laments, accusations, legal sentencings, and promises of hope reflect a biblical-economic ethos that recurs throughout the First Testament: the ethos of the community responsibility for the well-being of individuals. Despite its unpolished form, therefore, Micah is rich in ethical landscapes through which to explore poverty and other social justice issues, both ancient and modern.

14.1 MICAH'S HISTORICAL SETTING

The mid-to-late eighth century was marked by the rise of the Neo-Assyrian empire and its incursion into the southern Levant. While the northern Kingdom of Israel had already developed a political economy at this time, the southern Kingdom of Judah comprised scattered agrarian communities, which were largely autonomous. With the arrival of the Assyrians, however, Judean life changed at breakneck pace.

Socioeconomic Change in Late-Eighth-Century Judah

During the Assyrian incursion in which Israel was destroyed and Judah made a vassal state, Judah experienced massive population growth, a sevenfold extension of Jerusalem's fortified areas, the construction of massive defensive walls and fortresses in the Negev, and the introduction of standardized weights and scales. Judean agriculture witnessed the construction of irrigation systems and dams that established farming communities in previously uncultivated regions. In addition to the centralization of olive oil and wine production in the Shephelah, Judah experienced a boom in fruit processing facilities. All of this accompanied the sudden appearance of luxury imports in Jerusalem, including Nile River shellfish and precious woods. Developments such as these, all occurring within a single generation, required heightened administrative control, resource coordination, and increased interregional exchange.[1] Such rapid advances in a region previously dominated by scattered subsistence communities suggests the development of a political economy that eclipsed Judah's traditional low-maintenance subsistence strategies.

Effects on Farm Communities

The immense economic changes of the late eighth century undoubtedly had significant impacts on Judean farmers. In fact, there is a recurring and identifiable cross-cultural pattern to the changes in agrarian and practices land management strategies as communities, like Judah experienced, undergo rapid transitions from subsistence cultivation to the specialized production of revenue-producing crops. This pattern is explained through *cultural-evolutionary theory*.

As subsistence societies are absorbed into systems of centralized production and exchange, administrative elites employ debt schemes to refocus productive efforts from the needs of producers to the desires of administrators.[2] At this stage of the process, producers are coerced into trading risk-reducing subsistence strategies for the specialized farming of revenue crops. Due to the higher-risk nature of specialized farming, these crops are prone to failure and, as crop failure inevitably follows, administrators offer high-interest survival loans. These are intended to be impossible to sustain, as further crop failures ensue. The inevitable result is foreclosure, allowing administrators to consolidate family plots into large and manageable estates.[3]

---

[1] See C. L. Crouch, *The Making of Israel: Cultural Diversity in the Southern Levant and the Formation of Ethnic Identity in Deuteronomy*, VTSup 162 (Leiden: Brill, 2014), 8–82, with further references.

[2] See M. J. M. Coomber, *Re-Reading the Prophets through Corporate Globalization* (Piscataway: Gorgias, 2010).

[3] A. W. Johnson and T. Earle, *The Evolution of Human Societies: From Foraging Group to Agrarian State*, 2nd ed. (Stanford: Stanford University Press, 2001), 24–7.

As administrators hoard the benefits of the new economic landscape, rural producers suffer exploitation and displacement.[4] This pattern has resurfaced across culture and time, from Bronze Age Palestine to late-twentieth-century Vietnam.[5] Considering Judah's transformation under Assyrian vassalage, the presence of these cultural-evolutionary patterns would not be unexpected. Indeed, they appear to dovetail with Micah 2:1–2:

> Alas for those who devise wickedness and evil deeds on their beds!
> When the morning dawns, they perform it, because it is in their power.
> They covet fields, and seize them; houses, and take them away; they
> oppress householder and house, people and their inheritance.

In addition to also resonating with another late-eighth-century passage, Isa 5:8, this pattern may be reflected in Persian-period texts – another time of great transition and one in which much of Micah was written. In the Book of Nehemiah, for example, Nehemiah chastises his nobles for forcing their subjects to pledge their farmlands in order to acquire them for themselves (Neh 5:2–5).

In addition to affecting farming communities, the economic shifts witnessed in Assyrian Judah and Persian Judea adversely affected religious elites. This may have inspired Micah's wrath at the injustices perpetrated by corrupt priests and prophets.

Religious Elites in Times of Change

The massive sociopolitical shifts during the eighth century undoubtedly led to religious transformation in Judah, which may be found in Hezekiah's reforms. Since successful harvests are vital to agrarian societies, economic and religious practices become intertwined through rituals and feasts that determine farming and land management strategies. In time, these ritualized economic practices come to be seen as infallible as the deities to whom they connect, blurring the lines between religion and farming.[6] Judah's socioeconomic transformations would have rendered subsistence-focused religious practices obsolete barriers to new economic goals. This, too, is common during transitional periods. The augmentation of Chinese dietary taboos to facilitate sixteenth-century European trade, and the overhauling of religious

---

[4]   See Coomber, *Re-Reading the Prophets*.
[5]   See Coomber, *Re-Reading the Prophets*.
[6]   R. A. Rappaport, "The Sacred in Human Evolution," *Annual Review of Ecology and Systematics* 2 (1971): 23–44.

education and the Muslim calendar in Libya to engage in twentieth-century international capitalism are but two examples of how rapid economic transformation divides religious leaders – between those willing to adapt their faith to profit the elite and those who are killed, exiled, or simply rendered irrelevant. Perhaps such circumstances connect to the attacks against false prophets in Micah 3:5–7:

> Thus says YHWH concerning the prophets who lead my people astray, who cry "Peace" when they have something to eat, but declare war against those who put nothing into their mouths. Therefore it shall be night to you, without vision, and darkness to you, without revelation. The sun shall go down upon the prophets, and the day shall be black over them; the seers shall be disgraced, and the diviners put to shame; they shall all cover their lips, for there is no answer from God.

Perhaps this passage reveals the anger of religious elites displaced by a new order seeking to profit from Assyrian dominance and the changes that this brought to their traditional practices.

Connecting complaints against various injustices to a particular socioeconomic setting is useful, but connecting them to an overarching biblical ethos is especially beneficial when considering the ethical implications of Micah for modern audiences. The biblical-economic ethos of collective responsibility for the well-being of individuals is effective at facilitating such bridges.

14.2 ETHOS OF COMMUNITY RESPONSIBILITY

Blending an ancient Near Eastern economic ethos with modern poverty concerns is a minefield, fraught with potential missteps that range from veering into eisigesis – bending texts to fit modern contexts or agendas – to a postmodernist skepticism that discards the potential for connections. With proper respect for the dangers of either error, however, a middle ground is possible.

It must first be recognized that since biblical ethics is incredibly complex and diverse, no single economic ethos can be superimposed on the Bible as a whole. Its texts represent theologies and cultures spanning centuries. Genesis 41 encourages government control of production and distribution; Micah 2 encourages local control. Deuteronomy 15 calls for the care of the poor, regardless of how they became poor, but Proverbs 18 asserts self-determination as the path out of poverty. Furthermore, our modern economic philosophies and systems did not exist in Micah's time: Theirs was a world of subsistence and tribute economics. Nevertheless, despite the numerous differences separating biblical contexts and our own, the biblical ethos of community responsibility for the well-being of individuals offers a connecting thread between ancient texts and to modern poverty concerns.

The ethos of community responsibility – found throughout the Bible in laws, oracles, and stories – is reflected in Micah's attacks against those who worked to profit from their neighbors' poverty. What allows us to connect these texts to our time – in ethos and in practice – is what our worlds share: first, systems of poverty that profit the powerful and, second, a widely adhered-to set of religious texts that condemn such conduct.

The sabbatical laws of Deuteronomy 15 and the jubilee laws of Leviticus 25 offer two examples of the biblical ethos of community responsibility relevant to Micah. While the motivations behind writing these texts may have served elite interests, their laws reflect earlier legal traditions rooted in Israel's subsistence past.

Community Responsibility in the Deuteronomic Code

Deuteronomy 15:4–5 declares a radical idea: "There will, however, be no one in need among you, because the LORD is sure to bless you in the land that the LORD your God is giving you as a possession to occupy, if only you will obey the LORD your God by diligently observing this entire commandment that I command you today." It is clear, however, that the authors did not assume the commandment would be followed, for Deut 15:11 declares, "Since there will never cease to be some in need on the earth...'" While Deuteronomy 15 offers an idyllic vision for justice, it is also pragmatic: Any economic system, even one designed by YHWH, will be abused. According to Norman Gottwald, Deuteronomy 15:11 offers a perpetual challenge: to uphold the community's responsibility for the well-being of its individuals.[7] This understanding is supported by the verse's conclusion: "I therefore command you: open your hand to the poor and needy in your land." Such a command was particularly pertinent to the passage's primary audience: the elites who were able to access written texts.

To facilitate the protection of those who fell between the economic cracks, Deuteronomy 15 introduces the sabbatical year, which

---

[7]   N. Gottwald, "Early Israel as an Anti-Imperial Community," in *In the Shadow of Empire: Reclaiming the Bible as a History of Faithful Resistance*, ed. R. A. Horsley (Louisville: Westminster John Knox, 2008), 12.

demanded the clearance of debts every seven years. The intent was to take the bite out of debt; the Hebrew word for bite, *nšk*, is the word used for collecting interest. Not only does Deut 15:8–9 demand observance of the law and releasing borrowers from their debts, it warns against forgiving debts with a sour disposition:

> You should rather open your hand, willingly lending enough to meet the need, whatever it may be. Be careful that you do not entertain a mean thought, thinking, "The seventh year, the year of remission, is near," and therefore view your needy neighbor with hostility and give nothing; your neighbor might cry to the LORD against you, and you would incur guilt.

Whereas the sabbatical's safety net was designed to keep debt in check by limiting the lifespan of the debt, the Holiness Code's jubilee year was designed to protect families' access to the main economic driver of any substance community: arable land.

Community Responsibility in the Holiness Code

For agrarian societies around the world, access to arable land ensures access to livelihood and sustenance. The primary strategy for ensuring this access, from precolonial Australia to twentieth-century Tunisia, has been to make the sale of a plot of land's usufruct – the ability to access its productive capabilities – either illegal or religiously taboo, or both.[8] The authors of the Holiness Code similarly sought to forbid the permanent sale of usufruct. Using YHWH's voice, Lev 25:23–24 proclaims, "But the land must not be sold beyond reclaim, for the land is mine; you are but strangers resident with me. Throughout the land that you hold, you must provide for the redemption of the land." Like Deuteronomy 15, Lev 15:23–24 is both idealistic and pragmatic. For a family suffering successive crop failures, completely forbidding the exchange of usufruct for much needed foodstuffs could prove fatal. To protect families in desperate times, who are particularly vulnerable to those who have the means to permanently acquire their land, Lev 25:25–28 offered a series of safety nets to ensure family plots would be returned.

The first safety net demands, "If your kinsman is in crisis and has to sell part of his holding, his nearest redeemer shall come and redeem what his kinsman has sold" (Lev 25:25). In other words, if a struggling farmer needs to sell a portion of his usufruct (masculine pronouns are

8   Coomber, *Re-Reading the Prophets*, 60, 180–3.

used since only men could own land), it is the sacred duty of the farmer's nearest relative to buy it and restore his access to that land. Note the absence of stipulations; whether the land is in danger due to poor luck or poor decision making, the struggling farmer's kin is responsible for restoring the usufruct, if able.

If the nearest relative is unable to restore usufruct, but the struggling farmer falls upon good fortune, he is to repurchase the usufruct himself (Lev 25:26–27). However, the purchase price will reflect the remaining value of the agreement. If the farmer sold the usufruct for ten years of use in exchange for ten units of grain, and is able to repurchase after five years, only five units of grain is owed to the creditor, since the creditor benefited from five years of usufruct. Unlike economic systems driven by profit, this system's priority is equity and mutual benefit.

If these first two safety nets fail to restore the struggling farmer's usufruct, Lev 25:28 provided a final line of defense: the jubilee year. Since YHWH was deemed to own the land (25:23), no Israelite had the right to sell any part of it; the land's usufruct, alone, could be sold, and for a maximum of forty-nine years. In the fiftieth year, all usufruct returned to the original holders. Those who sold usufruct might not live to see the jubilee, but their families were protected from perpetual poverty.

City properties, which were not necessary for livelihood, were not protected by jubilee. If not reclaimed within a year, they belonged "to the purchaser in perpetuity" (Lev 25:30). This distinction between city and rural property highlights jubilee's intent: preventing the affluent from seizing their vulnerable neighbors' ability to access a livelihood. While these laws were likely written at the end of the Babylonian and beginning of the Persian periods, they reflect an ethos of community responsibility for the well-being of individuals that predates their authorship and permeated the culture in which Micah's authors lived.

Given Micah's historical setting in a period of radical economic transformation, coupled with an ethos of community responsibility that permeated Hebrew culture (even if reletaged to ancient equivalent of virtue signaling), any reading of poverty ethics in Micah should be considered through these lenses. The following section offers a few examples of reading Micah through its historical and ethical contexts to uncover ways in which the ethos of community responsibility for the well-being of individuals might be applied to modern conversations on poverty. While the concept of *debt* connects to the modern world, *land* does not hold the same meaning in modern nonagrarian societies.

However, by adjusting our hermeneutics to understand land through what it signified to ancient audiences – food security and livelihood – fruitful connections are possible.

14.3 READING MICAH IN MODERN ETHICAL CONTEXTS

Micah 2: Social Evils That Breach the Ethos of Community Responsibility

Concern for the ethos of community responsibility is reflected in the condemnation of those who planned and executed land seizures: "Alas for those who devise wickedness and evil deeds on their beds! When the morning dawns, they perform it, because it is in their power. They covet fields, and seize them; houses, and take them away; they oppress house-holder and house, people and their inheritance" (Micah 2:1–4). As the perpetrators of these evil deeds are not identified, scholars have long filled the vacuum with wealthy merchants, corrupt judges, and even organized crime cartels. In light of cultural-evolutionary theory, late-eighth-century Judah's socioeconomic transformations, and the preponderance of the biblical ethos of community responsibility, however, Micah 2:1–4 should be understood as a condemnation of people who have breached this ethos of community responsibility. Like other biblical figures who violated this ethos, such as King Ahab and those who moved boundary markers,[9] these perpetrators would face divine wrath. Micah 2:3–4 proclaims, "On that day they shall take up a taunt song against you, and wail with bitter lamentation, and say, 'We are utterly ruined; the LORD alters the inheritance of my people; how he removes it from me! Among our captors he parcels out our fields.'" The prophet makes clear that both the crime and its consequences for the perpetrators' neighbors had caught the attention of YHWH and would not go unpunished; those who inflicted this injustice would be visited by the same.

Micah 2:1–4 finds contemporary relevance when executives ship their workers' livelihoods overseas to increase profitability, or when corporations move agrarians off their lands for mineral exploration, as happened to the U'wa of Colombia, who threatened mass suicide to stop Occidental Oil from drilling their lands. While late-eighth-century Judean methods of debt, dominance, and extraction may differ from those employed today, the pain inflicted by the powerful upon their

---

[9] 1 Kgs 21; Deut 19:14; 27:17; Prov 22:28; 23:10; Job 24:2.

more vulnerable neighbors for the sake of self-enrichment, or under pressure from foreign powers, are similar.

Jubilee USA is one of the faith-based economic justice organizations that draw upon the ethos of community responsibility; their mission could benefit from a reading of Micah's second chapter. Jubilee USA's work focuses on poverty alleviation and is undertaken, in part, by addressing the corruption and unjust debt practices that exist in current modes of international financial assistance. One of the campaigns that the organization has worked on is the alleviation of Grenada's national debt. With the government as the primary employer and 50 percent unemployment, Grenada was hit hard by International Monetary Fund (IMF) austerity measures, which cut both government jobs and access to social services.

The lack of international economic regulations to protect highly indebted nations like Grenada has resulted in the proliferation of exactly the kind of predatory lending practices that the IMF was created to prevent. One such practice is the use of vulture funds: hedge funds that prey upon impoverished countries by buying their sovereign debt for pennies on the dollar, and then demand their repayment in full.[10] Since there is no equivalent of bankruptcy court for countries, impoverished nations facing massive debt have limited options.[11]

In addition to promoting debt forgiveness and protective regulations, Jubilee USA works with religious and political leaders to promote nonausterity alternatives to debt crises. Rather than using cutbacks on government programs to reduce costs, Jubilee USA encourages the IMF to pursue growth by curbing corporate tax avoidance.[12] Citing Pope John Paul II and Pope Francis, Jubilee USA's executive director, Eric LeCompte, asserts that wealthier nations must go beyond notions of forgiving debt and realize that national debt crises are symptoms of a "sickness in the international-financial sector," which needs to be reworked to protect the poor.[13] Akin to the biblical ethos from which Jubilee USA takes its name, the organization calls on the international financial system to put the onus of debt on those who can carry its

---

[10] T. R. Samples, "Rogue Trends in Sovereign Debt: Argentina, Vulture Funds, and Pari Passu under New York Law," *Northwestern Journal of International Law & Business* 35 (2014): 49–86.

[11] S. Winters, "Jubilee Aims to Ease Grenada's Debt Crisis," *National Catholic Reporter* June 20–July 3 (2014): 3.

[12] See Winters, "Jubilee Aims to Ease Grenada's Debt Crisis," 3.

[13] See Winters, "Jubilee Aims to Ease Grenada's Debt Crisis," 3.

weight, rather than on those who are struggling to keep their heads above water.

While Jubilee USA draws on the ethos of community responsibility with a foundation in the Bible's legal texts, the organization could strengthen and nuance its message by appealing to Micah 2. Specifically, Micah's calling out of those who scheme to take what is not theirs and to write unjust statutes to enrich themselves would serve Jubilee USA well. While there have been cases in which genuine help has been rendered, our system of international capitalism has shaped itself in ways that favor its elites and at the expense of those who are most desperate.[14] Drawing Micah 6:8 into the conversation, in which the prophet states all that God wants from the people, may be further used to highlight the incongruity between our current international economic practices and a core ethos of the Abrahamic faiths.

Micah 3: Corrupt Rulers and Prophets

Unlike the anonymous perpetrators in Micah 2:1–4, Micah 3 explicitly identifies those who used their power to callously profit off the misery of their people: the political and religious elites. Micah accuses the rulers of Jacob and the house of Israel of hating good and loving evil (3:2) and colorfully compares them to cannibals "who eat the flesh of my people, flay the skin off them, break their bones in pieces, and chop them up like meat in a kettle" (3:3). This violence is the result of their corruption. The prophet derides them, claiming, "Its rulers give judgment for a bribe, its priests teach for a price, its prophets give oracles for money..." (3:11a). As a result of reserving aid for those who can return favors, the impoverished are left completely vulnerable: "[the religious leaders] declare war against those who put nothing into their mouths" (3:5b). To compound this injustice, the religious elite deluded themselves into thinking they were fulfilling their duties: "yet they lean upon YHWH and say, 'Surely YHWH is with us! No harm shall come upon us'" (3:11b). Their failure to fulfill their community responsibility for the well-being of the individual, however, will result in annihilation: "because of you Zion shall be plowed as a field; Jerusalem shall become a heap of ruins, and the mountain of the house of wooded height" (3:12). While the prophet's accusations against these elites are powerful in their ancient context, reading Micah 3 alongside the wider biblical ethos of

---

[14]   See Coomber, *Re-Reading the Prophets*.

community responsibility helps to connect the chapter to ethical conversations pertaining to similar abuses today.

The book's concern with elites who follow their own interests and neglect those of their neighbors resonates in almost any culture and time. In the United States, allowing powerful financial interests to help craft legislation while cutting aid for vulnerable citizens is at odds with the biblical ethos of community responsibility. The Supplemental Nutrition Assistance Program (SNAP) is a government food program that costs less than 2 percent of the US budget. Eight and a half million American families rely on SNAP as their sole food source. Despite this, in 2016 House Speaker Paul Ryan sought to cut $23 billion from the $70.9 billion program. President Donald Trump's 2018 budget proposal went even further, seeking to cut SNAP by $192 billion over ten years. In 2016 Iowa Senator Joni Ernst called for an end to SNAP entirely. Significantly, Ernst's proposal aligned with the interest of her campaign benefactors, the financial elites David and Charles Koch. During his 1980 vice-presidential run on the Libertarian ticket, David Koch had proposed ending welfare, social security, and public education altogether. The Libertarian Party has declared a "war on the war on poverty." The following statement used to be on the party's national webpage and is now found on several regional pages, including the Libertarian Party of Alabama:

> We should eliminate the entire social welfare system. This includes food stamps, subsidized housing, and all the rest. Individuals who are unable to fully support themselves and their families through the job market must, once again, learn to rely on . . . family, church, community, or private charity to bridge the gap.

The words "once again" reflect a US myth that citizens were once entirely self-sufficient. This is not true. Federal money supported the unemployed as early as the late eighteenth century, the Civil War Pension Program assisted veterans and their families, European immigrants received lands stolen from Native Americans and utilized slave labor, and they all enjoyed the tax-funded infrastructure that enabled them to get their goods to market. The ethos of community responsibility, as expressed through Micah's oracles against those who deprive the vulnerable and aid the powerful, continue to speak to injustice, corruption, and anti-poor sentiment in the modern world.

Micah 7: Ensnaring One's Neighbors

Whereas Micah 3 lodges accusations against ruling and religious elites, Micah 7 turns its ire toward an entire Judean population that had abandoned the biblical ethos of community responsibility. Micah laments a kingdom full of inhabitants who "lie in wait for blood, and they hunt each other with nets" (7:2). The depravity is so great that Micah warns his audience:

> Put no trust in a friend, have no confidence in a loved one; guard the doors of your mouth from her who lies in your embrace; for the son treats the father with contempt, the daughter rises up against her mother, the daughter-in-law against her mother-in-law; your enemies are members of your own household (7:5–6). Any remnant of the ethos of community responsibility has been lost.

The animosity expressed in Micah 7 speaks to today. Citizens with purchasing power, but who are not among the financial elite or in political power, frequently engage in abusive systems. In an economy that labels a few products as *fair-trade*, *shade-grown*, or *conflict-free*, without labeling the majority of its goods as *sweatshop-produced*, *cultivated through deforestation*, or *mined by children and slaves*, it is easy for people to blind themselves to the systems of poverty and injustice in which they participate: in fact, most cannot afford to purchase ethically-produced products. Micah 7 sparks important ethical conversations about consumerism – a key driver of the US economic system – and about the moral implications of how our products, from low-cost items to luxury goods, are produced.

Another ethical dilemma to which Micah 7 might speak is the nation's growing student loan debt, currently totaling nearly $1.8 trillion. Secure and well-paying employment is a hallmark of the American Dream, which asserts that citizens can be prosperous if they are willing to work. Increasingly, secure and well-paying employment involves higher education. Those with college degrees earn, on average, almost $1 million more over the course of their careers and are more successful in weathering economic downturns.[15] But with ever-increasing tuition rates, only the wealthiest Americans can access college without incurring massive debts. This is a very profitable position for those controlling the levers of lending. Though farming is no longer a primary driver of employment in the United States, profiting off of our neighbors' debt is.

---

[15]   A. Berube, "Degrees of Separation: Education, Employment and the Great Recession in Metropolitan America," Brookings (November 5, 2010): www.brookings.edu/research/degrees-of-separation-education-employment-and-the-great-recession-in-metropolitan-america.

While college students voluntarily incur debt as an investment in their futures, the benefits are not theirs alone; all society benefits. College graduates become the medical workers, engineers, and educators that drive the nation. Yet, with an average undergraduate debt of nearly $40,000, these college graduates bear financial burdens that delay important life choices like buying homes and having children. Further injustice is found in how student loan debts are managed and exchanged. While most college graduates pay their debts in full, their loans are traded behind closed doors for pennies on the dollar.[16] The path to the American Dream thus winds through systems of debt and extraction that reinforce economic hierarchies; the fiscally powerful garner their neighbors' wages. As in Micah's time, community responsibility toward the well-being of individuals is lost, as our financial centers put profit above the well-being of the individual.

One justice organization that references the ethos of community responsibility for the well-being of the individual to address US student loan debt is Rolling Jubilee. Rolling Jubilee works to expose an unjust student lending system in which secondary markets purchase student debt for pennies on the dollar and then resell that debt at greatly reduced prices. In order to bring this system to light, cofounder Thomas Gokey started by using $400 of his own money to purchase and forgive $14,000 of student loan debt.[17] Rolling Jubilee's efforts, however, are not limited to student debt. Since the organization's 2012 inception, it has abolished nearly $32 million of student loan, credit card, and medical debt with $701,317.[18] According to Gokey, this strategy

> punches a hole through the morality of debt, through this idea that you owe x amount of dollars that the 1% says you owe. In reality, that debt is worth significantly less. The 1% is selling it to each other at bargain-based prices. [The debt holders] don't actually owe that.[19]

---

[16] J. Kasperkevic, "Occupy Activists Abolish $3.85m in Corinthian Colleges Students' Loan Debt," *The Guardian* (September 17, 2014): www.theguardian.com/money/2014/sep/17/occupy-activists-student-debt-corinthiancolleges.

[17] A. Frykohlm, "A Grassroots Jubilee," *The Christian Century* 132:11 (2015): 10–11, and Winters, "Jubilee Aims to Ease Grenada's Debt Crisis," 3.

[18] Rolling Jubilee, www.rollingjubilee.org (April 2019).

[19] See Kasperkevic, "Occupy Activists Abolish $3.85m in Corinthian Colleges Students' Loan Debt."

While "Rolling Sabbatical" may have been a suitable alternative name for an organization that encourages debt forgiveness, Rolling Jubilee offers another example of the ethos of community responsibility sparking the imaginations of activists in a modern struggle for justice. Similarly to how Micah 2 could augment Jubilee USA's desire to draw upon biblical texts in addressing international debt, Micah 7 could offer perspectives to further strengthen Rolling Jubilee's cause. By moving beyond the biblical legal texts to Micah 7, anti-debt campaigners could take their message beyond *debt forgiveness*, shedding light on the age-old propensity of those in power to abuse their status and conspire to ensnare their neighbors for profit.

Micah 6: Biblical Ethics in Micah, as Found through YHWH's Demands

Attacks on those who abandoned the ethos of community responsibility for the well-being of individuals in the second, third, and seventh chapters of Micah provide effective starting points from which to consider modern poverty ethics through a biblical lens. Equally important is the contribution of the trial setting in Micah 6:1–8 to conversations on positive ethical conduct.

With YHWH's people in the defendant's chair, the god charges them with returning numerous divine favors with disloyalty (6:3–5). The people's reaction and YHWH's rejoinder are telling. The people's response to YHWH's charges betrays a common misconception in Abrahamic faiths, both ancient and modern, namely, the idea that God's mercy is a haggled commodity. Projecting the modus operandi of their corrupt priests onto YHWH, the people ask if copious amounts of animal sacrifices, oil, or child sacrifice will abate YHWH's anger (6:6–7). These will not work. YHWH is not a god who shares in their depraved approach to power, giving favor only to those who can offer material gifts. Rather, Micah 6:8 responds with a review of proper ethical conduct for those who follow this god: "He has told you, O mortal, what is good; and what does YHWH require of you but to do justice (*mšpt*), and to love kindness (*ḥsd*), and to walk humbly (*hṣn ʾ*) with your God?" This verse offers a launching point to scrutinize our economic conduct toward our neighbor.

While the US may legally separate church and state, nearly half of its voting electorate participates actively in either Judaism or Christianity. Micah's instruction, read through the biblical ethos of community responsibility, brings both US economic policy and the sentiments and motivations that drive policy making processes into the limelight. Is a

Christian financier, whether running a pay-day loan store or trading in student loan debt, acting justly, kindly, and humbly before their god? What about factory owners who displace thousands of employees for profit? Are they acting justly, kindly, and humbly before their god? What about the politico calling for sweeping cuts for assistance programs, while offering tax breaks for the rich? Is he or she acting justly, kindly, and humbly before their god? Are the consumers buying products produced in sweatshops, or those sustaining systems that makes buying ethically sourced goods prohibitive, acting justly, kindly, and humbly before their god? Micah 6:1–8 can instigate numerous conversations on poverty and economics in our time – some of which are most uncomfortable.

14.4 CONCLUSION

A maxim attributed to Mark Twain, "History doesn't repeat itself, but it often rhymes," is applicable to the discussion at hand. The book of Micah's economic and religious systems are foreign to the modern reader, yet the injustices and sufferings it raises resonate with our modern ethical dilemmas. Land seizures continue to affect farmers, while prioritization of wealth over the needs of the vulnerable still drives our modern political, economic, and even religious machinery.

Even in industrial and postindustrial societies, where agriculture is practiced by few, the ethical core of the book of Micah finds footing. While "access to land" is no longer synonymous with "livelihood" in nonagrarian societies, readers can adjust the biblical ethos of community responsibility's focus to the things that land symbolized in ancient Judah – access to food security and livelihood. The ancient contexts of Micah may differ radically from our own, but what remains constant is the presence of those who use systems of debt and extraction to ensnare their neighbors and a collection of texts – still held sacred by many – that question and confront these systems.

FURTHER READING

Berube, A. "Degrees of Separation: Education, Employment and the Great Recession in Metropolitan America." *Brookings* (November 5, 2010): www .brookings.edu/research/degrees-of-separation-education-employment-and-the-great-recession-in-metropolitan-america.
Coomber, M. J. M. *Re-Reading the Prophets through Corporate Globalization.* Piscataway: Gorgias, 2010.
Frykholm, A. "A Grassroots Jubilee." *Christian Century* 132:11 (2015): 10–11.

Gottwald, N. "Early Israel as an Anti-Imperial Community." Pages 9–24 in *In the Shadow of Empire: Reclaiming the Bible as a History of Faithful Resistance.* Edited by R. A. Horsley. Louisville: Westminster John Knox, 2008.

Johnson, A. W. and T. Earle. *The Evolution of Human Societies: From Foraging Group to Agrarian State.* 2nd ed. Stanford: Stanford University Press, 2001.

Kasperkevic, J. "Occupy Activists Abolish $3.85m in Corinthian Colleges Students' Loan Debt." *The Guardian* (September 17, 2014): www.theguardian.com/money/2014/sep/17/occupy-activists-student-debt-corinthiancolleges.

Rappaport, R. A. "The Sacred in Human Evolution." *Annual Review of Ecology and Systematics* 2:1 (1971): 23–44.

Samples, T. R. "Rogue Trends in Sovereign Debt: Argentina, Vulture Funds, and Pari Passu under New York Law." *Northwestern Journal of International Law & Business* 35, 1 (2014): 49–86.

Winters, S. "Jubilee Aims to Ease Grenada's Debt Crisis." *National Catholic Reporter* June 20–July 3 (2014): 3.

15 War Violence in Hosea, Amos, and Nahum
STACY DAVIS

With few historical exceptions, it has been men who have initiated and fought in wars. Women keep the home fires burning, unless the fight reaches the home front, in which case they could become victims or casualties. With such historical tendencies acknowledged, the days of two clearly delineated, uniformed armies lining up and charging at each other are largely past, yielding to forms of combat where the distinction between combatant and civilian is often ambiguous. These changes have increased the dangers of war for women and children. While they still rarely fight in combat, they are often in the line of fire and may be viewed as legitimate collateral damage or as enemies to be conquered.

The continuing reality and negative effects of war violence against women, together with an evolving definition of "enemy" that includes not only formal combatants but anyone with whom one disagrees, make the biblical texts that describe war violence against women a pressing concern. Texts in Hosea, Amos, and Nahum describe the killing of unarmed women and children as a consequence of battle – occasionally a consequence sanctioned by God. These texts are problematic, even dangerous, from a feminist ethical perspective. Scholars debate whether their horrific descriptions of violence against some are literal or metaphorical – but this debate is arguably secondary to the way in which such texts have been used. A God who kills the families of "our enemies" may easily be used to sanction or minimize indiscriminate human slaughter at later times and in later places. This essay examines several prophetic texts describing war violence alongside three contemporary examples of modern ideological warfare, in each case perpetrated by lone male gunmen. Though who constitutes the enemy and what constitutes a battlefield differ in ancient and modern contexts, the ethical issues that violence against women raises are constant.

The biblical texts discussed in this essay have received little scholarly attention. While all three biblical books have been the subjects of feminist commentary, the focus has been on the marriage metaphor in Hosea, the calls for social justice in Amos, and the personification of Nineveh in Nahum. The scholarly debate regarding Nahum has often centered on whether the violence against the city is justified, rather than on the infliction of this violence upon a city personified as a woman.

Undergirding this prophetic literature is the theory of divine retribution, or the belief that God rewards the righteous and punishes the wicked. As Deut 30:16–18 states,

> If you obey the commandments of the LORD your God that I am commanding you today, by loving the LORD your God, walking in his ways, and observing his commandments, decrees, and ordinances, then you shall live and become numerous, and the LORD your God will bless you in the land that you are entering to possess. But if your heart turns away and you do not hear, but are led astray to bow down to other gods and serve them, I declare to you today that you shall perish; you shall not live long in the land that you are crossing the Jordan to enter and possess.

While Hosea focuses on this Israelite-centered view of retribution, Amos and Nahum apply it to non-Israelite nations – making God universal, as opposed to particular. Although Deut 30:7 suggests that God will curse Israel's enemies only after Israel has repented, there is no discussion of Israelite repentance in Amos or Nahum. Instead, God is unhappy with the enemies' own actions and responds to them accordingly.

In the book of Hosea, the prophet argues that Israelite idolatry is one of the causes of the northern kingdom's fall to the Assyrians in 722 BCE. Its collapse will leave no one unharmed: "the tumult of war shall raise against your people, and all your fortresses shall be destroyed, as Shalman destroyed Beth-Arbel on the day of battle when mothers were dashed in pieces with their children" (Hos 10:14). If Ps 137:8 is a parallel, death occurred by being thrown forcefully against rocks or walls. This killing of women and children represents the complete destruction of the community, because it literally destroys the future population. For Hosea, the deaths of these Israelite women and children happen with cause: "Samaria shall bear her guilt, because she has rebelled against her God; they shall fall by the sword, their little ones shall be dashed in pieces, and their pregnant women ripped open" (13:16).

Carolyn J. Sharp argues that Hosea destroys the disobedient rhetorically in order to encourage the Israelites to repent and to make

way for the righteous.[1] Beth-Arbel's fall acts as "a vivid contemporary
reference point for the prophet"; what happened there would be an
appropriate punishment for Israel's disobedience.[2] Alice A. Keefe inter-
prets the images as "a prophetic commentary upon the condition and
fate of the nation Israel in a time of intensifying societal disruption,
political strife, and the imminent threat of Assyrian invasion."[3] Because
of the cultural importance of fertility and family for social and economic
survival, Hosea's imagery of physical destruction intimates social
destruction as well. The violent deaths of women and children represent
the entirety of Israel's suffering and decimation as a result of Assyria's
conquest.[4]

Amos contains similar images and raises similar debates. The
Ammonites lose their capital city and go into exile, "because they have
ripped open pregnant women in Gilead in order to enlarge their
territory" (Amos 1:13). The text implies that these women were killed
in the process of Ammon's drive toward northern expansion. Paul
A. Kruger concludes that the actions are metaphorical, because "in
Assyrian art and the Assyrian royal inscriptions... children and their
mothers are mostly portrayed as deportees."[5] In one relief, however,
"women from an Arabic nomadic group are depicted as being hit and
apparently also being raped."[6] Kruger concludes that the images are
meant to depict war's horrors, not necessarily actual events.[7]

Even if imaginary, such images have theological implications; these
actions displease God and warrant punishment. Yet, as Mary Mills
observes, "If a city is founded on violent oppression, then it will find
a match in a religious belief which threatens it with like-minded
oppression."[8] Rabbah is violently destroyed because the Ammonites
killed pregnant women: Violence justifies violence. Moreover, when

---

[1]   C. J. Sharp, "Hewn by the Prophet: An Analysis of Violence and Sexual Transgression
      in Hosea with Reference to the Homiletical Aesthetics of Jeremiah Wright," in *The
      Aesthetics of Violence in the Prophets*, ed. J. M. O'Brien and C. Franke (New York:
      T&T Clark, 2010), 57.
[2]   Sharp, "Hewn by the Prophet," 62.
[3]   A. A. Keefe, "Family Metaphors and Social Conflict in Hosea," in *Writing and
      Reading War: Rhetoric, Gender, and Ethics in Biblical and Modern Contexts*, ed.
      B. E. Kelle and F. R Ames (Atlanta: Society of Biblical Literature, 2008), 113.
[4]   Keefe, "Family Metaphors and Social Conflict in Hosea," 117–20, 124–5.
[5]   P. A. Kruger, "Mothers and Their Children as Victims in War: Amos 1:13 against the
      Background of the Ancient Near East," *OTE* 29 (2016): 104; 103, 106.
[6]   Kruger, "Mothers and Their Children as Victims in War," 104.
[7]   Kruger, "Mothers and Their Children as Victims in War," 109, 111–12.
[8]   M. Mills, "Divine Violence in the Book of Amos," in *The Aesthetics of Violence in the
      Prophets*, ed. J. M. O'Brien and C. Franke (New York: T&T Clark, 2010), 169.

God is said to sanction the violence, it becomes a way for humans to release anger, hostility, and resentment – even if ostensibly only metaphorically.[9] Danger looms: What happens when humans have the power to transform symbol into action?

In Nahum's prophecy against Nineveh, the Assyrian city is warned that it will suffer the same fate as Thebes. Hosea claims that the Assyrians killed Israelite women and children; now Nahum declares that what happened to the Israelites will happen to the Assyrians. Thebes "became an exile, she went into captivity; even her infants were dashed in pieces at the head of every street; lots were cast for her nobles; all her dignitaries were bound in fetters" (Nah 3:10); Nineveh will suffer the same fate. Though such language may constitute an ahistorical justification of God's actions, the destruction itself was real: Both Nineveh and Thebes fell in the seventh century BCE. Some interpreters consider such violence an ethical response to Assyrian oppression, as a form of retributive punishment.[10] But Julia M. O'Brien points out that this conclusion depends on the interpreter's perspective: "the reader, depending on his or her location, might identify with Nineveh or perhaps with that other devastated woman – Thebes, whose children were dashed at the head of every street."[11] Read by an African American feminist rhetorical critic, attuned to the perspective of Israelite, Ammonite, Assyrian, and Egyptian women, these texts raise significant ethical questions about the way gender and war intersect.

Though these ancient texts may seem strange and distant to contemporary readers, ancient and contemporary warfare are similar in at least two ways. The first is a connection with ethnicity, apparent particularly in Amos and Nahum. Though civil wars are described in Judges 20 and Isaiah 7, Israelites do not usually fight each other. Their enemies are their non-Israelite – and usually more powerful – neighbors. Non-Israelites did not worship the God of Israel, and some biblical texts imply that, as a result, these outsiders lacked the moral standards of the Israelites – who are themselves regularly the object of God's ire for apostasy and other sins. The Ammonites destroyed pregnant women for territorial gain; it is the Ninevites' own brutality that will be visited upon them in turn.

---

[9]   Mills, "Divine Violence in the Book of Amos," 179.
[10] J. M. O'Brien, "Violent Pictures, Violent Cultures: The 'Aesthetics of Violence' in Contemporary Film and in Ancient Prophetic Texts," in *The Aesthetics of Violence in the Prophets*, ed. J. M. O'Brien and C. Franke (New York: T&T Clark, 2010), 125, 129, 113.
[11] O'Brien, "Violent Pictures, Violent Cultures," 118.

The second similarity between ancient and contemporary warfare is the frequency with which they are associated with sexual violence. Echoing Alice Keefe's remarks regarding Hosea, Ruth Seifert observes, "'If the aim is to destroy a culture, [its women] are prime targets because of their cultural importance in the family structure... Their physical and emotional destruction aims at destroying social and cultural stability.'"[12] Killing pregnant women destroyed the conquered community by destroying its next generation. In the ancient world women regularly became conquests of war, subject to physical and sexual abuse or slavery, though they were not always killed.[13] Especially violent female enslavement could be used as a form of vengeance against particularly resistant male fighters; women could be killed in those cases.[14] Referring to the modern movement to end war-related violence against women and girls, Kathy L. Gaca observes that this "amounts to an attempt to outlaw one of the most persistent and fundamental purposes of warfare as historically practiced from the Bronze Age to late antiquity and beyond."[15] The goal remains both noble and, as recent conflicts indicate, elusive.

With these similarities in mind, the remainder of this essay will compare biblical references to slaughtering women and children to three more recent instances of the slaughter of women and children in the United States and New Zealand: the shootings at the Emanuel AME Church in Charleston, South Carolina; at the First Baptist Church in Sutherland Springs, Texas; and at the Al Noor and Linwood mosques in Christchurch, New Zealand. Although in these cases mothers and children were not raped, ripped open, or smashed against rocks, they constitute instances of ideological warfare in which women and children were killed. In each case sacred space was reconfigured as a battle-ground, as the categorization of a person or a group as an enemy enabled a shooter to justify mass killing. Moreover, each provoked a public religious response to the violence.

Though war is traditionally defined as "a conflict carried on by force of arms... between nations or between parties within a nation," modern realities mean that the parties to war need no longer be national armies;

---

[12]   K. L. Gaca, "Girls, Women, and the Significance of Sexual Violence in Ancient Warfare," in *Sexual Violence in Conflict Zones: From the Ancient World to the Era of Human Rights*, ed. E. D. Heineman (Philadelphia: University of Pennsylvania, 2011), 73.

[13]   Gaca, "Girls, Women, and the Significance of Sexual Violence," 78–9.

[14]   Gaca, "Girls, Women, and the Significance of Sexual Violence," 84–6.

[15]   Gaca, "Girls, Women, and the Significance of Sexual Violence," 88.

paramilitary groups or terrorist organizations may also wage war.[16] Most essential to the genre is that it involves "active hostility or contention; conflict; contest." In the modern context, the rise of social media and the twenty-four-hour news cycle has exacerbated what appears to be a natural human tendency to segregate people into friends and enemies, and to demonize those deemed the enemy. Ancient and modern cases raise the same ethical questions: Who is my enemy? Why? How should I respond to my enemy?

*

In June 2015, Dylann Roof went into the Emanuel AME Church in Charleston, South Carolina, to start a war between blacks and whites. Having read white supremacist ideology online, he concluded that African Americans posed a threat to white American civilization.[17] Toward the end of a Bible study, Roof opened fire and killed nine parishioners, six of whom were women: Rev. Sharonda Coleman-Singleton, forty-five; Cynthia Hurd, fifty-four; Susie Jackson, eighty-seven; Ethel Lance, seventy; DePayne Middleton Doctor, forty-nine; and Myra Thompson, fifty-nine.[18] The church's pastor, State Senator Clementa Pinckney, died with members of his congregation.

In Pinckney's eulogy, President Barack Obama spoke of faith, grace, and history.[19] He began with Hebrews 11, the New Testament chapter that defines faith and names examples of faith from the Hebrew Bible. He called out the names of the dead, characterizing them as "good people. Decent people. God-fearing people" of faith. Obama wondered whether Roof knew the activist history of Emanuel AME in particular or of the black church in general, and suggested that Roof

> surely sensed the meaning of his violent act. It was an act that drew on a long history of bombs and arson and shots fired at churches, not random, but as a means of control, a way to terrorize and oppress.

[16] s.v. "War," dictionary.com.
[17] L. Bernstein, S. Horwitz, and P. Holley, "Dylann Roof's Racist Manifesto: 'I have no choice,'" *The Washington Post*, June 20, 2015: www.washingtonpost.com/national/ health-science/authorities-investigate-whether-racist-manifesto-was-written-by-sc-gunman/2015/06/20/f0bd3052-1762-11e5-9ddc-e3353542100c_story.html.
[18] "The Victims: 9 Were Slain at Charleston's Emanuel AME Church," NPR, June 18, 2015 : www.npr.org/sections/thetwo-way/2015/06/18/415539516/the-victims-9-were-slain-at-charlestons-emanuel-ame-church.
[19] The full video may be found on https://youtu.be/x9IGyidtfGI, and a written transcript at https://obamawhitehouse.archives.gov. All quotations in this paragraph come from these sources.

An act that he imagined would incite fear and recrimination, violence and suspicion. An act that he presumed would deepen divisions that trace back to our nation's original sin.

Instead, God's grace appeared. The congregation invited Roof into the Bible study, only an hour before he opened fire; some grieving families forgave him after the shooting. Hard conversations about removing the Confederate flag from the state capitol followed. Obama argued that this hard work needed to continue:

> It would be a refutation of the forgiveness expressed by those families if we merely slipped into old habits, whereby those who disagree with us are not merely wrong but bad; where we shout instead of listen; where we barricade ourselves behind preconceived notions or well-practiced cynicism. Reverend Pinckney once said, "Across the South, we have a deep appreciation of history – we haven't always had a deep appreciation of each other's history."

History, he implies, cannot be used to justify oppression or to avoid difficult dialogues. Obama then sang the first verse of "Amazing Grace," saying that those who died had God's grace, naming them again and concluding with an expression of hope that the congregation would make use of the grace left to them by the dead.

Obama's acknowledgment of the killings as hate crimes fits Roof's description of his own actions. Roof chose South Carolina because of its Confederate history and Charleston because it had been a majority slave city.[20] His language about African Americans as America's enemies has centuries-old history. Whether by a Northerner or Southerner, an active Ku Klux Klan member, or a passive lynching observer, language about and treatment of African Americans by white Americans has presumed African American inferiority and the need to control African Americans by any means necessary, including violence. Both legal and extrajudicial violence is an integral part of African American history.

Many of the white Americans who sanctioned that violence were regular churchgoers. In the last few decades, several scholars have analyzed the connections between American Christianity and systemic racism, as well as the use of the Bible to rationalize racist behavior.[21]

---

[20] Bernstein, Horwitz, and Holley, "Dylann Roof's Racist Manifesto."

[21] See, e.g., S. R. Haynes, *Noah's Curse: The Biblical Justification of American Slavery* (Oxford: Oxford University Press, 2002); E. J. Blum and P. Harvey, *The Color of Christ: The Son of God and the Saga of Race in America* (Chapel Hill: University of North

While Amos and Nahum have no concept of racism of the modern kind, their categorization of certain people as worthy of harm, particularly women and children, contributes to a moral logic in which anyone who mistreats you is your enemy; moreover, it allows you to harm those who have not harmed you. Nahum issues a blanket condemnation of the Ninevites for their treatment of Israel. Amos' critique of the Ammonites comes in the middle of a series of oracles against the surrounding nations; though most of these nations' actions are not directed at Israel, the prophet sees their activities as immoral and prophesies God's punishment. Dylann Roof acted out of a similarly generalized sense of threat when he killed six African American women at Emanuel AME: These were not black men raping white women, against whom he claimed he had to take up arms, but women who had just welcomed him into their church.

The prophets and Dylann Roof have one thing in common: rhetorical argumentation. For Amos and Nahum, the nations' evil conduct, especially as shown through their mistreatment of Israel, deserves God's punishment. Roof's manifesto claims that African Americans, naturally inferior and therefore violent, endanger white Americans. As the Ammonites and the Assyrians had to be stopped for the sake of Israel, African Americans must be stopped for the sake of America.

The primary difference is in execution. The prophets claim that God will destroy God's enemies – directly, in Amos, or through an unidentified army, in Nahum. Roof, a member of St Paul's Lutheran Church in Columbia, South Carolina,[22] decided that he was God's agent. Roof may not have seen himself as a prophet, but like Amos and Nahum he identified an enemy and decreed their punishment. At the church, he said, "I have to do it. You rape our women, and you're taking over our country. And you have to go."[23]

*

On November 5, 2017, Devin Kelley, a man with a history of domestic violence, decided to confront his mother-in-law at her church in Sutherland Springs, Texas. She was not in attendance at First Baptist at the

Carolina Press, 2012); and J. H. Fletcher, *The Sin of White Supremacy: Christianity, Racism, and Religious Diversity in America* (Maryknoll: Orbis, 2017).

[22] J. Kaleem, "South Carolina Lutheran Pastor: Dylann Roof Was Church Member, His Family Prays for Victims," *Huffington Post*, June 19, 2015, www.huffpost.com/entry/dylann-roof-religion-church-lutheran_n_7623990.

[23] Bernstein, Horwitz, and Holley, "Dylann Roof's Racist Manifesto."

time; instead, Kelley opened fire on her church family. Of the twenty-six persons killed, ten were women and nine were children: Shani Corrigan, fifty-one; Emily Garcia, seven; Emily Hill, eleven; Greg Hill, thirteen; Megan Hill, nine; Crystal Holcombe, thirty-six; Karla Holcombe, fifty-eight; Noah Holcombe, one; Sarah Johnson, sixty-eight; Haley Krueger, sixteen; Karen Marshall, fifty-six; Tara McNulty, thirty-three; Annabelle Pomeroy, fourteen; Therese Rodriguez, sixty-six; Brooke Ward, five; Joann Ward, thirty; Peggy Lynn Warden; and Lula Wolcinski White, seventy-one.[24] One week later, the church held its Sunday service in a large tent guarded by police.[25]

A combination of combat language and words of comfort characterized the hour-long service. Pastor Frank Pomeroy began by noting that it was Veterans' Day weekend and that the church, Texas, and the United States had been attacked. Those who had died, he argued, could also be called veterans: The apostle Paul warned that Jesus' followers would fight against principalities, and this is what the congregation is experiencing. Those who died are with God, their struggle over. Reading Gen 3:15 as a battle between the devil and Christians, Pomeroy assured the congregation that "victory has a price," but that ultimately Satan will lose. The shooting should not keep people out of church, because "Satan wounds those who worry him the most." Like Paul, the congregation must fight Satan until the end. Christians will have the final victory; the dead cannot be lost in vain. Pomeroy concluded by saying that salvation is available to all and that the congregation should remain strong and persist.

These words were the theme for the remainder of the service. Two praise songs and "Amazing Grace" were followed by plain words from Senator John Cornyn: "This hurts." Yet, though what happened is incomprehensible, God calls for trust; trials lead to strength and hope (Romans 5) and God will use all things for good (Romans 8). After three more praise songs, the former associate pastor spoke, saying that the devil did not win, because "we just smashed the attendance record"; God brings victory through Jesus, so "Satan has fumbled that ball" (2 Cor 2:14). The pastor then quoted various biblical passages as he challenged those present to ask whether they truly follow Jesus, for the

---

[24] C. Bailey and D. Arkin, "Texas Church Shooting: Who Were the Victims of the Sutherland Springs Massacre," NBC, November 8, 2017, www.nbcnews.com/ storyline/texas-church-shooting/texas-church-shooting-who-were-victims-sutherland-springs-massacre-n18356.

[25] The service may be viewed at https://youtu.be/_fY82IrFCYc; all direct quotations for the next two paragraphs come from this video.

dead are now in heaven and do not want anyone lost (Prov 3:5–6; John 8:32; 17:17). The service concluded with a lengthy altar call. Before the final song, the pastor said: "The Lord has a plan. We don't understand it. We don't know why."

Perhaps the greatest tragedy of the Sutherland Springs shooting is its almost basic comprehensibility. Devin Kelley already had a conviction for domestic violence that contributed to his dishonorable discharge from the Air Force. The Air Force's failure to report the conviction to the civilian authorities meant that Kelley was not flagged when he bought firearms. Kelley's anger against his wife and mother-in-law drove him to First Baptist, armed with weapons he should not have had. Those killed at First Baptist Church were victims of the violence against women that Kelley had already demonstrated.

To look for meaning in tragedy is natural, but the dead were martyrs, not veterans.[26] There is no mystery here. The women of First Baptist died for their faith, their deaths a result of a generalized expend-ability of women intrinsic to the patriarchal systems they inhabited. Kelley's war against one woman led him to open fire on others, collateral damage in his own private war. The enemy that day was not Satan but an angry man with a gun, who saw violence as the solution. This was a war on an all too human level. First Baptist Church endured a horrific act; its ordinariness makes it even more so. Domestic violence in the United States is a daily occurrence; what is most common is often the most difficult to see.

Allusions to violence against women and children do not especially stand out in Hosea, Amos, or Nahum, either, but these biblical texts contain disturbingly similar expressions of violence against women, particularly in war – driven by a patriarchal assumption of women's expendability. Hosea contends that the death of Israelite women and children is a necessary punishment for Israelite disobedience, a by-product of Assyrian conquest. As Alice Keefe notes, this devastation refers to "the end of Israel. Slaughtered mothers with their children figure the nation as a whole as it is devastated by war."[27] Amos insists that the Ammonites must be punished for destroying Israelite women in the name of territorial expansion. In Nahum, the murdered infants are Theban, but in every example men at war enact extreme violence

---

[26]   The pastors did not know at the time about Kelley's record of violence, so no words were said about a Christian response to domestic violence.

[27]   A. A. Keefe, "Family Metaphors and Social Conflict in Hosea," 125.

against women. These women are no more important to the foreign armies than the churchgoers were to Kelley.

*

On March 15, 2019, an Australian advocate of white supremacy killed fifty people at the Al Noor and Linwood mosques in Christchurch, New Zealand.[28] Among the dead were eight women and children: Husna Ahmed, forty-four; Ansi Alibava, twenty-five; Linda Armstrong, sixty-five; Karam Bibi; Mucaad Ibrahim, three; Sayyad Milne, fourteen; Muhammad Haziq Mohd-Tarmizi, seventeen; and Hamza Mustafa, sixteen. Because Friday services are not required for observant Muslim women, most of the dead were men.

One week later, the Muslim community and non-Muslim supporters gathered outside the Al Noor mosque for Friday prayer. Between the traditional prayers were praise of the Muslim dead and non-Muslim allies as well as passionate calls to resist Islamophobia and white supremacy.[29] As the imam addressed the congregation, he noted that the hatred of the previous week had turned into love and compassion. He suggested that the deaths of the worshippers were not meaningless, because people would now see the "beauty of Islam"; "hate will be undone, and love will redeem us." The terrorist had an "evil ideology," but "New Zealand is unbreakable... We are brokenhearted but not broken." The imam quoted a passage from the Qur'an about the dead being alive and declared that they had died in righteousness, martyrs of Islam and New Zealand. He connected another text, about all belonging and returning to God, to the persistence of the community in spite of suffering. After some prayers, the imam then spoke against religiously motivated violence. Citing examples from Canada, Norway, the United Kingdom, and the United States, he warned that "Islamophobia is real," a "targeted campaign to dehumanize and irrationally fear Muslims." What happened at the mosque was not an unexpected or sudden event but a consequence of political and media rhetoric: "Islamophobia kills." The imam called on his listeners to stop this hate speech and the

---

[28]   Prime Minister Jacinda Ardern asked people not to name the shooter, but to name those killed. On March 21, 2019, *The Guardian* heeded her advice, listing the names of forty-seven of the dead and telling their stories; "We Shall Speak Their Names," www.theguardian.com/world/ng-interactive/2019/mar/21/christchurch-shooting-remembering-the-victims.

[29]   The full video may be found on https://youtu.be/K8tPjSMZquo; all quotations in the following paragraph come from this source.

"politics of fear," acknowledging that the "evil ideology of white supremacy did not strike us first" and that "terrorism has no color, has no race, and has no religion." White supremacy is a universal threat. The imam concluded with prayers for paradise for the martyred, healing for the injured, strength for the affected families, and protection for New Zealand and the earth.

Especially striking was the imam's willingness to call this attack what it was: terrorism. By definition, terrorism is a tactic, but in recent decades it has been primarily associated with Muslim perpetrators. One result has been a reluctance by reporters and politicians to call white shooters "terrorists," even when white supremacist ideology leads them to terrorize the living by killing those of a different race or religion. Like Roof, the Christchurch shooter saw a nonwhite group as a threat and decided he had to "defend" his way of life.

Ethnocentrism as cultural superiority is common to both the ancient and modern worlds. Belief in the superiority of Israel's God made political alliances with other peoples morally problematic (Hosea); ethnocentrism rationalized the suffering of those who harmed God's people (Amos, Nahum). God is a warrior who avenges Judah by destroying Nineveh (Nah 2:13, 3:5). The ethical consequences of such attitudes arise when humans, rather than God, decide what others deserve for wrongdoing (real or imagined). Biblical texts that justify violence as God's will – even a cause for rejoicing (Nah 3:19) – scarcely offer a vision of how to protect the innocent from the self-righteous avenger. Calls to love the stranger may be insufficient: Strangers who worship the wrong deity may still be stoned (Lev 19:33–34, 20:2). Even the imperative to love one's enemies may be insufficient: Enemies (*echthrous*) are literally those one hates (Matt 5:44). Loving them certainly does not mean they will love you back. Yet, to "love the sinner but hate the sin" – purporting to love a person while hating their actions – borders on meaningless. "Hate" is too strong a word to be in the same sentence as "love"; to love means to abandon hate altogether. The imam's recognition of white supremacy and Islamophobia as a form of hate recognizes that the shooter did not love those he killed – and, perhaps, acknowledges that the love of Muslims toward the shooter might never have changed that. Roof sat in a church for an hour with the people he killed.

*

There are no clear solutions to the problem posed by men killing each other, women, and children. But language matters. What we call each other matters. Should we have "enemies" that God should avenge? As an Air Force brat, the daughter of a Vietnam veteran, the granddaughter of World War I and World War II veterans, and the great-niece of a Korea veteran, I do not call myself a pacifist. But I am a historian – and history suggests that war becomes harder to avoid and resolve once religion enters the picture. During the US Civil War, both the Union and the Confederacy claimed God was on their side. Compromise proved correspondingly difficult. Defeat left hard feelings in white Southerners, manifest in Jim Crow laws, voter intimidation, and lynchings.

The most vulnerable members of an enemy population bear the brunt of war's ravages. But not enemies all are created equal. Just war theory, developed by Christian theologians and employed by Christian nations, rationalizes armed conflict on the basis of "a gendered idea of the dichotomy between civilians and combatants that stereotypes men as 'just warriors' (righteous defenders of the innocent) and women as 'beautiful souls' (innocent of wars but a justification for fighting them)."[30] But those "beautiful souls" often become the victims of the very ideology meant to protect them. As Laura Sjoberg argues, "There is a significant risk that the performance of 'protection' not only fails to provide it but comes at a hefty cost, in terms of both war security and gender subordination, to those who appear to be protected."[31] This is equally the case after hostilities have ostensibly ended; thus, for example, violence against women has continued in the Democratic Republic of Congo long after fighting ended. As Serena Cosgrove observes: "Belligerent forces often become habituated to using violence to feed, clothe, and take care of themselves, but former soldiers who have been ordered or encouraged to carry out violent practices during the conflict are supposed to abandon them during peace."[32] This blurring of the distinction between war and peace, combatant and civilian is reflected in the fact that civilians are subject to violent attack in more than one-third of wars.[33]

---

[30] L. Sjoberg, "The Inseparability of Gender Hierarchy, the Just War Tradition, and Authorizing War," in *Just War: Authority, Tradition, and Practice*, ed. A. F. Lang, C. O'Driscoll, and J. Williams (Washington, DC: Georgetown University Press, 2013), 81.
[31] Sjoberg, "The Inseparability of Gender Hierarchy," 85.
[32] S. Cosgrove, "The Absent State: New Patriarchal Forms of Gender Subordination in the Democratic Republic of Congo," in *Gender Violence in Peace and War: States of Complicity*, ed. V. Sanford, K. Stefanos, and C. M. Salvi (New Brunswick: Rutgers University Press, 2016), 162.
[33] Sjoberg, "The Inseparability of Gender Hierarchy," 86.

These realities indicate that the biblical language describing military violence against women and children is not metaphorical. Failure to protect women was seen, in both ancient and modern times, as a failure of masculinity.[34] Whether expressed in the attention to the officers and their red clothing in Nahum 3:3–5 or the overwhelmingly male promotional video for the US Marine Corps, war is the business of real men.

*

How, in light of this, should we talk about the gendered implications of war? Laura Sjoberg offers a helpful way forward, as she suggests a reorientation of war away from the performance of protection:

> An ethics of war without civilians is one without us/them and public/private dichotomies, fundamentally altering the 'us' that might decide, ontologically, to make wars, and act to fight them. It is an ethics of war that needs an alternative justification for war than those who it cannot and will not be able to protect.[35]

In addition, any ethics of war must approach claims to moral superiority or moral judgments with great caution. Contra Hosea, apostasy should not justify the slaughter of apostate women and children. Contra Nahum, cruelty against one group of innocents should not be countered with cruelty against another group of innocents. If one must fight, one's opponents need to be one's equals. After describing Gilead's cruelty to pregnant women, Amos declares, "With shouting on the day of battle, with a storm on the day of the whirlwind; then their king shall go into exile, he and his officials together" (1:14–15). While this exile will undoubtedly create hardship for Ammonite women and children, pregnant Ammonite women will not be ripped open. Recognizing who is *not* the enemy is a first step in deciding not only who needs to be fought, but when, why, and – just as importantly – how. Women are not inevitably enemy combatants who must be destroyed.

FURTHER READING

Cosgrove, S. "The Absent State: Teen Mothers and New Patriarchal Forms of Gender Subordination in the Democratic Republic of Congo." Pages 158–70 in *Gender Violence in Peace and War: States of Complicity*. Edited by V. Sanford, K. Stefatos, and C. M. Salvi. New Brunswick: Rutgers, 2016.

---

[34] Sjoberg, "The Inseparability of Gender Hierarchy," 86–7.
[35] Sjoberg, "The Inseparability of Gender Hierarchy," 92.

Gaca, K. L. "Girls, Women, and the Significance of Sexual Violence in Ancient Warfare." Pages 73–88 in *Sexual Violence in Conflict Zones: From the Ancient World to the Era of Human Rights*. Edited by E. D. Heineman. Philadelphia: University of Pennsylvania, 2011.

Keefe, A. A. "Family Metaphors and Social Conflict in Hosea." Pages 113–28 in *Writing and Reading War: Rhetoric, Gender, and Ethics in Biblical and Modern Contexts*. Edited by B. E. Kelle and F. R. Ames. Atlanta: Society of Biblical Literature, 2008.

Kruger, P. A. "Mothers and their Children as Victims in War: Amos 1:13 against the Background of the Ancient Near East." *OTE* 29 (2016): 100–15.

Mills, M. "Divine Violence in the Book of Amos." Pages 153–79 in *The Aesthetics of Violence in the Prophets*. Edited by J. M. O'Brien and C. Franke. New York: T&T Clark, 2010.

O'Brien, J. M. "Violent Pictures, Violent Cultures: The 'Aesthetics of Violence' in Contemporary Film and in Ancient Prophetic Texts." Pages 112–30 in *The Aesthetics of Violence in the Prophets*. Edited by J. M. O'Brien and C. Franke. New York: T&T Clark, 2010.

Sharp, C. J. "Hewn by the Prophet: An Analysis of Violence and Sexual Transgression in Hosea with Reference to the Homiletical Aesthetics of Jeremiah Wright." Pages 50–71 in *The Aesthetics of Violence in the Prophets*. Edited by J. M. O'Brien and C. Franke. New York: T&T Clark, 2010.

Sjoberg, L. "The Inseparability of Gender Hierarchy, the Just War Tradition, and Authorizing War." Pages 81–96 in *Just War: Authority, Tradition, and Practice*. Edited by A. F. Lang, C. O'Driscoll, and J. Williams. Washington, D.C.: Georgetown University Press, 2013.

Part IV

Wisdom/Poetic Ethics

16 Teaching Complex Ethical Thinking with Proverbs

ANNE W. STEWART

From its opening words, the book of Proverbs suggests that ethical reflection is a complex task, requiring sophisticated faculties of discernment. It demands the ability to sift through competing sources of wisdom. Proverbs calls upon neophyte students and experienced sages alike to test their learning constantly in wisdom's laboratory of the world. Calibrating one's moral sensitivities is a lifelong pursuit that requires savvy and discipline, and the book of Proverbs in both its form and its function seeks to impart such skill.

The prevailing concern of the book of Proverbs is to equip its students with the intellectual framework and moral capacities to discern the way of wisdom in the world. The book's short proverbial sayings are deceptively simple; their form in fact reflects a complex and sophisticated understanding of the nature of ethical reflection. The longer poems that make up the first nine chapters of the book similarly assume a holistic understanding of moral formation, pointing toward the complex ways that human character is shaped and formed. The poems and sayings throughout the book appeal to the full range of the student's senses, emotions, and desires, not only the rational capacity of the intellect. They prompt the student to engage moral complexity and acquire the capacity to negotiate the way of wisdom in everyday contexts. Accordingly, it is a book that has much to offer contemporary reflections on ethics.

16.1 ETHICS IN THE ANCIENT WORLD: THE SOCIAL WORLD OF THE BOOK OF PROVERBS

The book of Proverbs represents a complex social reality and contains within its collections a vibrant conversation among social worlds and generations. Although it is typically understood as the example *par excellence* of the "traditional" pole of Israelite wisdom, the poems and sayings within the book contain a greater breadth of perspectives than may appear at first glance.[1] This too is part of the book's complex ethical reflection. Its collections hold diverse testaments to the nature of wisdom and its manifestation in particular circumstances. The book reflects a vibrant conversation, often just below the surface, about the way of wisdom, human nature, and the pursuit of righteousness and justice.

The poems and proverbial collections within the book were compiled over generations, and it is difficult to date the book with precision. While many scholars posit a date for the final composition of the book in the Hellenistic or Persian period, the book contains proverbial wisdom whose origins are nearly impossible to determine and likely reflect a variety of periods. Accordingly, the book does not represent a singular historical moment or static social world. Rather, as is the nature of proverbial sayings, it reflects wisdom accumulated and adapted over generations. As such, it invites dialogue with past generations and the lived experience of daily life in the present.

The book of Proverbs gestures to several contexts for its instruction. The book is traditionally ascribed to Solomon (Prov 1:1), and references to a royal context appear in superscriptions (e.g., 10:1; 25:1; 31:1) and proverbial advice (e.g., 23:1–4; 25:2). While the book was surely not authored by the monarch, the traditional ascription reflects a connection to the court and royal ideology. The king is the upholder of justice and righteousness. Thus Prov 16:12–13 observes, "It is an abomination to kings to do evil, for the throne is established by righteousness. Righteous lips are the delight of a king, and he loves those who speak what is right." Similarly, court officials participate in upholding moral order by advancing wisdom and righteousness. Thus the sages, "the wise ones," are charged to speak rightly and to make judgments in accord with moral order:

> These also are the sayings of the wise: partiality in judging is not good. Whoever says to the wicked, "You are innocent," will be cursed by peoples, abhorred by nations; but those who rebuke the wicked will have delight, and a good blessing will come upon them. (24:23–25)

This wisdom is in some measure a reflection of royal values. It vests authority in hierarchy and presents this as part of the natural order, vital to the health of the population. For example, Prov 29:4 notes, "By justice

---

[1]   See discussion in A. W. Stewart, "Wisdom's Imagination: Moral Reasoning and the Book of Proverbs" *JSOT* 40 (2016): 351–72.

a king gives stability to the land, but one who makes heavy exactions ruins it." At the same time, many sayings express suspicion of those who subvert or resist this order. Proverbs 25:6–7 warns, "Do not put yourself forward in the king's presence or stand in the place of the great; for it is better to be told, 'Come up here,' than to be put lower in the presence of a noble." Such sayings subtly undergird a particular view of the world and resonate with the court's interest in promoting and maintaining social order. Indeed, this is linked to the divine order: "My child, fear the LORD and the king, and do not disobey either of them; for disaster comes from them suddenly, and who knows the ruin that both can bring?" (24:21–22).

The book does not, however, represent an exclusively monarchical perspective. Other sayings hint at a critique of kingship, including Prov 29:4, referenced above. Similarly, Prov 20:2 warns of the king's capricious power: "The dread anger of a king is like the growling of a lion; anyone who provokes him to anger forfeits life itself."

Proverbs' pedagogical function leads many scholars to posit a setting in a school context. There is limited evidence for the existence of formal schools in ancient Israel before the Hellenistic period, though there is literary and epigraphic evidence for an educational system within Israel and among Israel's neighbors in the ancient Near East.[2] For the most part, this occurred not in formal schools with separate facilities and faculty, as in the contemporary context, but within the family or through an apprenticeship model with small groups of students. Its goal was not general literacy but training to facilitate administrative and economic functions. It also functioned to advance the ideology of the court and social elites. As David M. Carr explains, "the issue in Israel is not mastery of an esoteric sign system to achieve literacy but use of literacy to help enculturate, shape the behavior, and otherwise mentally separate an educated upper class from their noneducated peers."[3] Similarly within Proverbs, several sayings constitute overt instructions in court etiquette (e.g., 23:1–2; 25:6–7), and the values embedded within the book largely represent the ethos of an educated elite.

The book is overtly set in the context of the home. Its first nine chapters in particular are framed as an address of a parent to a son,

---

[2] Cf. Ben Sira's reference to a "house of instruction" (Sir 51:23). For a discussion of literacy and education in Israel and the ancient Near East, see D. M. Carr, *Writing on the Tablet of the Heart: Origins of Scripture and Literature* (New York: Oxford University Press, 2005).

[3] Carr, *Writing on the Tablet of the Heart*, 119.

providing instruction on the ways of wisdom. The book begins with an encouragement to adhere to the parents' wisdom (1:8–9). The purpose of such admonition, beyond mere parental advice, also relates to the transmission of certain values and the preservation of social order. As Carr reflects, "a key goal of such (largely) family-based education was the cultural reproduction of the parent/teacher: enculturating a son (and some daughters) to play a similar sociocultural role to that of the parent."[4] Accordingly, the parents' wisdom and activity is mirrored in advice directly from God. As Prov 3:11–12 encourages, "My child, do not despise the LORD's discipline or be weary of his reproof, for the LORD reproves the one he loves, as a father the son in whom he delights."

Even as the sayings reflect different social settings and origins, their final form reflects the editorial eye of the sages who compiled the book. As Michael V. Fox explains,

> Learned clerks – at least some of them the king's men, others perhaps serving post-exilic provincial administrations – were the membrane through which principles, sayings, and coinages, folk and otherwise, were filtered. The central collections of Proverbs are their filtrate, a largely homogeneous one. In the end, it is *their* work and *their* idea of wisdom that we are reading, and it is, not surprisingly, quite coherent.[5]

The book is surely a product of its context and reflects the perspective of those who edited and compiled it. Yet this is not to say that the book is *merely* a product of its time, but rather that it continues to call forth engagement with daily realities of the present moment. Nonetheless, it is important to recognize the operative commitments and values that its perspective presents, for this is part of acquiring the discernment to understand "the words of the wise and their riddles," as the book itself commends (1:6).

16.2 ETHICS AND WISDOM

Every culture has sets of wisdom sayings passed along from generation to generation, encoding certain assumptions about its values and visions of the moral life. Proverbs likewise reveals its assumptions about the

---

[4]   Carr, *Writing on the Tablet of the Heart*, 130.
[5]   M. V. Fox, *Proverbs 1–9: A New Translation with Introduction and Commentary*, AB 18A (New York: Doubleday, 2000), 11; emphasis original.

nature of ethical reflection and human flourishing through its wisdom poems and sayings.

The complexities of ethical reflection are apparent within the concept of wisdom itself. Within Proverbs, wisdom is not an abstract ideal, but acquires its rich dimensions from the nature of lived reality. Its nuances are closely connected to the book's vision of moral reasoning. In the first place, wisdom is practical, not book knowledge. It is rooted in experience and involves the ability to apply knowledge to daily life. The sages insist that the curriculum of wisdom comes from nature and everyday encounters. Even an ant colony (Prov 6:6–7) and a sick dog (26:11) serve as lessons in wisdom. Everything can be an occasion for moral reflection, if one has the eyes to see.

Second, wisdom is rooted in tradition. It reflects the accumulated and tested observations of those who have come before. Thus, much of the book is couched in the voice of a parent to a child, urging the student's close attention and adoption of the parents' authoritative guidance. Proverbs 6:20–22, for example, counsels:

> My child, keep your father's commandment, and do not forsake your mother's teaching. Bind them upon your heart always; tie them around your neck. When you walk, they will lead you; when you lie down, they will watch over you; and when you awake, they will talk with you.

Wisdom is found in adhering to parental advice. This exhortation is a constant theme throughout the book. Conversely, failing to listen to parents is a sign of foolish transgression: "Those who do violence to their father and chase away their mother are children who cause shame and bring reproach" (19:26).

Yet even as wisdom is rooted in tradition, it is not static. Wisdom has an inherent capacity for innovation and imagination. Simply knowing the content of tradition or a parent's instruction does not make one wise; true wisdom consists in the ability to apply that knowledge to unprecedented situations. The poems and sayings in the book are not codified dictates but must be interpreted in unfolding circumstances. Reading the book requires interpretive imagination, as it juxtaposes competing, even contradictory, sayings. For example, Prov 26:4 advises, "Do not answer a fool according to his folly, or you will be a fool yourself," while the very next verse declares, "Answer a fool according to his folly, or he will be wise in his own eyes" (26:5). What is a person to do? The wise person knows the right proverb for the occasion.

Such contradictions reveal the need for moral dexterity. Kathleen M. O'Connor notes that the literary form of Proverbs draws attention to the ambiguous nature of reality. In setting contradictory sayings side by side, the book "requires that readers enter into the ambiguity themselves and discover their own resolutions to the conflict of truths."[6] Life is not an unambiguous set of truths, but rather "a continual encounter with conflicting truths, each making competing claims upon the seeker. Wisdom views life as paradoxical, requiring discernment from situation to situation of how, when and if one should act."[7]

Moreover, the sayings invite an imaginative gaze at the world, compelling the reader to discern wisdom in the subtext. As William P. Brown attests, "the power of a good proverb lies in its ability to stimulate wonderment."[8] This is apparent not only in vivid descriptions of the natural world but in the incongruities to which the sayings point. Wisdom operates in the gray area of moral complexity. For example, the condition of the poor receives varying treatments. On the one hand, poverty is viewed as a consequence of negligence: "A slack hand causes poverty, but the hand of the diligent makes rich" (10:4). Yet other sayings suggest there is not a clear link between poverty and foolishness, for the discerning can be poor and the wealthy are not necessarily wise: "the rich is wise in self-esteem, but an intelligent poor person sees through the pose" (28:11). Wealth itself is not an inviolable indicator of wisdom. In fact, "better to be poor and walk in integrity than to be crooked in one's ways even though rich" (28:6). These sayings present a kaleidoscopic view that impedes simplistic, black-and-white judgments.

Finally, wisdom is elusive. Wisdom ultimately comes from God and is not fully accessible. There are frequent warnings not to rely on human wisdom (3:5, 7). Even as the book is ostensibly about the pursuit of wisdom, its confidence is not in humanity's ability to perceive wisdom, but in God's gift of knowledge (2:6–7a). As Prov 21:30–31 cautions, "No wisdom, no counsel, no understanding can avail against the LORD. The horse is made ready for the day of battle, but the victory belongs to the LORD." Humans can participate in the pursuit of wisdom and God's activity in the world, but it is ultimately God's domain.

---

[6] K. M. O'Connor, *The Wisdom Literature*, Message of Biblical Spirituality 5 (Collegeville: Liturgical, 1988), 20.

[7] O'Connor, *The Wisdom Literature*, 19.

[8] W. P. Brown, *Wisdom's Wonder: Character, Creation, and Crisis in the Bible's Wisdom Literature* (Grand Rapids: Eerdmans, 2014), 58.

Furthermore, wisdom is always just out of reach, sparking an insatiable desire within the one who pursues it. In this sense, wisdom is not a *thing* that can be possessed. Rather, it is a disposition that must be acquired through a lifelong process. Even the advanced sage must continue to seek wisdom. As the book's opening urges, "let the wise also hear and gain in learning, and the discerning acquire skill" (1:5).

In sum, the wise person must be rooted in tradition yet have the capacity to innovate. Applying traditional wisdom to new contexts requires a sophisticated capacity of moral discernment. Memorizing the book's sayings will not make one wise; wisdom is far more difficult than the sayings suggest. As Fox explains, "The reason that the wisdom the author is seeking to impart is at once difficult and obvious is that it is not reducible to the book's precepts."[9] Rather, it is an aspect of moral character, acquired in the disciplined acquisition of knowledge and submission to the wisdom of the community and of God.

16.3 THE CURRICULUM OF CHARACTER FORMATION

In accord with this conception of wisdom, Proverbs functions as a type of curriculum in the formation of character. Its purpose is the cultivation of discernment. Thus Prov 1:2–6 defines the book's objective this way:

> For learning about wisdom and instruction, for understanding words of insight, for gaining instruction in wise dealing, righteousness, justice, and equity; to teach shrewdness to the simple, knowledge and prudence to the young – let the wise also hear and gain in learning, and the discerning acquire skill, to understand a proverb and a figure, the words of the wise and their riddles.

The book's form develops this facility in the student, as different voices offer competing perspectives on wisdom that the student must negotiate. Wisdom sayings require interpretation and assessment against the backdrop of lived experience. The book itself is an education in comprehending the riddles within it.

Proverbs is not only a book *about* ethical reflection; it cultivates the very capacities for wise dealing that it imagines. It does this especially through its poetic form, both in the longer poems of the first nine

---

[9] Fox, *Proverbs 1–9*, 347.

chapters and in the shorter proverbial sayings. The literary form of Proverbs is closely connected to its pedagogical function.

The majority of the book comprises proverbial sayings. With few exceptions, one cannot discern an organizational principle in their ordering.[10] The sayings are not organized by topic or theme and, although the various superscriptions might suggest an overarching structure, even these do not exhibit a tightly constructed connection to the content. Rather, the sayings unfold over the course of the book at their own pace and in their own rhythm. This is no accident: it points to the nature of wisdom itself, which cannot be indexed in a reference book but is revealed in daily experience, as wise teaching brushes up against new contexts and situations.

Wisdom sayings are highly sensitive to context – they only sing when rightly understood and rightly applied. They are not the product of esoteric reflection but require conversation with lived reality. Discernment is such a prized virtue in the book because a saying wrongly understood or wrongly applied can be destructive. Thus Prov 25:11 celebrates the benefit of a saying spoken at the right time: "A word fitly spoken is like apples of gold in a setting of silver." Proverbs 26:9 warns, "like a thorn bush brandished by the hand of a drunkard is a proverb in the mouth of a fool." In this sense, the book provides one aspect of a wisdom curriculum but must also be joined by the education of experience. As Ellen F. Davis explains,

> The only way to learn from the Proverbs is by living with the book for a long time, dipping in and out with regularity... Then one discovers that progress through the book is movement along a spiral. The same relatively few themes recur, but each time we are looking at them from a different angle. The difference is both textual and personal: How does this proverb occur in light of those around it? What has happened in my life since the last time I thought about this?[11]

---

[10]   Though see Heim on repetition and variation as a possible editorial strategy (K. M. Heim, *Poetic Imagination in Proverbs: Variant Repetitions and the Nature of Poetry*, BBRSup 4 [Winona Lake: Eisenbrauns, 2013]); Brown proposes a "meta-narratival arch" in which the "woman of strength" (ch. 31) represents the ideal mate for the now-mature student introduced as the young son in chapters 1–9 (Brown, *Wisdom's Wonder*, 65; W. P. Brown, "The Pedagogy of Proverbs 10:1–31:9," in *Character and Scripture: Moral Formation, Community, and Biblical Interpretation*, ed. W.P. Brown (Grand Rapids: Eerdmans, 2002), 150–82.

[11]   E. F. Davis, *Proverbs, Ecclesiastes, and the Song of Songs*, Westminster Bible Commentary (Louisville: Westminster John Knox, 2000), 21.

In other words, the form of the book invites the engagement with contextual situations necessary to developing the capacity to discern the way of wisdom.

The book also contains competing – even contradictory – sayings that prompt moral evaluation. Not only is there opposing advice (e.g., 26:4–5), but there are divergent perspectives on common themes. For example, wealth is sometimes a benefit that comes to the wise (e.g., 10:15, 22), yet is also a liability that may lead to harm (11:4, 28). Similarly, Prov 17:27–28 qualifies the significance of restrained speech, frequently identified elsewhere as a marker of wisdom. Proverbs 17:27 lifts up the value of reticence: "One who spares words is knowledgeable; one who is cool in spirit has understanding." Yet 17:28 warns that such silence can also be deceptive: "Even fools who keep silent are considered wise; when they close their lips, they are deemed intelligent." Christine Roy Yoder argues that such contradictions serve an important peda- gogical function: "They call attention to incongruities in the world; they convey that the arena of wisdom is replete with competing discourses, with divergent perspectives on reality and morality."[12] Yoder argues that the existence of contradictory proverbs in the collections teaches something about the nature of the moral self:

> The sages thereby put readers in a position where no single response, no one proverb or perspective, can always work for them. By doing so, they point readers to a reality larger than the proverbs in question: the moral self inevitably holds views that are in conflict with one another and applies those views depending on the immediate circumstances. Readers cannot avoid the relativity of human knowledge – the fact that meaning is contextual.[13]

In this way, the book resists simplistic or rigid interpretation; it requires – even cultivates – sophisticated, thoroughly contextual, ethical reflection. As Davis explains, "the structure of Proverbs blocks the desire, so much encouraged by modern education, to look for solutions in the abstract. Rather we are constrained to cultivate a flexible moral insight into concrete situations, which are always fraught with ambigu- ity and tension, sometimes to an acute degree."[14]

---

[12] C. R. Yoder, "Forming 'Fearers of Yahweh': Repetition and Contradiction as Pedagogy in Proverbs," in *Seeking Out the Wisdom of the Ancients*, ed. R. Troxel, K. G. Friebel, and D. R. Magary (Winona Lake: Eisenbrauns, 2005), 180.

[13] Yoder, "Forming 'Fearers of Yahweh,'" 181.

[14] Davis, *Proverbs*, 21.

The short form of the proverbial saying also lends itself to the cultivation of moral discernment. For example, Prov 12:5 is marked by two short parallel phrases: "thoughts of (the) righteous: justice // counsels of (the) wicked: deceit" (my translation). In Hebrew, the saying is only six words, evenly balanced between two halves of the line, mirroring each other in number of words, syntax, and sound. The rhyme and balanced syntax hold the two halves together, even as the sense holds the two apart. Absent any conjunctions, particles, or other extraneous features, the saying starkly opposes the righteous and the wicked. Yet the paths so opposed sound strikingly similar, including an ironic wordplay that might cause the reader to stumble upon the distinction between *mišpat* ("justice") and *mirmâh* ("deceit"). While the meaning of the two words is opposite, the similarity in sound perhaps suggests a finer distinction between the two paths, requiring careful discernment. The form of the saying is not simply an embellishment to an otherwise straightforward point but a critical part of its pedagogical function.

Moreover, the short form often produces ambiguity, which prompts the student to engage more deeply by seeking understanding beneath the surface. For example, Prov 22:6 states, "train a child in his way, and when he is old he won't depart from it" (my translation). While the grammar and vocabulary are relatively simple, the meaning is ambiguous.[15] The sense could connote a directive to school a child correctly, that is, "train a child in the *right* way, and when he is old he won't depart from it." Or it could serve as a warning against indulging children in what they prefer, that is, "train a child in the way of *his preference*, and when he is old he won't depart from it." Or it could suggest training youth according to age, aptitude, or social position, that is, "train a child in the way *appropriate to him*, and when he is old he won't depart from it." The saying could sustain any of these interpretations. This ambiguity is part of its function, fostering the discernment the book seeks to cultivate. The form requires close reading and consideration of the context to which it might apply in order to unlock the meaning.

Form and function are magnified in the longer poems in the first nine chapters. Here, poetry permits the exploration of multiple perspectives, again prompting discernment. Several different voices vie for the attention and affections of the student. The guiding voice of the parent

---

[15] See discussion in M. V. Fox, *Proverbs 10–31: A New Translation with Introduction and Commentary*, AB 18B (New Haven: Yale University Press, 2009), 698–99; T. Hildebrandt, "Proverbs 22:6a: Train Up a Child?" *Grace Theological Journal* 11 (1988): 3–19.

orients and frames the pursuit of wisdom, counseling the student to heed the advice he offers and warning about those who seek to lead the student astray. Thus the father's voice anticipates the appeal that others may make: "My child, if sinners entice you, do not consent. If they say, 'Come with us, let us lie in wait for blood'... my child, do not walk in their way, keep your foot from their paths" (1:10, 11, 15).

Other voices also address the student. One of these is Wisdom, personified as a woman. She promises to satisfy the student's desires with health, wealth, and security: "I love those who love me, and those who seek me diligently find me. Riches and honor are with me, enduring wealth and prosperity" (8:17–18). Yet Wisdom has a negative counterpart, similarly attractive and appealing. She is foolishness personified – most notably as the strange woman ('išâh zārâh) – and likewise seeks to shape the character of the youth. Her appeal has striking overlap with woman Wisdom's. The strange woman also uses the language of seeking the object of her affections (7:15) and her appeal is based in the delights of love and lovely things: "I have perfumed my bed with myrrh, aloes, and cinnamon. Come, let us take our fill of love until morning; let us delight ourselves with love" (7:18). Both the strange woman and woman Wisdom address the student in the first person, drawing the reader-as-student directly into their gaze. There is also significant overlap in their appeals, even as the consequences of accepting their advances are starkly opposed. These two women present the student with two contrasting models, requiring discernment to choose the wiser course.

This dynamic of contested voices is particularly apparent in Proverbs 7. The chapter begins by positioning the reader as the son of the father, offering a preview of the special advice and warning he is about to receive:

> My child, keep my words and store up my commandments with you;
> keep my commandments and live, keep my teachings as the apple of your eye;
> bind them on your fingers, write them on the tablet of your heart.
> Say to wisdom, "You are my sister," and call insight your intimate friend,
> that they may keep you from the loose woman, from the adulteress with her smooth words. (7:1–5)

The poem nestles the student next to the father's side, gazing with him out of the window, as onlookers of a lesson in foolishness (7:6–8).

The poem thus differentiates the student whom the father addresses from the simpleton outside who is about to make some foolish choices.

Yet as this woman comes into view, she acquires her own powerful voice: "Then a woman comes toward him, decked out like a prostitute, wily of heart. She is loud and wayward; her feet do not stay at home" (7:10–11). After the father introduces the scene, the speaking voices shift and the strange woman addresses the simpleton directly, thus positioning the student – and the hearer of the poem – as the one to whom she appeals:

> So now I have come out to meet you, to seek you eagerly, and I have found you!
> I have decked my couch with coverings, colored spreads of Egyptian linen;
> I have perfumed my bed with myrrh, aloes, and cinnamon.
> Come, let us take our fill of love until morning; let us delight ourselves with love. (7:15–18)

With a quick shift in voice, the student has gone from the child of the father to the one led astray by the wayward woman. By featuring the strange woman's appeal directly, the poem acknowledges the enticement of her temptation. The spices and textures appeal to the senses and desires of the youth, describing with vivid language how the woman's love smells, tastes, and feels. This is not an appeal to the rational capacities of the intellect, but to the emotions and senses that in fact inform decision-making.

Yet the poem does not leave to the student to interpret this appeal independently. The father's voice interjects with an unambiguous evaluation.

> And now, my children, listen to me, and be attentive to the words of my mouth.
> Do not let your hearts turn aside to her ways; do not stray into her paths.
> For many are those she has laid low, and numerous are her victims.
> Her house is the way to Sheol, going down to the chambers of death. (7:24–27)

As the poem unfolds, it confronts the hearer with various voices and perspectives, all the while offering an interpretive lens through which to discern the voices of wisdom from the voices of foolishness. It carries the student through an imaginative journey, guided by the interpretive framework of the parent's direction. By use of first-person and second-person address, the poem alternately figures the hearer as the son of the father and as the simpleton to whom the strange woman appeals. Moving to its conclusion, the poem once again situates the hearer as the father's student. While the poem grants the appeal of the strange woman's plea, ultimately it offers the student the perspective to resist her appeal. The final line of the poem makes this point explicit: To follow the strange woman leads to *death*, the poem's final word.

Through its poetic form, Proverbs fulfills the mandate of its opening lines to cultivate capacities of discernment in the inexperienced student and wise sage alike. As Proverbs 7 in particular makes clear, the book is also steeped in a gendered discourse, explicitly addressed to a male student and thus positioning the reader as the son of the father, educated to look with suspicion upon women who threaten to harm his path.[16] The logic of this language is, of course, deeply problematic. Yet the book also provides the tools to resist its claims, for it emphasizes the value of the discerning ear as well as the capacity to distinguish the speech that is helpful from that which is harmful. In fact, the book presents a variety of voices and perspectives, mimicking the complex experience of lived reality, in which one encounters manifold choices and must discern the wisest course. As Prov 18:17 observes, "the one who first states a case seems right, until the other comes and cross-examines." In some sense the book as a whole presents this very point, as it provides perspectives that are then cross-examined in the juxtaposition of competing voices, claims, and concepts. In so doing, it prompts the reader to be an ethical critic of the language one encounters in the book and in the world.

16.4 PROVERBS IN THE REAL WORLD: CONTEMPORARY ETHICAL REFLECTION

Like a fine wine, Proverbs ages well, its depth and complexity becoming more apparent over time. The proverbial sayings, by their nature, transcend the particular social and historical moment of their origin and continue to resonate with vivid imagery and incisive observation of daily life. Their convictions and commitments provide a stimulating counterpart to the propagation of wisdom in the twenty-first century. In an age of rapid technological advances that require sophisticated

---

[16] For an analysis see C. A. Newsom, "Woman and the Discourse of Patriarchal Wisdom: A Study of Proverbs 1–9" in *Gender and Difference in Ancient Israel*, ed. P. Day, (Minneapolis: Augsburg Fortress, 1989), 142–60.

ethical reflection amid competing perspectives, Proverbs' wisdom resonates deeply. Proverbs is a book for our time. By way of conclusion,
I offer two areas in which Proverbs might provide wise food for thought.

16.5 WISDOM AND TECHNOLOGY

Through technology, information is more readily available at our finger-
tips now than ever before. We carry powerful computers in our pockets
in the form of phones and tablets that provide lightning-fast access to
knowledge. Opinions and insights are readily traded through digital plat-
forms. The effect is that competing voices inundate us daily through the
medium of advertising, music, entertainment, and social media. Sitting
before a phone or computer is the equivalent of standing in Times Square
at the intersection of commerce and entertainment, vivid imagery and
glitzy advertising flashing before our eyes while peddling their brands.

Proverbs suggests that the effect of such saturation is not purely
benign. Character is being shaped and formed by the voices we encounter and the company we keep. But not all voices have the same degree of
wisdom. Discernment is imperative for evaluating the claims and values
that different voices profess.

Precisely in this cultural moment, Proverbs offers a refreshing and
significant perspective on the nature of ethical reflection. As we have
seen, Proverbs is in many ways a book about discernment between
competing voices. The cacophony of choices before the student requires
careful deliberation about what is helpful and what is harmful. This is a
critical capacity for people in any age but particularly pressing in the
twenty-first century amid the technology revolution. Proverbs raises
questions about the way that we evaluate the wisdom proffered to us
and the values by which we measure its worth.

16.6 WISDOM AND COMMUNITY

Proverbs places an extraordinary emphasis on the value of the community as the arbiter of wisdom. As Prov 15:22 explains, "without counsel
plans go wrong, but with many advisors they succeed." Wisdom cannot
be sought in isolation from others, but rests upon collective discernment.
This is part of the reason that fools and the wicked are potentially so
threatening: they undermine the health of the collective body. Not only
do they resist counsel, but they offer bad advice (e.g., 15:2, 7). This means
that choosing the right company – seeking the companionship of those
who are wise and discerning – is critical to the task of ethical reflection.

This commitment to the primacy of the community sits in some tension with the dominant value of individualism in contemporary North American culture. At the same time, cultural forces, exacerbated by technology and media, have increasingly led to collectives of the like-minded. It is possible – and increasingly likely – to live both geographically and digitally in an environment primarily composed of those who think alike and look alike. Social media reinforces this tendency by curating the content that its users consume, showing more of the material that resonates with the user. Likewise, cable television and news media tailor their content to particular audiences, often cultivating partisan perspectives that appeal to certain demographics and reinforce their social, political, and ideological beliefs. The effect of this phenomenon is the formation of implicit communities of shared values. While such community formation is not necessarily or inherently bad, it can have a detrimental effect, insulating individuals from different perspectives and consequently warping the process of discernment. It is harder to negotiate competing perspectives if one only credits the legitimacy of a singular perspective.

The book of Proverbs is liable to a similar critique, insofar as it too largely represents the perspective of a particular social group. Yet it also provides a warning and set of tools to challenge the dangers of unbridled partisanship. Because the community is such a significant force in the cultivation of one's ability to discern, it suggests that we need many voices present in our communities if we are to do ethical reflection faithfully. The book of Proverbs offers one set of voices, but also points to the reality of daily experience as wisdom's playground, filled with many voices that warrant a discerning ear.

FURTHER READING

Brown, W. P. "The Pedagogy of Proverbs 10:1–31:9." Pages 150–82 in *Character and Scripture: Moral Formation, Community, and Biblical Interpretation.* Edited by W. P. Brown. Grand Rapids: Eerdmans, 2002.

Brown, W. P. *Wisdom's Wonder: Character, Creation, and Crisis in the Bible's Wisdom Literature.* Grand Rapids: Eerdmans, 2014.

Carr, D. M. *Writing on the Tablet of the Heart: Origins of Scripture and Literature.* New York: Oxford University Press, 2005.

Davis, E. F. *Proverbs, Ecclesiastes, and the Song of Songs.* Westminster Bible Commentary. Louisville: Westminster John Knox, 2000.

Fox, M. V. *Proverbs 1–9: A New Translation with Introduction and Commentary.* Anchor Bible 18A. New York: Doubleday, 2000.

Fox, M. V. *Proverbs 10–31: A New Translation with Introduction and Commentary.* Anchor Bible 18B. New Haven: Yale University Press, 2009.

Heim, K. M. *Poetic Imagination in Proverbs: Variant Repetitions and the Nature of Poetry*. BBRSup 4. Winona Lake: Eisenbrauns, 2013.

Hildebrandt, T. "Proverbs 22:6a: Train Up a Child?" *Grace Theological Journal* 11 (1988): 3–19.

Newsom, C. A. "Woman and the Discourse of Patriarchal Wisdom: A Study of Proverbs 1–9." Pages 142–60 in *Gender and Difference in Ancient Israel*. Edited by P. Day. Minneapolis: Augsburg Fortress, 1989.

O'Connor, K. M. *The Wisdom Literature*. Message of Biblical Spirituality 5. Collegeville: Liturgical, 1988.

Stewart, A. W. *Poetic Ethics in Proverbs: Wisdom Literature and the Shaping of the Moral Self*. New York: Cambridge University Press, 2016.

Stewart, A. W. "Wisdom's Imagination: Moral Reasoning and the Book of Proverbs" *JSOT* 40 (2016): 351–72.

Yoder, C. R. "Forming 'Fearers of Yahweh': Repetition and Contradiction as Pedagogy in Proverbs." Pages 167–83 in *Seeking Out the Wisdom of the Ancients*. Edited by R. Troxel, K. G. Friebel, and D. R. Magary. Winona Lake: Eisenbrauns, 2005.

17   Divine Justice in the Book of Job

C.-L. SEOW

Divine justice is a given throughout the Bible. The psalmists celebrate God's rule over the cosmos, emphasizing that "justice and rectitude" form the firm base of the divine throne (Pss 89:15 [14]; 97:2). This sovereign "loves justice" (33:5; 37:28) and performs it (9:5 [4]; 99:4). God is renowned for the exercise of justice (Deut 32:3–4; Pss 9:17 [16]; 36:7). The world is "firmly established" because God "judges with equity" (Ps 96:10). Indeed, the earth's stability depends on divine justice (58:2–3), and its foundations are shaken when that justice is lacking (75:3–4 [2–3]).

Psalm 82 illustrates what is at stake when there is divine injustice. God as the supreme deity of the divine assembly (82:1) judges the gods of the nations for their failure to ensure justice, the result of which is the destabilizing of the earth's foundations (82:2–5). So they are sentenced to die like mortals (82:6–7). Then the psalm concludes: "Arise, O God, judge the earth, for you are in possession of all nations" (82:8).[1]

Given such assumptions, suffering is as a rule regarded as just retribution for wrongs. The traditions affirm this doctrine as something like the laws of nature (Prov 22:8; Hos 10:12–13). At times confidence in divine justice is expressed in generalizations and hyperboles: YHWH does not permit the righteous to go hungry (Prov 10:3); trouble does not befall the righteous (12:21); rectitude delivers one from death (10:2; 11:4). Elders called upon experience to corroborate the truth of the doctrine (Ps 37:25–26). Yet there are passages that recognize contradictions of the dictum – instances where people receive the opposite of what they deserve (Jer 12:1; Ps 73:2–14; Eccl 7:15; Hab 1:4). Even if the wicked do thrive, their good fortunes are only temporary (Ps 37:1–2, 7–8; Prov 23:17–18). Justice will eventually prevail.

---

[1]   Unless otherwise stated, all translations are mine.

257

There are occasionally, however, more direct challenges to the
default view, as in Abraham's protest against YHWH's intention to
destroy Sodom and Gomorrah indiscriminately: "Shall the judge of all
the earth not do justice?" (Gen 18:25). Even if destruction is just retribution for the wicked, the corollary damage on the innocent is surely not.
An undifferentiated destruction would be "profanation" for God. YHWH
had in fact been wondering if Abraham should be apprised of the planned
destruction but decided in the affirmative on account of Abraham's call
(18:17–19; cf. 12:1–3). YHWH reflected that Abraham's election implies
"doing rectitude and justice" in order that the promise might be fulfilled
(18:19). So Abraham haggled with God about the issue until God simply
departed and "Abraham returned to his place" (18:33). Sure enough,
some were indeed spared destruction (19:15–23). While the injustice of
YHWH's original intention is called out, the narrator implies that justice
prevailed after all, through Abraham's mediation – just as YHWH willed.

In another context, Habakkuk undercuts the argument of retributive justice, contending that even if Israel deserved punishment, it is
unjust that the even more wicked Chaldeans should triumph (Hab
1:5–11). So he appeals to YHWH, implying that divine reputation is at
stake: "Are you not from of old, O YHWH? You will not die!" (1:12a–b).[2]
The prophet is perhaps alluding to the notion that a God who fails to
ensure justice is no better than a mortal (cf. Ps 82:7). Surely YHWH is
not such a deity; YHWH is too "pure of eyes" to countenance evil or
acquiesce when the wicked swallowed up those more righteous than
they (Hab 1:13). The question of divine (in)justice is raised in this oblique
manner, but it is not sustained.

The issue of divine justice or lack thereof is nowhere else more
rigorously debated than in the book of Job, which tells the story of a
person of impeccable character (Job 1:1, 8; 2:3), who nonetheless suffered
on account of a decision made in the divine assembly (1:6–11; 3:1–7). My
purpose in this essay is to explore how the question of divine ethics is
debated in this explicitly dialogical work.[3]

---

[2]   The MT here as *nāmût*, "we will not die" – an instance of *tiqqun sopherim*, that is, a
      deliberate scribal emendation of the consonantal text for theological reasons. The
      scribe apparently changed the text from *tāmût*, "you will not die," to the
      theologically more palatable *nāmût*, "we will not die."

[3]   Cf. M. Buber, *The Prophetic Faith* (New York: Harper & Brothers, 1960; based on a
      German essay published 1941), 188–202. He finds four views of God in the book: (1)
      the narrator's cruel God; (2) the retributive God of the friends; (3) Job's God, who hides
      his face; and (4) YHWH as the "I-Thou" God of "distributive justice." He leaves out
      Elihu as secondary to the book.

17.1 PROLOGUE (JOB 1–2)

One must not miss the implications of the divine assembly scenes in the prologue (Job 1:6–11; 2:1–7), for it is in just such a scenario that the deity condemned the gods of the nations for their failure to secure justice and sentenced them to death on account of it (Ps 82). At issue in the first assembly is the question of disinterested piety: "Has Job feared God for naught?" (Job 1:9). The question is ostensibly about human conduct, though it is more subtly also about divine conduct. Would a worshiper cease to worship God if God acts contrary to expectations? Indeed, divine conduct is explicitly in view in the corollary issue of disinterested divine beneficence. Are blessings intended to ensure a desired response from their human beneficiary? As the Adversary puts it to God: "Have you not put up a hedge around him, around his household, and around all that he has? You have blessed his deeds, and his substance has burst forth throughout the earth" (1:10). The Hebrew verb translated as "put up a hedge" is used also in Hos 2:8, which refers to God's putting up a hedge to block the way of Hosea's wife, who represents Israel, to prevent her from going astray. The Deuteronomic tradition to which Hosea subscribed is based upon a doctrine of divine retribution. Yet the case of Hosea's recalcitrant wife/Israel illustrates the insecurity of God. Despite the blessings Israel received, God takes drastic preventive measures to secure human devotion. The book of Job offers an implicit critique of such a theology.

Divine beneficence is perhaps an indication of divine insecurity, the Adversary implies.[4] God's hedge is ostensibly beneficent – to protect – but it really hampers human autonomy. This hedging is evident in God's blessing of what Job does. In fact, the expression, "to bless the deed of the hand" (*bārēk ma'ăśēh yād*) is distinctly Deuteronomic (Deut 2:7; 14:29; 15:10; 16:15; 24:19; 28:12). The idiom does not occur elsewhere. More specifically, the Adversary's language recalls Deuteronomic promises of divine blessing as a reward for fidelity.

Yet the proposal to test Job's disinterested piety entails not merely the withholding of divine blessing but rather a willful harming of Job: "But, stretch forth your hand and touch all that he has. Surely he will 'bless' you to your face" (Job 1:11). The Adversary implies that divine blessing of the human will bring human blessing of God, but the absence

---

4   M. J. Oosthuizen, "Divine Insecurity and Joban Heroism: A Reading of the Narrative Framework of Job," *OTE* 4 (1991): 300–3; A. LaCocque, "Justice for the Innocent Job," *BibInt* 19 (2011): 20–1.

of that divine goodwill will bring "blessing" of another sort, meaning its opposite.[5] So YHWH consents to let the Adversary do the dirty work of afflicting Job (1:12), which is no assuring affirmation of divine ethics. Indeed, God admits responsibility for Job's destruction, saying to the Adversary, "He still holds fast to his integrity, and you have incited me against him, to destroy him for naught" (2:3). The Hebrew verb for "destroy" (bl'), literally, "swallow up," echoes Hab 1:13, where God is not supposed to acquiesce when the wicked swallow up (bl') the right-eous; here it is YHWH who swallows up Job "for naught." The test of Job's character thus raises questions about divine character.[6]

YHWH turns Job over to the Adversary, who "struck Job with a terrible inflammation from the sole of his feet up to his crown" (Job 2:7). The wording echoes Deut 28:35, where amid curses for unfaithfulness Moses warns: "YHWH will *strike* you on the knees and legs *with a terrible inflammation* from which you will not be able to recover – *from the sole of your foot to the crown of your head*" (emphasis added).

17.2 THE DIALOGUE (JOB 3–31)

Readers of the book know more about Job's situation than his human interlocutors. The narrator is unequivocal about Job's impeccable char-acter (Job 1:1), and YHWH affirms the same (1:8; 2:3). Readers have been let in on deliberations in the divine assembly and know that Job's suffering is an injustice for which God is responsible. Readers know, too, that Job has been made to look like a sinner (2:7). Job and his friends do not know these things. They have been set up to misjudge the situation, for Job appears just like the sinner that the Torah describes (Deut 28:35).

Job's Friends

The views of Job's friends are traditional, not only in Israel but also elsewhere in the ancient world, as is evident in the "pious-sufferer texts" from the ancient Near East. The earliest of these is so-called "Sumerian Job" (*Man and his God*), the earliest extant copy of which

---

5   The Hebrew term *brk*, "to bless," occurs six times in the prologue (1:5, 10, 11, 21; 2:5, 9), meaning "bless" – its face-value meaning – or as a euphemism for its opposite, "curse" (as in 1 Kgs 21:10, 13; Ps 10:3). The interpreter must decide in each case which it is; at times one cannot be certain. See T. Linafelt, "The Undecidability of *brk* in the Prologue to Job and Beyond," *BibInt* 4 (1996): 154–72.

6   See Y. Raḥman, "The Satan in the Story of Job [Hebrew]," *Beth Mikra* 35 (1989–90): 334–40.

dates to the eighteenth century BCE,[7] though it was already known in the third millennium.[8] There are others like it: (1) an Old Babylonian version of *Man and his God* from the seventeenth century,[9] (2) an Akkadian Hymn of Thanksgiving to Marduk from Ugarit,[10] from the late thirteenth or early twelfth century, and (3) *Ludlul Bēl Nēmeqi* ("I will Praise the Lord of Wisdom"),[11] composed probably in the late twelfth century.[12]

All these assume that the suffering of the pious person in question is due to sin, even if the precipitating offense is unknown or perhaps unknowable (*Ludlul* II.33–38). As the Sumerian *Man and his God* has it, no one is perfect and no sinless person has ever existed, for humanity is fragile. These texts are all doxological. They point to the restoration of the sufferers, either experienced or anticipated.[13] They praise the gods even for afflictions, for though the afflictions are as scourges and barbs, the salves are soothing and revive the dying; the deity who presides over punishments also absolves one from sins (*Ludlul* I.21–24). The poet of *Ludlul* acknowledges that Marduk is heavy-handed, but his intention is mercy; his weapons are savage, but his goal is healing (*Ludlul* I.33–34). The dialectic suggests that the suffering experienced in the present is not indicative of divine will, which may in fact be benign. As Moran puts it, these texts urge readers to "make the problem of the mind a

---

[7] S. N. Kramer, "Man and His God: A Sumerian Variation on the 'Job' Motif," in *Wisdom in Israel and the Ancient Near East Presented*, ed. M. Noth and D. Winton Thomas, VTSup 3 (Leiden: Brill, 1960), 170–82; J. Klein, "*Man and His God*: A Wisdom Poem or a Cultic Lament?" in *Approaches to Sumerian Literature: Studies in Honor of H. L. Vantisphout*, ed. P. Michalowski and N. Veldhuis, Cuneiform Monographs 35 (Leiden: Brill, 2006), 123–43.

[8] S. N. Kramer, "The Oldest Literary Catalogue: A Sumerian List of Literary Compositions Compiled about 2000 B.C.," *BASOR* 88 (1942): 46, line 46.

[9] W. L. Lambert, "A Further Attempt at the Babylonian 'Man and His God'," in *Language, Literature, and History*, ed. F. Rochberg-Halton, AOS 67 (New Haven: Yale University Press, 1987), 187–202.

[10] D. Arnauld, *Corpus des textes de bibliothèque de Ras Shamra-Ougarit (1936–2000) un sumérien, babylonien et assyrien*, AuSorSup 23 (Barcelona: Ausa, 2007), 110–14.

[11] T. Oshima, *Babylonian Poems of Pious Sufferers: Ludlul Bēl Nēmeqi and the Babylonian Theodicy*, Orientalische Religionen in der Antike 14 (Tübingen: Mohr Siebeck, 2014), 3–114.

[12] W. L. Moran, "The Babylonian Job," in *The Most Magic Word: Essays on Babylonian and Biblical Literature*, ed. R. Hendel, CBQMS 35 (Washington, DC: The Catholic Biblical Association of America, 2002), 198.

[13] M. Weinfeld, "Job and Its Mesopotamian Parallels – A Typological Analysis," in *Text and Context*, ed. W. T. Claassen, JSOTSup 48 (Sheffield: JSOT, 1988), 217–26; K. van der Toorn, "Theodicy in Akkadian Literature," in *Theodicy in the World of the Bible*, ed. A. Laato and J. de Moor (Leiden: Brill, 2003), 57–89.

problem of the heart, and solve it with reasons of the heart. Instead of wisdom, belief; instead of reflection and argument, a hymn to paradox and contradiction. *Credo quia absurdum.*"[14]

This is precisely the perspective of Job's friends, as exemplified in the first speech of Eliphaz (Job 4–5). Eliphaz contends that (1) no human being is without sin because human beings are fragile (4:8–5:7); (2) the proper response to suffering is doxology (5:8–16); (3) suffering is not the final will of God, who wounds but heals (5:17–18); and (4) one should look forward to restoration (5:19–26). Eliphaz may be understood as someone who is trying to work out, however imperfectly, a theological anthropology that accounts for the apparent inevitability of human suffering. Shaped by his understanding of the widespread and age-old doctrine of the relationship between cause and effect, he concludes that suffering is inevitable because no one is perfect.

Bildad assumes that God does not pervert justice and rectitude (8:3). His allusion to the death of Job's children in 8:4 ("If your children sinned against him, he has dispatched them because of their transgression") has seemed gratuitous and mean-spirited to some. Yet he is concerned not so much with the culpability of Job's children as with Job's survival. He talks about the possibility of Job's children sinning and being "dispatched." Yet suffering is not the end of the matter, death is; Job, though suffering, is not dead, so it is premature for Job to conclude that God has perverted justice.

Like the first two friends, Zophar proffers a "theology from above," beginning with God: "Would that God might speak, and open his lips with you" (11:5). He emphasizes the transcendence and mystery of God (11:7–10). Job speaks his experience of pain, but Zophar points him to God's infinite power.

All three friends affirm the freedom of God, though their imaginations of divine freedom are restricted. Eliphaz praises God as creator, whose deeds are inscrutable and wonders innumerable (5:9), but his elaboration of the theme reveals a strictly retributive God (5:10–27). Bildad speaks of God's freedom to destroy even the good (8:18–19), but does not allow for the possibility of God acting against the norms (8:3, 20). Zophar waxes eloquent about divine mystery (11:6–10), yet his God is all about retribution (11:11–20). Indeed, as their later speeches confirm, the friends' views of God's possibilities are one-sidedly about God's retribution; they are concerned *exclusively* with what God will do to the

---

[14]   W. L. Moran, "Rib-Hadda: Job at Byblos?" in *Biblical and Related Studies Presented to Samuel Iwry*, ed. A. Kort and S. Morschauser (Winona Lake: Eisenbrauns, 1985), 177.

wicked, with nothing about what God might do to the upright (chs 15, 18, 20, 22, 25). The friends cannot see beyond the nexus of sin and punishment. There is no room for individual experience when experience contradicts systematized theology.

Job

The Sumerian and Akkadian sufferer texts mentioned so far all concur that suffering must be for cause. Yet the latest of them, *Ludlul,* seems less dogmatically so. While the cause of suffering is unknown, the sufferer has searched his conscience and comes to the conclusion that he has been faithful, as far as he knows. So he wonders if perhaps the gods have different values from mortals: "What seems good to one may be an offence to the deity, and what is bad to one's mind may be good to one's god" (*Ludlul* II.34–35). The sufferer does not quite claim innocence, but the text hints at the possibility that the sufferer may be innocent according to human understanding of right and wrong. The sufferer is eventually restored, but as Karel van der Toorn observes, "The happy ending does not mask the unease about the value of the traditional doctrines that transpires in this text."[15]

That unease gives way to an outright challenge in the *Babylonian Theodicy,*[16] composed probably near the end of the second millennium. Consisting of cycles of dialogue between a noble sufferer and an orthodox friend, the sufferer's speeches begin and end the dialogue, as do the speeches of Job (chs 3–31). Like Job, but unlike the pious suffer in the other texts, the sufferer insists on his innocence. The name of the author implies the same: Saggil-kīnam-ubbib ("O [E]Saggil, Clear the Just"). Here, for the first time in the ancient Near East, we have a story about a just sufferer.

Like his friends, Job has no access to information provided in the prologue and knows nothing about the deliberations in the divine assembly. All he has is the testimony of the traditions, his own experience, and his conscience. He does not rule out the possibility that he might have sinned (7:20; 19:3), but he knows of nothing that he has done that might have brought ruthless divine animosity against him.

---

[15] van der Toorn, "Theodicy in Akkadian Literature," 81.
[16] See W. Lambert, "The Babylonian Theodicy," in *Babylonian Wisdom Literature* (Winona Lake: Eisenbrauns, 1996), 63–91; T. Oshima, *The Babylonian Theodicy,* SAACT 9 (Helsinki: The Neo-Assyrian Text Corpus Project, 2013); T. Oshima, *Babylonian Poems of Pious Sufferers: Ludlul Bēl Nēmeqi and the Babylonian Theodicy,* Oriental Religions in Antiquity 14 (Tübingen: Mohr Siebeck, 2014), 115–67.

Divine enmity is not a new theme. YHWH is often depicted as an enemy of Israel's enemies and, less frequently, as Israel's enemy, though always for cause (Ps 38:2–9; Lam 2:4–5; Jer 30:14). The scandal of divine antagonism against Job is the injustice of it, as the prologue makes clear and Job insists. Worse yet, God as Job's enemy (see Job 16:9) is relentless and gratuitously cruel. Job says God scuttled him about, that is, swung him back and forth (16:12a). God then picked the creature by the scruff and smashed it again and again (16:12b). Then, as if the bloodlust remained unsatisfied, God set up the carcass as "a target for himself" (16:12c). The aggressor's archers surround Job (16:13a), God pierced the vitals of the victim, and – the text adds, needlessly – "he was unsparing" (16:13b), as Job's bile poured to the ground (16:13c). The climax is depicted as a relentless assault on a city, until the defenses are breached and, says Job, "he charged at me like a warrior" (16:14).

Job again accuses God of gratuitous animosity in 19:6–12. Although he does not rule out the possibility that he might have erred (19:4), he is convinced that the wrong ultimately lies with God. Indeed the difference between Job's inadvertent wrong (19:4a, "even if I have erred, my error...") and God's action (19:6, "God acted perversely against me") is stark.[17] This perversion is evident in God's enclosing of "his net" (mĕṣûdô) around him (19:6). In literature and iconography throughout the ancient Near East, the net was a symbol of power and sovereign control. God's action against Job is perverted, for Job is treated as if he were a chaos monster (cf. 7:12). This is also implied by a wordplay, lost in translation. God is supposed to be mĕṣûdâ, "a stronghold/bastion/ refuge," on which one can count on for protection (Pss 18:2–3; 31:4). God encloses Job not in protection but in hostility, so Job cries ḥāmās, "injustice!" (Job 19:7),[18] using a term used in the laments for enemies bringing false charges against the innocent (Pss 7:17; 11:5). In many cases, the victims are portrayed as creatures being hunted or besieged by an invading army. These laments appeal to God, confessed as mĕṣûdâ for those who suffer ḥāmās – the God who is supposed to hate those who "love ḥāmās" (Ps 11:5).

---

[17]   The verb is the same one used when Bildad insisted that God does not "pervert justice" and does not "pervert rectitude" (8:3; cf. Elihu: "Shaddai does not pervert justice," 34:12b). Against such a defense of divine justice, Job cites his own case as evidence of divine perversion of justice.

[18]   The common translation "violence" is inadequate. Here as elsewhere it has juridical connotations, even as the opposite of mišpāṭ, "justice" (cf. Jer 22:3; Ezek 7:23; 45:9). See Hans-Jochen Boecker, *Redeformen des Rechtslebens im AT*, WMANT 14 (Neukirchen-Vluyn: Neukirchen, 1974), 57–66.

As in Job 16, the scene in 19:8–12 is a city under siege, with God attacking Job "like his adversaries" (19:11). God seems paranoid about being attack by a plurality of enemies, though it is just Job. Indeed, so severe is this paranoia that it precipitates a mustering of God's "troops" (19:12; cf. 25:3), who "build up (*sll*) their way" against Job (19:12b), alluding to the construction of a siege ramp (*sllh*, 2 Kgs 19:32; Isa 37:33). The troops encamp, waiting for the right moment to mount the final assault on lonely Job in his tent.

These and other passages paint a picture of divine viciousness – and monotheism could not attribute such malevolence to any other power. The problem is stated in Job 9:22–24, a passage so vitriolic that some Jewish interpreters regarded it as outright blasphemy (so *b. B. Bat.* 16a):

"It is one," I say therefore,
　"The blameless and the guilty, it is he who brings to an end."
If a scourge kills suddenly,
　He mocks the despair of the innocent.
The earth is delivered into the hand of the wicked;
　The faces of its judges he covers.
　　If not he, then who is it?

Job has been challenging the assumption that suffering is a consequence of sin, which no human can deny: "Can a human be in the right before God / or can a mortal be pure before the maker?" (4:17). He uses the figure of a lawsuit – a metaphor of objectivity – to argue that the question is moot, for there is no way by which a mortal might be proven right with God (9:2–3). Job wants to prove he is in the right – but his opponent is one who, for better or for worse, controls the cosmos (9:4–19). His adversary, the accused, is also the judge; there is no go-between (9:19–33).

The entire speech (chs 9–10) is replete with forensic idioms,[19] which support Job's imagination of a legal dispute with God. He will return again and again to this metaphor (13:6–12, 17–28; 14:3; 16:8, 19–21; 23:6). This reaches a climax in Job's final speech (chs 29–31), in an expanded version of a legal genre attested in a seventh-century

---

[19]　*ṣdq*, "to be in the right" (9:2, 15, 20; 10:15), *rš*ʿ, "to be in the wrong, be guilty" (9:20, 22, 29; 10:7, 15), *hiršîaʿ*, "to condemn" (10:2), *tām*, "blameless" (9:20, 21, 22), *nāqî*, "innocent" (9:23), *niqqâ*, "to exonerate" (9:28; 10:14), *ʿnh*, "to answer" (9:3, 14, 15, 16, 32), *měšōpĕṭî*, "my (legal) adversary" (9:15), *hēʿîd*, "to testify" (9:19b), *ʿēd*, "witness" (10:17); *mišpāṭ*, "justice" (9:19, 32), *rîb* "(legal) dispute" (9:3), *ryb*, "to be in a lawsuit" (10:2); *šōpĕṭîm*, "judges" (9:24), and *môkîaḥ*, "arbiter" (9:33).

Meṣad-Ḥashavyahu (Yavneh Yam) inscription,[20] the form of which is a judicial complaint of power abuse.[21] Like the inscription, Job 29–31 contains a judicial complaint against wrongful conduct by someone in a position of power. The plaintiff lays out his case, rehearsing its circumstances, beginning with what he had in the past (ch. 29) and how everything had been taken from him (ch. 30). The accused abuser of power in this case is God (30:11, 20–31). Just as the plaintiff in the inscription swears his innocence (ll. 11–12), so Job makes a passionate asseveration of his innocence (ch. 31).[22] However, unlike the plaintiff in Meṣad-Ḥashavyahu, who has someone to hear his case, Job can only wish that he could have such a hearer (31:35a). His complaint has been issued and signed (31:35b), but he could only wish that a written response would be forthcoming (31:35c).

In chapters 29–31 we have the culmination of the juridical metaphor begun in chapter 9. The metaphor has resurfaced through the rest of Job's speeches, though the imagination of a lawsuit with God has always remained at a hypothetical level, a scenario Job wishes but does not attempt to actuate. While there are allusions to the legal process, no legal genre has been employed so far. Yet now one finds, for the first time in the book, a formal complaint of the abuse of power.

17.3 ELIHU (JOB 32–37)

Elihu is confident that God is just: "Indeed, truly, God does not act wickedly; Shaddai does not pervert justice" (Job 34:12). Yet Elihu does not assume Job's prior guilt, as the friends do. Rather, what incenses him is Job's self-justification and condemnation of God (32:2; 34:5–6, 17). For Elihu, Job's assumption that his suffering must be due to God's gratuitous enmity goes too far (33:8–11, cf. 13:24b, 27).

The problem is not necessarily that Job is a sinner who deserves punishment, but that he is actualizing his judicial metaphor. Job framed his charge in forensic terms, insisting that God had taken away his right (mišpāṭ, 34:5) and made him look like a liar (34:6; cf. 9:20). He fantasized

---

20   F. W. Dobbs-Allsopp, J. J. M. Roberts, C. -L. Seow, and R. E. Whitaker, *Hebrew Inscriptions: Texts from the Biblical Period of the Monarchy with Concordance* (London: Yale University Press, 2005), 358–70.

21   F. W. Dobbs-Allsopp, "The Genre of the Meṣad Ḥashavyahu Ostracon," *BASOR* 295 (1994): 49–55.

22   For ch. 31 as an "oath of innocence," see M. B. Dick, "The Legal Metaphor in Job 31," *CBQ* 41 (1979): 37–50; Dick, "Job 31, the Oath of Innocence, and the Sage," *ZAW* 95 (1983): 31–53.

about laying out his legal case ("Here now I have laid my *mišpāṭ*," 13:18a), directly before God ("I will lay my *mišpāṭ* before him," 23:4a). Yet whereas Job demands that God answer him (31:35), Elihu challenges Job to face him instead ("lay out before me," 33:5a). If Job has a dispute with God, it can only be via an intermediary.[23] God is too great to answer such a challenge (33:12–13). Elihu makes his point with a word-play on the verbs *rbh*, "to be great" (33:12a, *kî yirbeh mē'ĕnôš*, "for God is too great for people") and *ryb*, "to dispute" (33:13a, *maddûa' 'ēlâw rîbōtā*, "why do you dispute with him?"). Job uses the latter repeatedly in the forensic sense (9:3; 10:2; 13:8, 19; 23:6); its use here echoes Job's characterization of God as his juridical adversary, *'îš rîbî* (31:35).

Elihu further contends that retribution is not the only just cause for suffering; suffering may be a warning (33:16–30). The details of his exposition do not fit the case of Job, but he does not claim this as the explanation for all suffering. Rather, Elihu's point is that there may be other explanations besides the two options laid out by Job (that God is unjust) and his friends (that all suffering is due to sin). As the Karaite interpreter Yefet ben Ali explained in the tenth century CE, Elihu means that suffering may be retributive, like David's suffering because of his adultery with Bathsheba, but suffering may also be for future good, as in the case of Joseph. Elihu's approach is in some ways similar to the NT account of how Jesus sidestepped the issue of divine retribution in the case of the man born blind (John 9:1–5). Instead of being trapped in the proffered alternatives – who has sinned, this man or his parents? – Jesus averred that the suffering might be teleological: "so that God's work might be revealed in him" (John 9:3). Instead of pointing back to past offenses, suffering may point ahead. Suffering may not be punitive but purposive; it may be "to uncover human ears" (Job 33:16a). The guilt or innocence of the sufferer may be beside the point. Elihu reiterates that God makes people more amenable to revelation by opening their ears to discipline and hence turning them away from trouble in the future (36:10; cf. 36:15).

Unlike the friends, Elihu does not restrict God's freedom to act beyond what doctrine stipulates. He does affirm the doctrine of retribution and defends the character of God (34:10–27; 36:5–12). Yet he concurs with Job that God may be silent when the needy cry out (13:24); God may "hide his face" (34:28–29). Sufferers may become disillusioned and accuse God of neglect (35:9–16; 36:13–14). Elihu cautions against obsession with justice to the point that one loses perspective of one's

23 C. L. Seow, "Elihu's Revelation," *ThTo* 68 (2011): 253–71.

relation with God or goes astray because of the apparent injustice of suffering (36:17–21).

As many medieval Jewish commentators observed, Elihu's theology is like that of the poet of Psalm 73. Confronted with life's contradictions and divine silence amid injustices, the psalmist insists that one should stay faithful (Ps 73:13–17). In Elihu's view, ethics has consequences not for oneself, but for others (Job 35:6–8). Complaints in the face of suffering do not help and God may not respond anyway (35:9–12). Moreover, it is not true that God does not listen or has not taken notice of injustice, for "the case is before [God]" (35:13–15) – it is pending. Faced with suffering, one ought not to mouth empty words and speak ignorantly (35:16), but come before God in acknowledgment of God's transcendent goodness (ch. 36) and sovereign freedom (ch. 37).

17.4 YHWH'S RESPONSE (JOB 38–41)

The book reaches its theological climax in the second speech of YHWH (Job 40:6–41:26), which revolves around the issue of divine *mišpāṭ* (40:8). Unlike the juridical sense in which Job used it, this use of *mišpāṭ* has to do with a sovereign's jurisdiction or, more specifically, a creator's freedom to govern the cosmos as it seems fit.[24] This uncontestable prerogative is illustrated by the creation and existence even of monstrosities – even the monster that tradition associates with cosmic chaos and darkness, Leviathan (see 3:8). Indeed, the denouement of the speech is a paean to this monstrosity (41:1–34 [Heb 41:1–26]). The opening lines have proved especially challenging to interpreters:

> Behold, expectation of him proves false;
>> Even at his appearance one would be thrown off.
> Indeed,[25] the cruel one, surely he has roused him.
>> Who, then, will stand before me?
> Who will confront me that I should make whole?
>> Under the whole heaven, he is mine.
> I will not silence his outcries,
>> Talk of his might deeds and the grace of his array.

---

[24] Or as Buber has it, not (a judge's) "retributive justice" but (a creator's) "distributive justice" (*Prophetic Faith*, 195); cf. S. H. Scholnick, "The Meaning of Mišpaṭ in the Book of Job," *JBL* 101 (1982): 521–9.

[25] Assuming the asseverative *lamed*. See G. Fuchs, *Mythos und Hiobdichtung: Aufnahme und Umdeutung altorientalischer Vorstellungen* (Stuttgart: Kohlhammer, 1993), 232.

At the start, the poet signals the subversion of expectation, suggesting
that Leviathan contradicts what one anticipates (Job 41:9). The poet lays
out the nature of this astonishment in the next verse (41:10), though the
antecedents of the pronouns are difficult to pin down and it is unclear
who the "cruel one" is. Most interpreters also have trouble with the
adjective, ʾakzār, because they assume it refers to anyone who might
contemplate fighting the Leviathan. Yet the only other occurrence of
this term is in 30:21, where Job calls God ʾakzār, "cruel." The simplest
reading is thus that God is the "cruel one" and it is God who "roused"
Leviathan – just as Job had urged (3:8). The poet thus points to the
inadequacy of human demand for justice, for Job is shown to speak from
both sides of his mouth. On the one hand, he urged the rousing of
Leviathan (3:8). On the other, he charged God with abuse of power
(29:2–31:40) and, in particular, with cruelty (30:21).

The second line of 41:10 is also ambiguous, for it is unclear who
"he" is or who it is before whom "he" will stand. Commentators typically emend the text so that it refers to Leviathan's supremacy: "who will
stand before him?" Yet the witnesses overwhelmingly read, "he will
stand before me" – that is, before God. On the one hand, this "he" who
"will stand" may refer to Job, or indeed anyone who dares to challenge
God – even the one who chooses to rouse Leviathan (3:8). The point is
the sovereignty of God, who cannot be challenged, no matter how
preposterous that decision might be. On the other hand, "he" may point
to "him" in the preceding line – the one whom God has roused:
Leviathan. This one will not "stand before" God, either in defiance
(cf. Deut 9:2; Josh 1:5) or in subservience (cf. Exod 8:16; 9:9:13). The
monster that tradition held to be inimical to God is not, for it is the will
of God to rouse him.

The ambiguities in this couplet convey the difficulty of differentiating the monstrous from the divine, as if the two were somehow one and
the same. Job's expectation of Leviathan, as represented in his initial
outburst (Job 3:8), turns out to be fallacious: Leviathan, who is wholly
other, turns out to be indistinguishable from God. The cruel one, whom
Job accuses God of being (30:21), is the cruel one whom Job had wished
to be roused. Unlike Persian dualism, where good and light are attributed to one deity while evil and darkness are attributed to another,
monotheism entertains no such bifurcation.[26] God is solely responsible

---

[26]   Cf. C. -G. Kang, *Behemot und Leviathan. Studien zur Komposition und Theologie von
Hiob 38,1–42,6*, WMANT 149 (Göttingen: Vandenhoeck & Ruprecht, 2017), 276–77.

for all that happens in the cosmos, including the suffering of the innocent. The question of the next verse – "Who will confront me that I should make whole? Under the whole heaven, he is mine" (41:11, following the versions) – similarly signals the difficulty of separating God from Leviathan.[27]

Throughout his speeches, Job reiterated his desire to confront God directly, to get an explanation for his suffering and to demand just recompense. At the same time, he doubted that this would happen, recognizing that no one can ever challenge God and come out whole (9:4). Now, in this final divine speech, the poet avers that no one can confront God in order that God might make whole (41:11a). God is not subject to such demands and expectations, for the entire realm where mortals dwell belongs to God alone (41:11b). The sovereign deity presides over all, even if all is not whole.

The poet insists that God will "not silence his outcries" (41:12a).[28] The "outcries" echoes what Zophar says about Job's bluster (11:3a). The bluster in 41:12, though, is Leviathan's, and it is spelled out as "talk of his mighty deeds and the grace of his array." The "mighty deeds" may be an allusion to Leviathan's brute power or his formidable exploits, though the plural form is typically reserved for references to the wondrous deeds of God. Indeed the allusion to the "talk of his mighty deeds" echoes hymnic praises of divine power (Pss 71:16; 106:2).

The rest of the portrayal, which combines mythic elements and the stuff of legend, tells of the terrifying and unstoppable advance of the awesome one. Most of the words about Leviathan in Job 41:19–21 are elsewhere associated with theophany – "flames," "fire," "smoke," "coal," and "blaze" – and often occurring in a cluster. More specifically, the images of fire from the mouth and smoke in the nostrils and the mention of blazing coals are juxtaposed in the context of theophany (2 Sam 22:9 // Ps 18:8). "At his rising," says the poet, "the mighty/gods fear (Job 41:25a). Leviathan causes the deep to boil and generates a luminous wake, reminiscent of the turbulence of the primal waters when sea monsters emerge from them (Dan 7:2). Then, the poem concludes in

---

[27]   Cf. T. K. Beal, *Religion and Its Monsters* (London: Routledge, 2002), 50–4.

[28]   The Hiph. of *ḥrš* may be intransitive ("be silent," so 6:24; 13:5, 13, 19; 33:31, 33) or transitive ("silence," so 11:3). Yet in the thirty-seven occurrences of the verb as intransitive, the meaning is always simply "to be silent," never "to be silent *about* (something)."

Job 41:33–34 with language reminiscent of hymnic exaltation of God. Again, ambiguity: The verb *mšl* may mean "to be comparable" or "to govern." The poet means that Leviathan is without peer among all earthly creatures. At the same time, the point is that "there is no one on earth to control him." He is indomitable and, as such, transcends all mundane beings.

Then the paean reaches an even more surprising crescendo with the exaltation of the Leviathan as king. The pairing of "lofty" and "proud" recalls 40:10, where God mocks Job's pretensions to oversee worldly justice like a divine king. In that context, Job is challenged to "see every proud one and take him down" (40:11b) and "see every proud one, subdue him" (40:12a). He is in effect asked to play the role of a divine king, who pours out his angry outbursts and brings down the proud and the wicked. This is a role that Job is in no position to play; elsewhere it is God who brings down the proud and the wicked (Isa 13:9, 13; 14:6). Yet Leviathan does play this role: It is he who "sees all the lofty" (Job 41:34a). The poet triumphantly proclaims, in language that echoes the proclamation of divine kingship in the Psalms: "He is king!"

Throughout the ancient Near East, cosmic chaos is depicted in the form of terrifying monsters that can only be suppressed or destroyed by a divine warrior fighting on behalf of order and good. This mythic tradition is clearly known to the Joban poet (3:8; 7:12; 26:12–13). Yet here human demands and expectations are radically subverted. The terrifying beast, contrary to tradition, is not opposite to God. Whatever the earlier theological effects of the combat myth, the biblical writers of the Persian period insisted there must be no dualistic view of God as one from whom only good comes. Rather, God is the creator of all – light and darkness, weal and woe, alike (Isa 45:6–7). So, too, the poet of Job, explicating the divine *mišpāṭ*, challenges the dichotomy of good and evil, divine benevolence and malevolence, through his audacious and profound re-imagination of the chaos monster. Leviathan is an earthly creature (Job 41:34b). Yet he is no mundane beast, but a sublime reality at once terrifying and fascinating. Though there is no doubt about the aura of danger surrounding Leviathan, the poet does not paint a picture of an aggressive evil force.[29] This is not a being with whom a mortal dares tamper.

---

[29] In this sense, Melville's portrayal of Moby-Dick is an accurate reading of the Joban poem.

If one expects a word about divine suppression of this danger, one will be disappointed. On the contrary, Leviathan is depicted in terms reminiscent of the divine kingship and power and glory. Indeed, at points Leviathan and God seem to "morph" one into another, as if in encountering this terrible and dangerous reality one also encounters something of the divine – God as wholly other.[30] In refusing to domesticate the chaos monster, the poet resists the domestication of God, an awesome, mysterious, and dangerous reality. Indeed, in Leviathan – arguably more than in any of the other realities of God's creation (chs 38–41) – we encounter a God who is utterly sovereign, utterly free: God as *mysterium tremendum et fascinans*.

FURTHER READING

Arnauld, D. *Corpus des textes de bibliothèque de Ras Shamra-Ougarit (1936–2000) un sumérien, babylonien et assyrien.* AuSorSup 23. Barcelona: Ausa, 2007.

Dobbs-Allsopp, F. W. "The Genre of the Meṣad Ḥashavyahu Ostracon." *BASOR* 295 (1994): 49–55.

Dobbs-Allsopp, F. W., J. J. M. Roberts, C. -L. Seow, and R. E. Whitaker. *Hebrew Inscriptions: Texts from the Biblical Period of the Monarchy with Concordance.* London: Yale University Press, 2005.

Klein, J. "*Man and his God*: A Wisdom Poem or a Cultic Lament?" Pages 123–43 in *Approaches to Sumerian Literature: Studies in Honor of H. L. Vantisphout.* Edited by P. Michalowski and N. Veldhuis. Cuneiform Monographs 35. Leiden: Brill, 2006.

Kramer, S. N. "Man and His God: A Sumerian Variation on the 'Job' Motif." Pages 170–82 in *Wisdom in Israel and the Ancient Near East Presented.* Edited by M. Noth and D. Winton Thomas. VTSup 3. Leiden: Brill, 1960.

Kramer, S. N. "The Oldest Literary Catalogue: A Sumerian List of Literary Compositions Compiled about 2000 B.C." *BASOR* 88 (1942): 10–19.

LaCocque, A. "Justice for the Innocent Job," *BibInt* 19 (2011): 19–32.

Lambert, W. L. "A Further Attempt at the Babylonian 'Man and His God'." Pages 187–202 in *Language, Literature, and History.* Edited by F. Rochberg-Halton. AOS 67. New Haven: Yale University Press, 1987.

Moran, W. L. "Rib-Hadda: Job at Byblos?" Pages 173–81 in *Biblical and Related Studies Presented to Samuel Iwry.* Edited by A. Kort and S. Morschauser Winona Lake: Eisenbrauns, 1985.

Moran, W. L. "The Babylonian Job." Pages 182–200 in *The Most Magic Word: Essays on Babylonian and Biblical Literature.* Edited by R. Hendel. CBQMS 35. Washington, DC: Catholic Biblical Association of America, 2002.

---

[30] C. A. Newsom, *The Book of Job: A Contest of Moral Imagination* (Oxford: Oxford University Press, 2003), 252.

Newsom, C. A. *The Book of Job: A Contest of Moral Imagination*. Oxford: Oxford University Press, 2003.

Oosthuizen, M. J. "Divine Insecurity and Joban Heroism: A Reading of the Narrative Framework of Job." *OTE* 4 (1991), 295–315.

Oshima, T. *Babylonian Poems of Pious Sufferers: Ludlul Bēl Nēmeqi and the Babylonian Theodicy*. Orientalische Religionen in der Antike 14 Tübingen: Mohr Siebeck, 2014.

Seow, C. -L. "Elihu's Revelation." *ThTo* 68 (2011): 253–71.

van der Toorn, K. "Theodicy in Akkadian Literature." Pages 57–89 in *Theodicy in the World of the Bible*. Edited by A. Laato and J. de Moor. Leiden: Brill, 2003.

Weinfeld, M. "Job and Its Mesopotamian Parallels – A Typological Analysis." Pages 217–26 in *Text and Context*. Edited by W. T. Claassen. JSOTSup 48. Sheffield: JSOT, 1988.

18 Justice and Retribution in the Psalms

TARAH VAN DE WIELE

Moral discussions of the so-called psalms of imprecation tend to focus on the author as the mind behind their most violent imagery, with the retributions they invoke assumed to be a product of imaginative fantasy.[1] Debates pivot on whether this fantasy is born from justified or unjustified anger.[2] The following discussion breaks from these assumptions altogether, arguing not only that moral reasoning underlies the so-called psalms of imprecation, but that this reasoning is deeply informed by specific patterns of act and consequence attested across ancient Near Eastern legal cultures. These patterns include *talion*, *shame*, and *seat of the act*. The psalter's presentation of acts and their consequences draws on the features and logic of these patterns as they seek to compel YHWH to fulfil the retributive norms that the authors observe and therefore expect as a response to particular kinds of crime.

18.1 TALION

'Talion' is the term most frequently used to describe the 'like for like' statements in Exod 21:23-5, Lev 24:17-21, and Deut 19:21.

---

[1] G. Wenham, 'The Ethics of the Psalms', in *Interpreting the Psalms: Issues and Approaches*, ed. P. S. Johnston and D. G. Firth (Downers Grove: Inter-Varsity, 2005), 229-46.

[2] For examples of the former, see J. C. McCann Jr., *A Theological Introduction to the Book of Psalms: The Psalms as Torah* (Nashville: Abingdon, 1993), 119; N. L. DeClaissé-Walford, 'The Theology of the Imprecatory Psalms', in *Soundings in the Theology of Psalms: Perspectives and Methods in Contemporary Scholarship*, ed. R. Jacobson (Minneapolis: Fortress, 2011), 89; E. Zenger, *A God of Vengeance?: Understanding the Psalms of Divine Wrath*, 1st ed. (Louisville: Westminster John Knox, 1996), 85; J. L. Crenshaw, 'The Psalms as Prayers', in *The Psalms: An Introduction* (Grand Rapids: Eerdmans, 2001), 55-71. For examples assuming the latter, see C. S. Lewis, *Reflections on the Psalms* (London: G. Bles, 1958), 20-3; D. D. Hopkins, *Journey through the Psalms* (St. Louis: Chalice, 2002), 88-91; D. Firth, *Surrendering Retribution in the Psalms: Responses to Violence in Individual Complaints*, PBM (Eugene: Wipf & Stock, 2007), 141.

This principle's occurrence in the Hebrew Bible has been subject to debate because scholarship operates with such wide variation regarding its meaning and referent. There is a tendency in some quarters to identify any consequence resembling 'like for like' as talionic. Scholars drawing from legal theory, however, restrict talion to the specific crimes of murder, bodily harm, and false accusations in court. In the latter case, talion is identified as one of a few forms used to meet a more general principle of 'perfect fit', which underlies the ancient Near Eastern ideal regarding the appropriate form of justice for crimes. This essay follows the second approach, highlighting the presence of a talionic pattern in the moral reasoning of the psalmists who portray their enemies as intending murder, causing injury, or falsely accusing.

There are two features that characterise the ancient Near Eastern legal sources that call for the talionic punishment of murder, injury, and false accusation. The first feature is the matching of means, method, or language in such a way as to emphasise the perfect fit between the consequence and the harmful or deadly act. With regard to means and method, an Old Babylonian king's letter ordering a man to be 'thrown in the kiln' for doing the same to a boy (BIN 7 10) is exemplary.[3] A Neo-Sumerian prison sentence for wrongly imprisoning another (LU 3),[4] a Middle Assyrian punishment of sodomy for a man who has done the same to his comrade (MAL A 20),[5] and Lev 24:19's statement that 'Anyone who maims another shall suffer the same injury in return' reflect the same concern. With regard to matching language, the most obvious examples are the 'eye for eye' edicts of the Laws of Hammurabi and the Pentateuch (LH 196–197, LH 200; Exod 21:23–25; Lev 24:17–21; Deut 19:21).[6]

The second feature is the use of terms of 'payment' to describe the talionic punishment, highlighting its judgement on the victim's literal worth. In the Middle Assyrian Law collection, for example, a man who has struck a prostitute and caused her to miscarry is to be financially assessed 'blow for blow' (*miḫṣī kî miḫṣī*), so as to constitute a 'full payment of a life' (MAL A 52; cf. MAL A 50).[7] The language of payment is also present in the biblical material. Leviticus 24:21 calls for a

[3]   M. Stol (trans.), *Letters from Yale*, AbB 9 (Leiden: Brill, 1981), 126–7 no. 197.
[4]   Laws of Ur-Namma (LU), all cited from M. Roth, *Law Collections from Mesopotamia and Asia Minor*, 2nd ed., WAW 6 (Atlanta: Society of Biblical Literature, 1997), 13–22.
[5]   Middle Assyrian Laws (MAL), all cited from Roth, *Law Collections*, 153–94.
[6]   Laws of Hammurabi (LH), all cited from Roth, *Law Collections*, 71–142.
[7]   S. LaFont, 'Middle Assyrian Period', in *AHANEL*, ed. R. Westbrook, vol. 1, HOS 72 (Leiden: Brill, 2003), 558.

payment (*šlm*) of life for life, placed in parallel with a summons of capital punishment for killing. In Exod 21:22–23, the root *ntn* functions as a term of payment in addition to its meaning of 'give'. The attacker of a pregnant woman must 'give' (*ntn*) a payment of a fine if 'no further harm follows'. But if there is harm, the attacker must 'give' (*ntn*) (a payment of) 'life for life'.

The psalms use these same techniques to appeal for justice when enemies threaten either injury or death. Psalm 28:4, for example, calls on YHWH to respond to murderous (v. 1) foes 'according to their work and according to the evil of their deeds'. Psalm 143:12 calls for YHWH to 'destroy all my adversaries' because they have pursued the supplicant almost to his death (v. 3). Psalm 6 uses matching language to appeal for talion, calling for terror (*bhl*) (v. 10) because he has been terrorised (*bhl*) (vv. 2–3). In 35:3–5 the psalmist calls for pursuit (*rdp*) for being pursued (*rdp*).

The psalms also draw on this tradition when they use the words *gml*, *šwr*, *ntn*, and *šlm*, exploring the implications of talionic principles both for those who *preserve* life and do *no* harm, and for their malevolent counterparts. In the first category, for example, there is 18:20, which states that YHWH has 'rewarded' (*gml*) the supplicant 'according to my righteousness' and 'according to the cleanness of my hands'. Similarly, in 62:12 YHWH will 'repay' (*šlm*) to all according to their work'. Returning to 28:4, *ntn* and *gml* characterise the talionic exhortation: 'Repay them according to their work ... repay them according to the work of their hands; render them their due reward'. Psalm 54, however, is exemplary of the latter category: the 'insolent' have risen up against the supplicant and sought his life (v. 3). For their murderous intent, the psalm calls on YHWH to 'repay' (*šwr*) the evil of the foes back to them, naming their destruction as the payment (v. 5).

The psalms also use payment language to describe an enemy's behaviour as especially unjust – as *failing* to observe the principles of talion. For example, 38:20 and 35:12 portray their enemies as those who 'render' or 'repay evil for good'. In 7:3–5, the supplicant claims that if he were himself to commit this sort of anti-talion – to have 'repaid my ally with harm' – then his enemy should annihilate him for such a distortion.

Having examined manifestations of the talionic pattern arising from an attempt on a person's life through physical violence, we turn to attempts on a life through false accusation. The driving principle in these examples is that a false accusation for a capital crime deserves the death that would have occurred had the accusation been believed.

The association of false accusation with a talionic punishment is widely attested in the ancient Near East. Casuistic laws like those of Lipit-Ishtar, Hammurabi, and Deuteronomy explicitly draw a line from making a baseless accusation to bearing the penalty for the crime accused (LL 17; LH 1, 3–4; Deut 19:15–21). Trial records also attest to this association, as in the case of a Neo-Sumerian son who falsely accuses his father of a capital crime and is subsequently punished by death (RA 71).[8] Biblical narratives further confirm this association. First Kings 21:8–14, for example, demonstrates how false accusation, in this case Jezebel's claim against Naboth, is a form of murder. Accordingly, Jezebel meets a deadly end (2 Kgs 9:30–37).

The psalms use the same line of reasoning when they portray false accusers as hunters who fall into the very pits or traps that they have made. In Ps 7, they are lions pursuing the supplicant to 'tear apart' and 'drag away' (7:1–2). Psalm 57:4 also portrays false accusers as hunting lions 'that greedily devour human prey'. It is these hunters that Psalm 7 describes as digging a pit (v. 15), using a term that doubles in other psalms as 'grave' (28:1–2; 88:5; 143:7). In Psalm 57, the hunters have dug a pit as well, in this case a hunting trap (57:6). The psalm declares that, even though these hunters 'set a net for my steps' and 'dig a pit in my path', it is they who have fallen into it (57:6). Finally, 35:7–11 also portrays 'malicious witnesses' (35:11) as hunters who have 'dug a pit' (35:7) and 'ask me about things I do not know' (35:11). For these offences, the psalmist demands that 'the net that they hid ensnare them' (35:8).

The psalms also rely on expectations of talionic consequences for false accusation when they depict the mouths of false accusers as deadly weapons turned self-ward. Thus, the tongue is a sharp sword (57:4), the teeth are spears and arrows (57:4), and the throat is an open grave (5:9). Those who 'gnash their teeth' are 'the wicked who plot against the righteous' (37:12). The enemies who 'set their snares' are the ones who 'speak of ruin' (38:12). The ones who 'draw their swords' and 'bend their bows' (37:14) are those who 'plot against the righteous' (37:12). It is with this imagery in mind that the talionic pattern in Psalm 37:15 becomes apparent, as the supplicant declares that his enemies' 'sword shall enter their own heart, and their bows shall be broken'.

The psalms' use of the talionic pattern challenges the idea that, because the Pentateuch does not explicitly account for acts of bodily

---

[8]   B. LaFont and R. Westbrook, 'Neo-Sumerian Period (Ur III)', in *AHANEL*, ed. R. Westbrook, vol. 1, HOS 72 (Leiden: Brill, 2003), 221; B. Wells, *The Law of Testimony in the Pentateuchal Codes*, BZABR 4 (Wiesbaden: Harrassowitz, 2004), 150.

mutilation, ancient Israel regarded talion as a strictly financial compen-
satory system. The psalms never speak of or even allude to money, but
still adopt payment language. If financial compensation were the only
means of talion in ancient Israel, we would need to explain why the
psalms are so attentive to the explicitly physical responses that characterise the talionic pattern in ancient Near Eastern contexts beyond the
Pentateuch.

18.2 SHAME

Shame functioned in ancient Near Eastern cultures as both the result of
a criminal act and the aim of a sanctioned punishment. This is closely
related to the fact that these cultures were highly hierarchical in social
structure. Crimes of slander and unwarranted reproach, which publicly
damaged their victims, required responses that damaged the reputation
of the culprit to an equivalent degree. To this end, the shaming pattern
assumes a kind of talionic logic in its 'shame for shame' presentation of
act and consequence. It is distinct from the talionic pattern insofar as it
incorporates an observing community into how it achieves justice.

To punish someone by shaming them depends entirely on cues to
the community that it should shift its perception and treatment of the
punished. In the ancient Near East, this was frequently accomplished by
changing the personal appearance of the wrongdoer to that of a slave or
another person of low social status.[9] Shaming punishments of this sort
often took the form of bodily mutilations that could not easily be
undone or hidden. One attested example is the removal of hair from
the head or face of the wrongdoer. An Isin/Larsa document, for example,
reports on a son who has 'half his head shaved' for repudiating his
mother (*Ana ittishu* VII.A.1–6).[10] LH 127 prescribes the same punishment for a man who slanders another's wife. The Middle Assyrian laws
stipulate that a prostitute have 'hot pitch' poured over her head for
wearing a veil – that is, for adopting the outward signs of a higher status
than she was allowed (MAL A 40). In the same collection, slanderers had
their hair 'cut off' as punishment (MAL 18–19). The shorn appearance
of these wrongdoers would mimic that of a slave, inviting the surrounding society to treat them as such as the substance of their punishment

---

[9]   T. M. Lemos, 'Shame and Mutilation of Enemies in the Hebrew Bible', *JBL* 125 (2006):
      226.
[10] E. M. Tetlow, *Women, Crime, and Punishment in Ancient Law and Society. Vol. 1:
      Ancient Near East* (London: Continuum, 2004), 34.

(LH 146, 226–227; LE 51–52; CAD 5.130).[11] With regard to the removal of facial hair, Isa 50:6 and 2 Sam 10:4–5 both suggest that beard alteration constituted a shaming change in appearance. Isaiah equates 'smooth' cheeks to a punishing social disgrace, while David advises his clean-shaven, shamed servants to 'remain at Jericho until your beards have grown' (2 Sam 10:5).

A defining feature of the shaming pattern is the public nature of the punishment. Examples include an Old Babylonian man 'led around the city' with his newly shorn head for publicly slandering another (CT 45 18:14–16).[12] In LH 127, the man who slandered another's wife will, in addition to bearing a shorn head, be flogged 'before the judges' (cf. MAL A 18–19). A woman in Alalakh, whose claim against another has been rejected as slanderous, is to be struck by the accused in front of the court or in public (AT 11).[13] In Deut 25:5–10, a man has the choice of marrying his late brother's widow or of publicly refusing her. The latter shames her wrongfully and, in the event of such a refusal, the widow regains her honour not merely by spitting in his face, but by doing so in 'the presence of the elders' (v. 9). Deuteronomy 22:13–17 concerns the just response when a bride is slandered by her groom, calling for the public punishment of the latter. Thus, the bride's father publicly recounts the charges against his daughter (22:16–17), putting the groom's wrong on display to all in a 'shaming speech' about his behaviour.[14]

The psalms' moral reasoning around shame reflects an awareness of the pattern just outlined: the only justice for acts that cause shame is to shame the actor. The psalms thus participate in a wider system of expectations regarding how shame functioned in ancient Near Eastern legal cultures. The psalms also reflect on what it means to seek out justice that repairs the damage caused by slander and reproach.

The psalms usually convey the shaming pattern's 'change in appearance' feature through the use of clothing imagery. On the first instance, clothing terms describe the shameful state that results from slander and

---

[11]   Laws of Eshnunna (LE), all cited from Roth, *Law Collections*, 57–70; M. T. Roth et al. (eds), *The Assyrian Dictionary. Vol. 5* (Chicago: University of Chicago Press, 1956–2010), 130.

[12]   R. Westbrook, 'Old Babylonian Period', in *AHANEL*, ed. R. Westbrook, vol. 1, HOS 72 (Leiden: Brill, 2003), 423.

[13]   M. Malul, *Studies in Mesopotamian Legal Symbolism* (Neukirchen-Vluyn: Neukirchener Verlag, 1988), 432.

[14]   V. H. Matthews, 'Honor and Shame in Gender-Related Legal Situations in the Hebrew Bible', in *Gender and Law in the Hebrew Bible and the Ancient Near East*, ed. B. M. Levinson and T. Frymer-Kensky, JSOTSup 262 (London: T&T Clark, 2004), 111–12.

reproach. Disgrace, for instance, 'covers' the supplicant's face in Psalm 69:7. These same terms can then characterise the call for justice: YHWH is to 'clothe' enemies 'with disgrace' in 132:18, for instance, and 'cover' slanderous accusers 'with scorn and disgrace' in 71:13.

In the wake of slanderous claims by accusers, Psalm 109 uses clothing imagery to convey the shame that the supplicant will endure after his 'position' is 'seized' (109:8) and the implications reach his family (109:9–10). If his slanderous accusers are successful, he will wear the image they have painted of him 'like a garment that he wraps around himself, like a belt that he wears every day' (109:19). Accordingly, in 109:29, the call for justice articulates the retributive shaming of the slanderers by focussing on their outward appearance: they are to 'be clothed with dishonour' and 'wrapped in their own shame as in a mantle'. The psalm also plays on the talionic response of matching language to underline the 'shame for shame' logic: as the supplicant is 'clothed' (*lbš*), so shall they be 'clothed' (*lbš*) (109:18, 29).

Psalm 35 likewise identifies shame as both a wrongful act and a rightful punishment, but then goes further, identifying shame as integral to a proper relationship with YHWH. After presenting the supplicant as postured low and in sackcloth in a penitential effort on behalf of his friends (35:13–14), the psalm identifies the enemies' wrong: they rejoice at his stumbling and they 'tear' at his garment 'without ceasing (35:15)'. The enemies tear at the very clothing that signals a humble posture, forcing the supplicant into deeper ignominy – but for their sake, rather than YHWH's. In response, the psalm calls for a consequence that evokes the same change in appearance: let them 'be clothed with shame and dishonour' (35:26).

The psalms also reflect the public nature of the shaming pattern in their use of eye-related imagery and depictions of being 'seen'. Eyes become the instruments of shame in 17:11, wherein enemies 'set their eyes to cast' the psalmist 'to the ground'. Eye imagery is also used to depict YHWH as a complicit observer who witnesses the supplicant's loss of status at the hands of his enemies. Psalm 35, for example, accuses YHWH of taking part in wrongful public humiliation by asking, 'How long, O LORD, will you look on?' (35:17), and stating emphatically, 'You have seen, O LORD; do not be silent!' (35:22). Psalm 17:2 similarly exclaims, 'Let your eyes see the right!'

The psalms also use this imagery of the gaze or ability to see as a way to convey the supplicant's shamed status. In 40:12, for example, the supplicant 'cannot see', as a result of the 'iniquities that have overtaken' him. Similar imagery is also used to indicate the restoration of status.

Psalm 54:7, for example, ends with the victorious declaration that 'my eye has looked in triumph on my enemies'. In 18:27, God 'brings down' the 'haughty eyes' of enemies. The once superior are subdued into inferior positions in the public gaze.

These psalms' use of the shaming pattern raises important questions about the moral implications of including YHWH as part of the observing community. Insofar as the dimensions of shame are informed by the ancient Near Eastern legal milieu, this is a provocative image with which to wrestle: the one agent powerful enough to redeem the psalmist from shame may be participating in his shame, alongside the rest of the community, by virtue of the distance and silence he offers.

18.3 SEAT OF THE ACT

As the preceding has already hinted, speech acts carried considerable power in ancient Near Eastern legal cultures. Wrongfully used, they posed a serious threat. A false accusation for a capital crime was attempted murder, while slander or reproach sabotaged a person's livelihood by damaging their status in the social hierarchy. The speech act's power is evident in the oral nature of contract-making procedures. The thousands of written documents we categorise as 'contracts' are in reality aide-mémoires for agreements undertaken through the speech acts of ceremonies and oaths.[15] Documents in this category contain explicit citations of speech acts – 'he said these words' or 'it is we who have said to you' – and underscore the orality of the agreement taking place (ELTS 2; TPK 1 157–160; P. Louvre E 7856 and 7852).[16] Contracts for betrothal, adoption, and property contain directives for parties to speak key phrases. A Neo-Sumerian groom, for instance, is instructed to say, 'I will marry X daughter of Y' (NG 15:4–6, 16:4–6) or 'I am your son-in-law'.[17] An Old Babylonian man is directed to speak the words 'my children' to become an adoptive father and to make his adopted children the heirs of his property (LH 170–171). Correspondingly, a child's vocal challenge, 'you are *not* my father', was regarded as a genuine threat to an adoption contract's integrity (LH 192–193; cf. LH 160–161; EMAR 30;

---

[15] C. Wilcke, 'Early Dynastic and Sargonic Period', in *AHANEL*, ed. R. Westbrook, vol. 1, HOS 72 (Leiden: Brill, 2003), 165.

[16] Wilcke, 'Early Dynastic and Sargonic Period', 168; K. R. Veenhof, 'Old Assyrian Period', in *AHANEL*, ed. R. Westbrook, vol. 1, HOS 72 (Leiden: Brill, 2003), 461; R. Jasnow, 'Egypt: Third Intermediate Period', in *AHANEL*, ed. R. Westbrook, vol. 1, HOS 72 (Leiden: Brill, 2003), 810.

[17] LaFont and Westbrook, 'Neo-Sumerian Period (Ur III)', 202.

RE 10, 13).[18] The Pentateuch likewise assumes an oral contract culture when, for example, it addresses the covenant between YHWH and Israel.[19] Thus, Deuteronomy 32's Song of Moses assures the people of YHWH's personal commitment to the covenant by framing it as a speech act, in which YHWH says, 'For I lift up my hand to heaven and swear [lit: say]' (32:40).[20]

Spoken oaths featured in contract proceedings, serving to enforce the agreement.[21] The content of the oath compelled the party to keep it, insofar as it included a litany of curses that were self-directed and believed to be imminent if the speaker violated the terms of the contract. The spoken curse thus wished for evil but was not regarded as evil in and of itself, given its fundamental role in maintaining binding arrangements. This is useful to keep in mind when approaching the psalms' retributions against enemies, because the vitriolic language of the supplicant is often the focus of ethical critiques on the psalms. In an ancient Near Eastern context, however, an effective curse – no matter its purpose – is magnificently vitriolic. The level of its vitriol is not the basis upon which to judge whether it a 'good' or an 'evil'. Rather, its value is assessed by what the curse meant to accomplish as a result of its utterance. The psalms inherit this cultural context wherein vitriol, in the form of a 'good' curse, could accomplish a social good, compelling contracted parties to 'keep their word'.

The history of ancient Near Eastern law shows that a seat-of-the-act response was regarded as the most fitting justice for abuse of the speech powers integral to contract making. This response was defined by a conceptual understanding of the body that perceived a single body part as responsible for and representative of certain acts. In cases when contracts were broken or wilfully ignored and in cases of someone speaking a curse outside the parameters of oaths, the mouth is therefore overwhelmingly the focus of punishment. As with shaming, the seat-of-the-act pattern conveys a talionic logic at its root, while also displaying its own features.

---

[18]   R. Westbrook, 'Emar and Vicinity', in *AHANEL*, ed. R. Westbrook, vol. 1, HOS 72 (Leiden: Brill, 2003), 673.

[19]   T. Frymer-Kensky, 'Israel', in *AHANEL*, ed. R. Westbrook, vol. 2, HOS 72 (Leiden: Brill, 2003), 1020–7.

[20]   C. A. Strine, *Sworn Enemies: The Divine Oath, the Book of Ezekiel, and the Polemics of Exile*, BZAW 436 (Berlin: de Gruyter, 2013), 75.

[21]   A. Oppenheim, *Ancient Mesopotamia: Portrait of a Dead Civilization* (Chicago: University of Chicago Press, 1964), 338.

One of these is a concern to specify the mouth as the location of the wrongful act before carrying out a consequence directed at the same space. A good example is a Sargonic slave contract that describes a seller's act of fraudulently detaining a slave as 'putting deceit in her mouth'. The punishment is then mouth mutilation (SRU 43).[22]

A concern to specify the mouth as the 'seat' could also be accomplished by using a physical representation of the contract as the punishing instrument. An Emar tablet concerning the sale of land stipulates that 'if they contest, this tablet will break their teeth'.[23] Other cases use the nail or peg that attached the announcement of the agreement to a wall. Following the seat-of-the-act pattern, the nail or peg would be driven into the mouth of the contract breaker.[24]

These punishments – always focussed on the mouth – vary in their severity but present a discernible logic in their variation. Some punishment methods temporarily stopped the wrongdoer from speaking. For example, contracts from Alalakh and Ur call for filling the mouth of contract breakers with 'lead' or 'molten metal'.[25] The scarring from this punishment would be a mark for the community to see, warning them to be wary of taking these persons at their word. Crucially, however, the recipient would likely speak again.

Other methods, though, effectively stopped the wrongdoer from ever speaking again. Such cases suggest that the acts in question were considered ones from which a community needed protection, rather than simply a warning for caution. An Old Babylonian law, for example, stipulates that a son will lose his tongue if he says 'you are not my father/mother' to his adoptive parents (LH 192). Jacobs suggests that the punishment's severity arose because the child's words were regarded as a dangerous threat to social order, as a challenge to 'the normative authority of parents'.[26]

It appears that cursing outside the realm of oaths and contract making was also viewed as major threat to social order. Babylonian witchcraft literature reveals that the punishment for a 'witch' who has (illegally) cursed a victim is to 'tear out' her tongue (*Maqlû* 7.96–105;

---

[22]   J. Krecher, 'Neue sumerische Rechtsurkunden des 3. Jahrtausends', *ZA* 63 (1973): 188–92.

[23]   J. A. Hackett and J. Huehnergard, "On Breaking Teeth', *HTR* 77 (1984): 264–5.

[24]   Hackett and Huehnergard, 'On Breaking Teeth', 264–6.

[25]   Hackett and Huehnergard, 'On Breaking Teeth', 265–6.

[26]   S. Jacobs, *The Body as Property: Physical Disfigurement in Biblical Law*, LHBOTS 582 (London: T&T Clark, 2014), 140.

cf. 2.216; 3.92; 8.102; cf. VAT 35:1–3).[27] Removing the tongue is a response based in seat-of-the-act logic, as well as an act of disempowerment. Not only does a tongueless mouth warn onlookers that its owner abused the power of the curse or another speech act, but it also protects the community from future abuse.

In line with this understanding of contracts as fundamentally spoken agreements, the psalms describe the covenant between YHWH and his people in terms of speech acts and point to the mouth as pivotal to its integrity. Psalm 89:34, for example, assumes the covenant's spoken nature when assigning YHWH the words, 'I will not violate my covenant, or alter the word that went forth from my lips'. Likewise, in 50:16, YHWH asks the wicked what right they have to 'take my covenant on your lips'.

The psalms then use the seat-of-the-act pattern of justice to portray enemies as challenging this covenant by violating its agreements or lying about either party's fidelity to it. Like the legal examples above, the psalms show a concern to specify the mouth as the seat of the act before calling for the execution of justice focussed on the same space. Psalm 3 accomplishes this by quoting the enemies' spoken claim that 'there is no help for you in God' (3:2). Craigie and Tate suggest that the psalm's specification that the claim is directed 'to my soul' reflects the psalmist's concern for his 'most *essential being*, namely his relationship with God'.[28] In the rest of the Hebrew Bible, this relationship is defined as a covenant and its terms for fidelity. Thus, though these foes may rise against (3:1), outnumber (3:6), and completely surround the supplicant (3:6), this verbal challenge is the only offence to his soul because it challenges YHWH's fidelity to the covenant.

Psalms 63 and 31 specify the mouth as the seat of the enemies' wrongs by using *dbr* (speak) and *šqr* (lie): the enemies are 'the ones who speak a lie' (63:11) and have 'lying lips … that speak' (31:18). The term *šqr* has explicit associations with covenantal concepts and figures: false oaths in YHWH's name (e.g., Lev 19:12; Mal 3:5), lying scribes who interpret the terms of the covenant with YHWH (e.g., Jer 8:8; Mic 2:11), and false prophets who lead people away from that covenant (e.g., 1 Kgs 22:22–23; Isa 9:15).

In a similar fashion, Psalm 12 uses *dbr* with *šw'*, identifying the enemies as those who 'utter lies to each other' (12:2). The word *šw'* is the

---

[27]   T. Abusch, *Babylonian Witchcraft Literature: Case Studies* (Atlanta: Scholars, 1987), 109–110.
[28]   P. C. Craigie and M. E. Tate, *Psalms 1–50*, 2nd ed., WBC 19 (Waco: Word, 2004), 70.

key term in the covenant and Decalogue prohibition against using YHWH's name 'in vain' (Exod 20:7; Deut 5:11). It describes 'empty' oaths, taken when making a covenant that the oath taker does not intend to keep (e.g., Hos 10:4). Against this backdrop, the psalm places *šw'* directly in the foes' mouths, with their lips becoming its source (Ps 12:2–4) and their tongue being the only weapon needed 'to prevail' (12:4). Similarly, Psalm 58 couples *dbr* with *kzb*, declaring that the wicked 'err from their birth, speaking lies' (58:3). The latter term most commonly describes the divinations of false prophets (e.g., Isa 28:15; Ezek 13:6–9, 19). To lie in this sense is to present a reality wholly contradictory to one grounded in the covenant with YHWH.

Having now located covenantal challenges and violations in the mouths of foes, these psalms then follow with calls for justice carried out in the same space. Psalm 3 calls for YHWH to 'strike the cheek' (3:7) and 'break the teeth' of the supplicant's adversaries (3:7). As Sarna reasons, anyone surrounded by an overwhelming mass of enemy troops would surely pray for something more drastic.[29] But, when read within ancient Near Eastern legal context, the psalm is clearly using the norms of the seat-of-the-act pattern to name the enemies' offence, namely, challenging YHWH's fidelity to his covenant with the psalmist. The consequence the psalmist seeks is meant to render the enemies scarred: a warning to those around them. Psalm 58 similarly focusses on teeth, calling for de-fanged lions in a vivid portrayal of disempowered enemies in the same vein as Psalm 3.

Psalm 31 focusses on the enemies' lips, calling for them to 'be stilled' (v. 18). Though the NRSV translation of *'lm* suggests a metaphorical call for a bit of silence, the physical reality of this term finds support elsewhere in the Bible. In Ezekiel 3:26, for example, *'lm* describes the result of YHWH making the tongue 'cling to the roof' of the mouth. Along similar lines, Ps 63:11 calls for enemies' mouths to be 'stopped'.

Like the ancient Near Eastern legal examples above, Psalm 12 indicates an awareness of differentiated punishments for speech-act offences: those that should warn a community and those that should protect it. In Psalm 12 the call is for YHWH to cut off both the lips and the tongue of the enemies (12:3–4), mutilating these mouths beyond any function. The severity of the consequence seems to be a direct response to the enemies' ability to deceive and curse with so little recompense

---

[29]   N. M. Sarna, 'Legal Terminology in Psalm 3:8', in *Sha'arei Talmon: Studies in the Bible, Qumran, and the Ancient Near East: Festschrift Shemaryahu Talmon*, ed. M. Fishbane, E. Tov, and W. Fields (Winona Lake: Eisenbrauns, 1992), 175.

that they jest, 'who is our master?' (12:4). Recognition of the danger posed by such persons is affirmed by the language the psalm injects into the supplicant's plea for YHWH's help: he wants not only justice, but also to be in 'safety' (12:5) and 'guarded' (12:7).

The presence of this seat-of-the-act pattern in the psalms raises the possibility that contract breaking in the psalmist's community was punished with facial mutilation. Although there are no attestations of mouth-related punishment for contract breaking in the Pentateuchal codes, the psalmist has strong affinities with this pattern as it plays out in extant ancient Near Eastern sources; this suggests that the psalms may be another, non-Pentateuch window into ancient Israel's punitive norms. One may baulk at this suggestion, reasoning that the psalms' references are merely rhetorical. If that is the case, though, it is remarkable that the psalms are so precise, calling for a consequence that fits the enemies' actions in a manner that does not overstep that which is attested in the wider ancient Near Eastern material. If this is but rhetoric, it seems more likely that the psalms would call for consequences that exceeded the norm.

18.4 IMPLICATIONS FOR CONTEMPORARY ETHICS

Ethical discussion of these psalms has been stuck in a cycle of debate about how we 'contend' with the ways they wish to punish. More fruitful is a recognition that the moral logic underlying the talionic, shaming, and seat-of-the-act patterns of justice remains present in modern social consciousness.

In the case of talion, the psalms perceive no difference between false accusers who intend for their victim to be killed through a legal process and a murderer who carries out the act himself. Both share the same intent, so the subject of their intent is mirrored back upon them. Though such a blatant equivalence between intent and result breaks from contemporary legal practice, it adds urgency to two moral imperatives alive and well in our current climate: protecting our legal systems from those who manipulate them to harm the innocent, and pursuing justice for those who have already been made victims in this way.

With regard to shame, it is most important to recognise that this is not a tool solely for maintaining a social hierarchy. Rather, it is employed to maintain a cosmic hierarchy, checking those that the public might perceive as more powerful than God. The psalms remind us that the abuse of power damages the spirit of its victims as well as the observing public, because it tempts both to perceive the abuser as more powerful than God.

The seat of the act is perhaps the most intriguing. While its punishments for spoken crimes are abhorrent to contemporary ethics in terms of execution, they are strikingly reflective of contemporary ethics in terms of the gravitas that they recognise in the speech act. As is most evident in the age of information, social media, and billion-dollar advertising campaigns, words brandish an immense influence over the psyche and well-being of their hearers and readers. What at first seems like an archaic call to remove the teeth and tongues of those who speak crushing words to the supplicant is in its essence a prophetic call to acknowledge that cruel and manipulative words can be as deadly as any weapon.

In all of these patterns, the psalms draw us to questions of power and its abuse. This is a universal subject of ethical reflection. I hope I have laid some groundwork for future roads into how we might engage the psalter's calls for justice in response to abusive power, even as those calls manifest in bloodied and beaten foes.

FURTHER READING

Abusch, I. T. *Babylonian Witchcraft Literature: Case Studies*. Atlanta: Scholars, 1987.

Craigie, P. C., and M. E. Tate. *Psalms 1–50*. 2nd ed. WBC 19. Waco: Word, 2004.

Hackett, J. A., and J. Huehnergard. 'On Breaking Teeth'. *HTR* 77 (1984): 259–72.

Jacobs, S. *The Body as Property: Physical Disfigurement in Biblical Law*. LHBOTS 582. London: T&T Clark, 2014.

Krecher, J. 'Neue sumerische Rechtsurkunden des 3. Jahrtausends'. *ZA* 63 (1973): 145–271.

Lemos, T. M. 'Shame and Mutilation of Enemies in the Hebrew Bible'. *JBL* 125 (2006): 225–41.

Malul, M. *Studies in Mesopotamian Legal Symbolism*. Neukirchen-Vluyn: Neukirchener Verlag, 1988.

Matthews, V. H. 'Honor and Shame in Gender-Related Legal Situations in the Hebrew Bible'. Pages 97–112 in *Gendered Law in the Hebrew Bible and the Ancient Near East*. Edited by B. M. Levinson and T. Frymer-Kensky, JSOTSup 262. London: T&T Clark, 2004.

Oppenheim, A. *Ancient Mesopotamia: Portrait of a Dead Civilization*. Chicago: University of Chicago Press, 1964.

Roth, M. *Law Collections from Mesopotamia and Asia Minor*. 2nd ed. WAW 6. Atlanta: Society of Biblical Literature, 1997.

Sarna, N. M. 'Legal Terminology in Psalm 3:8'. Pages 175–81 in *Sha'arei Talmon: Studies in the Bible, Qumran, and the Ancient Near East: Festschrift Shemaryahu Talmon*. Edited by M. Fishbane, E. Tov, and W. Fields. Winona Lake: Eisenbrauns, 1992.

Stol, M. *Letters from Yale*. Leiden: Brill, 1982.

Strine, C. A. *Sworn Enemies: The Divine Oath, the Book of Ezekiel, and the Polemics of Exile*. BZAW 436. Berlin: de Gruyter, 2013.

Tetlow, E. M. *Women, Crime, and Punishment in Ancient Law and Society, Volume 1: Ancient Near East*. London: Continuum, 2004.

Wells, B. *The Law of Testimony in the Pentateuchal Codes*. BZABR 4. Wiesbaden: Harrassowitz, 2004.

Wenham, G. 'The Ethics of the Psalms'. Pages 229–46 in *Interpreting the Psalms: Issues and Approaches*. Edited by P. S. Johnston and D. G. Firth. Downers Grove: Inter-Varsity, 2005.

Westbrook, R., and G. M. Beckman, eds. *A History of Ancient Near Eastern Law*. Leiden: Brill, 2003.

Part V

Faithful Ethics

19 Jewish Ethics and the Hebrew Bible

DEBORAH BARER

The term "ethics" has a complicated history in Jewish tradition for two reasons. First, the term is not native to classical Jewish sources.[1] Second, in both Christian and secular discourse ethics is often contrasted with law, suggesting that the two are distinct and separate normative frameworks. This is problematic in a Jewish framework, where ethical discussions tend to focus on the question of proper behavior in specific situations and thus fall under the broader category of *halakhah*. Although often translated as "Jewish law," *halakhah* is better understood as a way of life, encompassing far more than the secular term "law" might suggest. Jews seek to live in accordance with the covenant established between God and the people of Israel; *halakhah* provides guidance about how to do this, whether the issue concerns interpersonal relationships, property law, or ritual behavior. As Chaim Saiman notes, "the rabbis use concepts forged in the regulatory framework [of halakhah] to do the work other societies assign to philosophy, political theory, theology, ethics, and even to art, drama, and literature."[2] As a result, many of the assumed distinctions between ethics and law do not apply easily or well to Jewish tradition.[3]

Despite these conceptual and terminological challenges, Judaism has a rich and extensive history of ethical reflection, in the sense of sustained engagement with questions about how to lead a good life.

---

[1] J. W. Schofer, *The Making of a Sage: A Study in Rabbinic Ethics* (Madison: University of Wisconsin Press, 2005), 313–14.

[2] C. N. Saiman, *Halakhah: The Rabbinic Idea of Law* (Princeton: Princeton University Press, 2018), 8.

[3] Much of the theoretical discussion about the distinction between Jewish law and ethics has centered on the idea of supererogation. For a brief overview of those debates, see A. Lichtenstein, "Does Jewish Tradition Recognize an Ethic Independent of Halakha?" in *Modern Jewish Ethics*, ed. M. Fox (Columbus: Ohio State University Press, 1975), 62–88, and L. Newman, "Law, Virtue and Supererogation in the Halakhah: The Problem of 'Lifnim Mishurat Hadin' Reconsidered," *JJS* 40 (1989): 61–88 and further references therein.

Although many of these discussions begin with the Hebrew Bible, which provides the primary and most direct source of divine instruction, extracting a practical guide for life from the biblical text is challenging for a number of reasons. First, there are many situations that the text simply does not address. Second, there are cases where biblical instructions may be unclear, or where the reasons for them may be opaque. Third, some readers may feel marginalized by the text or excluded from its assumed audience.[4] Finally, and perhaps most disconcertingly, there are biblical teachings that may strike the reader as directly harmful or immoral.

In this essay, I explore how Jewish readers have negotiated this last set of challenges: How should one interpret biblical instructions that seem morally problematic or inconsistent with the broader ethical message of the text? Since a comprehensive survey is far beyond the scope of the present essay, I focus on two paradigmatic examples: (1) the laws pertaining to the stubborn and rebellious son (Deut 21:18–21) as discussed in classical rabbinic texts, and (2) the law prohibiting sexual intercourse between two men (Lev 18:22), as explored in a 2006 *teshuva* by Rabbis Elliot Dorff, Daniel Nevins, and Avram Reisner (hereafter Dorff et al.). My goal is to introduce two prominent ethical dilemmas raised by the biblical text and to present some of the interpretive strategies that Jewish readers have used to address such dilemmas, focusing especially on the rabbis of antiquity (hereafter simply "the rabbis") and Dorff et al.

As I will show, there are several differences in the ways each of these sets of readers approach these verses. They have different assumptions about the origins of the biblical text, which impact their willingness to offer moral critique, and they employ different interpretive techniques. Yet, there are also marked similarities. While both seek to limit the potential harms caused by these commandments, neither is willing to reject or overrule them, and both acknowledge ongoing dissent about the ways these passages should be understood. Furthermore, both sets of responses can be understood – paradoxically – as a way of ethically resisting the biblical text, but also as a way of demonstrating fidelity to it.

---

4   This has been a central claim in feminist critiques. As J. Plaskow starkly frames the issue, "If the covenant is a covenant with all generations (Deut 29:13ff), then its reappropriation also involves the continual reappropriation of women's marginality." J. Plaskow, *Standing Again at Sinai: Judaism from a Feminist Perspective* (New York: HarperCollins, 1990), 26.

In what follows, I briefly introduce the two case studies, including the verse(s) in question, the challenges they raise, and the responses to them. I then offer a more detailed analysis of the interpretive assumptions and strategies each group of readers employs in responding to these texts, noting the similarities and differences. Finally, I consider the resources these examples offer to contemporary readers who struggle with their own ethical objections to specific biblical passages.

19.1 PROBLEMATIC VERSES: TWO CASE STUDIES

The Laws of the Stubborn and Rebellious Son

The book of Deuteronomy introduces the case of the "stubborn and rebellious son" (ben sorer u'moreh).

> If someone has a stubborn and rebellious son who will not obey his father and mother, who does not heed them when they discipline him, then his father and his mother shall take hold of him and bring him out to the elders of his town at the gate of that place. They shall say to the elders of his town, "This son of ours is stubborn and rebellious. He will not obey us [lit. "our voice," koleinu]. He is a glutton and a drunkard." Then all the men of the town shall stone him to death. So you shall purge the evil from your midst; and all Israel will hear, and be afraid. (Deut 21:18–21)

The meaning of the passage appears to be straightforward: A son who repeatedly refuses to obey his parents is subject to death by stoning. Rabbinic exegesis (midrash), however, rarely assumes that the peshat or plain sense of a verse conveys its entire meaning. In a characteristic move, the rabbis investigate the precise wording of these verses and their implications, elucidating a series of additional qualifications that must be met before the son in question can be executed. Their interpretations betray a sense of ethical discomfort with the death penalty prescribed by Deuteronomy: The rules they derive make it extremely difficult, if not impossible, to carry out this punishment.

Consider, for example, an interpretation offered in the *Sifre Devarim*, a compilation of tannaitic midrash on the book of Deuteronomy:

> "They shall say to the elders of his town" (Deut 21:20): ... If one of them, either his father or his mother, had a severed limb, or was lame, or mute, or deaf, or blind, he does not become a sorer u'moreh, as it is written "they shall take hold of him" – not if their hand was severed; "they shall bring him out" – not if they are lame; "they

shall say" – not if they are mute; "this son of ours" – not if they are blind; "will not obey us" – not if they are deaf. (Sifre Deut 219 on 21:20)[5]

In this passage, the midrashic interpreter, known as the *darshan*, investigates the series of steps that the parents must go through before the execution takes place. They must (1) physically take hold of their son; (2) take him out to the gates of the town; (3) speak to the elders of the town; (4) identify the child as their son; and 5) confirm that he does not listen to them. The *darshan* then identifies a series of physical limitations that the parents might have that could impede this process: (1) if one of their hands is severed, they could not physically seize the child; (2) if one of them is unable to walk, they could not physically bring him to the gates of the town; (3) if one of them is mute, they could not verbally declare him to be their son; and (4) if one of them is blind, they could not visually identify him as their child. The last clause is a bit more challenging, as it is not immediately clear why the *parents* being deaf would impede the *son* from listening to them and obeying their commands. There may be an assumption at work here that deaf people are not able to communicate verbally. Rather than simply reiterating the point about a mute parent, however, the *darshan* takes this opportunity to introduce a new limitation: deafness.

In Sanhedrin 71a, the Babylonian Talmud expands further upon the limitations implied by Deut 21:20, arguing that the mother and father must also speak in an identical voice for the execution to take place.

> Rabbi Yehuda says: If his mother is not identical to his father in voice, in appearance, and in height, he does not become a stubborn and rebellious son. What is the reason? As the verse states, "He will not obey *our voice* [*koleinu*]." (Deut 21:20)[6]

The Talmud here focuses on the grammar of the parents' statement. When the biblical text instructs them to say that their son "will not obey *our voice*," it must mean that their voice is functionally *one* voice to be heeded. Otherwise, the Torah would instruct them to say, "he does not obey *our voices*." While this might seem like an obscure grammatical point, the rabbis assume that the biblical text is perfect; as a result, these types of textual details function as coded instructions from the

---

[5] Hebrew text from *Sifre Devarim*, ed. L. Finkelstein (New York: Jewish Theological Seminary, 1969). Translation mine.

[6] Emphasis mine.

Divine, and new meanings can be derived from them. In this case, the Talmud concludes that the voices of the parents must be identical and indistinguishable from one another in order to charge their son as "stubborn and rebellious." The effect of imposing these limitations in both the Talmud and the *Sifre* is clear: They reduce opportunities for the punishment to take place. Eventually, the rabbis add so many limitations and qualifications to the rituals surrounding the execution of the stubborn and rebellious son that they ultimately dispute whether this penalty was ever intended to be carried out.

The Prohibition on Sex between Two Men

Leviticus 18:22 poses many of the same challenges for modern readers that Deut 21:18–21 posed for the early rabbis. While the plain sense of the text seems to be clear, the message is one that readers may find morally troubling. The verse states that "You shall not lie with a male as with a woman; it is an abomination" (Lev 18:22). Many readers, including numerous halakhic authorities, understand this verse to prohibit all intimate relations between same-sex partners. Relying on the same attention to linguistic details as we saw in the case of the *ben sorer u'moreh*, however, the rabbis in the Talmud read this verse as establishing a narrower prohibition. The grammar of the original verse is awkward: It literally states "You shall not lie with a man *the lyings of a woman* (*mishkeve 'isha*)." In b. Sanhedrin 54a, the Talmud concludes that there are two types of "lyings" with a woman: vaginal and anal intercourse. Since only one of these "lyings" can occur between two men, the verse must specifically prohibit anal sex between men. (The Talmud also considers other specific scenarios that might be prohibited by this verse but does not derive a blanket ban on same-sex intercourse.)

In a 2006 *teshuva* (responsum) submitted to the Committee on Jewish Laws and Standards (CJLS), the body that decides halakhic questions for the Rabbinical Assembly of the Conservative movement, Dorff et al. explore the scope of the prohibition in Lev 18:22 and its implications for gay and lesbian Jews. They begin by noting that "Judaism is based on how the Rabbis interpreted the Bible."[7] Drawing on the Talmudic passage discussed above, Dorff et al. therefore conclude that

---

[7]   E. N. Dorff, D. S. Nevins, and A. I. Reisner, "Homosexuality, Human Dignity and Halakhah: A Combined Responsum for the Committee on Jewish Law and Standards," *EH* 24b (2006): 4: www.rabbinicalassembly.org/sites/default/files/assets/public/halakhah/teshuvot/20052010/dorff_nevins_reisner_dignity.pdf

Lev 18:22 prohibits anal sex between men – and *only* anal sex between two men. While this is the only direct biblical prohibition, they acknowledge that later rabbinic law instituted several additional prohibitions, and that collectively these laws amount to a blanket ban on intimacy between same-sex partners.

Dorff et al. object to these additional prohibitions on several grounds, including the fact that sexual orientation is innate and cannot be changed,[8] that living a life of celibacy is not feasible (or desirable) for most Jews,[9] and the fact that these prohibitions are "deeply degrading to gay and lesbian Jews."[10] Ultimately, they view these collective prohibitions as unethical. They argue that a blanket ban on same-sex intimacy violates the core rabbinic principle of preserving human dignity.

> This dilemma is a matter of human dignity, כבוד הבריות [*kavod ha-briyot*], and as such it evokes the principle stated dramatically and repeatedly in the Talmud:... "So great is human dignity that it supersedes a negative commandment of the Torah."[11]

Identifying this conflict leads Dorff et al. to the question that lies at the heart of their *teshuva*: Given the centrality of this rabbinic principle, is it possible to overturn either the rabbinic or biblical prohibitions on same-sex intimacy out of concern for human dignity?

Surveying the classical literature and the rulings of previous authorities, Dorff et al. discover that although the principle of human dignity is invoked in several places to overturn rabbinic laws, "it is not considered capable of overturning an explicit biblical rule."[12] As a result, they conclude that (1) they cannot use this principle to override the biblical prohibition on anal sex between two men but (2) the other prohibitions on same-sex intimacy can and should be struck down out of concern for human dignity, since they are rabbinic rather than biblical in their origins. Furthermore, the authors note that if one wanted to override the biblical prohibition in Lev 18:22, this could be accomplished by issuing a *takkanah* (rabbinic decree). They decline to do so in this case, however, "because takkanah requires the consent of the majority of the population, and this subject remains quite controversial in the observant Jewish community."[13]

---

[8]   Dorff et al., 2–4.
[9]   Dorff et al., 9.
[10] Dorff et al., 10.
[11] Dorff et al., 10.
[12] Dorff et al., 10.
[13] Dorff et al., 10.

19.2 APPROACHES AND STRATEGIES

Both of the cases considered above illustrate how a set of rabbinic readers, writing in very different time periods, negotiated biblical laws that they found ethically problematic. In both cases, those rabbis sought to reduce the potential harms these verses might cause in their application. Although the ways in which they addressed these challenges were often quite different, the rabbis in both cases can be understood as staging a form of ethical resistance to the biblical text, as well as demonstrating a type of fidelity to it. This may seem like a paradoxical claim; in order to understand how this is possible, it will be helpful to trace some of the key elements of their respective interpretive approaches.

Interpretive Assumptions

The rabbis of antiquity approach the biblical text with a different set of assumptions than many readers today. In particular, they assume that the Torah or Pentateuch is a perfect text, given directly by God.[14] Since the text contains no errors, even the smallest linguistic details – such as grammatical oddities or unusual spellings – are potential sites for interpretive inquiry. Furthermore, the rabbis assume that the Torah is a fundamentally cryptic text, and that the instructions it contains require this type of intensive interpretation in order to be fully understood.[15] These combined assumptions are what allow them to derive additional qualifications for the execution of the stubborn and rebellious son – for example, their conclusion that when the Torah instructs the parents to declare that their son will "not obey our voice" (Deut 21:20), it means that the parents must speak in an identical voice.

The assumption that the Torah is a perfect text, however, has another implication: It means that it is impossible for any of the teachings it contains to be incorrect or immoral. If a reader has an ethical objection to a verse, it must signal a problem with the *reader*, not the text.

---

[14]   This assumption was widely shared among ancient readers of the biblical text, although many of the specific exegetical strategies used by the rabbis were unique to that reading community. See J. Kugel, *How to Read the Bible: A Guide to Scripture Then and Now* (New York: Free Press, 2007), 14–17. For more on specific strategies of midrashic interpretation, see also J. Kugel, "Two Introduction to Midrash" *Prooftexts* 3 (1983): 131–55 and D. Boyarin, *Intertextuality and the Reading of Midrash* (Bloomington: Indiana University Press, 1994).

[15]   Kugel, *How to Read the Bible*, 14–17.

Importantly, this does not mean that the reader's ethical intuitions are wrong; it may simply mean that they have misunderstood the verse in question. Like grammatical irregularities, ethical concerns are a goad, prompting the reader to engage in further exegesis. As a result, although ethical objections seem to hover in the background of rabbinic engagement with the laws of the stubborn and rebellious son, prompting them to interpret these verses in ways that make it (almost) impossible to execute such a person in practice, the rabbis never explicitly question or critique the morality of the laws themselves.

These assumptions, and their corollary implications, stand in sharp contrast to the approach of many Conservative rabbis today. As Gordon Tucker argues in a dissenting opinion to the 2006 *teshuva* by Dorff et al., the Conservative movement has affirmed that "the texts of the Torah itself, and of the Talmud, were the products of historically unfolding processes involving human hands, and not infallible, self-authenticating formulations of the transcendent divine will in human language."[16] On this view, such texts remain the primary sources of guidance about how to fulfill the covenant between God and Israel and lead a good life, but they are not perfect. The text may contain errors, including moral errors, as a result of human involvement in the revelation or transmission of God's word. As a result, even though the Hebrew Bible contains divine instruction, it is possible to critique some of its contents on explicitly ethical grounds.

Dorff himself offers such a critique when, reflecting on his own role in authoring the *teshuva* discussed above, he acknowledges that "sometimes rabbis *trying to make the law more moral than it was* must recognize that the perfect resolution is not politically or socially possible at this time."[17] Dorff expresses regret at his inability to lift the ban on anal sex between men entirely, and acknowledges the hardship that this commandment continues to place on gay Jews. In stating that his express goal was to "make the law more moral than it was," Dorff is not only willing to suggest that the Hebrew Bible is an imperfect text, but also that its laws should be modified based on evolving understandings of morality.

---

[16]   G. Tucker, "Drosh v'Kabel Schar: Halakhic and Metahalakhic Arguments Concerning Judaism and Homosexuality" *EH* 24g (2006): 1: www.rabbinicalassembly.org/sites/ default/files/assets/public/halakhah/teshuvot/20052010/tucker_homosexuality.pdf.

[17]   E. N. Dorff, *For the Love of God and People* (Philadelphia: The Jewish Publication Society, 2007), 235, emphasis mine.

Interpretive Strategies

Dorff et al. also rely on a very different set of interpretive strategies to address the prohibition on homosexual sex than do the rabbis in their treatment of the stubborn and rebellious son. These differences may be due in part to their respective understandings of the biblical text – for example, only a reader who views the text as perfect is likely to engage in the intensive linguistic scrutiny characteristic of rabbinic midrash – but they can also be attributed to differences in genre. Midrashic compilations, like the *Sifre Devarim*, represent a specific type of exegetical enterprise and tend to focus on the in-depth examination of a single biblical verse. They often list several different and competing interpretations of a given verse, with no effort to adjudicate between them. The Talmud is a sprawling compendium of rabbinic thought, which makes it difficult to categorize in terms of genre; as the case of the stubborn and rebellious son illustrates, however, it often interweaves midrashic exegesis with the discussion of specific legal scenarios and how they should be addressed.

Thus, the Talmud engages in halakhic discussions and sometimes issues legal rulings, but it does so in a way that differs markedly from *teshuvot*. A *teshuva* follows a specific format: It begins with a clear legal question, surveys existing sources that potentially address that question (including biblical and rabbinic teachings, as well as the rulings of previous halakhic authorities), and then issues a ruling or decision.

Such differences in genre may explain why Dorff et al. draw on the overarching principle of human dignity and its use in a variety of prior halakhic sources to interpret Lev 18:22, whereas the rabbis offer an intensive legal and linguistic analysis of a small set of verses about the stubborn and rebellious son, without reference to other cases or principles. While all of these strategies are common and frequently employed by Jewish readers of the biblical text, each is more common to certain types of literature than others, because the primary aims of those bodies of literature are different. Rabbinic midrash seeks to unlock new layers of potential meaning with the divine word; while it may have legal implications, it is not primarily concerned with determining practical law (*halakhah le-ma'aseh*). The primary purpose of responsa, on the other hand, is to resolve practical questions. While *poskim* (legal decisors) may draw on extant midrash or midrashic techniques to explain the relevant biblical texts and precedents, responsa are not primarily text focused; rather, they are case focused, seeking to resolve a specific legal question at hand. As a genre, midrash also displays no interest in systematic coherence; numerous contradictory midrashim may be offered on the same verse, as each provides a new layer of possible understanding. By way of contrast, since responsa issue practical legal rulings, it is necessary for the *posek* to systematically integrate their decisions into the broader body of Jewish law; this requires the consideration of previous rulings and overarching halakhic principles.

Dissent

In both of the cases considered here, I have provided only a brief sketch of the opinions and interpretations offered about the verses in question, and my discussion has left out an important component: dissenting rabbinic voices. It is an important feature of Jewish ethical engagement with the Hebrew Bible that there is no final authority who determines the "correct" interpretation of the text, regardless of genre. Although many will view the decisions of a specific rabbi as authoritative for their community, such conclusions are largely constrained to a specific time and place. Even the decisions of the most widely respected *poskim* are not unilaterally accepted by world Jewry. (Consider, for example, that the modern state of Israel has two chief rabbis – one for the Ashkenazi community and one for the Sephardi community.) Even when one rabbi issues a clear opinion, another is likely to disagree. Rabbinic texts and institutions largely embrace (or at least allow for) such disagreement.

The phenomenon of dissent can be clearly observed in both of the case studies considered here. After deducing an extensive list of additional criteria and restrictions on the procedures surrounding the punishment of the stubborn and rebellious son, the Talmud raises a question: Why did the Torah include these verses? After all, it seems unlikely, if not impossible, that a person would actually meet all of these criteria.

> Rabbi Shimon says: ... there never has been [a stubborn and rebellious son] and there never will be in the future. Why was this written? So that you may expound [i.e., have the opportunity to study and interpret new matters in the Torah] and receive reward. Rabbi Yonatan says: I saw one and I sat on his grave. (b. Sanhedrin 71a)[18]

R. Shimon argues that the Torah never intended for a stubborn and rebellious son to be executed since, when read through the lens of

---

[18]   Translation mine.

rabbinic interpretation, it would be impossible to ever meet the criteria that are laid out. He concludes that these verses must be given for a different reason: to prompt the reader to investigate the text and deepen his Torah learning. The verses are not actually written for the *ben sorer u'moreh* and his family but for the later reader, who will be rewarded by God for his devotion to Torah study. This view is promptly challenged by R. Yonatan, who claims he has first-hand knowledge that at least one such execution took place. As a result, these two rabbis understand the broader message of these verses in Deuteronomy quite differently. For R. Yonatan, the plain sense of the verses still applies, albeit in a highly restricted sense. Execution remains the appropriate and divinely intended punishment for a stubborn and rebellious child, even if the existence of such children is quite rare. For R. Shimon, God never intended for such children to be punished by death, which is why the criteria to become a *ben sorer u'moreh* are impossible to fulfill. Paradoxically, these verses ultimately teach that execution is not an appropriate punishment and is not divinely sanctioned in this case. The Talmud, as is its wont, does not adjudicate between these two opinions, but simply records them both.

A parallel phenomenon takes place within the Conservative movement surrounding the interpretation of Lev 18:22. In their *teshuva*, Dorff et al. rule that the biblical prohibition on same-sex intimacy only extends to anal sex between two men. On the basis of human dignity, they overturn all other prohibitions on intimate relations between same-sex partners. Their decision was ratified by the CJLS in 2006 and accepted as providing halakhic guidance on this question (although individual Conservative rabbis are still empowered to make case-by-case decisions for their own communities). And yet, in that same year, Rabbi Joel Roth submitted a *teshuva* to the CJLS that concluded that the prohibitions in Lev 18:22 are much broader. In fact, drawing on many of the same sources and authorities, he argues that the various and wide-ranging prohibitions on same-sex intimate relations are *all* biblical in origin, and therefore cannot be overturned on the basis of human dignity. Basing his arguments on the principle of *safek d'oraita le-ḥumra* (i.e., that when there is doubt about a Torah law, one must rule stringently), Roth concludes that all such prohibitions must be upheld. While gay and lesbian Jews should be welcomed in the Jewish community, they are expected to lead celibate lives.[19]

---

[19] J. Roth, "Homosexuality Revisited," *EH* 24a (2006): www.rabbinicalassembly.org/sites/default/files/assets/public/halakhah/teshuvot/20052010/roth_revisited.pdf.

Although the practical conclusions of these two *teshuvot* are contradictory, Roth's *teshuva* was also ratified by the CJLS in 2006. (Several other dissenting opinions were also submitted, but not ratified.) Individual Conservative rabbis must decide for themselves how to follow the competing guidance offered in these two *teshuvot*, just as individual readers of the Talmud must decide whether to understand the laws of the stubborn and rebellious son like R. Shimon or like R. Yonatan.

19.3 IMPLICATIONS

Above, I suggested that these two examples simultaneously demonstrate the ways in which rabbinic readers have offered forms of ethical resistance to the biblical text, as well as the ways in which they have demonstrated fealty to that text. How is this possible?

Consider the case of the stubborn and rebellious son. On one hand, one might conclude that the passages examined here demonstrate rabbinic resistance to the moral worldview contained within these verses. While they never come out and say it, the rabbis in these passages appear to be uncomfortable with the idea of stoning a child for disobeying his parents. Since they are unable to dismiss or reject a biblical commandment outright, they adopt a policy of subversion, adding so much legal "red tape" that the punishment to which they object is no longer feasible. On this view, the reader's moral discomfort indicates a problem with the text that must be resolved, and the reader's assumptions and ethical intuitions are affirmed.

On the other hand, one might conclude that these passages demonstrate rabbinic fealty to the commandments concerning the *ben sorer u'moreh*, because the rabbis base these new qualifications and restrictions on the details and grammar of the biblical text itself. Arguably, the rabbis are extracting a deeper ethical teaching than the plain sense of the passage might initially suggest. While a casual reader might conclude that the Bible condones the execution of rebellious children, the careful rabbinic reader knows that God has encoded a series of limitations to this practice within the text itself. To truly understand God's teaching, one must closely investigate the details of each word in a commandment. In the process of doing so, one may discover that its ultimate message contradicts the plain sense of the text itself: namely, that "stubbornness" and "rebelliousness" are highly technical qualities and that children who disobey their parents should not be subjected to drastic punishment. On this reading, moral discomfort signals a problem with the reader, who must question his own intuitions and assumptions in order to fully understand the biblical text.

The same is true in the case of Lev 18:22 and the interpretation offered by Dorff et al. On one hand, these rabbis seem to actively critique this prohibition on ethical grounds, suggesting that it violates human dignity. Much of their *teshuva* is dedicated to making this claim and to seeing if it is possible to overturn the prohibition as a result. This seems to be a case of active resistance to the ethical worldview articulated in this verse, which is read as degrading the dignity of gay Jews by prohibiting them from pursuing fulfilling sexual relationships.

On the other hand, Dorff et al. do not ultimately overturn this biblical commandment. They conclude that they are not able to do so on the principle of *kavod ha-briyot*, and then acknowledge that other remedies (such as the *takkanah*) are available but choose not to pursue them. In order to understand why, we need to understand the ways in which Dorff et al. are constrained by tradition and by their community. For these rabbis, life within the covenant requires fealty to rabbinic interpretations of the biblical text *and* to the community in which they live. This means not issuing a ruling that their community would perceive as uprooting or overturning biblical law, even when that law causes pain and suffering to some community members.[20] To act otherwise would undermine the legitimacy of their way of life and the entire halakhic system. While ethical considerations and concerns are important, these are not the sole factor in their decision making; the stakes are high, and their ethical, legal, political, and religious dimensions cannot be easily disentangled.[21]

19.4 CONCLUSIONS

To live an observant Jewish life is to strive to live within the covenant established between God and Israel. As noted at the outset of this essay,

---

[20] Dorff, *For the Love of God and People*, 235.

[21] For more on the way these factors shape the process of halakhic decision making, see J. Roth, *The Halakhic Process: A Systemic Analysis* (New York: Jewish Theological Seminary of America, 1986); A. Lichtenstein, "The Human and Social Factor in *Halakhah*," *Tradition* 36, 1 (2002): 89–114; M. Washofsky, "Taking Precedent Seriously: On Halakhah as Rhetorical Practice," in *Re-Examining Reform Halakhah*, ed. W. Jacob and M. Zemer (New York: Berghahn, 2002), 1–70; and A. Schremer, "Toward Critical Halakhic Studies," Tikvah Center Working Paper 04/2010, www.law.nyu.edu/sites/default/files/TikvahWorkingPapersArchive/WP4Schremer.pdf, among others.

the covenantal relationship is complex, and its dynamics cannot be reduced to the categories of either ethics or law. As Louis Newman has noted, all of the biblical commandments, "whether they concern the sacrificial cult or agricultural gifts to the poor, whether they relate to the Sabbath and festivals or to the administration of justice and civil damages, together... define the content of a life of holiness lived in accordance with God's revealed will."[22]

Figuring out how to live this "life of holiness" is challenging because the Hebrew Bible describes a social, political, cultural, and moral reality that would already have been quite foreign to the ancient rabbis and is often unrecognizable to modern readers. Despite this sense of distance, Jewish readers of various backgrounds continue to affirm that the text speaks to the reader in his or her own time and provides guidance for his or her own life. As a result, problematic verses cannot be ignored as irrelevant or outdated – but neither can the ethical challenges they raise be easily resolved. Although Jewish tradition provides a wealth of strategies and models for negotiating these challenges, and rabbinic authorities have issued rulings or offered interpretations of many problematic verses not considered here, in many cases, debate persists over how observant Jews should understand the instructions encoded in the cryptic and difficult text of the Hebrew Bible.

FURTHER READING

Boyarin, D. *Intertextuality and the Reading of Midrash*. Bloomington: Indiana University Press, 1994.

Dorff, E. N. *For the Love of God and People*. Philadelphia: The Jewish Publication Society, 2007.

Kugel, J. *How to Read the Bible: A Guide to Scripture Then and Now*. New York: Free Press, 2007.

Kugel, J. "Two Introductions to Midrash." *Prooftexts* 3 (1983): 131–55.

Lichtenstein, A. "Does Jewish Tradition Recognize an Ethic Independent of Halakha?" Pages 62–88 in *Modern Jewish Ethics*. Edited by M. Fox. Columbus: Ohio State University Press, 1975.

Lichtenstein, A. "The Human and Social Factor in *Halakhah*." *Tradition* 36 (2002): 89–114.

Newman, L. "Ethics as Law, Law as Religion: Reflections on the Problem of Law and Ethics in Judaism." *Shofar* 9 (1990): 13–31.

Newman, L. "Law, Virtue and Supererogation in the Halakhah: The Problem of 'Lifnim Mishurat Hadin' Reconsidered." *JJS* 40 (1989): 61–88.

---

[22]   L. Newman, "Ethics as Law, Law as Religion: Reflections on the Problem of Law and Ethics in Judaism," *Shofar*, 9 (1990): 24.

Plaskow, J. *Standing Again at Sinai: Judaism from a Feminist Perspective*. New York: HarperCollins, 1990.

Roth, J. *The Halakhic Process: A Systemic Analysis*. New York: Jewish Theological Seminary of America, 1986.

Saiman, C. N. *Halakhah: The Rabbinic Idea of Law*. Princeton: Princeton University Press, 2018.

Schofer, J. W. *The Making of a Sage: A Study in Rabbinic Ethics*. Madison: University of Wisconsin Press, 2005.

Schremer, A. "Toward Critical Halakhic Studies." *Tikvah Center Working Paper* 4, 2010. www.law.nyu.edu/sites/default/files/TikvahWorkingPapersArchive/WP4Schremer.pdf

Washofsky, M. "Taking Precedent Seriously: On Halakhah as Rhetorical Practice." Pages 1–70 in *Re-Examining Reform Halakhah*. Edited by W. Jacob and M. Zemer. New York: Berghahn, 2002.

20 Christian Ethics and the Hebrew Bible

JULIÁN ANDRÉS GONZÁLEZ HOLGUÍN

20.1 PROFANING THE HEBREW BIBLE: A TEXT OF TRAGEDY AND TERROR

I object to the unexamined assumption that the texts of the Hebrew Bible are suitable as a source of answers for ethical discussions of social, moral, and political questions of today. Readers with this hermeneutical supposition believe in finding rules in the biblical canon that they may enforce on modern society and church discipline.[1] The ethical relevance of the Hebrew Bible does not reside in accepting rules, principles, or ideas that come from the text and a reconstruction of its historical contexts based on sustained critical scrutiny of the will of God in scripture. It comes from a critical discussion with the text in light of current events, such as the migrant caravan moving from Central America to the southern border of the United States in 2018.[2] There were Christians advocating completely different political solutions and using passages of scripture to support their views, deeming it essential to their ethical stance to demonstrate a continuity between their claim and a biblical text. A critical exegesis of the Hebrew Bible, however, exacerbates rather than solves the problem because it heightens awareness of the ideological diversity within scripture and the infinite number of perspectives from which readers can interpret it. The only way that the Hebrew Bible can be regarded as straightforward and univocal in its message is if nobody bothers to read it. Even Augustine was

---

[1] For a presentation of this methodology consider the essay by O. Barclay, "The Nature of Christian Morality," in *Law, Morality, and the Bible*, ed. B. N. Kaye and G. J. Wenham (Leicester: InterVarsity, 1978), 125–50. See J. Rogerson, *Theory and Practice in Old Testament Ethics* (New York: T&T Clark, 2004), 12–18 for a critique of the legalistic use of the Hebrew Bible in moral issues.

[2] J. Barton argues that ethical insights from the Old Testament come not from trying to extract a message from it, but from the experience of reading these narratives and reflecting on the moral complexities of our world. See *Ethics and the Old Testament* (Harrisburg: Trinity Press International, 1998), 18.

dissatisfied with the Bible on ethical grounds, until he began conjuring allegorical interpretations to spiritualize the disturbing material away.[3] History has shown, again and again, that turning a simple message into a political position usually provides theological justification for oppression.[4] Is a critical reading of the biblical text relevant to deal with, comprehend, and use as a basis for action – as Christians – concerning the vicissitudes and problems that humanity faces in today's world? How can a text produced in a world so distant from our own be essential to inform how we act and be today?

The age of the Hebrew Bible, as an ancient document, has been problematic for modernity. The very notion of archaism suggests a distance between past and present that is radical and unbridgeable. This has forced interpreters to ask whether the Hebrew Bible is more than a repository of ancient customs and stories – to reinvest it with moral and pedagogical virtues to reappropriate it to the modern humanistic project.[5] This project brings the text closer to its audience, overcoming its distant origin – making familiar that which, in principle, is not. At the same time, it overcomes the uniqueness of the text and assimilates it by reproducing it. Both situations change how the text is received. Yet the modern project of biblical reappropriation fails, because our sense of the Hebrew Bible is limited, dulled, close-minded, and extremely pious. It leads to sanitized versions of its characters and narratives, exemplified in the abundance of so-called children's Bibles distributed among Christian communities around the world. These are often Christians' first contact with the Hebrew Bible, shaping their perception of what the stories and characters do and say. They play an essential role in shaping how certain events and characters are remembered later in life, normalizing embarrassing situations such as the binding of Isaac or the story of Noah. Their images not only provide a visual representation of biblical events but are interpretations with a story of their own.[6] Those who read the Hebrew Bible within the context of Christian ethics ought not to be

---

[3] He manifests his initial disappointment with the Bible in *Confessions*, books 3, 5, and 9.

[4] E. Seibert, *The Violence in Scripture: Overcoming the Old Testament's Troubling Legacy* (Minneapolis: Fortress, 2012) is an excellent analysis of cases in history about the relation between biblical interpretation and violence.

[5] J. Sheenah, *The Enlightenment Bible: Translation, Scholarship, Culture* (Princeton: Princeton University Press, 2007), 150–1.

[6] C. Vander Stichele and H. S. Pyper, *Text, Image, and Otherness in Children's Bibles: What Is in the Picture?*, Semeia Studies 56 (Atlanta: Society of Biblical Literature, 2012), 1.

interpreters who accept such received traditions passively or only listen to what religious leaders describe as the appropriate action. It may not be surprising that secular society does not read the scripture, regarding them as contrary to what matters in current understandings of reality, but it is a surprise to find faith communities dependent on ignoring critical examinations of scripture in order to preserve their traditions. Here, I propose to unsettle the old book and its readers by making constructive, profaning provocations. A close and careful reading of the Hebrew Bible is enough to profane its modern sanitized versions simply because, in many instances, the disturbances are self-generating. The Hebrew Bible contains the capacity to unsettle and puzzle its readers.

Reading the Hebrew Bible for ethical profanation means three things. First, it means that we prod the Hebrew Bible from its usual sacred space – pulpit, prayer room, Museum of the Ancient Near East – and bring it into the profane sphere in which we live, where its readers may critically engage it. The Hebrew Bible as part of the Christian canon is a set of writings that shapes individual and communal identity as well as informing Christian action. In one sense, to "profane" means to read the Hebrew Bible humanly, as a book of tragedy and terror, and to play with its density of ethical dilemmas. The sacred already implies that which is terrifying and mysterious.[7] To profane the sacred is thus already implicit in the nature of sacredness itself.

We will discuss the story of Abraham and Isaac as a narrative of tragedy and terror. Why does this story continue to exert significant power on the imagination of its readers? Why do the notions of binding, submission, obedience, and sacrifice haunt us as we wrestle with the text and its (un)ethical relevance? The richness of the Hebrew Bible resides in its constant invitation to rethink our ethical commitments and actions before a mandate like God's demanding Abraham's son for sacrifice. As a compelling narrative, its enduring ethical formative possibilities reside in its ability to perturb our confidence in our moral reasoning. In other words, it defies rational or moral explanation. As a story of tragedy and terror, the narrative invites an open conversation about its implications for Christian identity and action – and thereby keeps us reading it. It is not answers that we seek but a way to shock us out of security and complacency – out of the passivity of the subject as the origin of will, freedom, and the shaper of identity, and the idea that

---

[7]   R. Otto, *The Idea of the Holy: An Inquiry into the Non-rational Factor in the Idea of the Divine and Its Relation to the Rational*, trans. J. W. Harvey (Oxford: Oxford University Press, 1923), 12–42.

in our times we no longer practice the archaic activities of the biblical characters. A careful and imaginative reading of the story is more fruitful than an interpretation that takes Abraham and God off the hook and claims the tale as a moral resource.[8]

Second, to profane the text means that we resist modern tendencies that look at the Hebrew Bible as part of the foundation of Western civilization, or as a great monument to the modern world, or as the most significant contribution by the ancient Jewish people to current legal structures. In other words, it is to look critically at the assumption in American society that "the Bible is a central book in our culture."[9] This notion of the Bible, especially the Hebrew Scripture, is a precritical, pietistic, and vague idea that considers the Hebrew Bible as a container of morality, where readers may discover and find the practical, universal, and pragmatic guidelines for civil, democratic, and humane relationships. This concept perpetuates the illusion that the Hebrew Bible and the modern state are, loosely speaking, on the same page.[10] It is critical to explore how the Hebrew Bible is radically different from the modern project of the autonomous self. It threatens to shatter the idea of the Judeo-Christian God as the guarantor of my life, my plans, and the current sociopolitical status quo. In other words, to profane the Hebrew Scripture means to find alternative ways to dramatize it; its profanation should underline the human subjection to forces that exist outside of our control and exceed our limited comprehension. Profaning the scripture upsets the notion of what it means to be subject to these forces and to their influence on agency, choice, and freedom.

Third, to profane the scripture means to resist the modern impulse to secularize the Hebrew Bible, deconstructing it and rendering it another ordinary work from antiquity with sometimes vulgar depictions of relationships. In this sense, we must distinguish between the secularization and the profanation of the Hebrew Bible. The secularization of the Hebrew Bible moves its symbolism, metaphors, and archetypes from

---

[8]   Although the legal material may also provide a framework for a discussion of the ethical application of the Hebrew Bible, biblical stories are better suited for ethical analysis because in them the world is presented as a complex reality, their style is laconic, they are far from morally edifying, and it is difficult to decide what the story commends or deplores. See M. C. Nussbaum, *Love's Knowledge: Essays on Philosophy and Literature* (Hemel Hempstead: Prentice Hall, 1997), 37.

[9]   Sheenah, *The Enlightenment Bible*, 11.

[10]   A. Skinner, "The Influence of the Hebrew Bible on the Founders of the American Republic," in *Sacred Texts, Secular Times: The Hebrew Bible in the Modern World*, ed. L. J. Greenspoon and B. F. Lebeau (Omaha: Creighton University Press, 2000), 16, 31.

one place to another. For example, the transcendence of God as a paradigm of sovereignty is displaced from heavenly monarchy to earthly kingship, but leaves its power intact.[11] This is the problem with legalistic and literalist hermeneutics. They secularize the text by transferring its meaning into current social, political, and economic issues, without any critical perspective. The history of the (trans)formation of the Hebrew Bible since the Enlightenment offers us a vision of secularization in which biblical authority does not disappear but is reconstructed.[12]

Also, to profane the Hebrew Bible means to knock down the pedestal on which modern Western societies have placed it. That pedestal creates an insurmountable distance that can only separate and alienate the text from its readers. Once the pedestal is broken, the biblical text becomes available, *touchable* indeed.[13] The Hebrew Bible thereby loses its aura of unavailability and separation. To profane the Hebrew Bible means to neutralize and deactivate the apparatuses of power that, since the Enlightenment, have reconstituted the authority of the Bible as a model of social thought and to return the biblical text to everyday use in the spaces that power had seized.[14] In other words, to explore ethical profanation of the Hebrew Bible and Christian ethics is to subvert the either-or identitarian categories of modernity that place the biblical text as an authority for Christian faith and practice, as the foundation for Western culture, or as the outcome of the dirty work of human hands. Following Giorgio Agamben's analysis of the sacred and the profane, I study the Hebrew Bible with an aim other than its secularization. To profane the Hebrew Bible is a reading of the sacred that recognizes the authority that Christian communities have bestowed on this text. It is an approach that does not rely on reverence, fear, or blind obedience. To profane the Hebrew Bible is crucial for the life of those who engage with it as a sacred, even authoritative, source of religious identity and action. Otherwise, the text will continue to be secularized by those who read both it and themselves uncritically. Such an approach makes a critical commitment to the text itself, without regard for how it may conform to the profile of a believer or atheist. This restores the Hebrew Bible to its unique and distinctive voice – one that does not coincide with a utilitarian requirement that forces it to answer questions of moral identity

---

[11] G. Agamben, *Profanations* (New York: Zone Books, 2007), 77.

[12] Sheenah, *The Enlightenment Bible*, xi.

[13] This separation is exemplified with the "yad," the Jewish ritual pointer used by the reader to follow the text during the reading from the Torah scrolls.

[14] B. Hilton, *Age of Atonement: The Influence of Evangelicalism on Social and Economic Thought, 1795–1875* (New York: Oxford University Press, 1988), ix.

definitively or conceives it as a means to address the uncertainties of the world. Finding God in these texts becomes an exegetical experience, like the metaphor of Jacob fighting with the angel, rather than an abstract discussion about theological concepts.

Finally, to profane the Hebrew Bible is to play with the texts' meanings critically, while acknowledging the very indeterminacy and ambiguities at their core, especially regarding motives, moral character, psychology, power, duties, obedience, and so on. Connecting this to a study of ethics admits that the texts will be useful in their ambiguity, not in their descriptiveness. In playing with the text, I conceive meaning as a never-ending process that requires continual revision, both in the ordinary sense of reconsideration and in the etymological sense of "seeing again." In other words, there is a constant process of amendment and suspension of judgment, weighing multiple possibilities for ethical application, and brooding over the gaps in the information the text provides. To play with the Hebrew Bible is counterintuitive for Christian readers who believe the text is sacred and should be approached and interpreted with reverence.[15] But a playful reading follows some perspectives on rabbinic interpretation, in which we see that the rabbis' manipulation of the biblical text constitutes a "kind of joking, a learned and sophisticated play about the biblical text."[16] To play with the Hebrew Bible frees and distracts the reader from its sacred nature without simply abolishing the possibility that it may bring a word from the divine. In a global context where Christianity is perceived as false and oppressive, complicit with previous and current economic, political, and ecological catastrophes, to play is to undermine the use of the text in the sphere of public relations, where interpretations become frameworks by which Christians practice hospitality and solidarity. The claim that biblical texts form an ethical system for Western notions of personhood, rights, freedom, morality, democracy, and identity are usually connected with an affirmation that Christianity relies on scripture for authority and moral purpose. The biblical text enables the discovery of these distinctly modern goods as if they emanate diffusely from the ethical world of the text and its history of interpretation.[17] Instead of

---

[15] Y. Sherwood, *Biblical Blaspheming: Trials of the Sacred for a Secular Age* (New York: Cambridge University Press, 2012), 66.

[16] J. Kugel, "Two Introductions to Midrash," *Prooftexts* 3 (1983): 131–55.

[17] Rev. R. Warren's video-encyclical to Uganda's pastors in the matter of an anti-homosexuality law exemplifies the tension between the biblical mandate of loving the neighbor and the biblical rejection against homosexual practices. He balances the contradictory teachings of the text with a liberal discourse of democracy and rights

searching for ways to use the text to bolster claims we already want to
support, profaning the Hebrew Bible through play – through disassoci-
ating it from both religious tradition and secularization, through making
it immediately fresh and available – invites the power of a sacred text to
question who we are and what we do, not only as readers of but as
adherents to the wisdom of the Hebrew Bible. By reading, rereading,
and retelling the biblical stories we may find constructive, profaning
provocations and formative experiences that motivate individuals and
communities to reexamine their value judgments. This is the kind of use
that Walter Benjamin suggested when he wrote of Franz Kafka's *The
New Attorney* that the law that is studied but no longer practiced is the
gate to justice.[18] In the same way, if we can imagine the Hebrew Bible as
a textual ground for playing with ethics (not requiring that we limit
ourselves to discovering proscriptive ethics within it), we may find new
ways to show its connection to Christian ethics. Profanation may
become a gateway to new dimensions of political, economic, and religious solidarity in the global village.

20.2 BINDING ISAAC – BINDING US

Abraham and Isaac have traveled far from the mythical pages of the book
of Genesis to the political contexts of our modern and technological era.
They have not disappeared even as Christianity has gradually vanished
from much of modernity. Their appearances in places other than in
religious circles confirm that, even if the Hebrew Bible seems to vanish
from politics and public culture, it continues to shape the project of
modernity either as a bizarre presence of intolerance and hatred or as a
positive source in ethics of social justice and equality.

Cesar Vallejo's poem "No One Lives in the House Anymore" metaphorically explains the influence of the biblical story in our modern
society. His writing expresses the kind of passion that maintains our
returns to this tale.

> – No one lives in the house anymore – you tell me –; everyone is
> gone. The living room, the bedroom, the patio, are deserted. Nobody
> remains any more since each one has departed. And I say to you:
> When someone leaves, someone remains. The place through which

---

using the theological concept of free will to support respect and difference. https://
youtube.com/watch?v=1jmGu904fDE (accessed 15 March 2019).
[18]   W. Benjamin, "Franz Kafka," *Selected Writings, Volume 2, 1927–1934*, ed. M. W.
Jennings, H. Eiland, and G. Smith (Cambridge: Belknap, 1999), 815.

a person passed, is no longer empty. The only point that is empty, with human solitude, is that through which no one has passed. New houses are deader than old ones, for their walls are of stone or steel, but not of people. A house comes into the world, not when people finish building it, but when they begin to inhabit it.[19]

In the poem, we see an analogy of the ways the biblical story approaches us. Biblical times are not gone, because time is not a succession of events that cancel each other out as each new one appears. There is something that remains with us. Abraham and Isaac continually pass through us, via the sustained production of interpretations. The lives and relationships they have helped establish continue walking in our houses.[20] Our houses – that is, our bodies and our communities – are inhabited by presences that never leave – of ideas, feelings, and actions that circle back and continue passing through us.[21] Abraham and Isaac continue to be alive, though in different ways from the times when their story's emphasis was on revealing theological truths. For much of the Christian era, the story was safely unproblematic because it was considered to foreshadow God's willingness to sacrifice his son. It becomes challenging when paintings such as Caravaggio's *The Sacrifice of Isaac* emphasize Isaac's terror, giving priority to the subjective consciousness of the victim as something that forms the starting point for a new and reconsidered meaning of the story. The painting also portrays Abraham's seeming reluctance to stop the sacrifice, perhaps because the story reflects a culture in which the highest means of honoring the gods was by human sacrifice. With Caravaggio's painting, we see an early visual interpretation in which Isaac's consciousness no longer appears as provisional to the meaning of the tale.

Popular culture has exposed the text to a wide audience through spectacular exhibition. But at the same time popular culture has domesticated the text, creating the impossibility of using, dwelling within, or experiencing the text itself. That is why the process of constructive profanation is relevant: It affects how we organize our house and demands that we think critically about how we receive the story. To make it our story, we need to look carefully and slowly into its symbolic

---

[19]   C. Vallejo, *Los Heraldos Negros*, 1st ed. (1918), 269 (my translation).

[20]   I am grateful to Dr. J. Pimentel who pointed me to this idea in a panel discussion during SBL annual conference, Denver, 2019.

[21]   As literary scholar E. Auerbach says, biblical stories "seek to subject us." *Mimesis: The Representation of Reality in Western Literature*, trans. W. R. Trask (Princeton: Princeton University Press, 1953), 15.

roots, its process of recycling, and our interpretive positions. A hermeneutics of suspicion is ethically important to approaching Genesis 22 insofar as it continues to bind us to questions of sovereignty, subjectivity, submission, and sacrifice. A critical analysis counters the naive projections of the story in popular culture. It destabilizes and exposes both simplistic ideas about the text's moral perfection and the limited character of our interpretive categories.

I chose the story of Abraham and Isaac because of its deep connection with the rest of the biblical drama but also because of its uniqueness. The connection rests on its status as the last and most radical test of Abraham. It is this narrative that writers of the New Testament used to transform him into the paradigmatic model of faith.[22] Marc Chagall's 1966 painting *Le sacrifice d'Isaac* provides one of the most striking visual metaphors for understanding the place of this story in the Christian tradition. The story's themes of death and violence drive us off, for we prefer life. On the other hand, it provokes a disturbing fascination. Chagall communicates this conflicting entanglement of Christianity with Abraham and Isaac via the simply and starkly red, yellow, and blue colors, evoking perhaps the fundamental (basic) importance of the story as it creates a contrast between the tranquility of the blue and the terror and captivation of blood and flame via the red and yellow.

The divine promise appears in Abraham's story as an example of its importance in the complex biblical drama of ancestors and nations, reaching beyond the Hebrew canon to inform early Christian eschatological imagination.[23] Possessing the land, surviving by the production of male children, and receiving a name respected by all people are concerns of these stories in the book of Genesis. However, the idea of a promise is linked to the continuous threat that it may not be fulfilled. God's surprising command to slaughter Isaac is the epitome of this, although it reappears in Isaac's narrative as complications arise between Jacob and Esau. In many ways, Genesis 22 is a radical escalation of the theme of fulfillment and postponement of divine promise.

The ambivalence between these poles suggests a complex view of the divine in the biblical drama. The God of Mount Moriah seems to be an exception to the God of Mount Sinai. On Sinai, God commands not to take human life. On Moriah, God appears to demand human life as a test for Abraham. The latter represents God's ability to suspend the law

---

[22]   Matt 1:17; Luke 13:16; Gal 3:28; Heb 11:19.
[23]   G. von Rad, *Old Testament Theology: The Theology of Israel's Historical Traditions*, vol. 1, trans. D. M. G. Stalker (New York: Harper, 1962), 167.

against killing and portrays God as a sovereign power, with the right of life and death. Isaac becomes a paradoxical subject, because in relation to God he is neither dead nor alive; God exercises a sovereign right over his life.[24] God's command to sacrifice Isaac is an example of divine power capable of transgressing ordinary morality, suspending the law by placing Abraham outside of the sheltering embrace of norms and social order. As a sovereign power, God can take human life. The divine thus transits the boundary between chaos and order and embodies a threat to life. This resonates with C. G. Jung's opinion about God: "To this day God is the name by which I designate all things which cross my willful path violently and recklessly, all things which upset my subjective views, plans and intentions and change the course of my life for better or worse."[25]

The sovereign is the one who can take life or grant mercy without having to give any reason. Even divine mercy, exemplified in this story by the appearance of the angel, is evidence of God's sovereignty to grant grace or violence indiscriminately. The story thus shows a radical example of the idea of a sovereign – even a divine one – who uses terror and blood to shape human obedience. The story's uniqueness pertains to the absence of background information that might explain the divine violence. Genesis 6 represents divine violence as a reaction to the condition of lawlessness that prevailed upon the earth; the answer to human violence is divine violence, which is nearly all-consuming. But in Genesis 22, God is the power over life and death that grants one or the other without reason. The terrifying command demands Abraham's obedience and becomes exemplary for later Abrahamic traditions.

According to Genesis 22, the cornerstones of Abraham's covenant with God and the fulfillment of the divine promise are soaked with blood and terror. After the command, we want to know if the killing takes place or not; instead, we read of Abraham's preparations before the journey to Moriah, with the laconic narrative spending some lines describing all the activities. Abraham is not asked to kill Isaac immediately, which is already a horrific dilemma. Instead, we read of the perturbing preparations for the sacrifice and the journey, with the

[24] M. Foucault, *Society Must Be Defended: Lectures at the Collège de France 1975–76*, trans. D. Macey (New York: Picador, 2003), 240.
[25] From a 1961 interview of Jung, as cited in E. F. Edinger, *Ego and Archetype: Individuation and the Religious Function of the Psyche* (New York: G. P. Putnam, 1972), 101.

delay and its details intensifying the horrid nature of the command. The killing of Isaac threatens to suspend the promise, so the narrative seems to move toward the summit of the plot in a kind of suspended animation.

God blesses Abraham after suspending the sacrifice and replacing the victim with a ram. It is not surprising that the power of sacrifice is so productive in the Christian tradition; someone in obedience to God was willing to offer up the gift of death to his son. Abraham's disposition to sacrifice his son and the sudden presence of an animal that takes Isaac's place suggests Isaac's suspension between life and death. If we follow the biblical story Isaac is not sacrificed, but in the Jewish tradition the issue is more complicated. Midrash *ha-Gadol* 353 quotes Isaac saying, "Let a quarter of my blood be redemption for my people Israel." This portrays Isaac as a liminal life form that gets sacrificed on Mount Moriah for the sake of his people. It already suggests a striking resemblance to the Christian "lamb of God." Both sons are adult men who give themselves as offering to the father and as redemption for the people.

As Jon Levenson argues, Christianity is in a substantial measure a "midrashic system whose scriptural base is the Hebrew Bible."[26] Genesis 22 provides some of the fundamental idioms of Christian theological speculations, including the power of death to bring life in the context of terror, sacrifice, and blood. The narrative presents us with a notion of obedience that "involves giving up our very selves" to the point of annihilation or absorption.[27] Arguably, the story does not present Abraham and Isaac as heroes because it is a tale about giving up personal subjectivity. If the goal of faith is to lose ourselves, what is left of Abraham and Isaac's identity after this ordeal to meet the divine command? How are obedience and faith anything other than a long and dreadful path to self-destruction? The story ends by reporting only that Abraham returns to his servants (Gen 22:19), leaving the whereabouts of Isaac to the imagination of the reader. The raw ambition in the biblical tradition to glorify God obscures

[26]   J. D. Levenson, *The Death and Resurrection of the Beloved Son: The Transformation of Child Sacrifice in Judaism and Christianity* (New Haven: Yale University Press, 1993), 232.

[27]   B. S. Hook and R. R. Reno, "Abraham and the Problems of Modern Heroism," in *Sacred Texts, Secular Times: The Hebrew Bible in the Modern World*, ed. L. J. Greenspoon and B. F. LeBeau, Studies in Jewish Civilization 10 (Omaha: Creighton University Press, 2000), 135–61.

that this usually takes place at the expense of the human side of the story.[28]

Although Isaac is alive and will continue the biblical drama of the patriarchs, there is definitively an existential crisis as his life is suspended on a knife edge. This near-death experience becomes the condition upon which God bestows blessings upon Abraham: sons scattered upon the sky and the seashore and the dissemination of Abraham's blessings upon all the nations of the earth (Gen 22:16–18). Clinging to this promise, the Christian tradition portrays Abraham and Isaac as heroes, transforming the terror and tragedy of the story into the climatic portrayal of Abraham as a man of faith, willing to step beyond morality to fulfill the divine command.[29] The reader's stance depends on how we define heroism. Either it constitutes obedient endurance to participate in the glory of God – in this case, Abraham's laconic obedience is heroic – or we define it as obedience to conscience and individuality, wherein the appropriate response to the divine command is rejection.

It seems to me that one of the greatest powers of this story is its capacity to perturb modern sensibilities about obedience, submission, individuality, and sacrifice. Abraham's reaching out to grab his knife and the sudden cry of the angel stopping the killing communicate the precariousness of life. The liminal Isaac, who sees Abraham raising the blade to kill him, contributes to the in-between nature of the story and its appeal to ancient and modern readers. The story straddles fear with a promise, by way of a laconic unfolding of events that leaves out so many details we would like to know. The beginning of Genesis 23 tells us that Sarah dies, raising significant questions about the relation between her death and the test her family undergoes in the previous chapter. By the simple literary fact of juxtaposition, Sarah's death could be interpreted as a case of cause and effect. Her life has become an extension of the body of her son, which just underwent a traumatic experience at the hand of his father. But Sarah's response to the test was terminal. It seems that the story of Abraham and Isaac begins to darken once Sarah's grave sheds its perturbing light upon it. Chagall's painting incorporates Sarah as a minor character anxiously watching from behind a tree. It portrays the deep connection between Sarah and her son. She experiences the

---

[28]   F. Nietzsche addresses this by asking whether obedience and faith are existential blocks to human worth and distinctiveness; see Essay Three: Section 9–11, in *Genealogies of Morals* (New York: Dover, 2003), 159–66.

[29]   S. Kierkegaard, *Fear and Trembling*, ed. and trans. H. V. Hong and E. H. Hong, in *Kierkegaard's Writings*, vol. 6 (Princeton: Princeton University Press, 1983), 1–176.

same trauma Isaac suffers. In the end, Genesis 22 leaves us with two bodies. Isaac's remains a suspended life neither dead nor alive, while Sarah's becomes the actual dead body of the story.[30]

Although Isaac survives, the tale suggests that survival depends in part on the capriciousness of forces beyond our control. Genesis 22 articulates the conflicting collision between threat and promise, in which we may find that absolute submission and unexpected redemption keep us in suspense. Rather than resolving the tension, as traditional scholarly apologetic readings do when arguing that this is a story about the rejection of child sacrifice, we should work hard to keep the suspense.[31] Within modern notions of subjectivity, agency, subjugation, and freedom, a close reading of this account invites the exploitation of its rich ambiguity. The concepts of obedience and faith are likely to turn into ethical messiness when we look closely at them in conversation with the fullness of this particular story.

People often wield ownership over sacred texts for purposes of division, condescension, and judgment. When biblical interpretation is used to incite divisive behavior, profaning the story also provides us a way to experience the text in new and challenging ways, despite its serious implications. A playful approach to biblical interpretation is a political task by which interpreters reexamine value judgments. To profane the text is a way to plant openness, generosity, awareness, and solidarity with others who are also intellectually and existentially committed to the Hebrew Bible as a word from the divine. The act of profanation takes the text seriously as part of the tradition, yet pushes back against it in a wrestling dance of questions and adaptations. When interpretations of the biblical text become a mirror of our human condition and social realities, the hermeneutical task helps us look inward and evaluate our perspectives and compare them with different approaches. To play with the text challenges traditional assumptions and presumptions about the meaning of Genesis 22, suggesting possibilities by which we may reexamine the consequences of stereotypical readings for what we enact in the economic and political arena.

---

[30]   Sarah's attachment to her son Isaac was great enough to insist on the termination of another boy (and woman) who would seem to be competitors. Her attachment to Isaac reveals a frailty in her humanity and in her humane connectedness to life, so that if God seemed to give little thought for the son she adored she could no longer tolerate a life given as a blessing for herself.

[31]   N. Sarna, *Understanding Genesis* (New York: Jewish Theological Seminary of America, 1966), 75.

A profaned exploration of this – and other familiar texts – invites new ways for the sacred to become a stage for community building.[32]

FURTHER READING

Agamben, G. *Profanations*. New York: Zone Books, 2007.

Auerbach, E. *Mimesis: The Representation of Reality in Western Literature*. Translated by W. R. Trask. Princeton: Princeton University Press, 1953.

Barton, J. *Ethics and the Old Testament*. Harrisburg: Trinity Press International, 1998.

Edinfer, E. F. *Ego and Archetype: Individuation and the Religious Function of the Psyche*. New York: G.P. Putname, 1972.

Foucault, M. *Society Must be Defended: Lectures at the Collège de France 1975–76*. Translated by D. Macey. New York: Picador, 2003.

Hilton, B. *Age of Atonement: The Influence of Evangelicalism on Social and Economic Thought, 1795–1875*. New York: Oxford University Press, 1988.

Hook, B. S., and R. R. Reno, "Abraham and the Problems of Modern Heroism." Pages 135–62 in *Sacred Texts, Secular Times: The Hebrew Bible in the Modern World*. Edited by L. J. Greenspoon and B. F. LeBeau. Studies in Jewish Civilization 10. Omaha: Creighton University Press, 2000.

Kierkegaard, S. *Fear and Trembling. Vol. 6 of Kierkegaard's Writings*. Translated by H. V. Hong and E. H. Hong. Princeton: Princeton University Press, 1983.

Levenson, J. D. *The Death and Resurrection of the Beloved Son: The Transformation of Child Sacrifice in Judaism and Christianity*. New Haven: Yale University Press, 1993.

Nietzsche, F. *Genealogies of Morals*. Translated by H. B. Samuel. New York: Dover, 2003.

Nussbaum, M. C. *Love's Knowledge: Essays on Philosophy and Literature*. Hemel Hempstead: Prentice Hall, 1997.

Otto, R. *The Idea of the Holy: An Inquiry into the Non-rational Factor in the Idea of the Divine and Its Relation to the Rational*. Translated by J. W. Harvey. Oxford: Oxford University Press, 1923.

Rogerson, J. *Theory and Practice in Old Testament Ethics*. New York: T&T Clark, 2004.

Sarna, N. *Understanding Genesis*. New York: Jewish Theological Seminary of America, 1966.

Sheenah, J. *The Enlightenment Bible: Translation, Scholarship, Culture*. Princeton: Princeton University Press. 2007.

---

[32] Ted Merwin, "Sacred Texts As a Stage For Community Building," *The New York Jewish Week*, 1 May 2018, https://jewishweek.timesofisrael.com/sacred-text-as-a-stage-for-community-building/ (accessed 15 March 2019).

Index

Printed in Great Britain
by Amazon

46031485R00198